A COMPANION TO WITTGENSTEIN'S 'TRACTATUS'

Im Satz wird eine Welt probeweise zusammengestellt (wie wenn im Pariser Gerichtssaal ein Automobilunglück mit Puppen etc. ~~dargestellt~~ dargestellt wird.)

Daraus muss sich (wenn ich nicht blind wäre) sofort das Wesen der Wahrheit ergeben.

Denken wir an hieroglyphische Schriften bei denen jedes Wort seine Bedeutung darstellt! Denke wir daran dass auch wirkliche Bilder von Sachverhalten stimmen und nicht ~~stimmen~~ können.

„△×": Wenn in diesem Bild der Rechte den Menschen A vorstellt und bezeichnet der Linke den Menschen B so könnte etwa das Ganze aussagen „A ficht mit B", Der

EMERGENCE OF THE PICTURE THEORY
(from the original MS of the *Notebooks*, 29.9.14)

A COMPANION TO WITTGENSTEIN'S 'TRACTATUS'

BY

MAX BLACK

Professor of Philosophy
Cornell University

Cornell University Press

ITHACA, NEW YORK

© 1964 by Max Black

CORNELL UNIVERSITY PRESS

First published 1964

Second printing 1966

PRINTED IN THE UNITED STATES OF AMERICA

BY VALLEY OFFSET, INC.

BOUND BY VAIL–BALLOU PRESS, INC.

If a lover of truth finds a theory reprehensible and does not find plausible premises which remove its reprehensible character, he must not at once believe that the theory is false, but must inquire how he who has put it forward has arrived at it, must employ much time in learning this, and follow the systematic order corresponding to the nature of the topic. And if this is necessary in other sciences than metaphysics, how much more will this hold for metaphysics, since that science is so remote from the sciences built on common sense.

AVERRÖES, *Tahafut al-Tahafut*

At this period an insatiate appetite is accompanied by a fastidious palate. Nothing but the quintessences of existence, and those in exhaustless supplies, will satisfy this craving, which is not to be satisfied! Hence his bitterness. Life can furnish no food fitting for him. . . . 'Tis a sign, this sourness, that he is subject to none of the empiricisms that are afloat.

The Ordeal of Richard Feverel

PREFACE

My chief aim has been to make it easier for a serious student of Wittgenstein's early work to reach his own interpretation of the *Tractatus*. I hope I have been successful in this, whatever the fate of my own interpretation. There can be no question here of any 'definitive' reading: since my own views have oscillated while I was writing, I cannot be confident that my final judgement has always been the best.

I have followed the plan of dividing the text into a large number of 'instalments' which are introduced by preliminary statements that can be read consecutively. In the detailed notes on Wittgenstein's text, the following will be found: (1) Comments on the meaning of difficult or obscure expressions. (Although I have always worked with the German text, I have written with the needs in mind of an English-speaking reader, who may be occasionally misled by Ogden's translation or by that of Pears and McGuinness. All English citations are from the latter, except where otherwise indicated.) (2) Relevant quotations, chiefly from Wittgenstein's early sketches for the *Tractatus* (published as the *Notebooks*) and from unpublished manuscripts. (3) Explanations of the views, usually those of Russell and Frege, to which Wittgenstein refers. (4) Cross-references to related passages in the text. (5) Occasional free paraphrases (marked by the symbol '•' in the margin) of exceptionally cryptic or puzzling passages. In addition, I have provided a number of short articles, both expository and critical, on questions arising in the text (see small type headings in the table of contents).

My greatest obligation is to Wittgenstein's literary executors, Miss G. E. M. Anscombe, Mr Rush Rhees and Professor G. H. von Wright, for their kindness in allowing me to work with and to quote from Wittgenstein's manuscripts. The debt I owe to the valuable commentaries of Miss Anscombe and Professor Erik Stenius is great, perhaps especially where I disagree with them. Among the many others who have helped me, besides those already mentioned, I would like to express gratitude to Mr Rogers Albritton, Miss Hidé Ishiguro, Mr David Pears, Professor Gilbert Ryle and Professor David Shwayder. Cornell University gave generous assistance for typing the manuscript and for incidental expenses. I am particularly grateful to Mr Malcolm Greenaway for checking the numerous references and for helping with proof-reading, and to Mr James Shea for work on the index.

I have tried hard to keep this book reasonably short. If any reader feels I have not tried hard enough, I can only plead that I have withheld as much material as is here published.

MAX BLACK

ITHACA, NEW YORK
July 1962

CONTENTS

Contents

Contents

xi

Contents

Contents

Contents

LIST OF ABBREVIATIONS

Abbreviations used in referring to Wittgenstein's writings

Blue Book   *The Blue and Brown Books* (Oxford, 1958).

Foundations   *Remarks on the Foundations of Mathematics* (Oxford, 1956).

Investigations   *Philosophical Investigations* (Oxford, 1953).

Lecture   Unpublished manuscript of a public lecture on ethics.

Letters   Letters written by L.W. to Bertrand Russell, 1912–21, partly contained in *Notebooks*.

Logical Form   'Some remarks on logical form', *Proceedings of the Aristotelian Society* (suppl.), **9** (1929), pp. 162–71.

Math. MS.   Unpublished manuscript of part of a book. The portion used deals with the philosophy of mathematics and is entitled 'Grundlagen der Mathematik'.

Math. Notes   Notes by Norman Malcolm of lectures given by L.W. in the spring of 1939. Unauthorized copies on sale in San Francisco, 1954, with the title: 'Math Notes by Ludwig Wittgenstein' (*sic*), no publisher shown.

Moore Notes   Notes dictated by L.W. to G. E. Moore in Norway, April 1914, printed in *Notebooks*.

Notebooks   *Wittgenstein Notebooks 1914–1916*. Edited by G. H. von Wright and G. E. M. Anscombe with an English translation by G. E. M. Anscombe (Oxford, 1961).

Notes on Logic   Notes prepared for Bertrand Russell by L.W., September 1913, printed in *Notebooks*.

Phil. Bem.   Unpublished manuscript entitled 'Philosophische Bemerkungen'.

NOTE ON REFERENCES

I call the whole of any portion of the original text identified by a decimal (e.g. 5.552) a 'section', whether it consists of several paragraphs or only a single sentence. Each of W.'s sentences is referred to as a 'remark'. The portions into which I have divided the text are called 'instalments'. Paragraphs in the English translation are indicated by adding a numeral in brackets. Thus '5.552 (2)' indicates the second paragraph of section 5.552. Sentences are indicated by adding letters. Thus '3.24 *c*' means the third sentence of section 3.24; and '5.154 (3) *b*' the second sentence of the third paragraph of section 5.154. A colon is not counted as the end of a sentence. The text and translation used are those of the 1961 edition (Kegan Paul). Similar references are used for the *Notebooks* (and for the *Notes on Logic*, *Moore Notes*, and *Letters*, included therein as appendices). Thus '*Moore Notes* 108 (10) *c*' indicates the third sentence of the tenth paragraph on page 108 of the *Notebooks*. Each indented line in the original English text is counted as starting or as being a new paragraph. The continuation of a paragraph from a previous page is counted as the first paragraph on the page at whose head it appears.

References to Wittgenstein's unpublished manuscripts (*Lecture, Math. MS., Phil. Bem.*) are by page and paragraph numbers of the typescript in the possession of his literary executors.

GENERAL INTRODUCTION

The English translation of the *Tractatus Logico-Philosophicus* was first published in 1922; the original German version, under the title 'Logisch-Philosophische Abhandlung', appeared a year earlier. Parts of the book date back to 1913 and some of the concluding remarks on ethics and the will may have been composed still earlier, when Wittgenstein admired Schopenhauer.

No philosophical classic is harder to master. According to Wittgenstein himself, it was misunderstood by Russell, Moore and Frege; and even Ramsey, whose critical notice in *Mind* (reprinted in his *Foundations*) is the best short study of the text, sometimes went badly astray. The reader's difficulty is partly due to the extreme compression of Wittgenstein's often oracular remarks. Within a span of some twenty thousand words there are comments on the nature of the universe and the essence of language, important contributions to the foundations of logic and mathematics, penetrating criticisms of the work of Frege and Russell, the outlines of a theory of probability, revolutionary ideas about philosophical method, not to mention occasional remarks about philosophy of science, ethics, religion, and mysticism. Wittgenstein disliked circumlocution and found it painful to elaborate thoughts that were no longer fresh; his ideas would be valuable, he felt, only for those who had had similar ideas and could trace their implications unaided. He said: 'Perhaps this book will be understood only by someone who has himself already had the thoughts that are expressed in it—or at least similar thoughts' (first sentence of *Preface*). A serious reader must labour strenuously to reconstruct Wittgenstein's thoughts from cryptic and elliptical suggestions, getting what help he can from a succession of images that dazzle as much as they illuminate.

The difficulties can be overcome by patient collocation of the scattered passages where Wittgenstein re-examines a topic from a new perspective. His technical terms (*Sachverhalt, Tatsache, Sinn*, and so on) illuminate each other's meanings and very few passages fail to make good sense at last. Understanding is greatly helped by the 'Notes on Logic' prepared for Russell in September 1913, the 'Notes' dictated to Moore in April 1914, the letters sent to Russell between June 1912 and November 1921 and especially the *Notebooks* from which Wittgenstein quarried much of the final text. The reader will also wish to consider the criticisms of the *Tractatus* contained in the posthumous *Investigations*.

Familiarity does not blunt the pleasure of reading the text. If its intrinsic importance and its influence on the course of contemporary philosophy did not justify the present attempt at exegesis, it would be sufficient to say that a thorough grasp of the *Tractatus* is indispensable for a proper appreciation of Wittgenstein's later work. This was why he wished the text of the *Tractatus* to precede that of the *Investigations* (a course that has been followed in the German edition).

The book is arranged as a series of remarks, identified by decimal numbers purporting to indicate their 'logical importance' and the 'stress' they should receive. Possibly suggested by the similar system of reference in *Principia Mathematica*, the device is so misleading here as to suggest a private joke at the reader's expense. In later life, Wittgenstein proposed more in earnest than in jest to arrange the sentences of a philosophical book in alphabetical order: he always thought it harmful to force philosophical thoughts into linear deductive order. Adapting his remark about logic (6.127a) one might say that for him all philosophical pronouncements 'have equal justification' (*sind gleichberechtigt*); the *Tractatus* is a web in which almost every thought is connected with all the others. Its form has been aptly compared to that of a musical composition (cf. Stenius, *Exposition*, p. 5) whose leitmotifs reappear with subtle modulations. It has something of the spontaneity of its mode of composition— cf. his remark: 'Don't worry about what you have already written. Just keep on beginning to think afresh as if nothing at all had happened yet' (*Notebooks*, 30 (6)). Wittgenstein would have dismissed as idle pedantry an effort to impose the strait-jacket of conventional exposition.

System and order are present, nevertheless. Given the complexity and enormous difficulty of its main themes, the organic unity of the whole and its freedom from all but occasional inconsistency are impressive. The beauty of its lapidary German style will be best appreciated by readers who have suffered from the German philosophers of whom Carlyle once said that none could dive so deep or emerge so muddy.

Of strict argument, there is very little in the book. Wittgenstein occasionally uses informal argument to clinch a point, but his main insights are presented dogmatically. A sympathetic response calls for a willing suspension of disbelief in the visual metaphors ('pictures' Wittgenstein later called them) which lend those insights their force and their support.

Among the most important of these metaphors are those I shall call the *mosaic*, the *chain*, the *logical network*, the *picture*, and the *mirror*. The baldest summary of Wittgenstein's conception might run as follows: Reality ('the world') is a *mosaic* of independent items—the 'atomic facts'; each of these is like a *chain* in which 'objects' (logical simples) 'hang in one another'; the objects are connected in a *network* of logical possibilities ('logical space'); the simplest 'elementary' propositions are *pictures* of atomic facts, themselves facts in which names are concatenated, and all other propositions are truth-functions of the elementary ones; language is the great *mirror* in which the logical network is reflected, 'shown', manifested. If we add the notions of names *deputizing* for objects, of logical propositions as *limiting cases* of contingent propositions, and the pervasive notions of *logical form* and of *essence*, we shall have a serviceable list of Wittgenstein's chief leitmotifs.

How did it all begin? As an effort to answer certain fundamental questions in the philosophy of logic and mathematics, I believe. Here Wittgenstein shared Russell's preoccupations (the first volume of *Principia* appeared shortly before Wittgenstein began to study at Cambridge). The earliest notes for the *Tractatus* show a rooted dissatisfaction with Whitehead's attempt to reduce pure mathematics to logic and with Frege's heroic efforts to reach the same goal in the *Grundgesetze*. Behind the specific views attributed to Russell, that 'propositions correspond to complexes' (*Notes on Logic*, 93 (3) *a*), that completely general propositions must be 'simple' *qua* expressions of logical form, that logical connectives stand for 'logical objects', that 'laws of deduction' justify logical inference, and so on, there is plain to see a drastic rejection of the views about the nature of logic which Russell and Frege had reached. At that time Wittgenstein agreed with Russell that logical analysis was a prime concern of philosophy: when he said 'Philosophy is the doctrine of the logical form of scientific propositions (not primitive propositions only)' (*Notes on Logic*, 93 (2) *f*) he meant 'scientific propositions' to include the propositions of logic. So it is that in the *Notes on Logic* he constantly returns to questions about the 'indefinables' of logic and their proper expression in an adequate symbolism. No task could have seemed more fundamental, given his view that '[Philosophy] consists of logic and metaphysics, the former its basis' (*Notes on Logic*, 93 (2) *d*). Logic as the *basis* of metaphysics: throughout the book Wittgenstein expects a perspicuous view of the nature of logic to have ontological implications. Logic is important because it leads to metaphysics.

Concerning the nature of logic, Frege and Russell had little to say that Wittgenstein could use. Frege held it to consist of objective truths, *Gesetze des Wahrseins* (*Grundgesetze*, preface, p. xvi), and rested there, possibly believing there was no more to be said. Although our own nature and the external circumstances (*die äussere Umstände*) compel us to acknowledge logical truth as a necessary condition for making judgements, that throws no light on the nature and ground of logical truth (*op. cit.* p. xvii). Russell, however, tended to assimilate logical and mathematical truths to scientific truths in a way which Wittgenstein could not stomach. Logical truths are distinguished from empirical generalizations only by their superior generality (cf. *Principia*, vol. i, p. 93); logical words stand for subsistent 'universals', our apprehension of which is 'as ultimate as sensation' ('Mathematical Logic', p. 492); and logic is an abstract natural science which 'must no more admit a unicorn than zoology can; for logic is concerned with the real world just as truly as zoology, though with its more abstract and general features' (*Mathematical Philosophy*, p. 169). So Russell consistently took the primitive propositions of *Principia* to be hypotheses and held the chief reason for adopting his reduction of mathematics to logic to 'be inductive...[and to] lie in the fact that the theory in question enables us to deduce ordinary mathematics' (*Principia*, preface, para. 2). This view's deficiencies came to a head in the celebrated axioms of reducibility and infinity, which Wittgenstein must have been one of the first to criticize. Subsequent work in logic has shown how to dispense with the axiom of reducibility, but there can be no prospect for Russell or Frege either of doing without the axiom of infinity. If they were right, the truth of mathematics must rest in the end upon an unverifiable hypothesis concerning the 'subsistence' of sufficiently capacious sets of contingently existing entities. So mathematical talk about very large numbers might be self-contradictory, for all we could tell. Now something must be seriously wrong about a view that imagines it possible for mathematicians to exhaust the supply of numbers: the idea of a shortage of integers really is an absurdity.

The state of the philosophy of logic and mathematics therefore gave Wittgenstein good reason to revive the Kantian question 'How is pure mathematics possible?' Wittgenstein himself saw the analogy when he wrote 'Light on Kant's question "How is pure mathematics possible?" through the theory of tautologies' (*Notebooks*, 15(3) (see also Stenius, *Exposition*, ch. XI: 'Wittgenstein as a Kantian philosopher')). Kant in the *Kritik* held our undoubted knowledge of 'universal and necessary connexions' in logic and mathematics to be incomprehensible either from the standpoint of Hume's empiricism or from that of Leibniz's rationalism. Wittgenstein would have agreed that if experience is the source of all knowledge, mathematical conclusions ought to be tentative and approximate; while if reason supplies only analytical truth it remains mysterious how mathematics escapes triviality. Pure mathematics cannot be 'about' the world in the way that physics is; yet if grounded in thought alone, how can it *apply* to the world? Wittgenstein was absorbed by this ancient puzzle of the connexion between thought and reality: 'The great problem round which everything that I write turns is: Is there an order in the world *a priori*, and if so what does it consist in?' (*Notebooks*, 53(11)). That there must be 'an order *in the world*' was a conviction he never abandoned while composing the *Tractatus*;

though he came to see that *a priori* propositions 'say nothing' he still maintained that in them the 'logical form of reality' manifests itself.

Wittgenstein grappled with problems of the philosophy of logic as an ardent partisan, not as a dispassionate and neutral investigator. His interest in technical problems like the reduction of mathematics and logic to their 'primitives' was subordinated to an attempt to justify a conception of logic that was as compelling as it was difficult to defend. 'Men have always had a presentiment' he says (surely thinking of himself) 'that there must be a realm in which the answers to questions are symmetrically combined—*a priori*—to form a self-contained system' (5.4541(2)). It was a conception of logic as 'sublime' (*Investigations*, § 89), something of 'the purest crystal' (*ibid.* § 97)—self-contained, harmonious, perfect in its freedom from the imprecision and uncertainty of empirical knowledge.

How is this dazzling ideal of the 'essence of logic' to be justified? 'Logic takes care of itself; all we have to do is to look and see how it does it' (*Notebooks*, 11 (4)). 'All we have to do'—as a climber might say on starting the ascent of Everest, or rather of a mountain that wasn't there at all. I disagree with those like Stenius who take the interest of Wittgenstein's discussion of logic and mathematics to be 'merely peripheral' (*Exposition*, p. ix). This is about as plausible as saying that the hope of salvation is peripheral to religion.

Wittgenstein's pursuit of the 'essence' of logic engaged him at once in an equally arduous pursuit of the essence of language. It is easy to misconstrue his interest in the ideography (*Begriffsschrift*) or ideal language which Frege and Russell had already considered. Distrusting the ambiguity and formlessness of ordinary language, they had hoped for a symbolism that would perfectly reflect logical form. Although Wittgenstein also demands 'a sign-language that is governed by *logical* grammar' (3.325*a*), he thinks that ordinary language, just as we know it, is 'in perfect logical order' (5.5563*a*). So the ideography is for him merely an instrument in the search for the essence of representation that is present in all languages and in all symbolisms.

Wittgenstein's final conception of the nature of logic gave him stronger reasons to scrutinize the 'essence of representation' than, as with his predecessors, the desire to curb philosophical fallacies or to render the principles of deduction explicit. His first answer to the question 'How is logic possible?', given as early as 1914 and steadfastly defended thereafter, is that logical propositions 'signify' in a peculiar and distinctive way: unlike empirical propositions, they 'show' but do not 'say'. This 'means' that their truth can be established 'from the symbol alone' (cf. *Moore Notes*, 107 (2)). This, he significantly adds in the text, 'contains in itself the whole philosophy of logic' (6.113 a). (The *whole* philosophy of logic?—well, in the sense that the acorn contains the whole oak perhaps.) The lasting philosophical value of this idea must depend upon the perspicuity of the notion of 'showing' and this in turn upon the success of Wittgenstein's analysis of language *überhaupt*.

Truths of logic can be certified 'from the symbol alone'—here there is an important shift of interest from thought to language. Any number of philosophers had previously held *a priori* propositions to be verifiable by inspection of their meanings alone, by attention solely to the *thoughts* expressed; it was one of Wittgenstein's distinctive innovations to consider thoughts only as embodied in what he calls the 'significant proposition' (*der sinnvoller Satz*) and so to transform the question of the relation of thought to reality, which Anscombe considers a 'principal theme of the book' (*Introduction*, p. 19), into the more promising question of the relation of language to reality. No move in the *Tractatus* has proved more influential: here if anywhere we can see the beginning of the 'linguistic turn' in modern philosophy.

Wittgenstein's conception of the philosophy of language (the search for its essence) required a stand on ontological issues: anybody who hopes to delineate a *Begriffsschrift* that adequately manifests the grain of reality must have at least some schematic view concerning the true structure of thought and its true, if hidden, connexion with reality; for how is one to distinguish the 'accidental' from the 'essential' features of language except in terms of prior notions about what 'reality' is really like? Yet Wittgenstein hoped that comparison of alternative symbolisms, without explicit reference to the reality they represented, might serve to reveal their necessary features, their invariants, and so indirectly to reveal the form of the world. His ontology is on the whole suggested by his views about language, rather than the reverse, although the interaction between semantics and metaphysics in the book is too complex to be reduced to a simple formula.

Other philosophers, such as Hume and Leibniz, have arrived at a version of 'logical atomism' without considering what makes *language* possible: it has seemed to them that the existence of complexes in the world sufficed to imply the existence of absolute simples (logical atoms). But Wittgenstein's conviction that objects (logical simples) must exist seems to have been at least powerfully buttressed by his view that they are needed as a prerequisite for the possibility of *sense* (2.0201–2.0212). Also, his basic contention that the universe is an aggregate of facts, not of things, seems to have arisen from his insight that propositions signify in a way altogether different from that in which names do: in the early *Notes on Logic*, he was still treating 'fact' as an incomplete symbol and it was only after his conception of language had been fully elaborated that 'fact' became an indefinable.

If I am not mistaken, then, the order of investigation—from the nature of logic to the nature of language and thence to the nature of 'the world'—was roughly the reverse of the order of presentation in the final text. He said of his own inquiry: 'Yes, my work has stretched out from the foundations of logic to the essence (*Wesen*) of the world' (*Notebooks*, 79 (17)). It would be quite wrong, however, to treat the metaphysics as a mere appendage: indeed it would be plausible to read the book as being primarily concerned with metaphysics. Wittgenstein plainly attached great importance to his metaphysical conclusions; to treat his book as a positivistic tract, as the Vienna Circle tried to do, would be very perverse. Whatever the order of composition, the final conceptions of language, logic and reality are virtually inseparable.

The ontology of the *Tractatus* is a striking combination of an atomistic conception of the universe as an aggregate of mutually independent atomic facts, and an organic conception of logical form— or, what comes to the same, 'logical space'. The former is too prominent in the text to have escaped the attention of even the most casual commentators: the counterbalancing conception of the *necessary* features of the world (its 'essence') demands equal attention.

Wittgenstein calls the simplest kind of fact, one not analysable as a function of other facts, a *Sachverhalt* (best translated as 'atomic fact', I think, rather than 'situation' or 'state of affairs'—cf. the discussion at pp. 39–45 below). It is hard to get this fundamental notion clear. Since I shall discuss it later in this book, I confine myself here to pointing out that a *Sachverhalt* is of a radically different logical type from that of a *Gegenstand* (object). The opposition between the two cuts deep. Atomic facts are complex, are compounded of objects, their existence is contingent, they are symbolized by full sentences that 'say' something, and they are mutually independent—while objects are simple, combine to form atomic facts, their existence is necessary, they are symbolized by names that 'show' something, and they are mutually dependent.

Atomic facts are concatenations of objects in immediate combination. An important principle, nowhere explicitly formulated by Wittgenstein but implied by much of his discussion, is that *all* complexity is contingent and everything that is contingent is manifested in the occurrence of atomic facts. The 'objects', however, the stuff of every possible world, constitute together the *substance* of the world (2.021), they are what there is independently of what is contingently the case (2.024), are simple (2.02) and changeless (2.0271). (One might be inclined to add that they are changeless *because* they are simple.)

The atomic facts are mutually independent—each might have failed to obtain while everything else remained unchanged; but there is an important though difficult sense in which all the objects are interdependent. For all of them have being only as possible constituents of atomic facts, and all such possibilities must exist together and as it were timelessly. Wittgenstein here introduces the metaphor of (logical) 'space' (2.013). Objects are like the co-ordinates of empty positions in physical space, atomic facts are like the material points that sometimes occupy such positions. But just as talk about 'physical space' is a compendious way of referring to possibilities of spatial relation, so talk about 'logical space' proves to be a picturesque way of talking

9

about the logical relations between objects and atomic facts. The intelligible content of the metaphor finally depends upon the clarity of the notion of logical possibility: this is one point where the text is of little help and the reader is thrown back upon his own resources.

Some remarkable consequences can be drawn from this dominating metaphor of logical space. The properties of logical space must, of course, be without exception necessary (or 'internal' as Wittgenstein sometimes says). All that is contingent in the universe is comprised in the obtaining and non-obtaining of atomic facts; but in speaking of logical space we are referring to what could not have been otherwise. Just as it is nonsense to speak of physical space (*pace* some contemporary cosmologists) as being created or destroyed, enlarged, diminished or dismembered, so it is nonsensical to speak of the objects constituting logical space as coming into existence or ceasing to be—or of logical space as in any way changing its properties. Nor can there be any sense in speaking of 'logical spaces' in the plural; in alluding to objects we are really acknowledging the existence of a unique system, in which the existence of a part implicates the existence of the whole. It might seem to follow that acquaintance with even a single object would imply acquaintance with all. For to know such an object is to know the possibilities and impossibilities of its combinations with *all* other objects—and so in some sense to know them also.

This 'organic' view of the world's essence is in striking contrast with the atomism that Wittgenstein shares with Russell and other philosophers. Indeed there is in the book a sharp opposition between the contingent aspect of the world (whatever can be 'said' in language) and its essence (what must *show itself*). The intended subject-matter of metaphysics (the world's essence, logical space) displays regularity, coherence, necessary connexion. Contrasted with this is the realm of the empirical, where all is plurality, separation, and what Wittgenstein calls 'accident': here no fact is really connected with any other and knowledge is strictly speaking impossible. Given this stark bifurcation, it is no wonder that Wittgenstein located all that seemed most valuable to him—aesthetics, ethics and religion—in the transcendental heaven of substance, or beyond it.

General Introduction

Wittgenstein's final account of the nature of language divides into two parts—the 'picture theory' of elementary propositions, and the 'truth-function theory' of complex propositions—that can be considered separately. The first is to explain how certain propositions can be in direct contact with reality; the second is to explain how all other propositions are linked with the basic ones and so indirectly with the world. Wittgenstein seems never to have doubted that if language is linked with reality there must be some propositions directly connected with the world, i.e. not deriving their meanings from other propositions: these he called 'elementary propositions'. Non-elementary propositions are understood *via* elementary ones, i.e. their meanings are certain functions of selected sets of elementary propositions. Accordingly, Wittgenstein has two main questions to answer: How *are* elementary propositions linked with the world? and How *are* complex propositions related to elementary ones? He answers: Elementary propositions are 'logical pictures' of atomic facts and all other propositions are truth-functions of the elementary ones.

For the proper appreciation of Wittgenstein's solutions it is essential to hold steadily in mind that his pattern of analysis seemed to him necessitated *a priori*; he did not reach it by generalization from cases (e.g. by perceiving that given propositions *are* 'elementary' in his sense), was convinced that language must have the pattern envisaged in order for a connexion with the world to be *possible*. His philosophical semantics is that of a *lingua abscondita* grounded in 'elementary propositions' whose existence is guaranteed only by metaphysical inference. We can produce no elementary propositions and would not recognize them if we had them. Consequently, we can form no clear idea of what genuine 'names', the constituents of elementary propositions, are like, nor any clear conception of the nature and logical form of the objects for which those names stand. (The arguments in which some writers have engaged about whether objects are to be counted as particulars or universals, whether elementary propositions are relational or not, and so on, are bound to be futile.) The language of which Wittgenstein speaks with the confidence of *a priori* insight is a never-never language in which essence is adequately manifested. But he also holds that 'ordinary language', the language we *do* know, is logically 'completely in order' and shares the structure of the invisible language even if we cannot perceive it. (For instance, general propositions *must* be truth-functions.) Conflict between the two insights provides some dramatic passages in the *Notebooks* and is never satisfactorily resolved in the book. When Wittgenstein wrestles to accommodate specific types of propositions from 'ordinary language' (e.g. probability statements, statements of belief, scientific hypotheses) to his predetermined pattern of analysis, the material on which he works proves recalcitrant, for all his ingenuity, and threatens to burst out of the metaphysical strait-jacket into which he presses it.

In his conception of elementary propositions Wittgenstein introduced two important novelties which distinguish his view from the semantical theories of Russell and Frege: he insisted that propositions must be regarded as *facts*, not complex objects; and he extended a famous doctrine of Frege's by holding *all* names to have reference only in context. The two ideas together enforce a clear-cut distinction between the 'sense' (*Sinn*) of an elementary proposition and the 'meanings' (*Bedeutungen*) of its component names. Here, too, is the origin of the drastic contrast between objects and facts that recurs throughout the text.

Russell's philosophical grammar is dominated by the category of *name*: broadly speaking, words or symbols are ultimately acceptable for him only when they *stand for* real entities, are names of things. His 'incomplete symbols' are problematic, from a logical point of view, because they do not stand for objective constituents. Conversely, whenever we encounter symbols that cannot be construed as 'incomplete' we have good reason to acknowledge that corresponding entities exist or subsist. In particular, the 'logical constants' were taken to stand for 'logical objects'. Differences in the logical grammars of names are imputed, in these early views, to differences in the kinds of objects for which they stand: simplicity of the naming relation is paid for by complexity of ontology. That the naming relation, conceived as a link between a word and a real entity, is the only ultimately intelligible connexion between language and reality was, indeed, a common presupposition of nearly all philosophers prior to Frege: the assumption is, for example, just as pronounced in Mill's *Logic* as in *The Principles of Mathematics*. Frege took a decisive step forward when he introduced a radical distinction between 'functions' and 'objects'. The former, being 'incomplete', 'in need of supplementation', 'unsaturated', have to be symbolized by words of a peculiar and distinctive sort ('function names'), having 'gaps' that need to be filled by names of objects. Wittgenstein went still further: for him, it might be said, all simple symbols (names) were 'unsaturated' in something like Frege's sense. Names occur only in association with other names, and have no reference except in the propositional context (3.3); in elementary propositions they grip one another, without intermediaries, like the links of a chain (cf. 3.14); and their *esse* is to be eligible for such concatenation (3.203 + 3.21 + 2.0123). Hence the proposition itself *cannot* be another name (for else it would need to occur as part of another proposition): propositions are *facts*, and only facts (strictly speaking: atomic facts) have independent existence. In an elementary proposition, each of the concatenated names deputizes for a corresponding object and the unified sense of the proposition is that those objects *are* concatenated in a fact. The proposition *shows* by its configuration of names what fact it alleges to obtain, and it 'says' that the fact *does* obtain.

But *how* does an elementary proposition say that a certain fact obtains—how *is* the elementary proposition linked with the world? It will not do to say merely that each of its constituent names stands for a logical simple, for that happens only *because* the whole proposition has a unified sense. Nor will it do to say that the sense is the corresponding fact, for to false propositions no facts correspond. No problem gave Wittgenstein greater trouble. His final answer was that the elementary proposition is a 'logical picture' of what it represents or, more explicitly, that the picture and the fact pictured have 'logical form' in common. Every type of representation is based upon some general principle of representation, whether of approximate identity of spatial arrangement (as in a photograph) or something more sophisticated and 'conventional' (as in a musical score). The most general principle of representation which governs *every* symbolism

13

is that 'logical form of representation' that demands that the 'multiplicity' of the symbol shall answer exactly to the multiplicity of what is symbolized. Here is a *necessary* connexion between language and the world which guarantees that if we make sense it will be sense *about the world*. (The topic is hard to condense and the reader is referred to later discussions for more detail.)

The doctrine of identity of logical form between symbol and symbolized is quite central to the book and must be accepted if anything of importance is to survive. But it is hard to grasp and still harder to accept. In the first place, there can really be no question of strict identity of logical form between proposition and fact represented but at best a parallelism of form. Wittgenstein's conception of identity of logical form would be approximately satisfied if elementary propositions, which represent atomic facts, were themselves atomic facts. But this cannot be. The sentence-fact must have an attached sense and so needs to be *more* than an atomic fact; and in any case a 'significant *proposition*' must be a class or type of producible facts. The demand for strict identity of form cannot be met.

A more fundamental difficulty is this: the idea of shared logical form between sentence-fact and fact represented is attractive so long as that form is thought to be something intrinsic that might, as it were, be directly perceived in the marks on the page (as one *sees* the shape of the Great Bear in the sky). But logical form might better be called extrinsic and invisible, not something literally manifested in some fact. To say proposition and depicted fact have the same logical form comes to saying: to every sensible combination of some of the names with other names in elementary propositions there corresponds a possible combination in an atomic fact of the objects for which the names severally deputize—and *vice versa*, the powers of combination of the names exactly matching the powers of combination of their object partners. But this extrinsic conception of logical form, the only view that will stand scrutiny, fails to resolve the metaphysical perplexity (How *can* language be connected with the world?) that is its *raison d'être*. The mystery of the nature of the 'link' between an elementary proposition and what it represents in the world is only compounded by invoking a set of further elementary propositions, each needing its own objective counterpart. (If a child is puzzled why a stamp sticks to an envelope, it will hardly help him to be told that lots of other stamps *can* stick to envelopes.) The reference to *possibility*, which is a necessary part of the proposed solution, introduces problems at least as puzzling as those it is intended to resolve. I said before that Wittgenstein is pulled in opposite ways by a conception of the form of language as *hidden* and an opposing conception of language being 'perfectly in order' as it is; a closely connected conflict may be discerned here between the 'intrinsic' and the 'extrinsic' conceptions of logical form—between a conception of logical form as something that can be instantaneously 'shown' and 'seen' and a conception of logical form as manifested only discursively in a system of possibilities of related senses.

The weaknesses of the truth-functional theory of complex propositions are of a different sort. I have already mentioned the problems Wittgenstein found in exhibiting familiar types of propositions as truth-functions: it is doubtful whether his theory illuminates the mode of signification even of propositions that are explicitly truth-functional in form. Consider the following illustration: suppose somebody to be philosophically perplexed about the 'connexion' between a disjunctive proposition of the form $p \vee q$ and external 'reality', without being puzzled in the same way about p or about q. The perplexity might be expressed as follows: 'What *is* the case is either p, or else q (or both at once), i.e. in each case *something categorical*; so how can "p *or* q" mean anything when, as it were, there is nothing in the world for the "or" to correspond to?' (Cf. Wittgenstein on there being no logical objects.) The truth-functional answer amounts to displaying $p \vee q$ as the disjunction $pq \vee {\sim}pq \vee p{\sim}q$. And the philosophical gloss runs as follows: 'What is the case is either pq, or ${\sim}p\,q$, or $p \sim q$, or $\sim p \sim q$—in each case something categorical. The original proposition is verified by each of the first three cases and falsified by the last. Thus the complex proposition is rendered true or false, as the case may be, by what *is* the case—just as p and q are, though in a more complicated way.' Will this answer really satisfy? One might be inclined to object that it is as hard on Wittgenstein's principles to understand how $p \sim q$ can be the case as it is to understand how $p \vee q$ can be (the difficulty being that of grasping how negative propositions like $\sim q$ can be true in a world composed exclusively of atomic facts). And in any case, the explanation uses the very same connective ('or') that generated the original perplexity. If a man persuades himself that he cannot understand how $p \vee q$ is used, there is only an illusion of explanation in offering him a *disjunctive* normal form. The original trouble arose from a confused but pressing inclination to view only the categorical form of proposition as intelligible and can hardly be relieved by pretending that an adequate translation is anything but disjunctive again.

For the reasons outlined above, I am inclined to think that both parts of Wittgenstein's theory of language collapse. If his metaphysical preconceptions *forced* this view of language upon him, so much the worse, one might say, for the metaphysics.

Similar criticisms apply to Wittgenstein's final conception of the nature of logic. His basic idea is the following: Having arranged the 'truth-conditions' of molecular propositions in the form of truth-tables (4.31), he singles out 'tautology' as the 'extreme' or limiting case in which the proposition in question is true for *all* the combinations of truth-values of its components (4.46*ab*). So a tautology is seen to be true because it makes no demand upon the world (requires no verification), being so constructed that it will be 'satisfied' no matter what is the case. This way of looking at tautologies is persuasive and, on the face of it, genuinely illuminating. But I shall argue later (pp. 318–19) that there is an illusion here. The truth-table representation amounts to the translation of the original proposition into a new symbolism; the truth-table has to be *read* as a 'disjunctive normal form'. Thus the truth-table for $p \supset (q \supset p)$, for example, translates that proposition into $pq \vee \sim pq \vee p \sim q \vee \sim p \sim q$; and to say that the tautology 'exhausts all the possibilities' comes to saying that our new symbolism makes no provision for more than the four disjuncts. It might, therefore, be held that the outcome of the translation is philosophically no more satisfying than the original formula, since anybody perplexed as to how the one can be true *a priori* ought to be equally perplexed about the other. The difficulty resembles the one discussed above concerning the interpretation of any truth-

function. By his theory of tautologies Wittgenstein showed only how
to convert some *a priori* truths into the standard disjunctive normal
form. This fact is only obscured by his picturesque imagery of propositions delimiting regions of logical space (4.463) and the allied
imagery of one proposition 'containing' another (5.121–5.122).
When the imagery is discarded, what remains is the truism that
a priori propositions are—*a priori*. Wittgenstein's 'solution' merely
brought him back to his starting-point.

The disconcerting role of visual imagery in the book is nowhere
more disturbing than in Wittgenstein's account of what might be
called the epistemology of logical truth—his answer to the question
'How is logical truth recognized?' He replies 'from the symbol alone'
(6.113*a*). The same idea is expressed in repeated allusions to what
tautologies *show*—e.g. 'Every tautology itself shows that it is a tautology' (6.127(2)). But what *is* it to 'show'? The question is crucial,
since 'show' is a positive *verbum ex machina*. To conceive, naïvely, of
some perceptible manifestation would be to commit an elementary
error which Wittgenstein repudiates: what 'shows' is the sign
together with its use (3.326) and uses cannot literally be perceived. In
order to see what is shown, we must attend not to marks on paper but
rather to the *rules* governing the proper employment of symbols
(cf. 5.514*b* on rules as 'equivalent to the symbols'). But how do the
rules manifest themselves to us? Here we draw a blank. Rules of use
are so important for Wittgenstein's doctrine that one might have
hoped for some discussion of how they are expressed, how symbols
occur within them, how they fit into his general views about the
essence of language, and so on: instead, we get only the barest hints
as to what his views are on these matters. So the initial 'mystery'
about *a priori* propositions is supplanted by a mystery about rules.
But one might take 'rule', in the required sense, to be a more obscure
notion than that of logical truth, and wish, with apologies to Byron,
that Wittgenstein had explained his explanation.

I shall leave for later discussion the technical reasons why
Wittgenstein's account of logical truths as tautologies proves too
narrow to fit the whole of logic (see pp. 318–19, below). I shall also
defer consideration of the difficulties he met in trying to fit

mathematics into his 'picture' of the world (see pp. 313–14). The technical embarrassments are symptoms of a deeper malaise—a failure in the end to provide the metaphysical illumination that Wittgenstein so ardently sought.

How much weight should be attached to criticisms such as those outlined above? What is to be the final verdict on Wittgenstein's intricately woven fabric of metaphors? The relevant criterion, no doubt, is the power of the whole to illuminate and resolve philosophical perplexity (for whatever that all too familiar formula is worth). Certainly the book will seem not so much wrong as pointless to any reader who has not been obsessed by the 'transempirical' problems about the *a priori*, the nature of reality, the essence of reality, that held its author in thrall. Metaphysical obsession of this sort draws its force from a certain model which seems at once inescapable and intolerable: it is typically expressed in the form 'Things *can't* be that way—and yet they must!' The young Wittgenstein managed to invent a new model—a new philosophical myth, one might say, which displaced the old anxieties by a radical shift of vision. One can hardly indict a metaphor—or argue about a perspective (and this is perhaps why proof is so rare and unimportant in the book). The value of a philosophical myth may be tested either by its power of instant illumination or by its capacity to sustain coherent elaboration. That the *Tractatus* satisfies the first test no sympathetic reader can doubt; its real weaknesses emerge only when its doctrines are traced to their conclusions. I have outlined the reasons why I think Wittgenstein's conceptions of the nature of language and the nature of logic to be splendid failures; on the other hand, I disagree with the critics who have said that the *Tractatus*, on its author's own principles, ought to count as 'nonsensical' and hence unworthy of serious attention. I shall argue later (pp. 382–6) that the attempt to *extend* a given philosophical vocabulary in the service of metaphysical insight is a defensible procedure: Wittgenstein's sustained attempt to impose new meanings upon 'fact', 'logical form', 'sense', 'object', and the rest is legitimate in principle and can be criticized only in the light of its achievements. I judge its value to have been in the end almost wholly negative, as showing the limitations of one, enormously persuasive, way of looking at logic, language, and reality. (Any philosopher might have been proud to have achieved so much.) If the reader thinks otherwise, he must find Wittgenstein's use of his primitive terms more intelligible and more helpful than I have in the end managed to do. If my comments seem harsh, it should be remembered that Wittgenstein's own verdict on his earlier work was even harsher—and that equally grave objections apply to the competing philosophical mythologies that continue to flourish in the world of scholarship. What matters in a metaphysical system is not so much its conclusions as the force and originality of the insights that have inspired them. Here the reader of the *Tractatus* will not be disappointed. Prolonged study of this remarkable work only deepens one's admiration for the man who could overcome in himself the fascination of the grandiose philosophical myth so memorably expressed in his great book.

COMMENTARY

COMMENTARY

THE TITLE

Probably suggested by Spinoza's *Tractatus Theologico-Politicus*, it is said to have been proposed for the English edition by G. E. Moore. I take 'Logico-' to modify 'Philosophicus', so that the sense of the whole is 'A discourse in the kind of philosophy that uses logic as a basis'. (Cf. Wittgenstein's remark that philosophy 'consists of logic and metaphysics, the former its basis', *Notes on Logic*, 93 (2) *d*.) The relevant sense of 'logic' is a broad one, including whatever falls under 'logical syntax' (for which see p. 136 below).

WITTGENSTEIN'S PREFACE

It is noteworthy that Wittgenstein treats the famous concluding remark (7) as summarizing 'the whole sense of the book'. With this emphasis, the main purpose of the book would be the negative one of preventing the nonsense that results when the 'logic of our language' is misunderstood. This does injustice to Wittgenstein's positive achievements, especially to his investigation into the nature of logic, which was in the forefront of his interest while the book was being composed. There is a serious question whether a limit to the expression of thought can, on Wittgenstein's views, even be put '*in* language' (para. 4). His confidence in the unassailable truth of his position (para. 8) is piquant in view of his later rejection of the *Tractatus*. A reading of the *Notebooks* suggests that his views were in flux throughout the composition of the book. I believe his position was deliberately frozen for the sake of publication.

RUSSELL'S INTRODUCTION

Although Wittgenstein expressed some agreement with much that Russell had written (letter to Bertrand Russell, 9 April 1920) he later refused permission to have a German translation of it precede a proposed German edition of his work (letter to Bertrand Russell, 6 May 1920). I do not know whether the superficiality and misunderstanding he found in the German version of Russell's essay was merely a fault of the translation; at any rate he must have agreed to including Russell's introduction in the 1922 English edition. On the whole, Russell's discussion is an accurate and lucid summary of Wittgenstein's views, especially helpful in its analysis of the doctrine that all propositions are truth-functions of elementary propositions, and its explanation of Wittgenstein's notation. Its chief error was the assertion that Wittgenstein was 'concerned with the conditions which would have to be fulfilled by a logically perfect language' (p. ix(3) and *passim*). Since Wittgenstein was investigating the essence of all representation, his results must apply to ordinary language as much as to any other. To read him as proposing mainly an improved ideography is to misunderstand him. Russell takes a rather cool attitude towards the notion of 'showing' that is so important in the *Tractatus* and his remark that Wittgenstein 'manages to say a good deal about what cannot be said' (p. xxi (1)) must have been an irritant. Russell's tentative suggestion of an 'exit' from the identification of philosophy with the unsayable by means of 'a hierarchy of languages' (*ibid.*) will not fit into Wittgenstein's conception of language.

THE RELATION OF WITTGENSTEIN'S PROBLEMS TO RUSSELL'S PHILOSOPHY

In order to understand the questions that Wittgenstein tried to answer, it is helpful to bear in mind the conception of philosophical method held by Russell at the time that Wittgenstein was his pupil at Cambridge. This may be conveniently studied in Russell's 1914 lecture 'On Scientific Method in Philosophy' (reproduced in *Mysticism and Logic*) which a reference in the *Notebooks* (44 (13)) shows Wittgenstein to have read. Somewhat similar views were expounded by Russell in the second of his Lowell lectures (ch. 2, 'Logic as the Essence of Philosophy', in *Our Knowledge of the External World*, 1914).

We may pass over the part of Russell's programme that consists of the application of 'systematic doubt' to the uncriticized propositions of common sense and science, with the ultimate purpose of substituting propositions, constructed out of objects of acquaintance, having a better chance of being true than those they replace (see, for instance, *External World*, pp. 242, 244). Such 'philosophical criticism' and reconstruction, so important for Russell, had little or no influence on the earlier Wittgenstein, who was unattracted by epistemology.

There remains Russell's conception of 'philosophical logic' as consisting, first, of 'the analysis and enumeration of logical *forms*' in order to provide 'an inventory of possibilities' (*Mysticism*, p. 112), and, secondly, the assertion of 'certain supremely general propositions, which assert the truth of all propositions of certain forms' (*External World*, p. 67).

'Analysis', for Russell and for Wittgenstein, too, meant resolving some complex into ultimate elements incapable of further resolution. If the subject-matter of the kind of analysis envisaged in 'philosophical logic' consists of logical forms, the analysis should terminate in a set of logical simples. Thus Russell thought of himself as engaged in 'the discussion of indefinables—which forms the chief part of philosophical logic' (*Principles*, p. xv). Similarly, we find Wittgenstein in the *Notes on Logic* constantly returning to the theme of the 'logical indefinables' or the 'logical primitives'. We find him rejecting the idea that 'thing, proposition, subject–predicate form' are 'indefinables'; dismissing 'not' and 'or' as indefinables; asserting that 'indefinables are of two sorts: names and forms'; and so on. The search for the ultimate logical indefinables runs like a connecting thread through these earlier *Notes* and is present also, as a connecting principle, though less explicitly, in the *Notebooks* and in the *Tractatus*.

Coupled with this general task of arriving at a sort of philosophical morphology, is the 'applied' task of investigating the form of given propositions having philosophical interest. In the *Notebooks*, Wittgenstein uses as typical examples of philosophical questions: 'whether say "A is good" is a subject–predicate proposition'; or 'whether "A is brighter than B" is a relational proposition' (3 (4)). Similarly, he considers the question whether 'a point in our visual field [is] a *simple object*' (*ibid.*) and adds the illuminating remarks that he has envisaged such questions as these to be the 'truly philosophical ones' (*die eigentlichen philosophischen*). This interest in the analysis of the meaning of given propositions persists in the *Tractatus* in the discussion of belief statements, for instance.

To sum up: Wittgenstein's conception of the tasks of philosophical method at about the time he began the studies that culminated in the *Tractatus* seems to have been about as follows: Philosophy is a kind of analysis, aiming at the decomposition of propositional forms into simples, so as to provide both an inventory of such simples and of their modes of combination (a philosophical morphology) and specific answers about the forms of given propositions. How closely this conception agreed with Russell's view of philosophical method around 1914 may be seen by setting side by side some passages drawn from Russell and Wittgenstein respectively:

RUSSELL	WITTGENSTEIN
Philosophical propositions . . . must be *a priori* (*Mysticism*, 111).	Philosophy gives no pictures of reality, and can neither confirm nor confute scientific investigations (*Notes on Logic*, 93 (2) *c*).
Philosophy is the science of the possible (*ibid.*).	Logic deals with every possibility and all possibilities are its facts (2.0121 (3) *b*).
Philosophy . . . becomes indistinguishable from logic (*ibid.*).	[Philosophy] consists of logic and metaphysics, the former its basis (*Notes on Logic*, 93 (2) *d*).
Forms . . . are the proper object of philosophical logic (*External World*, 52).	Philosophy is the doctrine of the logical form of scientific propositions (not only of primitive propositions) (*Notes on Logic*, 93 (2) *g*).
Language misleads us both by its vocabulary and by its syntax. We must be on our guard in both respects if our logic is not to lead to a false metaphysic (*Logic and Knowledge*, 331).	Distrust of grammar is the first requisite for philosophizing (*Notes on Logic*, 93 (2) *f*).

Wittgenstein's interests broadened as he proceeded and the *Tractatus* contains much that cannot be called 'philosophical logic' in Russell's sense.

I

THE WORLD AS A TOTALITY OF
FACTS IN LOGICAL SPACE

(1–1.21)

The discussion of ontology, with which the book opens, was probably the last part to be composed. Wittgenstein's great contributions to philosophical insight—the so-called 'picture theory of meaning' (VI–XVI), the conception of 'logical syntax' (XX, XXII), the interpretation of logical truths as 'tautologies' (XLIII, XLVIII, LXXI–LXXII), the attempt to construe all propositions as truth-functions of elementary propositions (LI, LVI, LXIX), and the new conception of philosophy as 'critique of language' (XXIV, XXXI, LX)—are logically independent of his views about the nature of the world formulated in this instalment and the four that follow. But it should be remembered that Wittgenstein had a metaphysical goal. He did not regard the ontology to which he was led by his logical investigations as irrelevant or unimportant. The vision of 'the world' set forth in the earlier sections of the book is almost inexorably suggested by Wittgenstein's detailed investigations of the essence of language and contributes powerfully, in its turn, to the organic unity of the whole work. It is characteristic of Wittgenstein's thought that nearly every one of his main remarks about language or logic has an ontological counterpart, while, conversely, each ontological remark is reflected in some truth about the essence of language. The dominant image, throughout, is of language as a 'mirror' of the world (5.511).

Against the background of earlier metaphysics, the outstanding innovation of Wittgenstein's ontology is his characterization of the universe ('the world') as an aggregate of facts, not of things (1, 1.1). This sets him off sharply from Aristotle, Spinoza, Descartes—indeed from any of the 'classical philosophers' who come readily to mind, the earlier Russell not excluded. When metaphysicians search for truths of the highest generality about the universe, they usually

27

conceive themselves to be investigating some nameable entity or, in the language of the *Tractatus*, a *thing*. A supremely important one, to be sure—*summa rerum*, containing everything that is real as a part, but a thing nonetheless. Wittgenstein breaks sharply with this tradition. He rejects at the outset the traditional conception of the universe as something that can be referred to by a name.

'Fact' may be taken at the outset in its familiar, popular, sense of whatever answers to a true statement. But Wittgenstein at once conceives all such 'facts' to be compounded out of '*atomic* facts' (2) into whose make-up no other facts enter. Central to his metaphysical conception is the conviction that there must *be* such ultimate facts (see the important remark 4.2211) for there to be a universe at all. But he will be wholly unable to provide a specimen of an 'atomic fact': that there must be atomic facts, if there are any facts at all, is known only *a priori*, through philosophical reflection.

From the impossibility of reducing atomic facts to other facts, it is a short step to the idea of the mutual independence of atomic facts (1.21). The world is a mosaic of atomic facts, of which any selection might be imagined removed without detriment to the remainder, a view now known as 'logical atomism'. But there is an 'organic' as well as an 'atomistic' aspect to Wittgenstein's ontology. The bits of the factual 'mosaic' are not simple: it is of the essence of an atomic fact to be *complex*, to be a combination or a concatenation of 'objects' (2.01). These objects, however, *are* simple. As in the case of the atomic facts, we cannot produce a single instance of such an 'object', but we know *a priori* that they must be there, in order for the world to have a substance (2.021*a*). Objects belong to an altogether different logical category from 'atomic facts': it is, for example, senseless to think of *objects* as 'mutually independent'. In their totality, the 'objects' or logical simples constitute 'logical space' (1.13). The notion of 'logical space', here mentioned only in passing, will become increasingly important as the discussion proceeds. We shall have to bear in mind, throughout, that logical space is one and indivisible: the atoms of the great contingent mosaic are connected by the invisible web of formal connexions. This is what I called above the 'organic aspect' of Wittgenstein's ontology.

The World as a Totality of Facts in Logical Space

The most controversial sections in the present instalment are 1.11 and 1.21. The first plausibly, but in my judgement wrongly, suggests that there is something over and above the totality of facts (namely, some kind of super-fact to the effect of the atomic facts being *all* the facts). The second remark (1.21) is carelessly phrased (see notes below).

---

1 **world**: = 'universe' (a use more common in German than in English).

Cf. 2.04 (a similar remark about 'the world'), 2.063 (a link with the notion of 'reality'), 4.26 (analogous remarks about *describing* the 'world').

The definition of the world will soon be qualified in an important way (1.13) by reference to 'logical space' (for which see notes on 3.42 a).

Instead of saying 'the world', Wittgenstein occasionally speaks of 'total reality' (*die gesamte Wirklichkeit*, 2.063). Reality, or the world, consists of what is *contingently* the case; for the necessary aspects of the world he uses the labels 'logical space', 'the essence of reality', and 'the logic of the world' (6.22). He will talk about the 'substance of the world' (2.021, 2.0211, 2.0231) and about the 'form of the world' (2.022, 2.026). For reasons for treating both the substance and the form of the world as necessary, see notes on 2.021 below.

W. does not argue for the contention that the universe consists of facts, not of things. (Indeed his main contentions are usually offered without reasons; his metaphysics is not presented *more geometrico*.)

Facts are the supposed objective counterparts of true statements. So one way to find reasons for the claim that the universe consists of facts, not of things, would be to find reasons or plausible considerations in favour of the view that an adequate *account* of the universe must consist of statements, rather than of names or name-substitutes.

Let us then suppose that the task is set of describing everything that is real, i.e. the whole of the actual universe. Somebody might think that the task could be performed by producing an all-inclusive *catalogue*, i.e. a list of all the *things*, complex or simple, that exist. Against this it might be urged that such a hypothetical catalogue would have to be supplemented by an explicit or implied *statement* to the effect that all the listed things really existed. (In W.'s terminology, one might say that a list does not of itself *say* anything.) But if the single supplementary statement is true, as it must be in order for the catalogue to be correct, something about the universe must make that statement true and whatever *that* is it cannot be a further *thing*, since all of these are supposed to have been already listed.

Commentary

The list, together with the supplement, can be conceived as a single statement: so we end, not with a list or a catalogue, but rather with a single comprehensive assertion comprising the whole truth about the universe and verified, not by any object or by any set of objects, but rather by the *fact* that the corresponding objects exist. Such an inclusive statement might be called a *universal chronicle*. It seems then that reality must have the character of being what answers to a complete and perfectly faithful chronicle (a fact, or an aggregate of facts) rather than what answers to a catalogue or list (a thing or an aggregate of things). Once the necessity for reference to even a single fact in any adequate account of the universe has been admitted, the way is clear for further analysis of the universe into separate and independent contingent facts (cf. notes on logical atomism on p. 58 below).

The appeal of the argument I have sketched obviously depends upon the plausibility of the idea that a *list* of things, no matter how inclusive and accurate, *leaves something out*, namely the *fact* that the things in question exist. But could one not object that the all-inclusive list, without the addition of the 'supplementary statement', is complete and adequate *as it stands*? I believe so. In *one* sense of 'account', namely that in which an account *can* be a list, the all-inclusive list is a satisfactory account. One might therefore be inclined to object that somewhere in the argument a special and debatable sense of 'account', as something necessarily containing statements, has crept in. And, similarly, one might be inclined to say that a special use of 'universe', to *mean* an aggregate of facts, rather than an aggregate of things, has somewhere been smuggled in. If you start by thinking of the universe as a thing, *summa rerum*, the all-inclusive list will seem perfectly adequate; only if you somewhere find yourself induced to think of a universe as a fact, will the idea of the list seem unsatisfactory. Here, as elsewhere in metaphysics, extended argument serves only to underline the previous commitments of the disputants.

The following statement in Russell's lectures on logical atomism is probably inspired by the first section of the *Tractatus*: 'The first thing I want to emphasize is that the outer world—the world, so to speak, which knowledge is aiming at knowing—is not completely described by a lot of "particulars", but that you must also take account of these things that I call facts' (Russell, *Logic and Knowledge*, p. 183). But notice, here, how Russell calls a fact a 'thing', thereby smudging W.'s basic distinction.

Cf. such a statement as the following: 'The universe is the totality of things' (Milne, *Cosmology*, p. 49). But Peirce said: 'Reality belongs primarily to *facts*, and attaches to things only as elements of facts' (*Papers*, vol. 8, p. 87).

The World as a Totality of Facts in Logical Space

1.1 **fact** (*Tatsache*): always to be contrasted with 'thing' (*Ding*) or 'object' (*Gegenstand*). A further pair of important contrasts is with 'atomic fact' (*Sachverhalt*), for which see notes on 2, and with 'state of affairs' (*Sachlage*), for which see notes on 2.0121*a*.

Initially, at least, W. uses 'fact' in much the same way as that word is used in ordinary life—roughly speaking, to mean whatever is expressed by a true statement. Thus 'facts' may be either positive or negative (2.06*b*), and either elementary (= 'atomic') or complex (cf. 4.2211).

The natural reading of *Tatsache* as 'molecular fact' (or, 'complex fact') seems to have been contrary to W.'s original intentions: '*Tatsache* is what corresponds to the logical product of elementary propositions when this product is true' (*Letters*, 129 (3)). W. adds the tantalizing remark: 'The reason why I introduce *Tatsache* before introducing *Sachverhalt* would want a long explanation' (*ibid.*). (One may guess that the world is first conceived, superficially as it were, as a totality of *Tatsachen*. That these can obtain only if there are atomic facts or *Sachverhalte* is then discovered by reflection. We are unable to produce a single example of an atomic fact.)

If *Tatsachen* are to be understood as in the quotation from W. above, we might think of *Tatsache* as a collective noun for referring to sets of atomic facts.

THE 'TRACTATUS' CONCEPTION OF FACT

Uses of 'fact' in ordinary language

Both *Tatsache* and its English equivalent 'fact' occur frequently in laymen's talk; the philosophical uses of these words arise as extensions and modifications of these ordinary uses. The chief reason why the concept expressed by the word is so persistently unclear is that in its ordinary uses 'fact' shows marked deviations from those of a straightforward general term such as 'man'. A great deal of trouble in interpreting the book is caused by a stubborn but mistaken inclination, from which Wittgenstein himself may not have been wholly free, to treat 'fact' as a common *name*.

The chief ordinary uses of 'fact' are the following:

(i) In such contexts as 'It is a fact that Napoleon was born in Corsica' or 'Napoleon was born in Corsica: that is a fact'. It is important that, in such primary contexts, the word 'fact' is eliminable in a way which a genuine common name such as 'man' is not.

Each of the two illustrative sentences can be translated into 'Napoleon was born in Corsica' (and similarly for negative occurrences of the form 'It is not a fact that X', which is equivalent to 'not-X'). In such contexts, the phrase 'it is a fact' serves simply as an emphatic device for *assertion*. I call these contexts primary, because there is no way to identify a specific fact except by means of some true contingent assertion. It would be foolish to demand specimens of facts, as if they could be exhibited like lions in a zoo; it is a confusion to suppose, as some philosophers have done, that facts can be discovered by taking a sharp look at the universe. Yet F. P. Ramsey said that some facts could be 'perceived' (*Foundations*, p. 139) and Strawson says that facts are overlooked and noticed ('Truth', p. 136). Such views are encouraged by a tendency to infer from premises of the form 'I perceive that X' and 'That X is a fact' a conclusion of the form 'I perceive a fact'. There is no warrant in ordinary language for such an inference.

(ii) The word 'fact' begins to look like an authentic general name in such contexts as 'The fact of increasing poverty is alarming' or 'I am saddened by the fact that he has died'. But here, too, 'fact' can be eliminated, producing such variants as 'It is alarming that poverty is increasing' and 'I am saddened by his dying'. In such common uses, 'fact' serves again as a device for assertion; its occurrence marks the speaker's commitment to the truth of an implied sub-assertion ('Poverty *is* increasing' and 'He *has* died').

(iii) Consider, finally, the uses of 'fact' in contingent general statements, e.g. 'I am worried by some facts about the Eichmann trial'. In such occurrences 'fact' is not directly eliminable, and the inclination is correspondingly stronger to treat it as a general name for a class of entities. But our example can equally well be treated as a compendious way of making each of a class of related singular statements, of the form 'I am worried by the fact about the Eichmann trial that X', each of which can then be handled on the lines sketched above. To know how to make the correct transition from the general statement about 'facts' to each of the corresponding singular statements is to have a complete grasp of this last type of use. Here, as in the first two classes of occurrence, 'fact' functions as what Strawson calls 'One of the most economical and pervasive devices of language...to abbreviate, summarize and connect' ('Truth', p. 138). But useful as it is, the device is not *needed* for common-sense uses: we should lose nothing except convenience if its use were forbidden.

I neglect uses of 'fact' and such cognates as 'factual' to suggest something settled, accepted, or unquestionable, something contrasted with opinion. For such matters, and the consequent restrictions upon common-sense uses of 'fact', see Herbst ('Facts') and Lucas ('Facts').

I shall summarize the foregoing sketch by saying that 'fact' is *expendable* in its ordinary uses.

How Wittgenstein uses 'fact'

Two features of Wittgenstein's uses of 'fact' in the book show the extent to which he departs from the ordinary uses of that word: (i) As he uses 'fact', it is not expendable; (ii) all the statements in which he uses it are necessary statements. Both points can easily be confirmed by the reader.

The heart of Wittgenstein's conception is the idea that the truth of any contingently true statement is due to something non-verbal, 'out in the world'. (There is of course a basis for this in ordinary language.) The contingent statement cannot guarantee its own truth, but must point to a condition, a state of affairs, a fact, that *makes* it true. 'Reality is compared with propositions' (4.05, cf. 2.223).

The next step is to become clear that the non-verbal counterpart of a contingently true statement (a fact) cannot be *designated*, either by a name or by a description in Russell's sense. For assume, as Wittgenstein did, that every name, simple or complex, must have what he later called a 'bearer' (*Investigations*, §40), i.e. something that actually exists. If a whole sentence were a name (as Frege thought),[1] it could not have a meaning unless the corresponding bearer existed, i.e. unless there were a corresponding fact. Then no false statement could have a meaning, and no statement at all could be understood without prior knowledge of its truth. Frege escaped

---

[1] For W.'s criticism of Frege's position, see, for example, 4.063, 4.431 *d*, 5.02. It is significant that W. should have attacked Frege on this point so often.

such intolerable consequences by dividing meaning into 'reference' and 'sense'. So for him a false sentence could still have sense, whether or not it had reference. But for Wittgenstein, with his commitment to what might be called a single-factor theory of meaning, no such escape was open.

Again, it will not do to construe 'that'-clauses or full sentences as descriptions of facts, in Russell's sense of descriptions (cf. notes on 4.023 where the point is argued at length). Certainly a whole sentence cannot be a description, which, *qua* incomplete symbol, must always occur within a wider setting. But could we not understand 'That men breathe is a fact' as analogous with 'The king of France exists', taking 'is a fact' to play a role similar to that of 'exists'? I think not. For in the second case we are saying that some *man* exists; and by parity of thought we ought to mean in the first case that some *fact* exists. (And so in general: the existence of what is ostensibly identified by a definite description must be distinct from that thing itself.)[1] But it is an important feature of the intended use of 'fact' that it must be absurd to say of a *fact* that it exists; talk of a non-existent fact is a contradiction, as talk of a non-existent man is not. If we had an expression *existing-man* we would have a genuine analogue to 'fact'. But of course, 'existing man' does not make sense, except by way of allusion to some true existential statement (unless it means the same as 'living man'); no good case can be made for an analogous use of 'existing fact'.

Now if facts cannot be designated, if they can be only *stated* or *asserted*, general statements about facts (construed as pointing to objective counterparts, and not 'expendable' in the way I suggested as conforming to ordinary-language uses) become extremely problematical. Wittgenstein has deliberately departed from the ordinary uses of 'fact' without providing instructions for the new uses. The notion of a fact as a unique 'configuration' or 'concatenation' of objects, that is not itself a complex *object* (something, one might be tempted to say, whose essence it is to *obtain*), will have strong appeal for anybody who, like Wittgenstein, accepts a conflation of a corres-

---

[1] Cf. Moore's remark: 'Surely everybody can see that the fact that a lion does exist is quite a different sort of entity from the lion himself?' (*Problems*, p. 296).

pondence theory of truth with a bearer theory of meaning and Russell's theory of descriptions. If it is a mistake, as I think, its roots go deep. Nobody who has not felt its attraction can read the *Tractatus* with the sympathetic understanding it demands.

The work to which the notion is put

One might wonder how much difference would be made to the exposition if all references to facts were expunged. Well, in view of the tight connexions between Wittgenstein's uses of 'fact', 'atomic fact', 'object' and 'form', this would amount to a suppression of the whole of Wittgenstein's ontology. The reader soon discovers that the notion plays an essential part in Wittgenstein's thought. To take some crucial illustrations: (i) Recognition of facts is almost at once shown to require recognition of *atomic* facts. (ii) From necessary features of the latter (e.g. their mutual independence) corresponding inferences are drawn about the essence of language (e.g. that independent elementary propositions must exist (4.221), and that the propositional sign must be a fact (3.14)). (iii) From these linguistic consequences there follow in turn some of Wittgenstein's most striking conclusions about logic, mathematics and philosophy itself. Throughout the book, there is a systole and diastole of thought, a repeated movement from language to the world and back again.

If I am right in thinking that the universe, as Wittgenstein conceives it, is a projection of what he finds in language, it might be thought that the *détour* from words to facts and back again ought to be theoretically unnecessary. And somebody who rejected Wittgenstein's ontology might still be able to agree about important parts of his doctrine (notably the contentions that all complex propositions are truth-functions and that logical propositions are 'tautologies'). Yet his conclusions, as he presents them, depend strongly upon the metaphysical picture he has constructed. A positivistic rephrasing of the argument of the text, eschewing any reference outside language, would be flat and unpersuasive. There is an air of the improvised and contrived about the discussions of language by writers like Carnap who have been strongly influenced by the *Tractatus*, but have altogether rejected its ontology.[1] The ontology is integral to the work; 'facts' may be suspect, but they are put to work.

For recent discussions of the notion of a 'fact' see Austin ('Truth', pp. 116–18), Strawson ('Truth', pp. 133–43) and Austin, 'Unfair to Facts', ch. 5 of his posthumous *Papers*.

'The only plausible candidate for the position of what (in the world) makes the statement true is the fact it states; but the fact it states is not something in the world' (Strawson, *op. cit.* p. 135).

'The whole charm of talking of situations, states of affairs or facts as included in, or part of, the world, consists in thinking of them as things, and groups of things' (Strawson, *ibid.* p. 139).

'If we read "world" (a sadly corrupted word) as "heavens and earth", talk of facts, situations and states of affairs as "included in" or "parts of" the world is, obviously, metaphorical. The world is the totality of things, not of facts' (Strawson, *ibid.* p. 139, f.n. 6).

1.11 **determined** (*bestimmt*): this word is used a good deal by W. It occurs regularly when he wants to refer to a *stipulation* about the meaning of a word or the rules for the use of a notation. In this sense the 'determination' is often qualified as 'arbitrary' (e.g. at 3.315c, 3.342, 5.473 (2)d). In the present section, however, 'determined' is used in what might be called an 'impersonal' way (also at 2.0231, 2.05, etc.). *A* determines *B* in this sense if *B* (or sometimes the existence of *B*) is necessitated by *A* (or the existence of *A*).

● 'The world consists of *all* the facts, but there is no super-fact (or fact of higher order) to the effect that there are *no more* facts.'

Cf. 4.26a (specification of true elementary propositions completely describes the world), 5.524a (if the objects are given, *all* objects are given).

'It is perfectly clear, I think, that when you have enumerated all the atomic facts in the world, it is a further fact about the world that those are all the atomic facts there are about the world, and that is just as much an objective fact about the world as any of them are. It is clear, I think, that you must admit general facts as distinct from and over and above particular facts' (Russell, *Logic and Knowledge*, p. 236).

' "It is necessary also to be given the proposition that all elementary propositions are given." This is not necessary because it is even impossible. There is no such proposition! That all elementary propositions are given is *shown* by there being none having an elementary sense which is not given' (*Letters*, 130 (5)).

[1] See Carnap's *Syntax*, *passim*.

Stenius regards sections 1 and 1.1 as 'a kind of "persuasive definition"'. He takes W. to be saying, 'By the "world" I *understand* everything which is the case. By the "world" I *understand* the totality of all facts, not of all things'. And he adds that W. means 'that this is a "philosophically" *important* meaning of the word "world"' (*Exposition*, p. 22).

But it would be pointless to construct an arbitrary definition of 'the world'; W. is trying to reach necessary truths *about* the universe. It is as if he were to say: 'Consider what you mean by all that contingently exists, everything that makes the universe different from what it might have been. You will see that you must refer to a set of facts, not, as you might have supposed, to a set of things.' Here, and throughout, the metaphysical path leads from language to the world: as he said in the *Investigations*, 'We predicate of the thing what lies in the method of representing it' (§ 104).

He might also say: 'Consider what sort of language you would need in order to express the whole truth about the universe. You will find "fact" or some equivalent expression, such as "what is the case", indispensable. Were you to confine yourself to using "thing", or some synonym, you would be helpless to say what is contingently the case, helpless to characterize the universe, as you wished.' (Cf. discussion of the universal 'chronicle' in notes on p. 30 above.)

The two lines of thought reinforce one another. If 'fact', or some synonym, is indispensable for a general account of the universe, that can only be, it would seem, because the universe *is* a 'totality of facts'; and if the universe really does consist of facts, an adequate metaphysical vocabulary will have to make corresponding provision.

1.12   Cf. 2.05 (the same thought rephrased), 5.524*a* (a similar remark about objects).

1.13   Cf. 2.0121 (4) (objects must be thought of as in space), 2.013 (every thing is in a space of possible atomic facts), 2.11 (facts in logical space).

logical space: for discussion of this notion, see notes on 3.42*a* below.

Here W. is adumbrating the idea of the logical connexions between facts that will be central to the later development of the book.

1.2   **divides**: *zerfällt* is an emphatic word—the world *falls apart* into facts, we might say, because they are mutually independent, as explained in 1.21. The world is a mosaic of facts.

1.21   **Each item**: literally, 'each one' (*Eines*). If this is intended to refer to any complex fact (*Tatsache*), as it seems to do from its position in the text, it is a mistake. For instance, if $p \lor q$ is not the case, neither can $p.q$ be.

37

But perhaps W. had momentarily reverted to his earlier idea of a *Tatsache* as a conjunction of atomic facts. For it is certainly true that e.g. *p.q* may or may not be the case, while say *q.r* 'remains the same'. Alternatively, W. may really have intended to refer to *atomic* facts.

not the case: notice the awkwardness of saying here of a *fact* that it could not be the case, i.e. could not be a fact.

Cf. 5.135 (impossibility of inferring existence of one state of affairs from another).

'Either a fact (*Tatsache*) is contained in another one, or it is independent of it' (*Notebooks*, 90 (13)).

II

ATOMIC FACTS, OBJECTS, AND LOGICAL SPACE

(2–2.0141)

The emphasis in 1–1.21 has been upon facts and especially upon their relative independence. Now we turn to the complementary idea of 'objects' (logical simples) and their mutual connexions in 'logical space'. Here, we meet, for the first time, the difficult but quite central ideas of 'form' and 'possibility'. The easiest thing to say about them is that they are inseparable. Later on, we shall learn that form *is* the possibility of structure (2.033): every remark about 'form' can be made to yield a remark about 'possibility' and conversely. It is very difficult to advance beyond this point and to form a distinct idea of what Wittgenstein intends by either word. A section such as 2.0123, with its use of the substantive 'possibility' (*Möglichkeit*), might easily induce us to think of a 'possibility' as something quite substantial—a kind of Lockean power perhaps; but this is quite the wrong line to take. The situation becomes clearer when we turn from the ontological statements about possibility and form to their linguistic counterparts. The connexion between an 'object' and a 'possible atomic fact' (in 2.0124) has its counterpart in the connexion between a 'name' and the rules for its combination with other names in significant sentences. This is one of Wittgenstein's primary insights—that the use of a name is known only as part of the use of a *language*, so that knowing the meaning of a name includes knowing that name's 'syntax', the rules for its combination with other words. The object's 'possibility of occurrence in atomic facts' is the ontological counterpart of this essential feature of the use of names.

The reader should be warned that the appropriate translation of *Sachverhalt* (atomic fact) is controversial (see notes on 2, below). Particularly troublesome is the reading of the expression *möglicher Sachverhalt* ('possible atomic fact', as in 2.0124). There is some inclination to say that a '*possible* fact' is not a fact at all (whereas there is not the same resistance e.g. to the notion of a 'possible move' in a game). This has led some commentators to construe *Sachverhalt* as meaning a possibility rather than a fact. Of course, *möglicher Sachverhalt* then becomes pleonastic.

---

2 This statement might be called the principle of logical atomism (for which see discussion under III below). Cf. 2.06, with its mention of non-existence.

existence: *Bestehen*, the word regularly used by W. in this kind of context, can perhaps best be rendered as 'the holding' (of a fact). It is awkward to speak of the 'existence' of a fact.

state of affairs (*Sachverhalt*): here, and nearly always, I prefer 'atomic fact', as in the Ogden translation.

'Literally this word [*Sachverhalt*] simply means "situation". Etymologically it suggests "hold of things"—i.e. a way things stand in relation to one another' (Anscombe, *Introduction*, p. 29).

THE MEANING OF 'SACHVERHALT'

There has been a good deal of disagreement about this, and about the proper choice of a translation. Although 'atomic fact' for *Sachverhalt* had Wittgenstein's approval and was so used in Russell's introduction, it has been held to suggest misleadingly that an atomic fact is a *species* of fact. However, the suggestion of logical simplicity conveyed by the adjective exactly corresponds to Wittgenstein's intentions: he talks about a *Sachverhalt* whenever he wishes to refer to the objective counterpart of an *unanalysable* contingent truth (see, for instance, 4.2211). Pears and McGuinness's consistent use of 'state of affairs', without the adjective, blurs this important point.

Unfortunately, Wittgenstein is not consistent in his use of *Sachverhalt*. Most of the time, as in 2, he uses the word in the sense of (atomic) *fact*, i.e. for an actual, contingent combination of objects (as in 2.01, 2.011, 2.012, 2.0121 *b*, 2.0141, 2.0272–2.032). Occasionally, however, especially where he speaks of the non-existence (*Nichtbestehen*) of *Sachverhalte* (2.06, 2.062, 2.11, 4.1, 4.25, 4.27, 4.3) this reading will hardly do (see the further discussion below).

In Ogden's translation, the word *Sachverhalt* is always rendered as 'atomic fact'. Words of closely related meanings are *Tatsache* (translated by Pears and McGuinness as 'fact', e.g. at 1.1) and *Sachlage* (translated by them as 'situation' at 2.0122; Ogden has 'fact' at 2.11, 'state of affairs' at 2.0121, 2.014, 2.202, and elsewhere). 'Fact' is an acceptable translation of *Tatsache*; there is, however, a serious question as to whether 'atomic *fact*' will serve for *Sachverhalt* and a closely connected question about the proper way to understand *Sachlage*.

Stenius argues in his book on the *Tractatus* that 'a *Sachverhalt* is something that could *possibly* be the case, a *Tatsache* something that is *really* the case' (*Exposition*, p. 31). According to him, a 'that'-clause, e.g. 'that the earth is smaller than the moon', formulates what he calls the 'descriptive content of a sentence' (p. 30). And he thinks it conformable to German usage to call a 'descriptive content' a *Sachverhalt*, *independently* of its being a fact or not (*ibid.*).

Stenius's 'descriptive content' is somewhat reminiscent of Meinong's '*Objektiv*'. Cf. the following statement:

[Meinong] added to the realm of facts a set of entities which resemble facts in every essential respect, but differ from them in so far as they are not the case, that is, in so far as they lack the kind of being which is appropriate to facts. To the whole class of entities of which some are, and others are not, the case, he has given the name of objectives. Objectives are such things as 'that China is a Republic', 'that there is an integer between 3 and 4', 'that jealousy is a good emotion'. Meinong tries to prove that they are a unique and irreducible sort of entity, indispensable to our knowledge of reality and to reality itself (Findlay, *Meinong*, p. 60).

Stenius, however, does not share Meinong's views about the alleged ontological status of what a 'that'-clause stands for (cf. *Exposition*, pp. 114 ff. for his discussion of 'What is meant by an unreal state of affairs being "possible"?').

According to Findlay, Meinong considered using *Sachverhalt* in place of *Objektiv* but decided against so doing 'because it would be strange to say of an unfactual objective that it was a *Sachverhalt*' (*op. cit.* p. 90). Since Meinong often uses *Umstand* in place of *Objektiv*, Findlay proposes 'circumstance' as a suitable translation. Husserl uses *Sachverhalt* as equivalent to *Objektiv* (*Untersuchungen*, vol. II, p. 445) and other phenomenologists use the word in the same way.

If a 'that'-clause, such as 'that the earth is smaller than the moon', formulates a *Sachverhalt*, then a *Sachverhalt* need not be a fact (though some *Sachverhalte* are facts). I believe the best English expression for *this* conception would be 'possible (atomic) state of affairs', though '(atomic) situation' might also serve. A *Sachverhalt* would, on this view (call it the '*P*-theory') be regarded as a certain sort of *possibility*. An alternative view would be that a *Sachverhalt* is usually intended to be a *fact* (call this the '*F*-theory').

Suppose 'Jack loves Jill' and 'Jill hates Jack' express elementary propositions, of which the first is true and the second false. According to the *F*-theory, that Jack loves Jill is a *Sachverhalt*, but that Jill hates Jack is not; while according to the *P*-theory, that Jack loves Jill is a *Sachverhalt*, and that Jill hates Jack is also a *Sachverhalt*.

I shall now consider arguments in favour of these two theories: an argument in favour of one will usually be an argument against the other.

Arguments in favour of the F-theory

(1) Wittgenstein himself allowed 'atomic fact' to stand in the revised impression (1933) as well as in the original English edition, both of which he had an opportunity to correct. It is implausible to suppose he did not understand the difference between making *Sachverhalt* stand for a fact and making it stand for a possibility, or that his knowledge of English was unequal to the task of making the appropriate corrections. (Cf. similar comments by Anscombe, *Introduction*, p. 30 f.n.)

(2) Wittgenstein speaks of a *Tatsache* as being composed of (*besteht aus*) *Sachverhalte* (4.2211). Since a *Tatsache* is a (complex) fact, this speaks in favour of regarding a *Sachverhalt* as a fact.

(3) Several times Wittgenstein speaks of a *möglicher Sachverhalt* (possible *Sachverhalt*), e.g. at 2.0124 (cf. also 2.0123 and 2.0121 (5)). Now if a *Sachverhalt* is a possibility, the phrase *möglicher Sachverhalt* (= 'possible possibility'), italicized at 2.0124, becomes an absurdity.

(4) A 'configuration' (*Konfiguration*) of objects constitutes (*bildet*) the *Sachverhalt* (2.0272). Now the configuration is not determined by the substance of the world (2.0231) and is therefore (according to 2.024) not independent of what is the case: the configuration is mutable (2.0271). Throughout the text, the 'configuration' of objects is taken to be what is *contingent* about the world. If a *Sachverhalt* is a configuration of objects it cannot be a timeless unity of objects, independent of contingent fact. Whenever the objects are in a configuration, there will be a fact, not the possibility of a fact. Compare also 2.03 on objects hanging together in a *Sachverhalt*.

(5) If Wittgenstein held that objects are combined in complexes, which may or may not exist, he might have been expected to say so, and to use some word other than *Konfiguration* or *Struktur* (2.032) for the manner in which objects are so combined.

(6) If *Sachverhalte* were mere possibilities, how could Wittgenstein say that what is essential to an object is that it *can* occur in a *Sachverhalt* (2.012, 2.0121 *b*, 2.0123 *a*, 2.0141)? On the *P*-theory, Wittgenstein would surely be committed to saying that an object *must* occur in all the *Sachverhalte* of which it is a constituent.

(7) According to Wittgenstein, a name must have an object for which it stands (3.203) while nothing need answer to a meaningful description (3.24 (2)); it is therefore important that he speaks of a *Sachverhalt* as being described by a proposition (4.023 *c*). For, according to the *P*-theory, something *must* answer to a 'that'-clause, namely, the corresponding *Sachverhalt*. It would therefore be correct to treat such a clause as a compound name of the possibility for which it stands. But Wittgenstein says that names are simple (3.202) and argues against the idea that the proposition is a complex name

(3.143c). In the *Notes on Logic*, he chides Russell for still believing in complexes that are not facts: 'Frege said "propositions are names"; Russell said "propositions correspond to complexes". Both are false; and especially false is the statement "propositions are names of complexes"' (93 (3)).

(8) The 'picture theory' of the proposition recognizes co-ordinations between names and objects (3.2) and identity of logical form between the sentence-fact and the fact represented (2.151, 2.18). Wittgenstein does not say that the whole sentence-fact stands for some complex entity—indeed this way of looking at the sentence is alien to his standpoint.

The above considerations support the conclusion that Wittgenstein held that objects are not linked by necessary connexions, but only contingently *come together* in various mutable combinations.

I turn now to the reasons that have led others to suppose that a *Sachverhalt* must be a possibility rather than a fact.

Arguments in favour of the P-theory

(9) Wittgenstein often speaks of the *Bestehen* (= 'holding') or *Nichtbestehen* (= 'not holding') of *Sachverhalte*, e.g. at 2, 2.04, 2.05, 2.06, 2.062, etc. Now it is hard to think of a *fact* as not holding or, in Ogden's translation, not existing.

(10) Similar difficulties arise, though perhaps not so forcefully, in connexion with the phrase *möglicher Sachverhalt* (for which see point (3) above). One is inclined to say that a merely 'possible' fact is not *yet* a fact.

(11) The uses of *Sachlage* closely parallel those of *Sachverhalt*. Sometimes they are used almost as synonyms: cf. 2.012 with 2.0121a, the beginning of 2.0122a with its ending, 4.031 with 4.0311, 4.021a with 4.023c. The logical grammar of *Sachlage* is close to that of *Sachverhalt*: we have *mögliche Sachlagen* (2.0122, 2.202, 2.203, 3.11a, etc.), *Sachlagen* are configurations of objects (3.21), they can hold or exist (*bestehen*) (5.135, etc.). Hence, if *Sachlage* is properly translated as 'possible state of affairs', something that may or may not obtain, a parallel translation would seem to be required for *Sachverhalt*.

(12) A proposition (*Satz*) presents (*vorstellt* or *darstellt*) a *Sachlage* (2.11, 2.203, 3.02, 4.021, 4.031, 4.032*a*, 4.04*a*, etc.). A *Sachverhalt* is likewise presented (3.0321, 4.0311, 4.122*d*—notice that in the first of these passages we are dealing with a *false* picture). What a picture or a proposition presents (*darstellt*) is its *sense* (2.221 and *passim*). It would seem, therefore, that a *Sachlage*, *qua* *sense*, should be a possibility, not an actuality (cf. 4.061*a*: '...a proposition has a sense that is independent of the facts...'); and similarly for a *Sachverhalt*. When we read at 4.03*b* that a proposition communicates a *Sachlage*, immediately after being told that a *new* sense is what is communicated, the interpretation of a *Sachlage* (and hence also of a *Sachverhalt*) as a possibility becomes almost irresistible.

Comments on the foregoing arguments

Point (1) by itself seems to me a strong argument in favour of the *F*-theory and points (1)–(8) collectively to demonstrate that at least *most* of the time the *F*-theory must be correct. As for points (9)–(12), the following considerations may somewhat reduce their cogency.

With regard to (9): there is certainly some awkwardness in talking about facts not existing or not obtaining. But to say, for example, 'The fact that the moon is larger than the earth does not obtain', however clumsy it may sound, may be no more reprehensible than saying 'The present Queen of France does not exist'. The latter sentence does not mean the absurdity, 'There *is* a person who is the present Queen of France but does not exist' but rather 'There is no such person as the present Queen of France'. Similarly, the first sentence can be read as meaning 'There is no such a fact as that the moon is larger than the earth'. We could dodge the awkwardness by substituting 'state-of-affairs' for 'fact'.[1] But if so, we must not be tempted to suppose that 'a state-of-affairs' in the intended sense is some complex entity, also describable as a 'possible fact' and distinguishable from an 'actual fact'. A 'state-of-affairs', so con-

---

[1] '*State of things* or *affairs*: the way in which events or circumstances stand disposed (at a particular time or in a particular sphere)' (*O.E.D.*). In ordinary usage 'fact' is roughly (but only roughly) equivalent to 'state of affairs that *does* obtain'. 'Fact' is to 'state of affairs' approximately as 'existing person' is to 'person'. But this is not the sense that would be needed if 'state of affairs' were treated as a synonym for 'fact'.

ceived, is no more a *possible* something than a person (say 'the Queen of France') is a *possible* something. In using a description of a person, we are of course implying that it *is* (logically) possible for the person in question to exist, but 'possible person' has no good use. Similarly, in speaking of a certain 'fact' or 'state-of-affairs' (as a synonym for 'fact') we are implying that it is *possible for* there to be such a fact. The mistake to be avoided is that of peopling Wittgenstein's universe with *three* types of things (say: 'objects', 'facts' and also 'situations' or 'circumstances'). There are (timelessly) objects—and (contingently) facts or states of affairs. Reference to a 'possible state of affairs' should be regarded, according to context, either as a pleonasm or else as shorthand for reference to logical form. Similar considerations apply to point (10) above.

The moral of the considerations advanced at point (11) above is that *Sachlage* should sometimes be treated as an approximate synonym for *Tatsache* (compare 2.11 with 2). On the view I am advocating, all three words, *Sachverhalt*, *Sachlage*, and *Tatsache* are usually to be taken as standing for simple or complex states of affairs (*not* possibilities).

The plausible error behind point (12) depends upon supposing that if *A* is a picture of *B*, *B* must exist in some sense. But to say, correctly, that *A* is a picture of a centaur wearing a bowler hat is not to imply that there exists a centaur wearing a bowler hat of which *A* is a picture. Nor is it to imply, absurdly, that *A* is really a picture of a 'possible' centaur. Similarly, we can say, on Wittgenstein's view, that a proposition depicts (or presents) a fact, without in the least committing ourselves to the view that the fact in question must exist. If the proposition does depict a fact, it would be otiose to say that it *also* depicts something more, namely a possibility. As for Wittgenstein's implicit identification of a proposition's sense with the *Sachverhalt* or *Sachlage* depicted, this may be compared with his identification of the meaning (*Bedeutung*) of a name with its bearer (3.203). Both views are inadequate, as will appear later. But there is no ground here for thinking that Wittgenstein intended a proposition's sense to be a complex entity composed of objects in some non-contingent combination. If I am not mistaken, this interpretation is quite contrary to his intentions.

2.01 combination: cf. 2.03, 2.031 for further details. Approximately the same idea is rendered by 'configuration', for which see 2.0272. Stenius prefers the translation, 'connexion' (*Exposition*, p. 61 f.n.).

objects: here used in a technical sense for the logical simples (2.02) that must exist (2.0211–2.023). *Ding* ('thing') is often used by W. as a synonym for *Gegenstand*.

It is illuminating to read the six sections, 2.01, 2.02, ..., 2.06, consecutively, for a preliminary view of W.'s 'logical atomism'. The main points of his doctrine are that the universe consists of independent atomic facts (2, 2.061) which are composed of logical simples (2.01, 2.02) in direct connexion with one another (2.03) and also in direct connexion (in another way) with the names that stand for them (3.202, 3.203). For further discussion see notes on 2.02 below.

WHY THE SET OF ATOMIC FACTS MUST BE UNIQUE

I envisaged above (p. 30) the possibility of a universal record or 'chronicle' containing all the contingent truths about the universe. Any such record will contain many propositions that are theoretically superfluous, because they follow from other items of the record. Imagine propositions of this sort successively stricken, until no further deletions are possible, and call what remains a *basic universal record*. It will consist of a set of mutually independent contingent truths which jointly entail every contingent truth whatsoever. It is a natural, but mistaken, supposition, that a basic universal record, as so defined, must be unique.

For consider two sets of propositions, (A, B, C) and (K, L, M), having the following relations:

$$K . \equiv . A \equiv B$$
$$L . \equiv . B \equiv C$$
$$M . \equiv . BC \vee \bar{A}(B \vee C)$$

These can be equivalently expressed as follows:

$$A . \equiv . K(L \equiv M) \vee \bar{K}\bar{M}$$
$$B . \equiv . K(L \equiv M) \vee \bar{K}M$$
$$C . \equiv . \bar{K}(L \equiv M) \vee KM$$

It is easily verified that A, B, and C are mutually independent, that K, L, and M are mutually independent, and that ABC is logically equivalent to KLM. But we have just seen that the members of each set can be expressed as explicit truth-functions of the members of the other. Thus in reducing a universal record we might have arrived either at the first set or at the second. The view that there is a unique ultimate record must therefore be based upon other than purely logical grounds.

If we grant that an atomic fact is composed of logical simples in immediate combination, we shall soon see that it would be impossible for both of our supposed sets to consist of elementary propositions. For the sake of illustration, suppose that the atomic facts stated by A and B, respectively, had the structures (a, b) and (b, c), respectively, where the small letters stand for objects. Since our K was equivalent to $A \equiv B$, we must suppose all the objects involved in A and B to enter into K's make-up, which must therefore be $(a, b, c, ...)$. But we saw that A was also a function of K. Hence, by the same argument, the structure of A would have to be $(a, b, c, ...)$, contrary to our initial assumption. (I have assumed in the foregoing that atomic facts are uniquely determined by their constituents, for which see pp. 82–3 below.)

To put the matter in another way: It would be impossible for Wittgenstein to admit that (a, b), (b, c), and (a, b, c) might all be atomic facts, with the assumed logical connexions between the three. For then the three objects could not combine to produce the third atomic fact (a, b, c) unless something were *contingently* true about some subcombinations of those objects. This would clash with what might be called Wittgenstein's conception of the self-sufficiency of the objects—their power to unite in atomic facts, independently of whatever may be the case elsewhere in the universe. There cannot be, from Wittgenstein's standpoint, a remote influence of objects outside the atomic fact upon the objects inside it.

2.011   essential: see notes on 3.143 (2) below.

   should be: rather, 'can be' (*sein ... können*, as in O.). That the objects embody *possibilities* needs to be stressed. (Cf. 3.3421 on the importance of possibilities for philosophy.)

2.012   In logic...: for the converse see 6.3*b*. Cf. also 6.37*b* and 6.375 (there is only logical necessity).

written into: literally 'prejudged' (*präjudiziert*), or, 'presupposed'. (In the *Notebooks*, 60 (5), W. says that the existence of simple objects is *präjudiziert* by the existence of complexes.) Occurs again at 5.44 (3).

possibility: contrast the special sense (as possibility of structure) in which W. will use this word at 2.033 and subsequently.

● 'There is no open question as to whether a given simple can or cannot occur in atomic facts: a "thing" must be *able* to occur in atomic facts. We might say: "Thing" means the same as "possible constituent in an atomic fact".'

2.0121 (1)   situation: P.–McG.'s standard translation for *Sachlage*. O.'s 'state of affairs' is equally good.

(2)   can occur: here, and throughout, the reference is to logical possibility.

possibility: delete (corresponding word absent from the German text).

(3)*a* Nothing in the province of logic: literally, 'Something logical' (*Etwas Logisches*).

merely possible: should be hyphenated (*nur-möglich*). The intended sense is 'possible, and nothing more'. *That* something is possible always shows something about the essence of the world (cf. 3.3421*b*). Cf. also 5.473 (2)*b* (every logical possibility is permitted), 5.552 (2) (logic *precedes* every experience).

b 'We feel as if we had to *penetrate* (*durchschauen*) phenomena: our investigation, however, is directed not towards phenomena, but, as one might say, towards the "*possibilities*" of phenomena. We remind ourselves, that is to say, of the *kind of statement* that we make about phenomena' (*Investigations*, §90).

facts: a somewhat odd use of *Tatsachen*, which is usually reserved by W. for contingent facts. 'Possibilities' are, as it were, the hard data for subsequent logical investigation.

● 'That something is possible is necessarily the case: in *this* way every possibility belongs to the subject-matter of logic.'

(4)   temporal objects: i.e. things that are *in* time—events, continuants.

imagine: rather, 'think of', 'conceive' (*denken*): not to be taken in a psychological sense; cf. 3.02, for a similar use of 'think'. Similarly in (5).

excluded: or, 'apart' (literally, 'outside').

● 'Just as it is "unthinkable" (= logically impossible) that something having extension should not be in space—or something with a history should not be in time—so it is "unthinkable" that an object should be incapable of being combined with other objects in facts.'

For physical space, cf. 2.0131 *a* (a spatial object must lie in infinite space).

2.0122a **situations**: or, 'states of affairs'. 'Possible situation' (*mögliche Sachlage*) is a pleonasm. A *Sachlage* may usually be taken to be a complex or elementary situation, i.e. that which, if realized, is either a complex or an elementary fact. Accordingly, a *Sachlage* will be naturally expressed by a 'that'-clause (e.g. 'that men are warm-blooded'). On this view, it is natural to think of a *Sachlage* as being the sense of a proposition (cf. 2.202+2.221).

● 'An object (a logical simple) need not occur in any atomic fact (and is to that extent independent of all facts), but it *must* be *possible* for the object to occur in atomic facts (and so in *that* way, the object is dependent).'

b Cf. 2.0121 *a* (the connexion between an object and states of affairs is no accident). For dependence of words on context, see 3.3 (names have meaning only in a propositional context).

propositions: see notes on 3.1 below.

2.0123 (1) **know** (*kenne*): approximately in the sense of 'be acquainted with' (though not in Russell's sense of 'acquaintance').

its possible occurrences: i.e. in the light of 2.0141, its *form*.

Cf. 2.014 (objects contain the possibilities of all states of affairs).

'I asked W. whether, when he wrote the *Tractatus*, he had ever decided upon anything as an *example* of a "simple object". His reply was that at that time his thought had been that he was a *logician*; and that it was not his business, as a logician, to try to decide whether this thing or that was a simple thing or a complex thing, that being a purely *empirical* matter! It was clear that he regarded his former opinion as absurd' (Malcolm, *Memoir*, p. 86).

(2) **be part of**: literally, 'lie in' (or 'belong to').

2.01231 For the meaning of 'internal' see 4.122 (2), 4.123.

2.0124 **given** (*gegeben*): in approximately the sense in which a mathematician will say 'Given that *x* has the value 7 . . .'. W. is fond of this expression, which he uses at 3.24*b* (a complex given by its description), 3.42*a* (the whole of logical space is given), 4.12721*a* (a formal concept is given with an object), and elsewhere. The present remark can be collated with the preceding 2.0123 *a*, so that 'given' here equals 'known'. In general, for something to be 'given' is for it to be made available for reference by virtue of being symbolized—or for its existence to be implied by such a symbolization. Something is 'given' when it has been appropriately expressed in symbolic form. So W.'s thought can be rendered:

● 'A notation or language that provides names for all the logical simples (the objects) thereby provides means for expressing all possible atomic situations.'

On the above account, 'given' can often be replaced by 'expressed' (*ausgedrückt*) or the available synonyms of that word.

2.013 (1)*a* space: cf. 3.4 on 'logical space'.

b Possibly an echo of Kant: 'We can never represent to ourselves the absence of space though we can quite well think it as empty of objects' (Kant, *Kritik*, A24, B38). Cf. Martin, *Kant*, p. 32.

'Each thing modifies [or: conditions (*bedingt*)] the whole logical world, the whole of logical space, so to speak' (*Notebooks*, 83 (10)).

2.0131 (1)*a* Why **infinite**? Perhaps W. meant *unbounded* space, with the implication that no object has a privileged position (as objects on a boundary would have)?

b **an argument-place** (*Argumentstelle*): i.e. the place in a function sign held open for insertion of a constant, as at 4.0411 (2), 5.5351 *c*. This cryptic remark becomes clearer when collated with what is said later (4.12 *b*–4.1271) about formal concepts and their expression by variables. Cf. also 3.4–3.411 on the 'logical place'. Since space is a form of objects (2.0251), we may infer that 'space' alludes to a 'formal concept' (see 4.126 *a*). Thus 2.0131 *a* expresses an internal 'feature' (4.1221) of spatial facts. In a satisfactory notation, this internal feature would be *shown* by an internal property of the sign used—perhaps by the occurrence in it of a (three-dimensional) variable. When we talk about a 'spatial point' (or a 'position') we are not referring to a thing, but rather to a certain common internal feature of propositions 'about' that position.

● 'A "point in space" is adequately symbolized by the value of a certain variable, namely one requiring three independent determinations of each of its values.'

(2) speck: rather, 'patch'.

Atomic Facts, Objects, and Logical Space

THE CONCEPT OF SPACE

One of the least sophisticated uses of the word 'space' is in sentences of the form, 'There is a space between A and B', which may be taken to have roughly the same meaning as 'A and B are not in contact and there is no body C such that A is in contact with C and C with B'. It is here understood that A and B are 'bodies' or 'material objects' like pencils, books, and rulers. A 'body' in this sense must have a recognizable outline, shape, colour, etc., so that it can be identified when moved about. Uses of the sentence 'There is a space between A and B' presuppose a prior understanding of such phrases as 'This is *the same* pencil that I touched before', 'This book has just been *moved*', 'The two rulers are no longer *touching* one another', 'The chair is *closer* to the table than the sofa is', 'The pipe is *between* the ash tray and the inkwell' and so on.

Suppose now that A and B are two wooden cubes from a child's box of bricks, and consider the statement 'There is a cubical space of one inch side between A and B'. Call this statement S.

S expresses a complex relationship between A and B: in order to establish its truth, we need to determine whether other bodies can move freely *between A and B*, whether the distance *between one corner of A and a corner of B* is one inch, and so on. To put the matter in another way, 'the cubical space' in question is defined by reference to A and to B and to nothing else: if we can find the A and B in question, we can easily determine whether there is a space between them and if so how large it is, but if the bodies are removed or destroyed questions about 'the space between them' (e.g. 'Is the space still there?', 'Is the space still the same shape and size?') become senseless. They may be compared with the nonsensical questions 'What is the musical interval between two notes when no notes have been sounded?' and 'What is the family relationship between two non-existent persons?'

The word 'space', when used in the familiar ways here in question, may be compared with such words as 'gap', 'hole', 'void', 'room', 'hiatus', 'vacancy', 'place' (in one of its uses), 'cavity', etc., all of which suggest the absence of something. When a space (or a gap,

51

a hole, etc.) has been 'filled', the space no longer exists. Thus the primitive conception of the physical world is of bodies interrupted by spaces: the universe is conceived to be porous (cf. Leucippus's doctrine of 'the full' and 'the empty' as reported by Aristotle, *Metaphysics*, 985 *b*).

An extension of this primitive conception of a 'space' occurs in such familiar expressions as 'space (or room) *in which* to move'. The space defined by the walls, floor and ceiling of my study is partly occupied, partly not, I can move around inside it, etc. According to this conception 'the space' in question is still there, even when bodies are placed in it. But notice that the space is still defined by an identifiable and fixed boundary composed of material bodies. So long as the walls of my study stand, I can talk about the space defined by them, but once my house is pulled down, questions about that space become senseless, as before.

This idea is probably behind Aristotle's famous definitions of 'place' (*topos*). Consider, for instance, the following remarks from the *Physics*:

[Place is] the boundary of the containing body at which it is in contact with the contained body.
[By the contained body is meant what can be moved by locomotion] (212 *a* 5).

The innermost motionless boundary of what contains is place (212 *a* 20).

For this reason, too, place is thought to be a kind of surface, and as it were a vessel, i.e. a container of the thing (212 *a* 28).

The popular idea of Space (with a capital S) is that of 'room in which to move about'. We imagine Space as an enormous room—but one without walls, floor and ceiling.

Unquestionably we think of Space in ordinary life and in science as a single great box or container in which all physical objects are kept and in which all physical processes go on (C. D. Broad, *Scientific Thought*, p. 27).

Is this idea of Space as a great receptacle a bit of harmless imagery, or does it involve a conceptual error? (Is it like the idea of the Cheshire cat's grin that was supposed to remain after the cat itself had vanished?) If the concept of a space requires the existence of fixed material boundaries, the idea of a Space remaining even if all bodies were destroyed is a logical monstrosity. (If we try to imagine 'empty Space', we always imagine our own body moving freely *in* Space.)

The notion of physical space, as something existing independently of the presence of material bodies and having its own properties that can be stated without reference to such bodies, is comparatively modern, having been generally accepted only after the triumph of Newtonian mechanics.

The Schoolmen had no word for 'space' as we understand it; for *spatium* had rather the sense that 'space' has in the Authorised Version of the Bible, e.g. 'All with one voice about the space of two hours cried out "Great is Diana of the Ephesians"'; while *locus* meant the space occupied by a particular body (E. Whittaker, *Space*, p. 73).

The following is a good statement of the Newtonian conception of space:

We conceive Space to be that, wherein all Bodies are placed, or, to speak with the Schools, have their Ubi; that it is altogether penetrable, receiving all Bodies into itself, and refusing Ingress to nothing whatsoever; that it is immovably fixed, capable of no Action, Form or Quality; whose parts it is impossible to separate from each other, or by any Force however great; but the Space itself remaining immovable, receives the Succession of all things in motion, determines the Velocity of their Motions and measures the Distances of the things themselves (John Keill, *Natural Philosophy*, p. 15).

Keill speaks of Space as if it were something having various properties analogous to the properties of matter (it is penetrable, immovable, etc.). It should be noticed that the properties that are ascribed to Space are a *selection* of those that make sense when attributed to material bodies: Space has dimensions and position, but it makes no sense to ask about its density, colour, etc. The natural inclination to apply to Space some of the predicates that make sense when predicated of matter leads men to think of Space as an extraordinarily subtle or ethereal medium (might we not say 'an ocean of nothingness'?) in which bodies move around.

If we were to ask an unbiased, candid person under what form he pictured space, referred, for example, to the Cartesian system of co-ordinates, he would doubtless say: I have the image of a system of rigid (form-fixed), transparent, penetrable, contiguous cubes, having their bounding surfaces marked only by nebulous visual and tactual percepts—a species of phantom cubes. Over and through these phantom constructions the real bodies or their phantom counterparts move . . . (E. Mach, *Space*, pp. 83–4).

The temptation to substantialize space in this way can be illustrated by the simple case of a 'space between two objects' discussed above. There is a natural tendency to construe '*A* and *B* are separated by a cubical space of one inch side' as: 'There is something, *C* (namely a certain cubical space), standing between *A* and *B* in contact with both.' In other words, the original statement is taken as having a logical form closely resembling that of '*A* and *B* are separated by a cubical *body*, *D*, of one inch side'. The only difference between *D* and *C* on this view is that the former is composed of matter and the latter of space. This is to treat of space as if it were a kind of negative matter.

The following are among the considerations that lead people to substantialize space:

(*a*) It can be argued that the properties of the space between *A* and *B* are independent of those bodies. Thus if *A* is replaced by another cube of the same size in the same position, the space will be the same as before. From this standpoint it may seem that *A* and *B* serve only as ways of defining the space between them.

(*b*) It seems possible to determine the dimensions of the space between *A* and *B* by direct measurement, as in the case of a material body. Hence, a space may be thought of as a material body 'turned inside out'—in the case of a material body we are interested in what lies on one side of the bounding surface; in the case of a 'space' in what lies on the other side.

(*c*) 'Field theories' in physics seem to require the ascription of seemingly substantial properties (electrical potential, etc.) to empty points of space.

There is no harm in thinking of Space as a kind of receptacle, or as a kind of very ethereal medium, provided we draw no metaphysical conclusions that depend upon this imagery for their validity. But there is no need to think of Space in this way. For instance, we may prefer to think of Space as a system of *possibilities*: saying that there is a cubical space between *A* and *B* is now thought of as saying that a certain body *could be* interposed between the two bodies; the assertion that there is a certain electrical potential at some empty point of space becomes the assertion that if a charged particle *were to be* brought there, it would be subject to a certain force, etc. (No doubt this conception would also show strain if pressed too hard.)

The concept of space invites analogical extension. Somebody might be inclined to make the following assertions: (i) each position in a game of chess is a 'point' in 'chess space'; (ii) every game of chess consists of an ordered sequence of such 'points'; and (iii) all actual games of chess are '*in*' chess space. A detailed examination of such ways of talking (cf. the expression 'colour space') would lead to the conclusion that the word 'space', when used in such an analogical way, serves for making compendious allusions to a system of relationships. Talk about 'chess space' is shorthand for talk about the logical syntax of the symbolism of chess. Similarly, for Time, Light, and many other words that invite the dignity of a capital letter. The application of this suggestion to Wittgenstein's conception of 'logical space' will appear later.

2.014   An alternative formulation of 2.0123*a*.

2.0141   This important remark may be treated as a definition of 'the form of an object'.

THE FORM OF AN OBJECT

This expression is peculiar to Wittgenstein: other writers would prefer '[logical] type' or 'syntactical category'. Wittgenstein himself used the former expression in the *Moore Notes* (e.g. at 109 (3)). He is clearly thinking of the logical form of an object as if it were a power or capacity to combine with other objects in atomic facts: objects have different logical forms when they have different liberties of association. A physical analogy might be found in the shape of a material object as determining the capacity of a given object (a pencil, say) to combine with another of the right complementary shape (a pencil cap). Metaphorically, one might say that objects can have various 'logical shapes'.

The idea can be made more precise in the following way. When a given object, x, *can* combine with all the objects, $z_1, z_2, ..., z_n$, in a single atomic fact, let us call the set $(x, z_1, ..., z_n)$ a *combination*. (I leave it open whether or not a corresponding atomic fact answers to a given combination—a 'combination' must not be confused with an atomic fact.) Now let the set of all the combinations of which x is an element be called the *domain* of x. We shall say that x has the same logical form as an object y when the domain of x is converted into the domain of y (and *vice versa*) by replacing x wherever it occurs in a combination by y (and *vice versa*). The condition reduces to this: each set of z's, not containing y, with which x combines must be a set with which y also combines; and each set of z's, not containing x, with which y combines must also be a set with which x combines. A simple illustration follows:

$$\text{domain of } a: \quad (a, c) \quad (a, b, d);$$
$$\text{domain of } b: \quad (b, c) \quad (a, b, d).$$

Here, we can say that a and b have the same logical form. It will be noticed that the domains of a and b are parallel, but not identical.

The form of a given object can now be defined, 'by abstraction', in the usual way, as the class of objects isomorphic with it.

The foregoing account, like Wittgenstein's 2.0141, depends upon the idea of the *possibility* of given objects producing an atomic fact. It will appear later that such a possibility can only be shown in the 'formal features' of an *expression* (cf. 2.201, 2.203, 3.4–3.411, also 3.31 d). The logical form of an object is revealed by the class of different *names* that are allowed parallel occurrences in propositions according to the syntactical rules governing them.

III

OBJECTS AS THE SUBSTANCE
OF THE WORLD

(2.02–2.027)

Two complementary aspects of 'objects' (simples) are emphasized in this instalment. They are the materials of which atomic facts are constructed, the substance of the world (2.021). And they have form (2.025). (The form of an object, as has already been seen, is its possibility of occurrence in atomic facts. We may think of an object's form—provisionally, at least—as manifested in restrictions upon the sets of objects with which it can combine to produce atomic facts.)

Wittgenstein's view of 'objects' is very schematic. His conviction that propositions have a definite sense (that language is possible) drives him to postulate that there must be simples (cf. the important remark, 2.0211). But about the logical form of these objects he has nothing definite to say. It would certainly be a mistake to identify objects with what we commonly call 'individuals', or to suppose that they cannot be at all like what we commonly call 'relations'. Since objects constitute the substance of the world, it is natural to think of them as timeless (cf. 2.027) and so to imagine them as resembling 'universals' rather than 'particulars', but both of these traditional terms are inappropriate. All we can really know about the objects is that they exist.

2.02 The idea of the simplicity of the 'objects' is closely connected with that of the possibility of analysis (2.0201, 3.201, 3.25, 4.2211). If no final analysis were possible, every ostensible constituent of a proposition would be further decomposable, i.e. there would be no simples, and the world would have no substance (2.021). Since there are simples, analysis is possible. See *Investigations*, §§ 39, 46–50, 59.

It is useful to think of the 'objects' as the meanings of simple signs (cf. 3.203), i.e. as things that *could be* pointed at or designated by 'logically proper names'.

Commentary

'*Obviously* propositions are possible which contain no simple signs, i.e. no signs which have an immediate reference [or, which mean directly (*unmittelbar*)]. And these are really *propositions* making sense, nor do the definitions of their component parts (*Bestandteile*) have to be attached to them. But it is clear that components of our propositions can be analyzed by means of definitions, and must be, if we want to approximate to the real [or: actual (*eigentlichen*)] structure of the proposition. *At any rate, then, there is a process of analysis*' (*Notebooks*, 46 (4–5)).

'The reference [or: meaning] of our propositions is not infinitely complicated (*unendlich kompliziert*)' (*ibid.* 46 (10)).

'The *monad* of which we shall here speak is merely a simple substance, which enters into composites; *simple*, that is to say, without parts. And there must be simple substances, since there are composites; for the composite is only a collection or *aggregation* of simple substances' (Leibniz, *Monadology*, §§ 1,2).

LOGICAL ATOMISM IN THE 'TRACTATUS'

The label 'logical atomism' was introduced by Russell into modern philosophy for 'the view that you can get down in theory, if not in practice, to ultimate simples, out of which the world is built, and that those simples have a kind of reality not belonging to anything else' (*Logic and Knowledge*, p. 270). In some form, this position has been defended by philosophers as diverse as Hume, Leibniz, and Hegel. A view of this sort dominates the *Tractatus*, although Wittgenstein's reasons for holding it were not entangled in epistemological considerations as Russell's were. The 'principle of reducibility to acquaintance', for instance, is absent from the *Tractatus*.

Russell's definition of logical atomism has the serious defects of not explaining what is to be understood by 'ultimate simple' and what it means to say that they 'have a kind of reality not belonging to anything else'. In the *Tractatus* there are two types of 'ultimate' units: 'atomic facts' and 'objects'. The former are ultimate in being indecomposable into other facts; the latter in being indecomposable into other objects. But what does 'indecomposable' mean? What reasons are there for holding that such ultimate units exist? In what sense, if any, supposing them to exist, should they be held to have a kind of reality not attaching to complexes?

58

Objects as the Substance of the World

In what follows, I shall consider only what might be called *contingent complexes*. I call a complex K contingent when the following conditions are satisfied: (i) K is composed of a set of parts P_i; (ii) each P_i might have existed, without any of the others existing and so without K existing; and (iii) the existence of all of the P_i's in question is a necessary and sufficient condition for the existence of K. A special case of a contingent complex is an *aggregate*, i.e. a K defined as being simply P_1 *and* P_2 *and* ... *and* P_n, or what would nowadays be called a 'class taken in extension'. Wittgenstein's facts (*Tatsachen*) may be considered to be contingent complexes, although they are not mere aggregates.

Let us call a contingent complex, *all* of whose parts (at no matter which level of analysis) are themselves contingently complex, *irreducibly* complex. Many philosophers have thought it impossible for irreducibly complex contingent complexes (I shall not consider non-contingent complexes) to exist.

Thus Leibniz says: 'I believe that where there are only beings by aggregation, there will not even be real beings; for every being by aggregation presupposes beings endowed with a veritable unity, because it derives its reality only from that of those of which it is composed, so that it will have none at all if each being of which it is composed is again a being by aggregation' (Gerhardt, ii, 96, quoted from Russell, *Leibniz*, p. 242).

'A body is not a true unity; it is only an aggregate, which the Scholastics call a being *per accidens*, a collection like a herd' (Loemker, ed., ii, 1013). Similar passages abound in his writings.

And Hume: ''Tis evident that existence in itself belongs only to unity, and is never applicable to number, but on account of the *unites*, of which the number is composed. Twenty men may be said to exist; but 'tis only because one, two, three, etc., are existent; and if you deny the existence of the latter, that of the former falls of course' (*Treatise*, book i, part ii, §ii). Some such ideas may have influenced Wittgenstein when he wrote 4.2211, on the need for simple objects and atomic facts, even in an infinitely complex universe.

But why are irreducibly contingent complexes impossible? If they

59

exist they must have infinitely many parts, but this will offend only those, unlike Wittgenstein at the time he wrote the *Tractatus*, who reject the 'actual infinite' (cf. 4.2211). It will hardly do to argue that the existence of such a complex would depend upon the existence of each of a set of its parts, and each of those upon the existence of other parts and so on without end. For it remains to be shown that this is a vicious regress: *if* all the infinitely many parts exist (and why should they not?) the complex will exist too, for we assumed that the existence of the parts was a necessary and sufficient condition for the existence of the whole. What lies behind remarks like those of Leibniz and Hume quoted above is the conviction that it is impossible that all existence should be conditional. And if this view were correct, the existence of simple parts would at once follow. But this is no more than a metaphysical prejudice. So far as I can see there is no logical absurdity in the idea of there being contingent complexes that are irreducibly complex.

The reasons why Wittgenstein was nevertheless forced to reject this idea become clearer when we consider his views about the relation between language and the world (e.g. 2.0211–2.0212). If *all* facts were irreducibly complex contingent complexes, i.e. if there were no ultimate objects in *direct* connexion with the names standing for them, no proposition could say anything definite, i.e. no proposition could say anything at all. This is nicely brought out at 2.0211: 'If the world had no substance'—i.e. if there were no objects—the resolution of the apparent complexity of a given proposition could have no terminus. The sense of S_1 would depend upon the truth of some other sentence S_2 (affirming the existence of a complex apparently mentioned in S_1) and the sense of S_2 would depend upon the truth of some other S_3, and so on without an end. This would be a *vicious* regress: we could never know what the sense of a given S_1 was without first, *per impossibile*, knowing an infinity of other propositions to be true. More simply: unless *some* signs are in direct connexion with the world (as names are when they stand for objects) no signs can be in indirect connexion either. Thus the sense which we find attached to the propositions we encounter in ordinary life forces us to believe in elementary propositions and so to believe in objects. It is by this semantical route, rather than by the traditional arguments in favour of substance, that Wittgenstein must have arrived at his own version of logical atomism.

2.0201 Cf. 3.24 (2) (truth-value of propositions containing complexes), 3.3442 (analysis of complexes), 5.5423*a* (how complexes are perceived).

that describe the complexes completely: in the corresponding section of the *Notes on Logic* (99 (6)*c*), W. adds 'i.e. that proposition which is equivalent to saying the complex exists'. In short, what W. has in mind here is Russell's well-known procedure for analysing propositions containing definite descriptions.

'It may be suggested that the ultimate factors in a fact are the factors which are simple or have no part (in the widest sense of part). But this is a mistake. . . . McTaggart's theory of the infinite divisibility of substance is not incompatible with the theory of atomic facts. On the other hand, though what "this" names may have parts, the parts must all be of the same logical type, and if what "this" names is a particular then all the parts must be particulars. This is because to say of a factor that it is ultimate is to say that it is a block, and not a unity or a construct. To say of a factor that it is ultimate is not to say that it has no parts but that it has no elements. A particular is not a unity, nor is a perfectly determinate shade of red—they may have parts but they have no elements. They are homogeneous wholes—they are blocks' (Wisdom, 'Constructions', pp. 212–13).

Similar views are expressed in Hall, *Value*, p. 23 f.n. He there contrasts 'entities' with 'facts': 'They [entities *named*] may be made up of parts having the same status, ontologically, as the whole; e.g. particulars may be made up of particulars, universals of universals. . . .'

2.021*a*   make up: 'constitute' or, simply, 'are'.

Substance is defined at 2.024 as what exists independently of what is the case, i.e. as what necessarily exists. This is the *totality* of objects (5.5561*a*).

b **composite**: or, 'complex' (*zusammengesetzt*)—opposed to 'simple'.

It is a basic principle for W. that every combination is contingent (cf. 2.0271 on the 'configuration' as mutable). If objects were complex, their existence would be a contingent fact and hence they could not collectively constitute the substance of the world.

2.0211

● 'If it were not *necessary* that objects existed (as in 2.021*a*), it would always be a question of *fact* whether a constituent of a proposition stood for anything. For the proposition to have sense, each of its constituents must stand for something (or be part of a complex sign signifying a complex). Thus, in the absence of substance (= the totality of objects), a proposition's having sense would depend upon whether further propositions were true, namely those stating that the complexes signified really existed.'

'The question whether a proposition has sense (*Sinn*) can never depend on the *truth* of another proposition about a constituent of the first' (*Moore Notes*, 116 (6)).

'Whether a proposition is true or not is decided by experience—but not its sense' (*Phil. Bem.* 9, 1).

Cf. 4.061 *a* (propositions have a sense independent of the facts).

2.0212 sketch out: or, simply, 'produce' (there is no implication of incompleteness in the German text).

If a proposition had no final analysis, there would be an infinite (and vicious) regress. In order for p to have sense we should first have to determine by experience that some other proposition q was true (2.0211). But before doing so, we should have to know that q made sense, i.e. we should have first to verify some *other* proposition r, etc.

An alternative argument runs as follows: A 'picture' is constituted by a set of word–object co-ordinations (2.13). Unless the objects were 'given' to us, i.e. unless we *knew* they existed, we could not set up the correspondence—could not make a picture, could not say anything.

2.022 imagined world: rather, 'a world which is thought about (*gedacht*)'. For 'thought', see 3 and accompanying notes.

a form: in the light of 2.024 and 2.025, this might equally well have read 'a form *and* a content' (= 'a substance').

THE USES OF 'FORM' IN THE 'TRACTATUS'

Wittgenstein uses the word 'form' in a strikingly wide variety of distinct, though related senses. These uses include the following:

(*a*) As a synonym for 'shape' (cf. the 'form' [= 'shape'] of a spot, 4.063*a*; the 'form' of clothing, 4.002 (4)).

(*b*) As a synonym for 'kind' or 'sort' (e.g. at 2.0122*a* in speaking of the 'form of independence').

(*c*) As a synonym for 'constitution' or 'make-up' (cf. 5.6331*a* on the 'form' of the visual field).

In these and similar contexts, 'form' is used in a loose popular sense and could be replaced by a synonym (as is sometimes done in the translation) without damage to Wittgenstein's thought.

(*d*) In the crucial technical sense in which a proposition (*Satz*) has a specific form that can be exhibited by variables (instances occur at 3.311*a*, 3.312, 3.333 (2), 4.012, 4.5, 5.131, 5.156*b*, 5.24*ab*, 5.47*a*, 5.5422, 5.55*a*, 5.556*a*). I shall speak in this connexion of the *specific logical form* of a proposition.

(*e*) In an equally important, but distinct sense, in which constituents of propositions have logical form (form of *expressions*, 3.31*d* ff., cf. also 4.242 and 5.5351*a*; form of the *term of a series*, 5.2522*b*).

(*f*) The form of atomic facts (2.031 + 2.032 + 2.033).

(*g*) The form of non-atomic facts (*Tatsachen*) (inferred from 2.034 + 2.033).

(*h*) The form of objects(= logical simples) (2.0141, 2.0233, 2.0251).

It will be noticed that (*g*) offers an ontological parallel to (*d*) and (*h*) to (*e*). Eventually Wittgenstein *identifies* the form of a proposition with the form of the fact it represents and the form of a name (a simple expression) with the form of the object for which it stands.

(*i*) The form of a proposition's sense (3.13*e*).

(*j*) The 'form of representation' of a picture or a proposition (2.15*b*, 2.151, 2.173, 2.174).

In the cases (*d*)–(*j*) listed above, Wittgenstein is referring to specific forms, of which one may be contrasted with another. But he also has a use in which 'form' admits of no plural:

(*k*) *The* 'form of the world' (2.022, 2.026), the 'form of reality' (2.18). In this sense, 'form' is an approximate synonym for 'logic'.

A full survey of Wittgenstein's reliance upon notions of form would require attention to the related notion of 'structure' (2.032) and the favourite phrase *die Art und Weise* (the mode or fashion, 2.031).

2.023 Here, as in the preceding remark, a reference to 'content' would also fit.

2.0231*a* **material properties**: also called 'external properties' by W., as in 2.0233. Contrasted with 'formal' (= 'internal') properties, for which see 4.122.

b **represented**: P.–McG.'s usual translation of *dargestellt*. I prefer 'presented'.

configuration: cf. 2.0272 (the configuration constitutes an atomic fact).

produced: or, 'constituted' (*gebildet*).

2.0232 In a manner of speaking: in O., 'roughly speaking'. The German expression, *beiläufig gesprochen*, also has the force of 'incidentally' or 'in passing'.

● 'That some thing is coloured is expressed in a proposition (2.0231 *b*). But objects themselves have neither colour nor any other contingent (= "material, external") properties. Objects are propertyless.'
Cf. 3.221 *d* (propositions as saying *how* things are, not *what* they are).

2.0233 external properties: = 'material properties' (in 2.0231 *a*). For the meaning of 'external property', see 4.123.

● 'For the sake of illustration, treat red and green as objects. The two colours differ in their "external" properties, since they are not ingredients in the same facts (my pen is green, but not red). Although they have the same logical form ("red" and "green" can occur in the same propositional contexts), they must be different objects. Yet there is no *respect* in which they differ.' (We might say that the colours differ in 'content'— for which see 2.025.)

2.02331 This can be read as a destructive dilemma in support of 2.0233. If one of the two objects (of the same logical form) had a uniquely distinguishing property, we could produce a description of that object by using that property. But this would be incompatible with what has already been said about the simplicity of objects (2.02) and the character of descriptions (2.0201). If, on the other hand, neither object has a property that distinguishes it from the other, it must be impossible to distinguish them (i.e. by means of any property). (Of course this does not mean that we are unable to *refer* to objects—cf. 3.263 on the 'elucidation' of primitive signs.)
Anscombe (*Introduction*, p. 111) thinks that W. may have been thinking of what is involved in distinguishing particles of matter. If so, his remark is consistent with 5.5302.

2.024 Cf. 2.021 *a* (objects as substance of the world).
subsists (*besteht*): it might be more natural to say 'there is'.
'If one says substance is indestructible (*unzerstörbar*) one *means* that it is senseless to speak in any connexion—whether affirmative or negative— of the "destruction of a substance"' (*Phil. Bem.* 40, 3).

2.025 The substance of the world consists of the objects (2.021 *a*). Considered as determining the atomic facts in which they can occur, each of them has its own form (2.0141)—together, they constitute in this aspect *the* form of the world (2.026, cf. 2.023). But objects are also the stuff of which facts are made. From this standpoint, then, objects also have content. Compare also notes on 2.0233 above.

This section is discussed by Stenius (*Exposition*, pp. 79–81).

2.0251 In talking about 'space' we are not talking about an 'object' (or a set of objects) but rather indicating (alluding to) certain formal features of certain propositions, namely those that we call 'propositions about space'. And similarly for 'time' and 'being coloured'. Compare notes on 2.0131 above.

2.026 Cf. 2.023 (the unalterable form consists of the objects).
unalterable: literally, 'fixed' (*feste*).

2.027 **subsistent**: or, 'persistent' or 'immutable' (*das Bestehende*). Stenius construes this as 'persistent in time' (*Exposition*, pp. 81–2). This seems to be a mistake.

'Every term is immutable and indestructible. What a term is, it is, and no change can be conceived in it which would not destroy its identity and make it another term' (Russell, *Principles*, p. 44). (Russell has previously defined a 'term' as 'whatever may be an object of thought, or may occur in any true or false proposition, or can be counted as *one*' [*op. cit.* p. 43].)

On the indestructibility of objects, cf. *Investigations*, § 55.

IV

THE STRUCTURE AND FORM OF ATOMIC FACTS

(2.0271–2.034)

The timeless objects in their internal relations constitute the system of 'logical space'. But the actual world is contingent: logical space might have been 'empty', there might have been not a single atomic fact. The contingent aspect of the world is conceived by Wittgenstein as constituted by the clinging together of objects (like the links of a chain, *without intermediaries*) in atomic facts. The particular way in which the objects cohere in a given atomic fact is the 'structure' of that fact; the possibility of that structure is the 'form' of that fact. Wittgenstein's distinction between 'structure' and 'form' has troubled commentators as able as Ramsey. It is doubtful whether it is needed.

2.0271   unstable: or, 'variable', 'mutable' (*das Unbeständige*).

2.0272   configuration: = 'hanging in one another' (2.03) = 'being combined in a definite way' (2.031).
   produces: or, 'constitutes' (*bildet*).

2.03   fit: literally, 'hang'.
   links: the point here is to deny that there is anything substantial in a fact (a bond, tie, connexion) holding the components together. They hang *in one another*—i.e. without the intervention of anything further. Compare Frege on functions as 'unsaturated'. It is rather odd to think of the eternal 'objects' as 'hanging together'.
   Gasking (*Anderson*, p. 4) counts a relation (*darker than*) as an object. But we must not suppose that the 'objects' are linked by anything like what we call relations.

2.031   stand in a determinate relation: or, 'are combined', 'are arranged with respect to one another'. Literally, 'behave with respect to one another' (*verhalten sich*, with a possible allusion to *Sachverhalt*).
2.032   way: literally, 'manner and fashion' (*Art und Weise*). (W. is rather fond of this expression.)
   the determinate way: this must always refer to an actual concatenation in a fact and not, say, to a formal relation or a possible mode of combination of the elements. Compare last part of notes on 2.033 below.

   structure: notice the contrast with 'form' in 2.033. Cf. 2.15*b* for a definition of 'structure'.

2.033   its: delete (not in the text).
   Its form: presumably the form of an atomic fact.
   In the light of this remark, one would expect that a fact has structure *and* form, while a possible state of affairs has only form. Two distinct facts can have the same form: can they also have the same structure? The correct answer seems to be that distinct facts must have distinct structures, even in a case in which the facts have the same form.

'The only point which I can see in the distinction between structure and form, is that the insertion of "possibility" may include the case in which the alleged fact whose form we are considering is not a fact, so that we can talk of the form of the fact *aRb* whether or no *aRb* is true, provided it is logically possible' (Ramsey, *Foundations*, p. 271). If it is correct to think of the 'form'–'structure' contrast as parallel to the 'possibility'–'actuality' contrast, Ramsey was mistaken here.

possibility: in ordinary language, use of the noun 'possibility' can normally be replaced by use of the adjective 'possible': instead of 'Is there a possibility that . . .?' we can say 'Is it possible that . . .?' and similarly in other cases. This type of use of 'possible' or the cognate substantive is common in the text. However, in the present passage, the substantival use cannot be replaced by the adjectival one: no sentence containing the expression 'it is possible for there to be a structure . . .' will adequately express W.'s thought. Thus, 'possibility' and 'form' become something quasi-substantial, and we can, for example, speak of the form of a fact (e.g. at 5.156*c*). Thus there arises a serious problem of how such references to possibility are to be interpreted.

THE FORM OF AN ATOMIC FACT

Wittgenstein's thought in this part of the book, and throughout, is strongly influenced by the analogy of a *spatial arrangement* of a set of material bodies (cf., for example, 3.1431). There is a clear sense to the notion of the 'way' in which a set of material bodies are put together or arranged. The question 'How are these cubes to be arranged?' might be answered by saying 'With the red one underneath, then the blue on top, and the green uppermost'—and similarly for the arrangement of guests around a dinner table, of books on a shelf, etc. We say what the mode of arrangement is by mentioning relations between the things in question, using relevant properties to identify them where necessary ('husbands and wives alternating' or 'in order of size'). Two sets of arranged objects (let us call them *arrays*) count as being arranged *in the same way* when the same or parallel descriptions apply to both. Suppose we have some set of material objects, $a_1, a_2, ..., a_n$, a set of properties, $P_1, P_2, ..., P_j$, and a set of *spatial* relations, $R_1, R_2, ..., R_k$, such that each P is a property of at least one of the a's and each R relates at least one subset of the *a*'s. Call all this a *system*. Suppose we also have a system involving the material objects b_1, b_2, ..., b_n (not necessarily differing from the *a*'s) and the same *P*'s and *R*'s as before. Suppose, finally, that each a_i has a property *P* when and only when the corresponding b_i has the same property and that each relation *R* holds between a set of the *a*'s when and only when the same relation holds between the corresponding *b*'s. We shall then be entitled to say that the array of the *a*'s and the array of the *b*'s have the *same spatial arrangement*, are arranged in the same way.

The generalization to non-spatial arrangements is obvious: all we need do is to remove the restriction that the relevant set of relations (the *R*'s above) shall be spatial. In this way, our definition of 'same mode of arrangement' can be extended to cover any kinds of entities, standing in any kinds of relationships. We can now speak, in a perfectly clear and literal sense, of the mode of arrangement of the elements of a sonnet, a fugue, a sentence, etc. In order to pass to Wittgenstein's notion of the 'form' of an atomic fact, or as we might say, of the 'logical arrangement' of the objects in such a fact, we need only conceive our 'systems' as follows: the objects are Wittgenstein's logical simples; the only relevant 'properties' are what he calls their 'logical' ones, which for present purposes can be identified with the logical form of each (cf. notes at 2.0141 above for the meaning of this); and the sole 'relation' (now something of a misnomer) is the *concatenation* of the objects in an atomic fact. Since objects can, on Wittgenstein's view, only be combined by 'concatenation' (and, as I shall argue later, pp. 127–8, in only one way), we can derive the following simple formula for the form of an atomic fact: an atomic fact composed of the objects a_1, a_2, ..., a_n, has the same logical form as one composed of the objects b_1, b_2, ..., b_n, if and only if there is a one–one correlation between the *a*'s and the *b*'s such that the correlated objects are isomorphic. That is to say, atomic facts are isomorphic if and only if they are composed of the same number of mutually isomorphic elements. Hence, the logical forms of objects uniquely determine the logical forms of the atomic facts in which they can combine. For discussion of the extent to which the converse is true, see pp. 127–8 below.

Of course, we must beware of treating 'the logical arrangement of F' or 'the structure of F' as designating-expressions, i.e. of supposing that the universe contains 'structures' or, for that matter, 'forms', over and above objects and facts. 'Structure' and 'form' are incomplete symbols; what we say with their aid is exponible, as we have seen, into talk about the 'logical forms of objects' and so eventually into remarks belonging to logical syntax.

A further extension of the notion of 'same arrangement' will be needed when we come to discuss the form of logical pictures. Modify the above account of 'systems' so that the second system does not consist of the *same* properties and relations as the first but rather of *correlated* properties, P'_i, and relations, R'_j. Suppose also that properties and relations apply to objects in the first system when and only when the correlated properties and relations apply to the correlated objects in the second system. That is to say, $P_i a_j$ if and only if $P'_i b_j$, and $a_i R_j a_k$ if and only if $b_i R'_j b_k$, etc. I shall then say that the two arrays have *parallel arrangements*, are *homomorphic*. (The language used by mathematicians and logicians in this connexion fluctuates: some would use 'isomorphic' where I propose to use 'homomorphic'.)

2.034 This should be compared with 4.1. The 'fact' here is a complex fact (*Tatsache*): the 'atomic facts' (*Sachverhalte*) ('states of affairs' in P.–McG.) are those involved in the former.

V

REALITY AND THE NON-EXISTENCE OF ATOMIC FACTS

(2.04–2.063)

The chief novelty here is the introduction of the puzzling notion of reality (*die Wirklichkeit*). The apposition of 2.04 and 2.06 suggests an intended contrast between 'the world' and 'reality'. The former seems to be the totality of atomic facts, while the latter is constituted by the non-actualization of some atomic situations (the 'non-existence' of some atomic facts) as well as by the actualization of others (the 'existence' of some atomic facts). The world, one might be inclined to say, is the positive core of 'total reality'. Unfortunately, 2.063 refutes this plausible gloss. In the light of 2.05, perhaps the right answer is that 'the world' and 'total reality' are synonyms; the world has both negative and positive aspects, the former of which are emphasized by using the expression 'total reality'. The use of 'reality' is especially appropriate whenever there is later occasion to speak of the truth-conditions of non-elementary propositions.

2.04 existing states of affairs: here, and in 2.05–2.062, I agree with P.–McG. in thinking that *Sachverhalt* should be read as meaning 'elementary *situation*', i.e. something that *could* be the case.

2.04 follows from 1+2.

2.05 Cf. 1.12 for another expression of this thought.

2.06 (1) By collating 2.06 (1) with 2.1–2.12 we get: 'reality' (*die Wirklichkeit*) = a complex fact (*Tatsache*). 'Total reality' (2.063) would then be the totality of facts, i.e. the 'world' (1.1, 2.063). On the other hand, it is sometimes more natural to read '*die Wirklichkeit*' as synonymous with '*die Welt*' (e.g. at 4.462 *a*).

'We might say that the World is Reality distributively analyzed into facts and Reality is the World collectively organized into a single whole' (Shwayder, *Thesis*, p. 559).

(2) negative fact: for further uses of this expression, see 4.063 *b*, 5.5151 *b*.

'There are *positive and negative facts*: if the proposition "This rose is not red" is true, then what it signifies is negative. But the occurrence of the word "not" does not indicate this unless we know that the signification of the proposition "This rose is red" (when it is true) is positive. It is only from both, the negation and the negated proposition, that we can conclude about a characteristic of the signification of the whole proposition' (*Notes on Logic*, 94 (5)).

NEGATIVE FACTS

The present section seems to affirm the reality of negative facts and this is confirmed by 2.062, with its reference to the non-existence of states of affairs. Can Wittgenstein allow irreducibly negative facts to be part of the world (as $2.06 + 2.063$ would imply)? He has said, at 2, that a fact is the *existence* of atomic facts (and here, we notice, there is no reference to their non-existence); at 1.1 he said that the world is the totality of facts; taken together, these remarks seem to say that the world consists of nothing but 'positive facts'. That this was Wittgenstein's intention is confirmed by 2.05, with its implication that the sum-total of positive facts (atomic facts) suffices to determine what is *not* the case.

Consider a model universe, containing three logical simples, a, b, and c, respectively designated by the names, l, m, and n. Suppose the elementary propositions are lm, mn, and ln (with the order of the letters immaterial). There are then just three elementary propositions, P_1, P_2, and P_3: suppose the first two are true and the last false. The universe in question may then be held to consist of just the two atomic facts, ab and bc, and the conjunction $P_1 . P_2$ might be held to express the whole truth about it. But suppose it were objected that something is left out by $P_1.P_2$, the non-existence of the remaining combination of a and c. Then we would need a further negative proposition, $\sim P_3$. This proposition would have to count as true, and so something in the universe would have to *make* it true: what could this be? Obviously, neither the fact ab nor the fact bc will serve; the only possibility is the *non*-existence of the combination of a and c (cf. 4.25). This fact, if it were admitted to be a genuine fact, would be independent of the atomic facts ab, bc (contrary to 2.05): we would then have an unanalysable negative fact. This is quite incompatible with Wittgenstein's conception of the concatenation of objects in unanalysable facts (2.03). For in the supposed fact answering to $\sim P_3$, a and c would *not* be 'in immediate combination' (4.221): what makes $\sim P_3$ true is that a and c are not combined at all. (It would be preposterous to say that a and c are combined—but in a 'negative' way.) I therefore hold that Wittgenstein is committed to the view that $P_1 . P_2$ does express the *whole* truth about the imagined universe: that universe consists of ab and bc and *nothing else*. But we are not required to *say* that we are speaking the whole truth: it is enough to affirm P_1 and P_2 and to say nothing more. If I am right, a perfectly adequate language might contain no provision for negation (or any other logical operation). I shall call this a *primary language* for future reference. In a primary language, the whole truth about the universe would be expressed by affirming each of a set of unanalysable propositions, respectively asserting the existence of the corresponding atomic fact. But nothing in the above precludes the possibility of higher-level languages, containing the usual logical operators.

2.061 Cf. 1.21 (a similar idea), 4.211 (no elementary proposition is contradicted by an elementary proposition), 4.27 (2) (possibility of existence of combinations of atomic facts), 5.134 (impossibility of inferences from elementary propositions).

independent: for definition of this, see 5.152 a.

2.062 Elaboration of the preceding remark.

There seems, on the face of it, to be a conflict between 2.062 and 2.05.

2.063 **sum-total of reality**: or, 'total reality' (*die gesamte Wirklichkeit*): for the only other occurrence of this expression, see 4.12 a.

VI

PICTURES OF FACTS

(2.1–2.15 (1))

Having concluded this account of the world as a mosaic of atomic facts embedded in logical space, Wittgenstein now turns to consider what is necessarily involved in any symbolic *representation* of the world. The leading question might be expressed as: Given that *this* is what the world must be, what *must* language be, in order to be capable of representing the world adequately? The task may be called, in Wittgenstein's own phraseology, that of clarifying the essence of all language, provided 'language' is taken to include any system of signs, not necessarily verbal, that is adequate for making all possible assertions about reality. Clarification of the essence of all language will be a central preoccupation in instalments VI–XVI:

everything of importance in the book depends, in one way or another, upon what Wittgenstein has to say about this topic.

One way to appreciate the point of Wittgenstein's doctrine of symbolism is to allow oneself to feel the force of the nagging question that provokes it: How is a proposition linked with the world, in such a way that the facts make it either true or false? We may begin with elementary propositions, composed wholly of names (4.22), leaving questions about non-elementary propositions for later discussion (see, for instance, instalments LXI–LXII on general propositions). Suppose, for a start, that the connexion of *names* with the world is unproblematic: each name, by convention, stands for one 'object' (a logical simple) which, according to Wittgenstein, is its meaning (3.203). But then the whole sentence, *pace* Frege, cannot be a complex name of its truth-value or of anything else: it cannot, for example, be a designation of its verifying fact—for then where is to be found the meaning of a false elementary proposition, to which *no* atomic fact answers? We understand a proposition before we know its truth-value, as a unified whole, not a mere bundle of its constituents, and in so doing we know what *in the world* makes it either true or false, as the case may be. So the proposition is connected to the world by something more than the individual correlations between the names and their objects. How are we to make sense of this? How are we to understand the 'common bond' (what Wittgenstein in the *Notebooks* called *das gemeinsame Bindemittel*) between proposition and reality—or, what comes to the same thing in the end, between thought and reality?

In brief, Wittgenstein's answer is this: The sentence by which an elementary proposition is expressed has to be regarded as a *fact* (3.14*b*) in which the elements, the words, are united in a definite structure—a definite arrangement or mode of combination (3.14*a*). If the proposition happens to be true, the objects severally coordinated with its words are combined in a fact having the same structure as the sentence-fact. But wherever there is structure, there is also 'form', the corresponding 'possibility of the structure' (2.033). Since the true proposition and its verifying fact have the same structure, they must also have the same form. And even a false proposition (here is the decisive point) will display a *form*, a possibility of combination in a perfectly definite way of the objects co-ordinated with the elements of the sentence-fact (the words). The proposition presents or exhibits or shows the form in question by actualizing it in the sentence-fact. By seeing *that* the words are combined on the page in just one way, and not another, we understand how the corresponding objects *may be* combined in the world—we understand the proposition's truth-condition. Of course, in understanding the proposition we also understand that the objects in question are being *said* to be combined in just the way in which the words that go proxy for them actually are combined (cf. 4.022*c* on what a proposition 'says'). Later, I shall try to show that this view is exposed to serious objections.

Wittgenstein introduces his analysis of the essence of language by first considering the related question of how a *picture* can depict a possible state of affairs in the world. (For him, a proposition *is* a picture of a certain sort—a '*logical* picture', as he will say.) In this instalment, and subsequently, Wittgenstein is not using 'picture' in some figurative sense. His remarks should be taken as intended to apply literally to all representational paintings, photographs, or diagrams such as maps, that can be 'read' as depicting how things stand in reality. Nearly everything said about 'pictures' in general will later be found to apply to the important special case in which the picture is a 'logical picture', i.e. a proposition.

THE SEMANTICAL TERMINOLOGY OF THE 'TRACTATUS'

It will be useful to consider together most of the expressions which Wittgenstein uses in connexion with the symbolizing relation.

Abbilden: The active verb corresponding to *Bild* (picture). This is a general label used by Wittgenstein to stand for the connexion between a picture or a proposition (a logical picture) and whatever the picture depicts. It is natural to translate it as 'to picture' or 'to depict', which I prefer, with Pears and McGuinness, to the expression, 'to represent', that is regularly used in Ogden. Wittgenstein's uses of the verb and the corresponding noun are strongly influenced by the mathematical senses of those words in which, for example, there may be said to be an *Abbildung* of a non-euclidean geometry upon a euclidean space. (Compare note on 'projection' at 3.11 (1) below.) In the mathematical sense, an *Abbildung* is approximately the same as a model.

What are depicted? According to 2.1, *Tatsachen* (facts), according to 2.19, *die Welt* (the world), according to 2.17, *die Wirklichkeit* (reality), etc. A picture might be said to picture the fact or facts which make it true, if there are such facts.

Darstellen: This word occurs much more frequently than the previous one. We might try translating it as 'to present', contrasting 'to present' with 'to picture'. (I prefer this to Pears and McGuinness's use of 'represent'.) Such a contrast is often implicit in Wittgenstein's usage: for example, what is presented (*dargestellt*) in 2.201–2.203, 2.22, 2.221, 4.031 (2), is clearly a possibility (notice especially that the *sense* is said to be *dargestellt* by a picture in 2.221). Similarly, in 4.124 (1), 4.125, 4.462 *b*, a possible state of affairs (*mögliche Sachlage*) is said to be *dargestellt*. To 'present' then, would be much the same as to 'show' (*zeigen*), while 'picturing' would be the same as 'saying'. Unfortunately, Wittgenstein sometimes uses '*darstellen*' as a synonym for *abbilden* (see, for example, 4.12 (1)). And he also uses *darstellen* more widely, so that what is *dargestellt* can be a material property (2.0231), the general propositional form (3.312 *a*), a proposition (5.21), and even a contradiction (6.3751 (2)). On the whole, it may be best to translate *darstellen* by 'to present', when its meaning is contrasted with that of *abbilden*, by 'to represent' or 'to picture' when it is a synonym of *abbilden*, and by 'to express' elsewhere.

Bedeuten, bezeichnen, nennen, stehen für, vertreten: These are approximate synonyms for the relation between a propositional *component* (a sign or a name) and its meaning. *Bedeuten*, = 'to mean', is regularly used for the relation between a *name* and the object it stands for. *Bezeichnen*, = 'to signify', is the general term for the relation between any sign and what it stands for (e.g. at 3.24(3), 3.261 *a*, 3.334). (A numeral signifies a number, 4.126 (3); a variable signifies a formal concept, 4.127; a proposition is signified at 4.442; and a relation at 5.5541, etc.) *Nennen*, = *bedeuten*, = 'to name', is used only of names. *Stehen für*, = 'to stand for', is approximately the same as *vertreten*. The last word is the most interesting of the group. It is always used of the relation between a name and an object. In line with Wittgenstein's analysis of the proposition, it should be rendered as 'to stand proxy for' or 'to deputize for', rather than by the colourless 'to represent'. A central idea for Wittgenstein is that the names combined in the propositional fact deputize for, take the place of, the objects for which they stand.

Aussagen, aussprechen, behaupten, sagen: Used only of entire propositions. All have the force of 'say' or 'assert'.

Aufweisen, spiegeln, zeigen: exhibit, reflect, show. Used in connexion with 'logical features' of the world. Strongly contrasted with the previous group.

Beschreiben = 'to describe'. Contrasted at 3.144 with naming, and at 6.124*a* with *darstellen*. Nevertheless, Wittgenstein talks of describing an object (2.02331*a*, 4.023*d*, 5.02 (2)), a complex (3.24*b*), a proposition (3.317*b*, 4.5*a*, 5.501 (4)), an expression (3.33), etc. The term is used very loosely, as approximately equivalent to *bezeichnen* (to signify), but with a relatively strong implication of a contrast with naming. See also note on 4.023 (4) below.

There is an elaborate discussion of the meaning of *Bedeutung* and related German words in Gätschenberger's *Symbola* (ch. 17: 'Eine sematologische Untersuchung'). Ingenious tests lead him to conclude that there are many different nuances of meaning in the actual uses of such words as *bezeichnen, vertreten, nennen*, etc. No unified meaning can be found for the word *bedeuten*. It is an extremely many-sided, ambiguous, and almost empty (*nichtsagend*) word.

2.1 to: or, 'for'. The literal rendering is 'We make pictures of facts for ourselves'.

picture: W. is mainly concerned with '*logical* pictures' (2.181), i.e. with propositions (3, 3.1). But his remarks in 2.1 onwards are intended to apply to *any* picture (cf. 2.171*b*, where spatial pictures are discussed).

2.11 presents: P.–McG.'s rendering of *vorstellt*, which is, however, used interchangeably with *darstellt* by W. Cf. 2.15*a*.

in logical space: for this expression, cf. 1.13.

For a similar statement, with 'proposition' replacing 'picture', see 4.1. See also 2.201 (and notice the reference to 'possibility' there).

By collating 2.11 with 2.06a, we get: 'A picture presents reality', which is equivalent to 2.12.

2.12 model: used interchangeably with 'picture' at 4.01 and 4.463b. But notice the addition of the words, 'as we think it is' (P.–McG.: 'as we imagine it') in 4.01b. These words might properly be added to 2.12.

THE PICTURE THEORY

The idea of the 'picture' or 'model of reality', that was to be of such importance in the *Tractatus*, appears quite late in Wittgenstein's writings [*Notebooks* (7 (2–7))]: many of Wittgenstein's most distinctive views, notably his theory of truth-functions, the recognition of logical propositions as tautologies, and the distinction between 'saying' and 'showing', precede his introduction of the idea of a 'logical picture' and can be developed independently of it. At the time he hit upon the idea, he was much preoccupied with questions about the correct analysis of propositions, i.e. with questions about their logical form. (Following Russell, he held this to be a major task of philosophical investigation, cf. *Notes on Logic*, 93 (2)g.) But how is the true logical form of a proposition to be discerned, disguised as it is by the irregularities of ordinary language? Not by any transcendental *Wesensschau*, whose possibility Wittgenstein never seriously entertained: the symbol alone, the propositional sign with its attached meaning, must be able to reveal its logical form. But this means that the signs themselves will have all 'the logical properties of what they represent' (*Notebooks*, 11 (1)): there must be a 'logical identity of sign and thing signified' (*ibid.* 3 (3)). The nature of the connexion between the two, Wittgenstein says, is a main feature (*Hauptansicht*) of 'the whole philosophical problem' (*ibid.*). He finds it hard to grasp the character of this connexion. A relational proposition, '*aRb*', presumably means that a state of affairs *cSd* obtains; the arbitrary co-ordinations between '*a*' and *c* and between '*b*' and *d* do not worry Wittgenstein, but the required link between the linguistic relation ('*R*' standing between '*a*' and '*b*' in that order) and its signification

77

gives him endless trouble. He considers, only in the end to reject, the idea of some super-relation binding the two relations together. He is unable to find a way in which the propositional fact '*aRb*' shall mean *cSd*, when there may be no such fact as the latter. There seems to be a gulf between thought and reality—and yet the thought 'reaches right up to' reality, because it has a truth-value, is made true or false, as the case may be, *by* reality. Some philosophers have tried to bridge the gap by interposing between the spoken words and reality an ideal 'proposition'. But this is an unsatisfactory device: even if we could form a clear conception of what such a proposition was supposed to be, the very same perplexities would arise again when we wondered about the relation of the proposition to the world. The true proposition is certified by the existence of a corresponding fact; but then what makes the false proposition false? The gulf between the ideal proposition and the world seems as unbridgeable as that between a sentence and the world.

The same problem arises about a proposition of unknown truth-value. When we set out to test such a proposition by confronting it with the facts, we must already know what that proposition means—for else there would be nothing to test. So the proposition's sense must be known prior to and independently of what the proposition represents as being the case. Once again, the question is how to locate this sense in the world, how to understand the bond between a proposition and what confers a truth-value on it. Wittgenstein's problem might be expressed as the question 'Given that the world consists of facts, how can propositions have meanings independent of facts?'

At this point, Wittgenstein hits upon the saving conception—the release from his 'mental cramp', he might have said in later life. Consider the representation of some state of affairs by means of a scale-model (his example was the reconstruction of a traffic accident in a law court): the toys on the table stand as *proxies* for the pedestrians, cars, traffic lights, etc., that they represent. The decisive point is that the *how* of the accident, the way in which the original participants were mutually disposed at the time of the affair, is shown *here and now* by the spatial arrangement of the proxies. The *meaning* of the model is, as it were, right before our eyes. The reconstruction by the model of the alleged accident is a *picture*; we can see *in* it what was supposed to have happened. The key to the possibility of sense independent of fact seems to lie in identity (or at least homology) of spatial structure: substitute the general notion of *logical* structure and we shall have the answer we sought. Language, thought, the world, are bound together by identity of logical form (2.18).

2.13   objects: i.e. those represented by the picture.

elements: a picture will be said to be a fact (2.141); the 'elements' will be the objects concatenated (or 'configured') in the picture-fact. For the 'elements' of a proposition, see 3.14a, 3.2–3.202. W. sometimes uses 'constituent' (*Bestandteil*) as a synonym for 'element', e.g. at 3.315a, 3.4.

In a spatial picture, such as a 'naturalistic' painting of some actual scene (Frith's *Derby Day*) or a photograph, we can isolate parts (blobs of paint, black and white patches) which resemble what they represent. The smallest such parts bearing a visible resemblance to their objects might be called *graphemes*, by analogy with linguists' analysis of language into 'morphemes'. Although the sense in which graphemes resemble the originals they depict is a sophisticated one (as shown by the difficulty that children and aborigines find in understanding even the most 'faithful' paintings), the 'method of projection' or the principle of element–thing co-ordination is, broadly speaking, that of physical similarity: graphemes stand for their objects iconically (to use Peirce's terminology). The spatial arrangement of the graphemes in the painting or photograph (suitably defined so as to exclude irrelevancies) shows the imputed spatial arrangement of the things depicted: the principle of representation of spatial structure is, broadly speaking, *identity* of arrangement. Since a given picture represents what it does by virtue of *conventions* (however natural these may seem in some cases), every representational picture belongs to an enveloping system of pictures governed by the same principles of representation: I cannot understand a picture of a dwarf without knowing what it would be like to have a picture of him shown taller, scowling instead of smiling, and so on. All three features—the element–thing co-ordinations, the transmission of structure from picture to what is represented, and the part played by the 'enveloping system' will figure prominently in W.'s account of *logical* pictures.

2.131   are the representatives: or, 'stand for' (*vertreten*), in the sense of 'stand proxy for' or 'take the place of'.

Commentary

2.14 in a determinate way: for this expression cf. 2.031, 3.14. 'Determinate' can be read here as a contrary of 'vague': a smudged or blurred picture is not a picture at all; the sense of the picture must be precise, even if the picture depicts a non-atomic situation and thereby leaves much unspecified. (A Turner painting of a foggy sunset is a precise representation of what it purports to depict.) 'Determinate' can also be opposed to 'indefinite': the blobs of paint of which a picture is made must be organized in a single, definite way, out of the many that are possible (must be intended to be seen in a unique way), in order to constitute a determinate picture.

● In the light of 2.032, 2.14 could be rephrased as, 'A picture consists in its elements being combined in a definite structure'.

2.141 Cf. similar remarks on propositions at 3.14 *b*, and see 3.143 *a*.

It sounds paradoxical to call a photograph, for example, a fact (or even a set of facts), but *only* facts can be complex, according to W., and a photograph, like any representation, is of course complex. A fact, considered by itself, is not yet a 'picture' in W.'s sense: it becomes one through its 'projective relation to the world', i.e. by having objects co-ordinated with its elements. A 'picture' is a fact *used* in a certain way in accordance with a system of conventions of designation.

2.15 (1) The fact that: delete (nothing corresponds in the German).

in a determinate way: in any fact, the constituents are combined 'in a determinate way' (cf. 2.031 on atomic facts), i.e. every fact has a definite structure. So, what W. is saying here may seem to be merely a corollary of his conception of the picture as a fact (2.141). But there is a further point intended. Consider the following 'picture':

$$\bigcirc \quad + \qquad\qquad . \qquad\qquad (*)$$

whose meaning is defined by the following stipulations:

(i) the circle stands for Russell;

(ii) the cross stands for Frege;

(iii) that the circle is immediately to the left of the cross means that whatever the former sign stands for admires what the latter sign stands for. (The whole picture therefore means that Russell admires Frege.)

One is inclined to talk about 'the fact (*)', as if merely putting a circle and a cross side by side on paper uniquely generated a certain fact, which could then be identified without ambiguity or misunderstanding. But the figure shown at (*) above could be made to yield any number of facts, and in all sorts of ways. For example, it might be conceived to involve three elements (a circle, a horizontal stroke, and a vertical one) and a certain relation between these elements. The particular stipulations (i)–(iii) that

I have chosen imply one definite way of articulating the figure shown at (∗) as a fact. And so in general: the definition of the picture-fact in question goes hand in hand with the definition of the fact as a picture of *something*. Assigning a definite sense to a given picture implies the selection of a definite articulation of the picture elements; and, conversely, the selection of such an articulation determines the *possible* sense of the picture.

represents (*stellt vor*): this is easily confused with the semantical relation between an element of the picture-fact and the corresponding object in the world. In the light of 3.1432, *stellt vor* as here used has the same force as 'says' (*sagt*).

VII

THE FORM OF REPRESENTATION AS A LINK BETWEEN PICTURE AND REALITY

(2.15 (2)–2.17)

Wittgenstein now introduces the notion of the picture's 'form of depiction' (*Form der Abbildung*) which I prefer to Pears and McGuinness's 'pictorial form'. 'Form of representation', as in Ogden, might serve. This notion, with which the present instalment and the next are largely concerned, is likely to give trouble in what is otherwise a clear and straightforward account.

Given that the picture is a fact (2.141), it must necessarily have both a structure and an associated form (the possibility of that structure). Wittgenstein at first seems to identify the 'form of depiction' with the form of the picture-fact (2.15*b*). But it is necessary to distinguish between the picture as a fact in its own right (an arrangement of blobs of paint on a canvas, without any associated meaning) and the picture *as a picture* (a fact that *depicts* something, a possible state of affairs). Let us call the picture 'as a fact in its own right' the picture-vehicle. The vehicle becomes a picture in the full sense when its elements have been co-ordinated in a determinate way with objects (2.1514), upon the understanding that those objects are supposed to be connected as their proxies are in fact connected in the vehicle. A complex stipulation to this effect defines what Wittgenstein calls the 'picturing relation' (*die abbildende Beziehung*, 2.1514). It is tempting to say that this 'picturing relation' should itself have both a structure and a form, and to identify the latter with the 'form of depiction' of the picture. For further discussion of this controversial matter, see the notes below.

2.15 (2) Let us call: Wittgenstein is offering a definition of 'structure'.

● 'When a fact is being treated as a picture (either because definite assignments of objects have been made, or because the ranges in which such assignments shall be made have been stipulated), let the structure of the fact be called the structure of the picture, and the form of the fact be called the form or the form of representation of the picture.'

The contrast between structure and form made here parallels 2.032 + 2.033.

pictoral form: or, 'form of depiction' (*Form der Abbildung*).

CAN A SET OF OBJECTS UNITE IN MORE THAN ONE ATOMIC FACT?

Wittgenstein's references, at 2.15 and earlier at 2.032, to the 'determinate way' in which objects combine may well suggest an affirmative answer. If so, the character of an atomic fact is not solely determined by its constituents: it has one structure among the several to which it is limited by the logical forms of its objects. The dominant image of the chain of objects (2.03) does not preclude this, since the links of a chain can be rearranged. Although Wittgenstein may sometimes have thought that different logical arrangements of the same objects might occur, the following objections seem conclusive.

(1) If given objects could combine in more than one way, the sense of an elementary proposition would not always be a unique function of the references of its component names, for the co-ordinated objects would be able to combine in several structures, all but one of which would have to be somehow excluded in order for the proposition to have a determinate meaning. This conflicts with 2.1514 (the picturing relation consists of the name–object co-ordinations),

with 3.318 (where the intention, shown more clearly in the German text than in the translation, seems to be that a proposition is uniquely determined by its constituents) and by the remarks at 3.4 (implying again that the sense is a unique function of the references of the names).

(2) If there were two distinct elementary propositions composed of the same names, there would be a logical operation converting the one into the other. Such an operation could not be truth-functional, since all elementary propositions have independent truth-values. Now Wittgenstein admits only truth-functional operations on propositions (cf. 5.54).

(3) Suppose the objects mentioned by a given elementary proposition could unite in either one or the other of *two* atomic facts: the proposition might then represent either of these equally well, and a further *arbitrary* convention about the use of the sentence would be needed in order to resolve the ambiguity. So a proposition would not be automatically linked with the fact it pictures, *via* identity of form (contrary to 2.161 + 2.17).

I conclude that an atomic fact is uniquely determined by its constituent objects. It follows, as I assumed in my discussion of logical form (under 2.033 above) that the form of an atomic fact is a unique function of the forms of its objects. When Wittgenstein says that the elements of a complex are combined 'in a definite way', the structure in question is not contrasted with some other structure that the same elements might have had, but rather with the different structures that combinations of objects having other logical forms might have had.

2.151 If we compare this with 2.15b, we seem to have 'two different definitions of the form of representation' (Ramsey, *Foundations*, p. 272)— or of the 'pictorial form', according to P.–McG. In the first passage, the form of representation is defined as the possibility of the configuration of the elements of the picture-fact, i.e. as the form (in the sense explained at 2.032 + 2.033) of the picture-fact; in the second passage, the form of representation is said to be the possibility of the configuration of the objects that the elements of the picture-fact stand for (i.e. the form of the corresponding fact, if there is such a fact). These two accounts of the form of representation are consistent (in spite of Ramsey's contrary verdict):

Commentary

for, as stated at 2.17, the form of the picture-fact is the very same as the form of the state of affairs depicted.

In view of the connexion established at 2.033 between 'form' and 'structure', we might have expected Wittgenstein to speak also, as he does not, of the 'structure of representation'. This would presumably be the pattern of the *actual* representation, defined by a set of determinate correlations between the picture elements and the objects they stand for—as contrasted with the possibility of this pattern of representation, defined by the logical categories of the picture elements.

Pictorial form: here, as elsewhere, I prefer 'the form of representation' or 'form of depiction'.

things (*die Dinge*): can be taken to refer to the objects depicted and also to the picture elements that deputize for them.

2.1511 *That*: the German *so* may refer back to the use of the same word in the preceding remark.

'I have said elsewhere that a proposition "reaches up to reality" and by this I meant that the forms of the entities are contained in the form of the proposition which is about those entities' (*Logical Form*, p. 169).

● 'The picture is connected with reality because *its* form is the same as that of the state of affairs it depicts—in this way, as it were, it makes contact with, or "reaches up to" reality.'

2.1512 In other writings W. sometimes compared a proposition to a standard by which reality was judged.

2.15121 **touch** (*berühren*): cf. the use of this image at 5.557 (4).

● 'All we learn about a body whose length is measured is that its ends coincide with two definite marks on a ruler, the properties of the body being immaterial except as determining its *length*. Similarly, when we "apply" a picture, i.e. use it to make an assertion, we are able to do so because of the identity of *form* between sign and signified (cf. note to 2.1511 above). Nothing more than this identity of form is needed to make the assertion possible.'

2.1513 conceived in this way: the conception explained in 2.141–2.1511 of the picture as linked with reality by having its constituents combined in the way in which the corresponding elements of the world *might* be combined in a fact.

also includes: Anscombe holds the corresponding translation in O. as 'also belongs' to be misleading and suggests the reading, 'According to this conception, the picture must have in addition the depicting relation *which makes the picture into a picture*' (*Introduction*, p. 68, italics added). If the depicting relation 'makes the picture into a picture', it would seem natural to count the relation as part of the picture, as Ramsey did (see quotation below). The point may turn upon what we mean by a given 'picture'. If we think of it as a fact whose constituents have not yet been co-ordinated with elements in the world, that fact is already connected with reality through its form; but the 'depicting relation' will be something 'quite external' (Anscombe, *Introduction*, p. 67) that will still be needed to make the picture a definite representation of a definite state of affairs. This would be to identify the picture with a certain complex *sign* (cf. 3.32 for the distinction between 'sign' and 'symbol'). However, if we think of the picture as not existing before the correlation of its constituents with objects have been supplied, that correlation becomes internal to the picture. On this view (the more natural one, perhaps), the picture is treated as a complex *symbol*. Two verbally identical sentences with different meanings attached would then count as *different* pictures (cf. 3.32–3.321 for differences in symbols).

'This [i.e. 2.1513], I think, means that whenever we talk of a picture we have in mind some representing relation in virtue of which it is a picture' (Ramsey, *Foundations*, p. 271).

'The representing relation by which the proposition is to touch reality is part of the proposition. It is not a question of the proposition resembling what it depicts and then our depending on some psychological process to signal this resemblance to us. ... We do not require any sign to stand between the words 'true' or 'false' and their application. ... The essence of this matter of language and logic is that nothing can stand between language and its application' (Watson, *Physics*, p. 31).

pictorial relationship: I prefer 'picturing relation' or 'representing relation' (as in O.).

2.1514 correlations: I prefer 'co-ordinations', as in O.

Stress on **things**. The connexion of the unified proposition with the corresponding state of affairs is wholly achieved by the element–thing co-ordinations. That is to say: the meanings (*Bedeutungen*) of the propositional constituents uniquely generate the sense (*Sinn*) of the whole proposition to which they belong.

elements: what features of a picture are to be counted as elements? The fact that a black blob of paint is *above* a white blob may mean that a hat is *on* a head. It would seem, then, that the spatial relationship of *being above* has a representative function and must count as an element. (However natural it may be to co-ordinate this relationship, iconically, with the relationship between hat and head, the co-ordination still results from an arbitrary convention.)

85

2.1515 feelers: or, 'antennae'. The only occurrence of this word. One might think of them as (ethereal) rays connecting propositional elements with the things they stand for.

2.16 in common with: here means 'identically the same as' (as in 2.161). If there were not something identically the same in the picture and the pictured, the picture would be incomplete because a further convention would be needed to render the picturing relation determinate.

2.161 In the *Notebooks*, W. connects this idea with that of logical multiplicity (for which see 4.04). 'The logical identity between sign and thing signified consists in its not being permissible to recognize (*wiedererkennen*) more or less in the sign than in what it signifies' (3 (8)). 'It must be possible to distinguish just as much in the real [or, actual (*eigentlichen*)] propositional sign as can be distinguished in the situation [the *Sachverhalt* pictured]. This is what their identity consists in' (37 (2)). Compare the variant rendering of this idea at 4.04.

2.17 'The things with which its [the picture's] elements are co-ordinated by the representing relation are of such [logical] types that they *can* be combined in the same way as the elements of the picture' (Ramsey, *Foundations*, p. 273).

way (*Art und Weise*): the determinate way in which the picture pictures (as resulting uniquely from the determinate co-ordinations of its elements with their meanings).

VIII

THE IMPOSSIBILITY OF DEPICTING THE FORM OF REPRESENTATION

(2.171–2.174)

At this point in his exposition, Wittgenstein has already presented the main points in his conception of the essence of a picture (and so, by an implication to be made explicit later, of the essence of a proposition). His key contentions have been: that a picture is a fact, that a given fact becomes a picture when objects have been co-ordinated with each of its elements, and that the picture has the same form as the state of affairs that it depicts. Very soon, Wittgenstein will amplify these insights and will apply them to the case in which the 'picture' is a verbal proposition. But already he is in a position to draw a restrictive consequence of great importance, upon which will eventually be seen to depend his conception of logic, of mathematics, of philosophy, and of the *a priori* in general.

We have seen that a picture depicts a state of affairs; we can now easily see that no picture can depict the 'form of depiction' or the 'form of representation' that enables the vehicle of that picture (the picture-fact) to be the definite picture that it is. In order for a picture to depict its own 'form of representation' it would need, *per impossibile*, to 'place itself outside its form of representation' (2.174), i.e. to use some other form of representation in order to depict its own original form. And this is plainly impossible. The self-reference necessitated is enough to render the attempt nugatory. (See also the further discussion in the notes on 2.172 below.) So far, the argument seems to leave open a prospect of depicting a given picture's form of representation by means of some other 'higher order' picture (as Russell in his introduction to the book, and Carnap subsequently, held to be possible). Full insight into the reasons why a 'form of representation' cannot be depicted at all may be postponed. For the time being, I shall say dogmatically that a 'form of representation' is not a 'possible combination of objects', not a 'possible state of affairs', and therefore cannot be depicted. To reject this inference it is necessary to reject Wittgenstein's fundamental principle that all 'depiction', all 'representation', requires objects to go proxy for objects, with the actual combination of the symbol-objects signifying a corresponding possibility of combination of the co-ordinated objects. (For further discussion, see the notes on 2.221 below.)

It should be noted that Wittgenstein is not saying that the 'form of representation' is ineffable—for in understanding a picture we necessarily grasp its form of representation, though not in the mode of 'depicting' or 'saying'. A picture *exhibits* or '*shows forth*' (2.172) its form of representation. This crucial notion will become increasingly prominent as the discussion progresses.

2.171 (1) can: should be stressed. The picture's form is a possibility— cf. 2.15*b*.

any reality: notice the generic use of 'reality' (*Wirklichkeit*) here.

form: this should be distinguished from the *specific* 'form of representation' of the picture.

2.172 A very important statement. Cf. 4.12, 4.121 (propositions cannot represent logical form).

displays it: or, 'shows it forth' (*weist sie auf*). In the light of 4.121, we can equate this with the more frequent 'shows' (*zeigt*).

2.173 a position outside: or, simply, 'outside' (*ausserhalb*) as in the German. For the only other use of the word in this sense see 4.12*b*.

its subject: the state of affairs depicted.

incorrectly: literally, 'falsely' (*falsch*). Similarly in 2.18. Cf. 2.21.

● 'The relation between the picture-vehicle and the *particular* state of affairs which is its sense (2.202 + 2.203) is *external*, i.e. contingently determined by stipulations (but the identical form of the picture and the pictured is *internal* to both). The picture has a truth-value precisely because its elements have been co-ordinated with objects *outside* the picture.'

2.174 Cf. 2.1513 (the representing relation belongs to the picture).

IX

THE LOGICAL PICTURE

(2.18–2.21)

A representational painting or a photograph is what Wittgenstein calls a 'spatial picture' (2.171*b*). Imagine a coloured photograph of a red ball on a white tablecloth and think of it as a complex assertion about some state of affairs. The fact that a certain patch in the photograph is red means that the corresponding physical object (the particular ball now in my possession, say) is also red; the fact that another patch is white means that another definite physical object (the kitchen tablecloth, say) is also white; and the fact that the red patch is just above the white patch means that the ball is just above, is 'on', the cloth. In short, certain 'spatial' properties and relations of elements of the photograph are co-ordinated with the *same* properties and relations in what is depicted: the picture is partly 'iconic', as people say nowadays.

Not all features of even the most faithful coloured photograph exactly resemble the objects they represent: the colour of the red patch only approximates to the true colour of the ball and the circularity of the patch means that the ball is *spherical*. A perfectly iconic 'picture' would have to be a three-dimensional replica of the situation to which it refers. But Wittgenstein does not demand perfect resemblance in a 'spatial picture'. Although a map is less iconic than a photograph, it would still be counted as a spatial picture by him, because some spatial properties and relations in it mean somewhat similar spatial properties and relations of the coast-lines, lakes, etc., depicted.

A sentence is not iconic in this way at all. In the sentence, 'The red ball is on the white cloth', the expression, 'the red ball', does not at all resemble my red ball, and the relation between the two expressions, 'the red ball' and 'the white cloth' (of being on either side of the expression, 'is on'), is quite unlike the spatial relation of contiguity between ball and cloth. But it is not hard to see why Wittgenstein still wants to call the sentence (or, rather, the corresponding sentence-fact) a picture of a certain state of affairs. According to his conception, the three elements of the sentence-fact (the expressions, 'the red ball', 'the white cloth', and the relation between them) 'hang together' or are concatenated. That the three elements are united in the sentence-fact means that the corresponding physical elements *are* united. Since concatenation of elements in the sentence-fact means concatenation of the co-ordinated elements in the represented state of affairs, it is not far-fetched to detect a residual 'iconicity' even in a sentence. Identity of concatenation in the sentence-fact and in what the fact represents is an essential feature of what Wittgenstein calls a 'logical picture' (2.181).

A picture counts as a 'logical picture' (soon to be identified with a proposition) when the form of representation is the logical form of representation, i.e. when the structure of the picture-fact shows that the co-ordinated objects *can be* structured in exactly the same manner (i.e. by concatenation) and when the picture means ('says') that the objects are thus combined. Since every picture can be regarded as a fact, every picture satisfies the essential conditions for being a logical picture (2.182*a*). To be a logical picture, says Wittgenstein, is to present certain atomic situations as obtaining and others as not obtaining (2.201). The truth-value of a logical picture, and so of any picture whatever, consists in agreement with reality (2.21). Here, and elsewhere (e.g. at 2.223), Wittgenstein accepts something like a 'correspondence theory of truth'.

2.18 Cf. 4.12*a* (propositions cannot represent logical form). 2.16, 2.17, 2.18 express a consecutive train of thought.

PICTURES IN GENERAL

A spatial picture, as we have seen (notes on 2.13 above), is a system of 'graphemes' (smallest significant parts) related to their objects by approximate visual resemblance, with the spatial arrangement of the graphemes meaning approximately the *same* arrangement of the depicted objects. In order to make this conception fit the most general case of a representation, including such diverse cases as a diagram of an electrical circuit, a map, a printed record of a game of chess, a sentence, the following modifications in the earlier account are needed:

(i) While each of the representations mentioned in the preceding sentence consists of significant elements in a significant arrangement, the relation between an element and its significate ceases to be one of similarity. There are no relevant similarities between a circle on a map and the city it stands for, or between the mark 'P' and the pawn for which it stands. Each element need only stand in *some* way, no matter which, for an identifiable significate; the abstract notion of a one–one correlation between picture-elements and their significates replaces the earlier, more concrete, notion of *resemblance*.

(ii) It is no longer possible to say, even approximately, that the relation between the significant arrangement of the picture-elements and what that arrangement represents is one of identity. The spatial order of the notes in a musical score is not identical with the temporal order of the sounds represented. The notion of *identity* of arrangements must make place for the more general one of *homology* of arrangement.

(iii) Homomorphic structures may still be held to have something 'in common' (cf. 2.17), namely a *pattern* of relationships, indifferently exemplified by each member of a class of mutually homomorphic structures. So, in a *very* abstract sense of 'same form', we might still say that a representation and what it represents have the same form (in my terminology, are homomorphic).

The reason why Wittgenstein says that *any* picture has logical form (2.18) is that any representation can be regarded as an assembly of facts, each of which means, according to the governing conventions of the mode of representation in question, the existence of a corresponding state-of-affairs (cf. note on 2.181 below).

2.181 logical form: here, as in 2.182, logical form is to be contrasted with spatial form and, presumably, with temporal form, with the form exhibited by coloured pictures, etc. A picture has spatial form if one of the conventions defining the specific depicting relation in question is that spatial relations shall signify spatial relations; a picture has logical form if the concatenation (the hanging together in a fact) of elements of the picture-fact means the concatenation of the things for which the elements severally stand.

The words 'logical form' should here be taken as elliptical for 'logical form of representation' (as in 2.2).

2.182a Because every picture is a fact (2.141), and so the elements of the picture *could* be correlated with objects and used as names in a proposition. (Cf. Anscombe, *Introduction*, p. 67, for a similar comment.)

2.19 Cf. 2.171a (a picture can depict every reality whose form it has).

2.2 Follows from 2.17+2.171+2.182+2.19.

logico-pictorial form: I prefer 'logical form of representation', as in O.

2.201 At 2.11 the picture was said to assert 'the existence and non-existence' of atomic states-of-affairs. But now there is reference to the 'possibility' of the same. Accordingly, *darstellen* should here be taken in the sense of showing, i.e. the symbolization of something *internal* to the proposition (cf. 2.203). This section should be compared and contrasted with 4.1 and 4.2 (the notes on which should be consulted).

2.202   Here, too, *stellt . . . dar* should be rendered as 'presents' or 'shows'.
   possible situation: or, 'possible state of affairs' (*mögliche Sachlage*). A pleonasm.
   'If you make an actual judgment properly expressible by the words "men exist", you must have before your mind a conceptual complex which these words may be said to stand for or name. And one important thing about this complex is that it is a "possibility", which is susceptible of being "realized". . . . But there is another thing that can be said about this conceptual complex which is perhaps even more important, and that is that it is itself a *fact*' (Lewis and Langford, *Logic*, p. 472).

2.203   The intention here may be to stress **contains**. The picture 'contains' the possibility by actualizing it.
   Cf. 2.221 (the picture presents its sense).
   For comment on this section see Stenius (*Exposition*, p. 99).

2.21   To be read in apposition with 2.22: The picture agrees or disagrees with reality (an external relation) but it *contains* its sense (an internal relation).

X

THE SENSE OF A PICTURE

(2.22–2.225)

The main point of interest here is the important principle that the sense of a picture is independent of the picture's truth-value. This may well recall the earlier demonstration that there must be objects (whose existence is not contingent) in order for propositions to have sense (2.0211, 2.0212). As we have already seen, the set of objects determined by the constituents of the proposition uniquely determines that proposition's sense. A point that will be very important later is that the sense of a picture is *shown*, not 'said' or asserted (inferred from 2.221, where the use of 'represents' is misleading).

2.22 ● 'The picture has a sense (or meaning), whether it is true or false, because the concatenation of its elements (in the picture-fact) is logically possible and is sanctioned by the rules of representation governing the picture. *This* possibility guarantees the logical possibility of concatenation of the things signified, i.e. guarantees that the picture can represent an actual state of affairs.'

2.221 Apart from a passing use at 2.0211, we have here the first occurrence of the important notion of the 'sense' of a picture (or of a proposition).

Cf. 2.11, 2.201, 2.202 and 4.031 (2), for connected remarks.

By comparing 2.221 with 4.022*a*, we see that *darstellt* must here be taken as equivalent to 'shows' (as in 2.2–2.22 above). It would be a bad mistake to suppose that the picture 'represents' its sense in the way that picture-elements represent, go proxy for, the corresponding objects.

See also notes on 4.1 below.

2.222 **agreement**: cf. 2.21, 4.2, for other occurrences of this notion.

2.223 Echoed at 4.05 (reality is compared with propositions).

compare (*vergleichen*): for discussion, see Schlick, 'Facts', and Hempel, 'Remarks'.

THE VERIFICATION OF PROPOSITIONS

We can distinguish a non-epistemic sense in which a proposition is 'verified' if it 'agrees' with the world (2.21), i.e. if it is true, from an epistemic one implying some human activity of confrontation with the atomic facts. Wittgenstein's use of the simile of 'comparison' for the latter derives from the supposed analogy between a proposition and an iconic picture such as a naturalistic representation of some landscape. In checking a painting against a scene that it represents, we might look *at* the picture and at the scene it is supposed to portray, check that each picture-element sufficiently resembles the corresponding item 'out there', and confirm that the landscape's features are arranged in approximately the same ways as the corresponding patches of paint. This might reasonably be called 'comparison' of picture and scene depicted. But in verifying a proposition we do not look *at* it; when I wonder whether a given animal is a lynx, I look at the beast, but not at the words that express my question. Apart from exceptional cases like checking a text for typographical errors, we seldom inspect words, and especially not when we read them. In order to verify the presence of a lynx, it is necessary and sufficient to see that the animal is a lynx, while affirming, silently or out loud, that it is one. Had the proposition to be tested been written out beforehand, it might be necessary to refer to the words composing it, but only as a reminder of their meaning, so that the correct proposition might be affirmed or denied. Reading a sentence in order to be reminded of a proposition is quite different from looking at a patch of paint in order to observe its physical characteristics. Because words are not iconic, the idea of 'comparison' cannot be taken literally: a rule of designation cannot literally be 'seen'. Using words is not comparing them with anything, any more than hailing a man by his name is comparing a person with a proper noun.

Since a name has reference only in the setting of a proposition (3.3), scrutiny of a name requires scrutiny of some proposition to which it belongs; and, correspondingly, confirmation of the presence of the designated object requires inspection of some fact of which it is a constituent. But the only way in which I can register a fact is to affirm its existence (cf. 5.5423*a* on the perception of a complex). Now in registering the existence of the verifying fact, in order to check that the bearer is present, I have already performed the act of verification, and there is no point in some further act of 'comparison'. Indeed, in recording the existence of the verifying fact, I might have used the very form of words by which the proposition to be verified was originally expressed. Verification reduces to the assertion of the proposition in the presence of the requisite fact.

Observation can be only of what is contingently true. So all that can result from the alleged 'comparison' is knowledge of the fact that the designated objects are indeed concatenated. But this again can only be registered by making an appropriate assertion. The idea of 'comparison' dissolves into the more appropriate, if less picturesque one, of true assertion.

The same conclusion might have been reached directly from Wittgenstein's principle that we cannot get 'outside' language or 'outside' the world (cf. 4.12b). For in order literally to compare a proposition with a fact, I would need to be 'outside' both, i.e. in a position to refer to each and also to some correspondence between them.

2.224 Cf. 3.04 (condition for a thought to be *a priori* correct), 5.634c (everything describable might have been different).

2.225 Restatement of 2.224. We can infer that Wittgenstein understands by an *a priori* proposition one whose truth-value is wholly determined by its meaning, independently of any comparison with the world. This definition agrees as well as can be expected with common philosophical usage of this unclear expression (cf., for example, Broad, 'A Priori', p. 102). It will be noted that W. is not equating *a priori* and 'analytic' by definition, if 'analytic' is taken to mean 'demonstrable solely from logical principles, with the help of definitions'. It is, at this stage, still an open question for W. whether there might be 'synthetic *a priori* propositions'. Some of his rules of logical syntax might be regarded as 'synthetic', but the traditional terminology has little point in a discussion of W.'s views.

XI

THOUGHTS AS LOGICAL PICTURES

(3–3.05)

In previous instalments, Wittgenstein has been exploring the connexions between 'pictures' and the world, always with the special case in mind in which a picture is a logical picture, a proposition. Now he turns to the 'projective relation' (3.12b) between the sentence and the world, i.e. to what on the side of the sentence-user confers sense upon a sentence and thereby makes it a significant proposition. A single 'thought' is not a complex of images, or the like, but, as Frege held, something sufficiently abstract for various persons to possess in common. Because a thought is the projection of a possibility upon the world (as the picture on a lantern slide is projected on to a screen), there cannot be an 'illogical' thought. For the same reason, a thought cannot be true *a priori*. (The suggestion that a thought has a direction, conveyed by the figure of 'projection', will be elaborated later.)

Discussion of propositions as pictures will be resumed at xxv. Much of the intervening discussion is relevant to the same topic.

---

3 logical picture: this expression was introduced at 2.181, to which 3 and the immediately following sections can be regarded as a sequel.

thought (*Gedanke*): the present statement should be collated with 3.11 and 4.

W. was undoubtedly familiar with Frege's use of *Gedanke*, for which see his paper, 'Thought'.

Frege says: 'Without wishing to give a definition, I call a thought something for which the question of truth arises . . . the thought is the sense of the sentence. . . . We say a sentence expresses a thought' (*op. cit.* p. 292). An important aspect of Frege's conception of 'the thought' is its objectivity: 'The thought . . . is timelessly true, true independently of whether anyone takes it to be true. It needs no bearer' (*op. cit.* p. 302). 'The thought belongs neither to my inner world as an idea nor yet to the outer world of material, perceptible, things' (*op. cit.* p. 308). Alonzo Church renders Frege's use of *Gedanke* consistently as 'proposition' (see for instance his 'Review of Black').

I think W. deviates from Frege in regarding a 'thought' as the propositional sign *in use*, i.e. as the sentence *with* its sense, i.e. as the *significant* proposition (4). The 'thought' is not, as with Frege, the ideal sense of the proposition.

' "Does a Gedanke consist of words?" No! But of psychical constituents that have the same sort of relation to reality as words. What those constituents are I don't know' (*Notebooks*, 130 (2)).

'Thinking is a kind of language. For a thought (*der Gedanke*) too is, of course, a logical picture of the proposition (*Satz*), and therefore it just is a kind of proposition' (*Notebooks*, 82 (14)).

'As to the relation between a proposition and a thought Mr W. is rather obscure; but I think his meaning is that a thought is a type whose tokens have in common a certain sense, and include the tokens of the corresponding proposition, but include also other non-verbal tokens' (Ramsey, *Foundations*, p. 274).

3.001 picture it: cf. *Investigations*, §§ 395–7 on 'imaginability'. 'Instead of "imaginability" one can also say here: representability by a particular method of representation' (§ 397).

thinkable: = *das Sagbare*, 'the speakable' (4.115), = 'what can be said' (4.022*c*). The corresponding passage in the *Notebooks* (24 (1)) is immediately followed by the remark that a proposition must determine a logical place (= first clause of 3.4).

3.01 A linguistic pendant to 1 and 1.1. The remark is very important as indicating that W. wished to include more than elementary propositions under 'pictures'.

3.02*a* Follows from 3+2.202+2.203.

b Of course, the converse is also true.

3.03 Cf. 5.4731*b* (connexion with *a priori* character of logic).

3.031 **The reason being**: W. is offering *his* reason, not that of the persons he is talking about.
'He had said previously "I can't say what reality would have to be like, in order that what makes nonsense should make sense, because in order to do so I should have to use this new grammar" [i.e. one in which the nonsense became sense]' (Moore, *Papers*, p. 278).

3.032 For the analogy between logic and space, see 2.013, 2.11, 3.4, etc.
co-ordinates: cf. notes on 3.41 below.
'An illogical language would be one in which, e.g., you could put an *event* into a hole' (*Moore Notes*, 107 (5)).
'If a point in space does not exist, then its co-ordinates do not exist either, and if the co-ordinates exist, then the point exists too. That is how it is in logic' (*Notebooks*, 69 (1)).

3.0321 **geometry**: cf. 6.35*b* (geometry as *a priori*).

3.04 Cf. 2.225 on there being no *a priori* true pictures.
3.04 complements 3.03: the latter says there is no thought expressing a contradiction; the former that there is none expressing a tautology.
possibility: cf. 2.202 (a picture presents a *possible* state of affairs).

3.05 For the truth would be guaranteed by the possibility of the thought (3.04) and the thought (= the 'picture') *contains* that possibility (2.203).
anything to compare it with: literally, 'object of comparison' (*Vergleichsobjekt*). W. means a corresponding fact.

XII

THE PROPOSITION
IN ITS PROJECTIVE RELATION TO
THE WORLD

(3.1–3.13)

In this instalment and the next, Wittgenstein elucidates the crucial concept of a proposition. Much that he says here follows from his previous remarks about the nature of a picture. For a proposition is a *logical* picture (3 + 3.12). Many readers find 3.13, with its use of the new expressions, 'form of sense' and 'content of sense', confusing. But what Wittgenstein wants to say is clear enough. Articulated as some determinate fact, a sentence has a determinate logical form *before* correlations have been supplied for its elements, i.e. before it has been converted into a definite picture. (Here, it is helpful to compare what is said at 3.315 about a proto-picture or *Urbild*.) Any co-ordinations introduced cannot be entirely arbitrary, since the objects correlated must be able to combine as the elements of the sentence-fact do, must be able to constitute a state of affairs having the same form. It is in this way that the sentence-fact, through its determinate logical form, 'contains' only the '*possibility* of expressing' a determinate sense (3.13c). The form of the as yet uninterpreted sentence-fact settles the *class* of admissible senses that may be assigned (*via* co-ordinations of objects with the sentence elements), but does not yet settle what determinate sense of the given form will be chosen. (A definite 'thought' arises when such a determinate sense has been supplied, cf. 3.11b.) So, Wittgenstein is once more stressing two inseparable aspects of the depicting situation: arbitrary, though not wholly arbitrary, references of the elements of the sentence-fact, and necessary identity of logical form between the sentence-fact and the sense assigned to it by a thought.

3.1 From here until 3.144, W. is elucidating the crucial concept of a proposition.

proposition: the word *Satz* is used in German to stand for what we would call a 'sentence' as well as for what we would call a 'proposition' (or 'statement'—or, in other contexts, 'principle', 'law', etc.). Wittgenstein sometimes distinguishes the two senses by using 'propositional sign' (*Satzzeichen*, 3.12a) for the sentence. Only the particular context can show whether 'sentence' or 'proposition' is the better translation. It is essential to Wittgenstein's conception that the proposition should be expressed *in* a sentence, or some equivalent sign (cf. for example, 3.12b). A disembodied proposition would be an absurdity. Thus it is natural for him to use *Satz* to cover *both* aspects—the 'perceptible' sign and its sense. In Wittgenstein's use of *Satz*, a proposition is defined without reference to any particular speakers or any occasions of its use (cf. the notes under 3 above on the abstract nature of a 'thought'). Nor is it material whether the proposition is actually asserted or not (cf. notes under 4.442b). But it is essential to a proposition that it makes an abstract truth-claim, whether it is asserted or not.

Schlick (*Gesetz*, p. 82) distinguishes between *Satz* and *Aussage* (say, 'statement'). A *Satz* is a series of perceptible signs (cf. W.'s *Satzzeichen*): the *Aussage* is such a *Satz* 'together with its *sense*' (*ibid.*). Schlick adds that the 'sense' is to be thought of as the rules for the use of the *Satz*.

For current uses of 'proposition' and 'statement' see, for instance, Carnap, *Semantics*, pp. 235–6 (article on 'Proposition') and Strawson, *Introduction*, pp. 3–4.

Stenius usually translates *Satz* as 'sentence' (cf. *Exposition*, p. 6 f.n.).

by the senses: P.–McG.'s translation is somewhat laboured. W. is saying: 'In a sentence the thought expresses itself perceptibly.' Here, 'sentence' rather than 'proposition' (as in P.–McG.) seems right.

3.11 (1) Cf. 2.202, where the possible state of affairs is said to be 'presented' by the picture. The idea of 'projection' is no doubt suggested by the 'projection' of a geometrical figure on to a plane (e.g. in descriptive drawing). It can serve as a reminder of the necessity of some rule or 'law of projection' (cf. 4.0141c) and of the 'distortion' resulting—the 'accidents' of the resulting representation. For many purposes, 'project' (*projizieren*) can be taken as synonymous with 'present' (*darstellen*) or 'depict' (*abbilden*).

'In connection with this question of the similarity between experiential "propositions" and pictures, he frequently used the words "project" and "projection" . . . [he said] that "2+3" really is a picture of "5" "*with reference to a particular system of projection*" . . .' (Moore, *Papers*, pp. 263–4).

'But is not "projecting with the common method of projection" merely a metaphorical way of saying "using in accordance with the established rules of grammar"?' (Moore, *op. cit.* p. 270).

(2) **method of projection**: the only occurrence of this expression. It has approximately the same meaning as 'representing relation' (*abbildende Beziehung*)—cf. 2.1514.

think out: rather, 'think' (*denken*): there is no suggestion of task accomplishment in the original.

● 'The possible state of affairs (the sense) is brought into relation with the sentence by using the latter to mean (or "think") that the corresponding state of affairs obtains.'

3.12a 'He seemed to be making a distinction between a proposition and a sentence, such that no sentence can be identical with any proposition, and that no proposition can be without sense. But I do not think that in his actual use of the term "proposition" he adhered to this distinction. He seemed to me sometimes so to use "proposition" that every significant sentence *was* a proposition, although, of course, a significant sentence does not contain everything which is necessary to give it significance' (Moore, *Papers*, pp. 262–3).

b Cf. 2.1513. The proposition *is* a 'picture', but the 'propositional sign' (= 'sentence') is something that is made into a picture by being brought into 'projective relation with the world', i.e. by being given a determinate sense.

I infer from 3.1+3.12*b* (a thought is perceptibly expressed in a proposition, a proposition is a propositional *sign* in a certain relation to the world) that it is essential to a proposition that it *can* be expressed in signs—a non-expressible proposition is an *Unding*. The point is especially important in view of W.'s equation of 'thought' with 'significant proposition' (3+4). A thought is not some ideal complex of objects but a concrete fact, composed of words, images, or other things, to which a sense has been attached in virtue of syntactical and semantical rules.

3.13 Throughout this section, *Satz* is best translated as 'sentence'.

(1) **all that the projection includes**: all that is *internal* to the representing relation, i.e. the logical form that the sentence has in common with the state of affairs it represents (2.18).

what is projected: the sense.

(2, 3) Cf. 2.203 (the picture contains the possibility of a state of affairs).

(4) Cf. 3.32 and 3.326 for contrast between sign and symbol.

proposition that has sense: literally, 'significant proposition' (*sinnvollen Satzes*), cf. 4, where this is identified with a 'thought'.

(5) **form of its sense** = 'form of the possible state of affairs presented' = 'the logical form'.

● 'A sentence, considered as a fact (3.14), in abstraction from any use to which it is put (3.326), i.e. from any determinate sense attached to it has an internal structure (2.032) that determines the *form* of any sense that the sentence *could* have. But the determinate sense must come from "outside" the sentence (2.173) by the correlations that the users of the sentence supply. Thus we can say that the not-yet-significant sentence "contains" only the possibility of its sense, but not yet the "content" of that sense.'

If we thought of 'Tom loves Mary' as an example, we might say that W. was claiming that sentence to 'contain' no more than would be 'contained' by *aRb*—like a propositional function, as it were. Only when *a*, *R*, and *b*— or 'Tom', 'loves' and 'Mary'—are co-ordinated with objects, *from the outside*, does determinate sense accrue.

Cf. also Anscombe, *Introduction*, pp. 68–9.

XIII

THE PROPOSITIONAL SIGN
IS A FACT
(3.14–3.144)

The central thesis follows from Wittgenstein's earlier account of a proposition as a logical picture. (A proposition signifies that there is a certain fact, i.e. a complex. But identity of logical form between picture and what it pictures requires the proposition, *qua* picture, to be complex. And only facts are complex.) The contention is of the utmost importance in Wittgenstein's philosophy of language, and any attempt to reject it plays havoc with the remainder of his analysis. For example, if a significant sentence were a complex name (which Wittgenstein is emphatically denying—cf. 3.143*c*), it would have to stand for something, even if it should happen to be false (for a name always has a bearer). But then a false proposition could not be a picture of a fact, for a false proposition has no correlated fact. Again, it is only by hanging together in a fact that the elements of a sentence constitute a unity, instead of merely being jumbled together in a heap (3.141). Also, if there were not a radical difference between a proposition and a name, the distinction between 'sense' and 'meaning' (*Bedeutung*) would collapse (cf. 3.142) and with it the entire distinction between 'fact' and 'object'. The contention that a propositional sign must be a fact can be taken as a special case of the identity of logical form between sign and what is signified. Since a proposition *can* depict a fact and cannot refer to an object, it must differ in logical form from a name, that *can* stand for an object and cannot depict a fact.

It would seem to follow that it is impossible to *refer to* propositions, on the general principle that facts cannot be the subjects of assertions, although here and throughout Wittgenstein constantly sounds as if he *were* talking about propositions.

3.14 'Propositions (which are symbols having reference to facts) are themselves facts: that this inkpot is on this table may express that I sit in this chair' (*Notes on Logic*, 98 (3) *d*).

Cf. 2.14, 2.141 for parallel statements about pictures.

(**1**) **its elements, the words**: we must also count the significant properties and relations of the words as *material* components of the sentence-fact.

(**2**) The converse is not true, though *any* fact can become a picture by being brought into 'projective relation' with the world, i.e. by having a sense attached to it.

3.141 (1) 'Owing to the way in which the verb actually relates the terms of a proposition, every proposition has a unity which renders it distinct from the sum of its constituents' (Russell, *Principles*, p. 52).

medley: literally 'mixture of words' or 'jumble of words' (*Wörter-gemisch*).

(**2**) **articulated**: cf. 3.251 for an expansion of the thought. *Gegliedert* (composed of members), with approximately the same meaning, occurs at 4.032 *a*. In the *Notebooks* (40 (2)), W. says that *language* is articulated.

'All I want is only for *my meaning* to be completely analysed! In other words the proposition must be completely articulated. Everything that its sense has in common with another sense must be contained separately in the proposition' (*Notebooks*, 63 (3)).

'The hope, the thought, the wish, that *p* will occur are so called only when these events have the multiplicity expressed in *p*, i.e. when they are articulated' (*Phil. Bem.* 12, 2).

The idea of the proposition as 'articulated' implies (i) its being composed of parts, (ii) those parts being connected together or 'configured' (2.0272) in a definite way, i.e. the proposition's having a structure (2.032).

3.142 **set**: or, 'class' (*Klasse*). To be taken in the extensional sense of an aggregate.

'Indefinables are of two sorts: names and forms. Propositions cannot consist of names alone, they cannot be classes of names' (*Notes on Logic*, 98 (3)).

'As Mr Russell has said, a fact has a *sense*. It has a logical arrangement' (Wisdom, *Constructions*, p. 197).

'There is a fact when and only when one or more things are tied to one another' (Wisdom, *op. cit.* p. 199).

3.143 (1) **propositional sign**: or, 'sentence'.

(2) **essential** (*wesentlich*): an important notion for W., especially in the context of his discussions of symbolism. It is contrasted with the 'accidental' (*zufällig*) and the 'arbitrary' (*willkürlich*). The essential is that which is not contingent, not a matter of fact, but logically necessary— that which shows itself as invariant in equivalent modes of representation.

(3) **composite name**: or, 'complex name'.

Frege regarded declarative sentences as designations of truth-values (cf., for example, *Translations*, pp. 62 ff.).

3.1431 (1) **imagine**: rather, 'think' (*denken*).

very clearly seen: because we have to bring the physical objects into relation with one another before a thought can be expressed. The physical properties of the things used are of no importance—the 'spatial objects' function just as words do in a sentence, and their combination in a fact produces a propositional sign (cf. Rhees, 'Anscombe', p. 26).

(2) **spatial arrangement**: literally, 'mutual (*gegenseitige*) spatial position', as in O.

CONVENTIONAL EXPRESSION OF SENSE

In the general case of a 'logical picture' something other than the 'spatial arrangement' of names or symbols will signify; but what? Consider an elementary proposition, *ab* (with the order of the letters indifferent), where '*a*' is a name for *c* and '*b*' for *d*. Considered as a fact in its own right, *ab* will have a logical structure. But the logical form of *ab* cannot be identified with the logical form of the situation it represents. For one thing, we have seen that homomorphy (similarity of form) rather than isomorphy (identity of form) is the best that can be expected in the general case. But even this weaker condition is seldom satisfied by languages and other systems of representation. The logical form of colour (to use Wittgenstein's terminology) is partly shown by the logical impossibility of anything's being red all over and green all over at the same time. But it is quite possible to construct the two sentence-facts, '*A* is red all over at time *t*' and '*A* is green all over at time *t*' (where *A* and *t* respectively refer to the same material object and the same time in both cases). If the conjunction of the corresponding propositions results in 'nonsense' (= logical impossibility), that is due to the associated syntactical and semantical rules and not to any mutual incompatibility of the respective sentence-facts in themselves.

The case would be different were elementary propositions to be expressed by sentence-facts that were *atomic*. Then some atomic fact, $\phi_1(a, b)$, say, would mean the obtaining of the atomic fact $\phi_1(c, d)$, say, in which the bearers, c and d, would be united in *the very same way* (the ϕ_1-way) in which their names, a and b, were united in the sentence-fact.[1] If a further object v, say, had the name, u, and it were impossible for c and v to combine in the ϕ_1-way (a feature of the logical form of c), this would show itself in the logical impossibility of constructing a sentence-fact in which a and u were combined in the ϕ_1-way. The appropriate licences and restrictions upon combinations of the names in sentence-facts would take care of themselves, without appeal to linguistic conventions. It is doubtful whether such reduplication of logical form is possible in any language (compare the footnote below); in any case, it is plain that identity of logical form between a sentence-fact and its significate cannot be a *necessary* condition for linguistic representation, since it fails to be satisfied by the

---

[1] Since each member of a *class* of sentence-facts must be counted as expressing the same proposition (cf. notes on types and tokens under 3.203*c* below) and therefore as each containing the same names, it seems doubtful if the hypothesis can be satisfied. Even in the most favourable circumstances, the linguistic correlate of an atomic fact is a *class* of atomic sentence-facts.

languages we know. In the general case, an elementary proposition is not expressed by an atomic fact and consequently its 'names' (the smallest elements to which reference attaches) are not logical simples. Thus the mode of combination of the words is *not* that of objects in an atomic fact, although it means that mode of combination. We might say that a higher-level structure of the sentence-fact is treated *as if* it were the structure of an atomic fact: a conventional structure is *imposed* upon the sentence-fact by virtue of the syntactical and semantical rules for its correct use. It is easy to see, in a general way, what form these rules must take. We have seen that the logical form of an atomic fact manifests itself in restrictions upon the possible combinations of objects. For each such restriction, there must be a *conventional* prohibition upon the concatenation of the corresponding names. (Thus if a, b and c have the names, n_1, n_2 and n_3 and if the form, ϕ_1, of $\phi_1(a, b)$ is partially manifested by the absence of the pair (a, c) from the range of ϕ_1, there must be an understanding that a combination of n_1 and n_3 shall not *count* as significant.) We might say that propositions of a language have a *conventional* form that is homologous with the form of the states-of-affairs they signify.

Of course it remains true that the concatenation of words in such a language still means the concatenation of their bearers. Here we have a general connexion between propositions and the world (cf. 2.18) which must not be confused with the specific way in which the *linguistic* form of the sentence-fact signifies the form of the situation represented. The foregoing emphasis upon the conventional aspects of the relevant form of the proposition agrees well with Wittgenstein's remarks about the 'general rule' or 'law of projection' at 4.0141.

3.1432 in a certain relation: the relation between a and b that consists in the first standing to the left of R and the second to the right of R.

I take W. to be denying that the complex sign is a *name* of the situation described: a *fact* is needed to refer to a fact.

'Symbols are not what they seem to be. In aRb, R looks like a substantive, but it is not one. What symbolizes in aRb is that R occurs between a and b. Hence R is *not* the indefinable in aRb' (*Notes on Logic*, 99 (3)).

'In *aRb* it is not the complex that symbolizes but the fact that the symbol *a* stands in a certain relation to the symbol *b*. Thus facts are symbolized by facts, or more correctly: that a certain thing is the case in the symbol says that a certain thing is the case in the world' (*ibid.* 105 (4)).

For a further reference to *aRb*, see 4.012.

For what the sentence-fact 'says', see 4.022 (2).

This section is discussed by Anscombe (*Introduction*, p. 89). She points out that a sign such as '*aRb*' could be interpreted as 'expressive' in many different ways (some features of the letters are significant, others immaterial to the intended meaning). She concludes that a sentence expressing *how* '*aRb*', say, is to be understood formulates 'a genuine proposition . . . according to the conceptions of the *Tractatus*' (*loc. cit.*). This is an important and controversial point.

Copi ('Objects', pp. 155–6) argues that the negative injunction of 3.1432 applies only to an 'adequate notation' (presumably the *Begriffsschrift*), in which the fact that *aRb* must be expressed 'by a proposition containing only the words *a* and *b*' (p. 156). Both points seem mistaken.

3.144 (1) A crucial case of a category-distinction.

described: not in Russell's sense of 'description'.

given names: or, simply, '*named*'. 'Facts cannot be named' (*Notes on Logic*, 93 (3) *c*).

(2) 'Naming is like pointing' (*ibid.* 100 (3)).

'Names are points, propositions arrows—they have *sense*. The sense of a proposition is determined by the two poles *true* and *false*. The form of a proposition is like a straight line, which divides all points of a plane into right and left. The line does this automatically, the form of the proposition only by convention' (*ibid.* 97 (1)).

The point of the simile is that an arrow is *aimed* at something: we might say that a proposition has a target, the fact it represents, and might count the proposition as reaching it if true and missing it if false. The analogy breaks down, however: a misfired arrow fails to hit a real target, but a false proposition has no fact that it fails to reach. W. is anxious to stress the double aspect of a proposition as prescribing falsifying, no less than verifying, conditions. If, *per impossibile*, I knew only what verified a proposition I would not have understood it. (But of course in knowing what would verify the proposition I must already know also what would not verify it.) This double aspect sharply distinguishes a proposition from a name, on W.'s conceptions of both. W. liked to think of this 'bi-polarity' by imagining the proposition to draw a boundary in 'logical space', with the verifying conditions on one side and the falsifying ones on the other.

The need for a proposition to specify both falsifying and verifying conditions then appears as the truism that a boundary must have two sides to it.

sense: mathematicians speak of the 'sense' of a directed line, so there is a double meaning here: 'sense' as direction and 'sense' as meaning.

Cf. 4.0621 (3) on 'opposite sense'.

XIV

COMPLETELY ANALYSED PROPOSITIONS AS COMPOSED OF NAMES

(3.2–3.221)

This instalment makes plain the dependence of Wittgenstein's philosophy of language upon his view that the meaning of a name is a co-ordinated object (a view that he was later to attack in *Investigations*). His claim that propositions are 'configurations' of names (3.21) applies only to elementary propositions. For, as he will argue later, molecular propositions and general propositions have complex and indirect projective relations with the world, *via* the elementary propositions. Wittgenstein certainly thought that every proposition had a unique and complete analysis (3.25) and therefore must have had in mind any thought whatever when he said (3.2 + 3.201) that a thought can be expressed in a completely analysed proposition. The difficulty of understanding what such an analysis would be like is formidable. The problem of understanding how general propositions symbolize (with which he wrestled arduously but in the end unsuccessfully) is crucial for his doctrine, for all the propositions that we can produce are 'general' in Wittgenstein's sense. The claim that language *as we know it* can be analysed into functions of elementary propositions is untenable. Yet Wittgenstein did not wish to be discussing some hypothetical, 'ideal' language; his chosen subject was the essence of all language (including the ordinary language we now use).

3.2 Perhaps better expressed in reverse: 'A thought can be so expressed in a proposition that', etc.

W. can hardly be thinking here of general propositions containing variables (for which see, for instance, 4.0411). The propositions in question can only be atomic ones (or, conceivably, finite truth-functions of atomic propositions).

'The trivial fact that a completely analysed proposition contains just as many names as there are things contained in its reference [or, meaning (*Bedeutung*)];—this fact is an example of the all-embracing representation of the world through language' (*Notebooks*, 11 (2)). It is an example of the identity of logical multiplicity between the proposition and what it depicts.

3.201 This cannot serve as a useful definition of 'simple sign' since we have no way of telling when we have reached the complete analysis of a proposition (cf. 5.55 (2)).

Cf. 3.25 (the uniqueness of analysis).

3.202 Parallels 2.02 on objects. W. is here introducing a philosophical definition of 'name' (approximately in the sense of Russell's 'logically proper names'): what we ordinarily call 'names' (e.g. of persons) do not qualify. In sentences of ordinary English, word-order, marks of inflection and conjugation, intonation, must all be included in W.'s 'simple signs'. His 'names' are the linguists' 'morphemes', the smallest units of meaning in the sentence.

● 'When a simple sign is used in a sentence-fact we shall call it a "name".'

3.203 *ab* **means** (*bedeutet*): here, and elsewhere, W. does not use *bedeuten* in Frege's special sense of 'refer' or 'denote'. (Also, W.'s use of *Sinn* does not coincide with Frege's use of that word.)

If 'objects' (simples) can be regarded as analogous to universals, rather than particulars, W.'s 'name' would approximate to what Frege meant by 'function-name' (*Funktionsname*).

Stenius regards 3.203 as 'a kind of definition of the concept of a name' (*Exposition*, p. 121).

Section 3.203 might easily convey a one-sided impression of W.'s conception of the meaning of a name. We must remember that according to W. all symbols, including names, have both 'content' and 'form' (cf. 3.31*d*, and the quotation from Moore in the notes on that remark). The object co-ordinated with a name is the content of that name's meaning; the form of the name is a complementary aspect of the name's meaning.

W. criticized 3.203 severely in later life. The following comments are characteristic:

'[One is tempted to say] *a name ought really to signify a simple*' (*Investigations*, § 39).

'It is important to note that the word "meaning" is being used illicitly if it is used to signify the thing that "corresponds" to the word. That is to confound the meaning of a name with the *bearer* of the name' (*op. cit.* § 40).

Cf. also *op. cit.* § 46 (with its reference to the *Theaetetus*).

c 'It is to be remembered that names are not things, but classes: "A" is the same letter as "A". This has the most important consequences for every symbolic language' (*Notes on Logic*, 104 (6)).

IS THE PROPOSITIONAL SIGN A TOKEN OR A TYPE?

When we normally speak of a sentence, we use the word 'sentence' in a 'type-sense' rather than a 'token-sense'; we count two occurrences of the words 'a proposition is a complex' as two instances of one and the same sentence, not as instances of two synonymous sentences. That this is the way Wittgenstein himself uses the expression 'propositional sign' (which takes over the role of 'sentence' in his conception) is made quite clear by his remark at 3.203*c*: '"A" is the same sign as "A".' If two propositional signs consist of physically similar words respectively attached to the *same* bearers, Wittgenstein counts the two as instances of the *same* propositional sign. Indeed, he has to do so in explaining his conception of the elementary proposition. He speaks, as we have seen, of objects (logical simples) being attached or assigned to the elements of the propositional sign in accordance with conventions or stipulations. But it would make no sense to speak of conventionally attaching a bearer to a particular mark, a token, having a unique occurrence. If we stipulate, explicitly or implicitly, that 'Hitler' shall stand for a certain person, we mean that *all* marks of a certain class, resembling one another within an admissible range of variation, shall stand for the man, whenever and wherever they occur. And similarly for all conventions of reference or meaning: all of them must concern classes of marks or sounds. Wittgenstein, as we know, says that the propositional sign is a fact

(3.14*b*). If I am right in contending that 'the propositional sign' is a *class* (identified partly by physical similarity of its members and partly by identity of the relevant word–object co-ordinations), Wittgenstein's account will need amendment. There is no *single* fact constituting the proposition 'in its projective relation to the world' (3.12*b*) but a class of such facts. Or, if we prefer, there *is* such a fact, but it is a conjunctive one. If this is correct, Wittgenstein's account of the essence of propositional representation will have to be modified in a number of places. Roughly speaking, we need to change his remarks into the plural: instead of saying that the picture is *a* fact, we must say that it is a class of similar facts; instead of saying that the propositional sign consists in *the* fact of combination of its elements (cf. 3.14*a*) we must say that it consists of the definite mode of combination of elements in *each* fact of a certain class of facts. And similarly in other cases.

3.21   There seems no reason to invert the original. Read: 'To the configuration of simple signs, etc. corresponds', etc.

   configuration (*Konfiguration*) = 'arrangement of parts in a form or figure' (*O.E.D.*). Thus 'configuration' is closely related in meaning to 'structure' (2.032). For the configuration of objects in a fact, see 2.0231, 2.0272.

   situation: or, 'state of affairs' (*Sachlage*). It might be argued that unless the proposition is true, there is no 'configuration' of the objects to which it refers. If so, *Sachlage* ('state of affairs') ought here to have been replaced by *Tatsache* ('fact'). Or else, *Sachlage* should be read as 'fact'.

3.22   This can be read as following from 3.21 (i.e. 3.22 *because* 3.21) or as a restatement of 3.202+3.203.

   is the representative of: or, simply, 'represents' (*vertritt*): an alternative to 'means' (*bedeutet*), as in 3.203, 3.221.

3.221 *a–c*   A pendant to 3.142.

c   *put them into words*: too specific a rendering of *aussprechen*, for which '*express*' seems about right. The obscurity of W.'s remark is removed by *d*.

d   For the contrast between 'how' and 'what' cf. 5.552 (3). In order to express 'what' a thing is, I need to convey its internal features—and these can only be *shown*.

XV

THE ANALYSIS OF PROPOSITIONS

(3.23–3.261)

A reader may sometimes wonder whether Wittgenstein's remarks about propositions were intended to fit all propositions or only those 'elementary' ones composed wholly of names. If the latter, a separate discussion would be needed for the propositions of ordinary language. It seems certain that Wittgenstein must have intended his remarks to fit the propositions we know rather than the hypothetical elementary propositions. If so, his view of a proposition as a picture loses much of its attraction, in view of the important consideration, to be emphasized later by Wittgenstein, that 'logical constants' do not represent. The sense in which a general proposition is a 'logical picture' can hardly be exactly the same as the sense in which an elementary proposition is one. No problem gave Wittgenstein more trouble than this.

The present instalment, with its emphasis upon analysis and definition, may be regarded as a necessary preliminary to the later discussion of non-elementary propositions. A crucial remark is 3.25, postulating the 'complete analysis' of every proposition. Its importance is underlined by the remark that immediately follows it (3.251): only if a proposition has a unique and complete analysis can its sense be definite. For Wittgenstein, a fragmentary sense was no sense at all—general propositions, for instance, must express with absolute precision the ranges of objects over which they generalize. It may be thought unfortunate that Wittgenstein did not enlarge upon his concept of 'analysis'. From 3.26 and 3.261, we may conjecture that analysis consists of replacing all defined terms by their definitions, until a proposition is reached in which only names and logical signs remain. Section 3.24 suggests that Wittgenstein accepted Russell's theory of descriptions and would have regarded as an admissible method of analysis the 'contextual definitions' employed by Russell.

3.23 requirement: or, 'demand'. The reference here is to 3.2.

'The demand for simple things *is* the demand for definiteness of sense' (*Notebooks*, 63 (8)).

● 'Unless it were possible to use "simple signs" (names for the simple objects) it would be impossible for a proposition to have a definite sense. That is to say, unless the proposition, just as it stands, is a structure of signs referring, even though indirectly, to simples, it cannot have a definite meaning—i.e. cannot have a meaning at all.'

3.23 is an important remark, foreshadowing one of W.'s leading ideas in the remainder of the book. He was convinced that all sense must be 'determinate', i.e. that there is no such thing as an inexact meaning. This is why he says later that all the sentences of our everyday language, just as they are, are 'in perfect logical order' (5.5563) and that 'Everything that can be said can be said clearly' (4.116*b*). General statements are no exception to the principle that a proposition must 'completely describe' its meaning (cf. especially 5.156 (3)). As W. said in the *Notebooks*, it was clear to him 'that what we MEAN must always be "*sharp*"' (68 (6)).

It is very interesting to find him, here at 3.23, explicitly regarding the possibility of simple signs (and so of direct reference to objects) as a stipulation (*Forderung*) arising from the demand that sense should be determinate. There is no place in this conception for what is sometimes called the 'open texture' of language.

3.24 (1) For the meaning of 'internal', see 4.123*a*.

● 'If a complex K has a as a constituent then any proposition about K entails an associated proposition about a.'

(2) *a* **given**: cf. note on 2.0124 above.

right or wrong: literally, 'will agree (*stimmen*), check, or not'. That is to say, either the object answering to the description will exist or it will not exist.

b **mentions**: literally, 'talks about'. Here W. is following Russell's theory of description, according to which any statement about the king of France is counted as false if the king of France does not exist.

(3) *a* **indeterminateness**: to be contrasted with the determinateness of simple signs (3.23). In the light of (**2**) the proposition is 'indeterminate' to the extent that the contingent question whether the description of the complex refers to anything remains to be answered. Alternatively, on Russell's analysis of descriptions, as here accepted by W., any statement containing a description is necessarily general—and in this way 'indeterminate'.

b **we know**: to understand the proposition, we have to know *that* it is indeterminate (and, we might add, exactly in which respects it is so).

c **prototype**: or, literally, 'proto-picture'. See notes on 3.315*e*. Cf. also 5.522. It is essential to a general proposition that it makes use of the range of values of a propositional function.

(4) Cf. 4.241 *ab* for W.'s conception of definition.

simple symbol: or, 'single symbol', i.e. one that *seems* to be used as if it were simple (a name for an object).

3.25 Cf. 3.2 (how propositions may be presented as analysed), 3.201 (for use of 'completely analysed').

'A proposition is logically completely analysed whose grammar is completely clarified (*klargelegt*). No matter in what mode of expression (*Ausdrucksweise*) it has been written down or pronounced' (*Phil. Bem.* § 1).

3.251 **articulated**: cf. 3.141 (2), also 4.032*a*, for parallel uses of this word.

3.26 Cf. 3.263*a* (the meanings of primitive signs cannot be given).

'Of course it cannot be said either of a thing or of a complex that it is not further analysable' (*Notebooks*, 9 (12)).

primitive sign (*Urzeichen*): approximately the same as 'indefinable' (the term used in the *Notes on Logic*). It is worth noting that W. uses 'sign' here in speaking of names—cf. 4.24*a*, where names are called 'symbols'.

3.261 (1) The stress upon *via* (*über*) suggests that the definition is part of the 'defined sign': to know how to use a complex sign we must know the rules for changing sentences containing it into those composed solely of 'primitive signs' (names).

point: or, 'show' (*weisen*): with the implication that definitions do not 'say' anything (cannot be true or false).

(2) *b* This implies that the name does not signify 'in the same way' as a complex sign (i.e. that the two must be of different logical types).

c **independently**: i.e. of definitions. Even names, according to 3.3, have meaning only in the context of propositions and so depend for their meaning upon the symbols with which they combine.

XVI

THE MEANING OF NAMES
(3.262–3.3)

Wittgenstein rounds off his account of the meaning of names (begun in XIV above) by stressing the dependence of the name–thing co-ordination upon the setting in which the name occurs. The principle that a name has meaning 'only in the context of a proposition' (3.3) is of capital importance. It would be a harmful over-simplification to think of a name in Wittgenstein's sense as being merely an arbitrary tag attached to an object. For it is of the essence of a name to have the capacity to unite with other names in complete pro-positions—like a cogwheel designed to mesh with other wheels in a working mechanism. Consequently, a given name is subject to rules of combination (which Wittgenstein later calls 'rules of logical syntax', 3.33) through which the form of the name is manifested. For names, like all 'expressions', have both 'form' and 'content' (cf. 3.31 d): a name has, as it were, lateral connexions with its eligible partners as well as a forward connexion with the object that is its meaning. The two types of connexion are inseparable, and neither can hold without the other; together they constitute what Wittgenstein calls the 'application' of the sign (3.262), i.e. what distinguishes a meaningless mark or sound from a significant symbol having a role *within a language*. These remarks about the double aspect of a name's meaning—its form and its content—parallel what was said much earlier about objects (cf. 2.021 + 2.025). Just as objects must be 'in logical space', so names—and, indeed, all symbols—must belong to a language. This important idea Wittgenstein never abandoned: it runs like a connecting thread through his *Investigations*.

In this instalment, also, Wittgenstein considers the question of how the meanings of names can be communicated. His disturbing answer (3.263) is that it is impossible to explain a name's meaning explicitly: the only way to convey the meaning is to use the name in a proposition, thereby presupposing that the meaning is already understood. On this view, the achievement of common reference by speaker and hearer becomes mysterious. We may guess that Wittgenstein would have retorted that the question of how mutual understanding is achieved belongs to psychology or sociology and is of no concern to philosophy. It just is a fact, for which causal explanations of the scientific sort can be provided, that we do sometimes make ourselves understood. There can be no philosophical question here, because it is logically impossible for there to be any philosophical answer.

3.262 application: or, 'use'. Cf. 3.326 on 'significant use' and 3.32 on the difference between symbol and sign. In the light of 3.5, 'applied' = 'thought'.

'By application I understand whatever makes combinations of sounds or strokes into a language. In the sense in which it is the application which makes a rod with strokes on it into a *ruler*. The *laying* (*Anlegen*) of language against reality' (*Phil. Bem.* 20, 12).

In the *Tractatus*, 'application' does not mean 'use' in the sense of the *Investigations* (cf. Anscombe, *Introduction*, p. 91—I agree with her that 'application' means 'that kind of difference between the syntactical roles of words which concerns a logician'). Cf. 3.327 on 'logico-syntactic application'.

3.263 5.526 (2) suggests a more explicit way of explaining the meanings of names.

elucidations: presumably, *true* propositions whose senses are grasped by identifying the facts which they state. If this is the only way in which the bearers of names can be recognized, it follows that every object (logical simple) must be a constituent of at least one fact. There is no logical necessity for this, of course—but it is implicated by the existence of an understood language.

W. once said (*Phil. Bem.* 3, 1) that there is a sense in which the employment of a language cannot be taught, namely by talking about it. Suppose somebody hears me using the word, 'Orosius', which he correctly takes to be the proper name of some person. If he asks, 'Who is Orosius?', i.e. 'Whom does "Orosius" stand for?', the correct answer, '"Orosius" stands for Orosius' is useless. For in order to understand it, he must already know whom 'Orosius' stands for, and that is just what he wants to find out. Of course, in ordinary life, the question would be answered

115

informatively by giving some description of Orosius, such as 'a fourth-century historian and theologian', etc. But W.'s simples cannot be identified by definite descriptions. For the difficulty involved here, cf. Reach, 'Name', p. 99, and Anscombe, *Introduction*, p. 84.

'An explanation [according to W.] is always of the same kind as a definition, namely "replacing one symbol by another"' (Moore, *Papers*, p. 264).

DIFFICULTIES ABOUT THE NAMING RELATION

Wittgenstein seems to have found surprisingly few philosophical puzzles in the name–object co-ordination. But it ought to have seemed as puzzling as anything it was used to explain.

Consider some propositional sign (a fact F) whose elements a, b, c are respectively attached to the objects o_1, o_2, and o_3. Then F, in its 'projective relation' to the world, i.e. F together with its links to o_1, o_2, and o_3, is a complex fact including, but not identical with, F. It is only *contingently* the case that the elements of F have the bearers that are attached to them, since it is perfectly conceivable that F might have had a different sense. We are therefore entitled to think of F with its meaning as a more inclusive fact—say G. It would seem that G must be a conjunction (or aggregate) of F and some other fact F', with the latter dividing into the facts corresponding to the links a–o_1, b–o_2, and c–o_3, respectively. Consider the fact answering to the a–o_1 link. We have seen that, apart from certain restrictions of logical form, any object can stand for any object—it is an integral feature of Wittgenstein's conception that the name–object relation shall be arbitrary. But now the character of the fact supposedly establishing the a–o_1 link becomes mysterious: one is tempted to affirm the absurdity that the mere existence of things, a and o_1, of the same logical forms suffices for the existence of the fact in question.

The difficulty seems to be connected with an inclination to treat the name–bearer relation as if it were simple and unanalysable. But the relation is always exponible, even when the name is literally attached to its bearer, like a label stuck on a bottle. (If every member of a tribe had his name permanently tattooed on his skin, we should still need to explain the *use* to which the tattoo-mark was put in that tribe.) From the standpoint of common sense, there is no mystery about how names get attached to bearers—we are sufficiently familiar with the practices of baptism and other ways of bestowing personal names; in case of doubt we verify that a man has a certain name by observing whether he answers to it, uses it in signing cheques or other documents, and so on. But the Wittgenstein of the *Tractatus* would have to exclude this kind of story as 'merely psychological' or perhaps 'merely sociological'. A description of naming practices could hardly qualify as displaying the essence of naming; there is no room in his austerely abstract world of atomic facts for this kind of analysis. Or if there is, he does not supply it.

3.3 **'nexus'**: I prefer 'context' (as in O.).

The first clause may be connected with 3.142 (only facts can express a sense).

The second clause must be an echo of Frege's statement in *Foundations*: 'Only in the context of a proposition do words mean something' (§ 62, p. 73). Frege's original German is identical with W.'s formulation except that he has *Wörter* in place of *Name* and *bedeuten etwas* instead of *hat...Bedeutung*. These differences are unimportant.

A little earlier, Frege says that 'only in a proposition have words really a meaning' (§ 60, p. 71). And in the introduction to the same book, Frege lays it down as one of his fundamental principles (*Grundsätze*) 'never to ask for the meaning of a word in isolation, but only in the context of a proposition' (p. x). Frege's reason seems to have been that ascription of meanings to words, in isolation from the propositions in which they occur, leads to the mistake of identifying the meanings with subjective images (pp. x, 71). The correct view, he urges, is that the meanings of words are determined by the senses of the propositions in which they occur: 'It is enough if the proposition as a whole has sense; thereby its parts also acquire their content (*Inhalt*)' (§ 60, p. 71). This position, which is the opposite to W.'s view that the sense of the proposition is a unique function of the meanings of its component words, is barely intelligible. In his later writings, when Frege had introduced the distinction between sense (*Sinn*) and reference (*Bedeutung*), he abandoned his earlier view and recognized that names and other designations have meaning (both sense and reference) outside propositions (see, for instance, his essay, 'Sense and Reference', in *Translations, passim*).

Since W. identified the meaning of a name with an object (3.203) he did not have Frege's original reason for adopting the principle in question.

W.'s thought may have been that names have no use except as parts of propositions—certainly a plausible view. The chief function of a word is to be conjoined with others in meaningful propositions. We can say that a given name has a kind of 'meaning' outside a proposition, but this meaning is then, as it were, potential: it is the word's capacity, when used in propositions, according to standard conventions, to stand then for a definite thing. We cannot idly correlate a name with a thing: the correlation succeeds only when we want to say something about that thing, to make an assertion about the connexion of that thing with other things.

W. does not imply that the meaning of a name must shift with the senses of the various propositions in which it occurs; on the contrary, in making the name stand for something in a given proposition, we are also settling how it is to be used in other propositions of the same form (cf. the reference to 'form' in 3.31 (4) and see also 3.203c).

For discussion of W.'s principle and Frege's version of it, see Dummett, 'Nominalism', pp. 491 ff. and Geach, 'Subject', p. 462.

In *Phil. Bem.* W. compares 3.3 to the remark that a cog functions only when it makes contact with another cog—or that a rod is a lever only when used as such.

'Naming and describing do not stand on the same level: naming is a preparation for description . . . *nothing* has so far been done, when a thing has been named. It has not even *got* a name except in the language-game. This was what Frege meant too, when he said that a word had meaning only as part of a sentence' (*Investigations*, § 49).

'On the statement "Words, except in propositions, have no meaning", he said that this "is true or false, as you understand it"; and immediately went on to add that, in what he called "language games", single words "have meanings by themselves", and that they may have meaning by themselves even in our ordinary language "if we have provided one"' (Moore, *Papers*, p. 261).

For further elaboration of 3.3, see 3.314a (generalization to all expressions) and 4.23 (restriction of the context to elementary propositions).

SUMMARY:
HOW AN ELEMENTARY PROPOSITION REPRESENTS

I shall now try to bring together the main points that Wittgenstein has made about the connexion of language with the world, confining myself for the present to the case of an elementary proposition. We have seen that Wittgenstein conceives an elementary proposition as a 'sensibly perceptible' fact, consisting of a concatenation of words or morphemes, to the whole of which a certain sense attaches in consequence of certain conventions of designation and of the interpretation of structure. An appropriate diagram for the sentence-fact might be as given in Fig. 1: in which the three elements, *a*, *b*, and *c*, have been so shaped that all three hang together ('like the links of a chain'), while any two of them would 'fall apart'. The shapes chosen for the three elements are meant to suggest their 'logical forms' (the same for *a*, *b* and *c* in the diagram), i.e. the sustaining conventions determining the

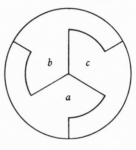

Fig. 1

permissible unions of the elements with other elements of the language to which they belong. Each element has a co-ordinated object (a logical simple) for which it deputizes. When the name–object co-ordinations are shown, the diagram becomes something like the following (Fig. 2):

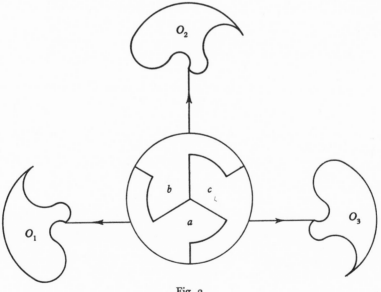

Fig. 2

119

The *O*'s have been shaped (like *a*, *b*, and *c*) to hang together. The contrasting shape of the attached objects is a reminder that the logical form of the represented state-of-affairs parallels, but is not identical with, the form of the sentence-fact. The arrows are intended to recall the 'projective' or 'truth-claiming' aspect of the proposition. The key to the entire conception is the reflection that the form of what is represented by the entire proposition does not need to be separately shown (e.g. by means of a shadowy replica of the circumference drawn around the *a–b–c* complex). In assigning references to the words, we necessarily make just the right provision for the possibilities of concatenation of the intended objects. Everything shown in the last figure may be taken as actually present in the world (with some residual questions about the name–thing connexions). The attraction of the analysis arises from this concreteness, from our apparent freedom to consider the proposition as an embodied arrangement of actual elements standing for actual objects. Instead of needing to think of the proposition's sense as some mysterious complex object, we have succeeded in 'exploding' its real elements into the complex situation graphically depicted in our diagram: instead of some mysterious ideal entity that is the proposition's meaning, we think of a concrete propositional sign-fact *having* sense—a *sinnvoller Satz*, as Wittgenstein calls it.

If the foregoing view of Wittgenstein's intentions is correct, there is more than a superficial resemblance between the course of his analysis and Russell's 'relational theory' of judgement (for which see his 'Truth', and many later writings, notably *Principia*, vol. 1, pp. 43 ff.). Russell summarizes his view by saying that 'a judgement does not have a single object, namely the proposition, but has several interrelated objects. That is to say, the relation which constitutes judgement is not a relation of two terms, namely the judging mind and the proposition, but is a relation of several terms, namely the mind and ... the constituents of the proposition' (*Principia*, p. 43). Thus both Russell and Wittgenstein agree[1] in rejecting the idea of a single

---

[1] In *Mysticism* (p. 220, f.n. 1), Russell says that he has been persuaded by W. that the earlier form of his theory as expounded in 'The Nature of Truth' was 'somewhat unduly simple'.

complex object of judgement or thought. (And this, as we have seen, is the clue to overcoming the puzzle about the mode of signification of the false proposition or the proposition of undetermined truth-value.) The chief difference between the two positions is that whereas Russell thinks of the 'self' or 'the judging mind' as a term in the complex relation between the propositional elements and the objects in the world, Wittgenstein explicitly rejects the notion of any such 'judging self' (cf. 5.542).

In the light of our discussion, we must resist any temptation to think of a proposition's sense as anything substantial. To identify a proposition's sense is to articulate the analysis graphically represented in our diagram. Upon becoming clear as to what the several name–thing co-ordinations are, and how they implicate syntactical rules for the permissible combinations of the words in question, we have become as clear as we can be *about* the sense. Thus Russell calls the phrase expressing a proposition an 'incomplete symbol' (*Principia*, p. 44) and in much the same vein Wittgenstein said, 'Neither the sense nor the meaning of a proposition is a thing. These words are incomplete symbols' (*Notes on Logic*, 94 (3)).

This conception has the appearance of resolving the philosophical puzzle about the ways in which false propositions and propositions of undetermined truth-value signify. But like most philosophical solutions, the answer given can be made to seem as problematic as the original question. I said that the image of the traffic accident model seemed to dissolve Wittgenstein's initial perplexity because it seemed to bring the meaning right before our eyes. Given that the puppets are proxies for the participants in the accident, we can literally *see* what happened. This fits the case of a spatial picture or model in which it makes sense to speak of perceiving the imputed arrangement. But we cannot literally see the specific logical form of a sentence-fact (nor can that fact literally show it). The logical form of the sentence-fact is an affair of the permissible transformations of the proposition (the admissible combinations of its elements with other elements); it can no more be perceived than can the moves of the bishop be seen in the wooden object placed on the chess-board. The logical form of an object is a potentiality of transformation and recombination, not a perceivable structure in the sentence-fact: the rules of logical syntax, one might say, are necessarily invisible. To be *shown* the relevant logical form is to be correctly instigated to use one's knowledge of the controlling logical or syntactical rules; to grasp the form is not to have an intuitive perception of something directly perceptible but rather to be ready to perform discursive procedures of transformation, logical inference, and so on. If this kind of gloss has to be discounted, from the standpoint of the *Tractatus*, as 'purely psychological', it seems hard to see what can take its place. As in the case of the name–thing co-ordination (for which see notes on 3.263 above), the apparent simplicity of the picture that Wittgenstein has constructed, with the structure of the sentence-fact embodying the elusive form of the fact depicted, threatens to disappear upon closer inspection. In the end, the attempt to visualize the essence of all picturing by means of some privileged picture must be self-stultifying. The later Wittgenstein made a penetrating criticism of his early work when he said 'Impressed by the possibility of a comparison [between stating a fact and using what is literally a picture] we think we are perceiving a state of affairs of the highest generality [the essence of picturing, the essential picture]' (*Investigations*, § 104). Wittgenstein's later criticisms of the picture theory are conclusive.

For discussion of the application of the picture theory to complex propositions, see below under 4.4.

XVII

EXPRESSIONS AND VARIABLES
(3.31–3.314)

This instalment and the next deal with the expression of logical form. The present instalment can be regarded as a preparation for the important conception of the proposition as a function of its constituent expressions (3.318).

Wittgenstein defines an expression as any propositional element having a determinate symbolic function in the propositions in which it occurs. (In the limiting case, a full proposition is also called an 'expression'—perhaps on account of the role it can play in truth-functional compounds.) Thus definite descriptions and other complex symbols must count as 'expressions'. The principle that an expression has meaning only in a proposition (3.314*a*) is a generalization of the corresponding principle for names (3.3), discussed in the last instalment. Indeed, the present instalment can be viewed as a natural extension of Wittgenstein's standpoint with respect to the simple symbols he calls 'names'.

The chief novelty introduced at this point is the symbolizing of the form of an expression by means of a variable (3.313*a*). One is tempted to think of the form of a given expression as somehow crystallized in a specially designed symbol (as the form of 'Russell' in 'Russell admires Frege' might be 'presented' in the 'propositional variable', 'Russell *x*'s *y*'). This is, of course, an illusion. Just as the meaning of a definite symbol, e.g. a name, is partially determined by the rules of combination that are one aspect of its 'application', so also the meanings of the letters we call 'variables' are determined by the rules of their use. The contrived notation, 'Russell *x*'s *y*', is a reminder, for a special purpose, of the propositions, 'Russell admires Frege', 'Russell admires Peano', 'Russell dislikes Hegel', etc. This is perhaps what Wittgenstein had in mind at 3.316*b* when he said that the determination of the values of a variable *is* that variable.

3.31 (1) **characterizes**: i.e. 'partially or wholly determines'. Cf. 3.318 on the proposition as a function of its component expressions.

expression (*Ausdruck*): here, and in the succeeding sections, always used in the narrowed sense of 'significant component'.

or a symbol: this may be misleading. Wittgenstein is not defining this sense of 'symbol' but merely adding that an expression is a symbol.

symbol: to be contrasted throughout with 'sign'—cf. especially 3.32 and 3.326.

(3) **have in common**: cf. 3.343 *b* for the intended meaning.

(4) mark: in the sense of a *distinctive* mark.

For the whole remark cf. 2.025 on combination of form and content. On 'form' see, for instance, 6.23 (2) and 4.0141. The same idea is otherwise expressed at 3.327.

Since propositions can have *forms* 'in common' and such forms are 'essential to their sense', the expressions of which they are composed must determine those forms.

'Names signalise (*kennzeichen*) what is common to [or, the unity (*Gemeinsamkeit*) of] a single form and a single content.—Only *together with* their syntactical use do they signalise *one particular* logical form' (*Notebooks*, 53 (5)).

This is an important idea, which will reappear in one way or another many times.

'About the meaning of single words, the positive points on which he seemed most anxious to insist were, I think, two, namely (α) something which he expressed by saying that the meaning of any single word in a language is "defined", "constituted", "determined", or "fixed" (he used all four expressions in different places) by the "grammatical rules" with which it is used in that language, and (β) something which he expressed by saying that every significant word or symbol must essentially belong to a "system", and (metaphorically) by saying that the meaning of a word is its "place" in a "grammatical system"' (Moore, *Papers*, p. 257).

3.311*a* **presupposes**: in order for the meaning (use) of an expression to be definite, the rules governing all the combinations in which it can occur must have been previously determined.

the forms: the plural suggests that an expression can belong to propositions of various forms. This might be questioned.

3.312 (1) presented: or, shown (*dargestellt*). This seems to be the first place at which the form of a proposition is held to convey anything.

(2) Cf. 4.126 (8) on the expression of a 'formal concept', and 4.1271 for a variable as the sign of a formal concept.

3.313 (1) Collating this with 3.312*a* might tempt us to identify the variable with the 'general form'—which would be a mistake. According to what W. is saying here and at 3.312*b*, the predicate of 'Tom is happy' would presumably be 'presented' by 'X is happy'. So, what W. calls a 'propositional variable' (3.313*c*) approximates to what Russell and others have meant by 'propositional function'.

(3) such a variable: the reference can be taken as being to (1), in the light of 3.314*b*.

3.314a   Cf. the parallel statement for names, 3.3.

b   Follows from ***a***. In assigning a definite use to a variable, we necessarily refer to a definite class of meaningful statements. It is natural, therefore, to think of the *propositional* variable as basic.

   Even: or, 'also' (*auch*).

XVIII

THE LOGICAL PROTO-PICTURE; PROPOSITIONS AS FUNCTIONS OF EXPRESSIONS

(3.315–3.318)

Wittgenstein here concludes, for the time being, his discussion of the logical form of a proposition. When all the constituent expressions of a proposition are converted into variables, there results what he calls a 'proto-picture' (*Urbild*) that presents the proposition's logical form (3.315). Thus the proto-picture answering to our example, 'Russell admires Frege' (cf. notes under XVII above), would be expressed by the complex symbol, $x\,y$'s z, composed wholly of variables.

   To understand a proto-picture is to understand its 'values'—i.e. the propositions instantiating the form in question; we must have at our disposal what Wittgenstein calls a 'description' of the range of values (3.317*b*). He will specify later some of the ways in which such 'description' is achieved (5.501 (3)–(6)).

   His conception is hard to follow. An important part of it is his insistence that the 'description' must involve no reference to the meanings of symbols, 3.317*c*. (We may remind ourselves at this point that any 'description' of meanings is impossible according to Wittgenstein—cf. 3.263 above.) Thus the 'description' of the ranges of variables belongs to logical syntax (in which there is no mention of meanings). According to Wittgenstein, there can be no such thing as 'semantics' in the way that Tarski, Carnap, and others have conceived that discipline. To 'describe' the range of values of each of the constituent expressions of a proposition (in the manner already explained at 3.311–3.313) is to determine uniquely the sense of the entire proposition: the proposition's form is a unique resultant of the forms of its constituents, and its content is a unique resultant of the contents of those expressions. When the expressions are names, this principle can be stated more simply as: The sense of a proposition composed of names is uniquely determined by the 'meanings' of those names. A mathematician might ask: If the sense of a proposition is *a* function of the meanings of its names, *what* function is it? The answer is: The 'concatenation' function; the sense of the proposition emerges when the names 'hang in one another', i.e. are combined in the *only* fact in which they can be properly united.

The reader might wish to consult xxxv, on variables as signs of formal concepts.

3.315 *a* **constituent**: an 'expression', in the sense explained at 3.31 *a*.
variable proposition: = 'propositional variable' (3.313 (3)).

b **the meaning that**: literally, 'what we intend by'.
conventions: or, 'agreement', as in O.

e **logical prototype**: or, 'proto-picture'. An *Urbild* is literally a 'primitive picture'. The word also occurs at 3.24 (3) *c*, 3.333 *a*, 5.522, 5.5351 *b*. It can sometimes be taken as a synonym for *Urzeichen* (= 'primitive sign', e.g. at 5.45 *a*) and has approximately the force of 'indefinable'. '*Ur*' suggests 'ultimate' (unanalysable), and hence something beyond our control. In the *Notes on Logic*, W. often speaks in this connexion of a 'type' or a 'logical type': 'In a proposition convert all indefinables into variables, there then remains a class of propositions which does not include all propositions, but does include an entire type' (106 (2) *c*, cf. also the remainder of 106 (2)). *Urbild* is perhaps an unfortunate neologism. For the *Urbild* is not a picture of the form in the sense of W.'s 'picture theory', but rather embodies the form; it shows what every proposition that is an instance of the *Urbild* has in common with its sense.

'A prototype sometimes is what Russell might call a fundamental irreducible form of proposition. It is a pattern for sentences, as often presented by such expressions as "*xRy*" and the like' (Shwayder, *Thesis*, p. 81). Anscombe identifies the proto-picture with the 'picture, without individual correlations' (*Introduction*, p. 67).

The Logical Proto-picture

The word *Urbild* occurs quite often in the *Notebooks*. W. says, for instance, that the simple proposition (*einfacher Satz*) must contain its own un-analysed proto-picture (*Urbild*), suggests that the picture is not the simple proposition, but the *Urbild* contained in it, and says that the *Urbild* is not a proposition but has the aspect of one (29 (11, 12)). In the proposition, we hold up or apply (*anlegen*) proto-pictures to reality (32 (5)). There cannot be propositions asserting the existence of proto-pictures, for this would be to give logic an impossible reality (*unmögliche Realität*): there would have to be, *per impossibile*, co-ordination (*Koordination*) in logic (i.e. logic would have a genuine subject-matter) (48 (9)).

● 'If we change the subject expression of "Tom is happy" into a variable, we get the class of statements "x is happy" determined by the arbitrary meaning of the constant predicate expression. (If instead of "happy" we had "sad", a different class of statements would have resulted.) But if the surviving constant is also changed into a variable, the class of statements "x is Y" is independent of the specific meanings of the constants in the original statement (but is determined only by their logical forms). "x is Y" shows the indefinable logical form of the original statement. And so in general.'

For this section, see Anscombe, *Introduction*, pp. 95–7.

HOW FAR DOES THE LOGICAL FORM OF A COMPLEX DETERMINE THE LOGICAL FORM OF ITS ELEMENTS?

I shall consider only elementary propositions and atomic facts. Consider a two-termed elementary proposition mn. (I have argued above, on pp. 82–3, that choice of the names m and n uniquely determines the sense of the proposition, hence the order of the letters in the symbol mn is immaterial.) Wittgenstein says that the proposition's form can be reached in any one of the following three ways: (i) First replace m by a variable, x say, and form the class of all propositions, xn. For each such proposition, an, say, replace n by another variable, y, say, and then form the class of all the values of ay. In this way we get a class of propositions that may be called the *extension* of the form exemplified by the original proposition. (ii) Start again, but this time first replace n by a variable and replace m by a variable subsequently. (iii) Replace m and n simultaneously by variables, say u and v, and form the class of all values of uv. Wittgenstein certainly holds that all three procedures will produce the same result, for otherwise the form of the proposition would be ambiguous. I propose to say that the extension of the form must be unique. A corresponding principle will apply to the analysis of the form of an atomic fact. I shall call the set of possible combinations of objects arising from the analysis of the form of an atomic fact the *extension* of that form; and I shall represent each such combination by grouping the corresponding names of objects in brackets. If a combination is realized, i.e. constitutes an atomic fact, I write the object names without brackets.

The demand that the extension of a form shall be unique imposes certain restrictions upon the relations between the forms of objects and the corresponding forms of atomic facts, as the following example will make clear. Imagine a universe of four objects, with one atomic fact, and two further possible combinations of objects, thus:

$$ab \quad (ac) \quad (cd).$$

Analysis of the form of ab by procedure (i) above yields the extension as (ab) and (ac), while analysis by procedure (ii) yields (ab) and (ac) and (ad). So here the condition of uniqueness of extension is violated. (The difficulty arises because a can combine with objects, b and c, which are not isomorphic.)

The following example will show that satisfaction of the condition of uniqueness of extension is compatible with a certain kind of ambiguity in the analysis of form. Imagine a universe of four objects with the following possible combinations

$$(ab) \quad (ac) \quad (bc) \quad (ad) \quad (cd).$$

It will be found that all the forms of atomic facts here shown have the same extension, the set of *all* combinations. But writing 'ϕ' for the form of an object, it is easily verified that $\phi(a) = \phi(c)$, $\phi(b) = \phi(d)$, and $\phi(a) \neq \phi(b)$. So we have two forms of objects, say ϕ_1 and ϕ_2, and the form of an atomic fact may prove to be either $\phi_1\phi_2$ (as in (ab)) or else $\phi_1\phi_1$ (as in (ac)). This seems sufficient reason for saying that the forms of the atomic facts are different.

3.316 (1) Cf. 5.501 (3) for a similar statement. The reference is to the procedure described at 3.317, rather than at 3.315. If we arrive at a propositional variable by successively substituting variables for constants in a definite proposition (as in 3.315), there is no room for stipulation. It is only if we start at the other end, as it were, with a sign to be used for a variable, that we are required to decide what values we intend it to have.

is: or, 'gets' (*wird*).

(2) Here the variable seems to be identified either with the rule for finding its values or with the set of such values. (Cf. 5.514*b* for a similar identification.) As one might perhaps say: 'If you know what substitutions to make for the variable, you know how to use it—and there is nothing more to know.'

3.317 (1) common characteristic: or, 'common mark' (*Merkmal*). Cf. 3.311*b* for a parallel usage.

(2) Cf. the echo at 5.501 (4).

(3) An important assertion, connecting with 3.33.

symbols: 'signs' would be more appropriate, as in 3.33.

therefore: why does W. say this? Perhaps because 'description' in (2) is contrasted with 'use' (cf. 3.326): in talking *about* a class of signs, you cannot be *using* any of those signs to refer to their meanings.

● 'The rule that determines the values of a variable concerns only the logical form of signs and not their "contents" (their specific meanings). For the determination of the values of a variable is the determination of a logical form.'

(5) For alternative modes of 'description', see 5.501 (6).

is produced: literally, 'occurs' (*geschieht*).

3.318 Cf. 4.24*b* (elementary propositions as functions of names).

An important difference should be noted between Russell's and Frege's conceptions of a function. Russell's definition of 'propositional function' (the kind of function here in question) runs as follows: 'Let ϕx be a statement containing a variable x and such that it becomes a proposition when x is given any fixed determined meaning. Then ϕx is called a "propositional function"' (*Principia*, vol. I, p. 14). According to Russell, then, a 'propositional function' is a certain kind of *expression*, namely one obtainable from a sentence expressing a proposition by replacing in it one or more names by variables, such as x, y, etc. But it is asking for trouble to use 'function' in this sense, especially since Russell is led when quantifying over functions to shift the meaning of the word to something like 'attribute'. Quine's use of the expression, 'statement matrix', in his writing, obviates the ambiguity. It is fair comment to say that 'The propositional function is . . . just the old-fashioned "predicate", with the copula treated as an indistinguishable part of it' (Prior, *Categoricals*, pp. 191–2).

Frege, on the other hand, repeatedly protested against mathematicians' identification of a function with a certain symbolic expression (e.g. at *Translations*, p. 22). For Frege, an expression such as '*x* is human' (a propositional function in Russell's sense) is properly called an expression '*for* a function'—which signifies the function but is not itself the function. The nearest that Frege comes to a positive characterization of the notion of function is when he says that 'the essence' of a function comes out in a 'correspondence' between its values and the values of its arguments.

W.'s notion of 'function' in 3.318 approximates to Frege's conception, rather than to Russell's.

XIX

SIGN AND SYMBOL CONTRASTED; MODES OF SIGNIFICATION

(3.32–3.322)

Wittgenstein has already emphasized the distinction between a sentence considered as a fact in its own right and considered as a significant proposition in 'its projective relation to the world' (3.12*b*). There is a parallel distinction (implicit in several previous remarks) between an object to which no meaning has been attached and the same object as standing for some other object. Wittgenstein now explicitly marks these distinctions by stipulating contrasting uses for the words 'sign' and 'symbol' (3.32). A symbol is a sign together with its meaning or sense. (Heretofore, he has used 'sign' and 'symbol' as approximate synonyms: e.g. names were called signs at 3.202, but expressions were called symbols at 3.31*a*.)

When we call an object a symbol, we are presupposing that it has a 'use' in a language (3.326) and therefore that it is governed by syntactical rules determining its logical form (3.327). An important part of Wittgenstein's conception is that one and the same sign can belong to different symbols (3.321, with examples given in 3.323). Two symbols having a common sign have different 'modes of signification' (*Bezeichnungsweise*), says Wittgenstein, now using this expression for the first time (3.322). Two symbols have different modes of signification, we may infer, if they stand for different objects, or have different logical forms, or both. Symbols are individuated by their 'modes of signification', not by the arbitrary signs that render them perceptible. In xxii, the idea of a mode of signification will be used in connexion with the distinction between the essential and the accidental features of symbols.

3.32   what can be perceived: or, 'the perceptible aspect'.

'About propositions ... he made a distinction ... between what he called "the sign" and what he called "the symbol"', saying that whatever was necessary to give "a sign" significance was a part of "the symbol", so that where, for instance, the "sign" is a sentence, the "symbol" is something which contains both the sign and also everything which is necessary to give that sentence sense. He said that a "symbol", thus understood, *is* a proposition and "cannot be nonsensical, though it can be either true or false". He illustrated this by saying that if a man says "I am tired" his mouth is part of the symbol; and said that any explanation of a sign "completes the symbol"' (Moore, *Papers*, p. 262).

See also 3.262 + 3.326 on the distinction between sign and symbol.

3.321   See the supplementary remarks at 5.47321 (2) and 5.4733 (3) *b*.

3.322 *a*   characteristic: or, 'mark' (*Merkmal*), here a distinctive property.

modes of signification: in the *Notes on Logic*, W. uses the expression, 'ways of designation'. To the passage that became 3.322, he added: 'Nevertheless one is always tempted, in a difficulty, to take refuge in different ways of designation' (104 (5) *b*).

The meaning of the expression 'mode of signification' is very closely related to that of the expression 'logico-syntactical employment' that occurs at 3.327. Cf. also the expression 'method of projection' at 3.11 *b*, and the expression *Art und Weise* (e.g. at 2.17, 3.261 *b*).

In the *Notebooks*, Wittgenstein says that only a sign and its mode of signification *together* are 'logically identical' with what is signified (19 (7)). Similarly he says that what represents is not merely the sign or picture alone, but also the method of presentation (*Methode der Darstellung*) (21 (10)).

c   **on the signifying side**: literally, 'in the signification'.

XX

CONFUSIONS IN ORDINARY LANGUAGE AND THE NEED FOR AN IMPROVED IDEOGRAPHY

(3.323–3.33)

In these important remarks, Wittgenstein for the first time criticizes ordinary language in a way which has led some readers to suppose he wished to replace it by an improved notation. The logical form of ordinary language is not perspicuous, because different symbols, having different modes of signification, are expressed by physically similar signs (3.323 a). This provokes the kind of confusion on which philosophy thrives (3.324). A cure would be to introduce an ideography (*Begriffsschrift*) that would render logical form more obvious. (Of course, no alteration would thereby have been made in the essence of the language; and conventions that *could* be misunderstood would still be in effect. Wittgenstein is thinking of an 'expedient' to combat confusion of thought, a practical measure to facilitate conceptual clarity.) Such an ideography would manifestly obey the rules of logical syntax, as ordinary language must already do—though covertly. (It is therefore somewhat misleading for Wittgenstein to say that the improved language *would* obey the rules of logical syntax (3.325 a)—for ordinary language already does that in its own fashion.) Plainly, one guiding principle in the construction of the new notation would be to eschew homonyms. But all we are told about 'logical syntax' at this point is that its rules make no reference to meanings (3.33). We learn regrettably little, here or later, about the specific forms that the rules of logical syntax take.

xxiv may be read as a sequel.

3.323 For this whole section, cf. 4.002.

(1) everyday language: ordinary, non-technical, language.
word: here used in the 'type-sense', not in the 'token-sense'.

'The structure of the proposition must be recognized and then the rest is easy. But ordinary language conceals the structure of the proposition: in it relations look like predicates, and predicates like names', etc. (*Notes on Logic*, 96 (3), end).

(2) **word**: here used in the 'token-sense' (cf. corresponding note on (1) above).

we speak of *something*, **but also of** *something's* **happening**: both 'of' and 'something' must be regarded as having distinct senses in the two different uses.

(3) 'The reason why "The property of not being green is not green" is *nonsense*, is because we have only given meaning to the fact that "green" stands to the right of a name; and "the property of not being green" is obviously not *that*' (*Moore Notes*, 115 (4)).

'But suppose that one gives a particular lion (the king of lions) the name "Lion"? Now you will say: But it is clear that in the sentence "Lion is a lion" the word "lion" is being used in two different ways (*Tractatus*). But can't I count them as *one* kind of use?' (*Foundations*, p. 182).

'We see from this quotation [3.323 (3)] that W.'s concept of a symbol, though it includes the "way of symbolizing" of a sign does not include its meaning. One and the same symbol might be used in different meanings' (Stenius, *Exposition*, p. 189).

3.324 This remark is elaborated at 4.003.

3.325 (1) **superficially**: or, 'externally' or 'ostensibly'. Notice that W. seems to be saying the same thing twice: the same sign is not to be used in different ways (prohibition of homonyms). W. did not exclude synonyms from his 'sign-language'.

logical syntax: the first occurrence of this important notion.

In this section W. seems to be subscribing to the ideal of an 'ideal language'. But cf. 5.5563*a* (ordinary language is perfectly in order). The apparent conflict might be resolved by supposing that in 3.325 W. was concerned only with a notation for logic. Yet in *Investigations* (§ 81, p. 38) W. suggests he had been misled into thinking that to understand means 'operating a calculus according to definite rules'.

'By syntax in this general sense of the word I mean the rules which tell us in which connexions only a word gives sense, thus excluding non-sensical pseudo-propositions' (*Logical Form*, p. 162).

(2) **conceptual notation**: *Begriffsschrift* (Frege's word)—literally, 'concept writing' or 'ideography'.

One example of a proposition of logical syntax cited by W. (*Math. MS.* 567) is the angle-sum theorem in plane euclidean geometry. The theorem means, he explains, that if the sums of the measured angles should not be two right angles, one will always assume some error of measurement. Accordingly, it is a postulate about the mode of description of states of affairs, hence a proposition of syntax.

'Above all, our grammar lacks *perspicuity* (*Übersichtlichkeit*)' (*ibid.* 1, no. 10).

3.326 Can be read as a complement to 3.32. See also 3.262.

used with a sense: 'used significantly' (*sinnvoll*). Cf. 3.13 (4) for another occurrence of this word.

3.327 logico-syntactical: adjectival form of 'logical syntax' (3.325 a). Cf. 3.334 on the connexion between logical syntax and signification.

The phrase '*syntaktische Anwendung*' (or, *Verwendung*) occurs occasionally in the *Notebooks* (e.g. at 59 (10), 61 (6), 64 (3)). Cf. also notes on 'mode of signification' at 3.322 a above.

Notice that part of the 'logico-syntactical employment' of a given proposition is shown by specifying the propositions it entails.

'We might demand (*fordern*) definiteness in this way too: if a proposition is to make sense then the syntactical employment of each of its parts must be settled in advance.—It is, for example, not possible *only subsequently to come upon* the fact that a proposition follows from it. But, for example, what propositions follow from a proposition must be completely settled before that proposition can have a sense' (*Notebooks*, 64 (6)).

'Names [i.e. what we call names in our ordinary language] may and do stand for the most various forms, and it is only the syntactical application (*syntaktische Anwendung*) that signalises the form to be presented' (*Notebooks*, 59 (10)).

● 'A sign determines a logical form only when account is taken of the ways in which it may combine with other signs according to the rules of logical syntax.'

'[A symbol] has a certain logical form which we bring to light ... by asking what signs we may substitute in the propositional sign and still preserve the logical form' (Watson, *Physics*, p. 14).

3.328 (1) *useless*: rather, 'not used'.

Occam's Maxim: cf. 5.47321 for a similar statement.

point: literally, 'sense' (= meaning).

● 'A sign that stands for nothing is not being used; if a sign is found to be used as part of a statement, it necessarily stands for something—has meaning.'

3.33*b* establish: or, 'formulate'.

description of expressions: cf. 3.317.

For an example of the use of the principle that logical syntax does not mention meanings, see 6.126 (2).

W.'s exclusion of reference to meanings in logical syntax follows at once from the principle, to which he is committed, that it is impossible to state the meanings of expressions. This imposes no restriction in the present context. Since the rules determining the logical form of a given symbol will be the same for all isomorphic symbols, we can confine our attention to the rules governing the appropriate variables. As W. says in *Logical Form* (p. 162), 'the rules of syntax which applied to the constants must apply to the variables also'. Now rules for the use of variables in meaningful combinations make no reference to meanings—cf. 4.1271*b*, also 3.316–3.317. For the idea of 'description of expressions' that arises in connexion with the determination of variables, see 3.312–3.317, 4.126 (6)–(8), and especially 5.501.

According to Moore, W. was anxious to insist that rules of grammar 'treat only of the symbolism' (*Papers*, p. 277).

'Of *what* symbols did he suppose that "3 + 3 = 6" was treating? He did indeed actually assert . . . that the proposition "red is a primary colour" was a proposition about the word "red"; and, if he had seriously held this, he might have held similarly that the proposition or rule "3 + 3 = 6" was merely a proposition or rule about the particular expressions "3 + 3" and "6". But he cannot have held seriously either of these two views' (Moore, *Papers*, pp. 290–1).

'[In opposition to Frege's view that mathematics deals with "what is symbolized"] he went on to express his own alternative view by saying "What is essential to the rules is the logical multiplicity which all the different possible symbols have in common"; and here, by speaking of "all the different possible symbols", I take it he was admitting, what is obvious, that the *same* rules which are expressed by the use of the Arabic numerals may be expressed by ever so many different symbols. But if the rules "treat only of the symbolism" how can two rules which treat of *different* symbols, e.g. of "3" and "III", possibly be the *same* rule? I suppose he must have thought that we use the word "same" in such a sense that two rules, which are obviously *not* the same, in that they treat of different symbols, are yet said to be the same, provided only that the rules for their use have the same "logical multiplicity" (whatever that may mean)' (Moore, *Papers*, p. 291).

Commentary

LOGICAL SYNTAX AND THE 'BEGRIFFSSCHRIFT'

The expression, 'logical syntax', first occurs at 3.325a, where it is used as a synonym for '*logical* grammar'. (This is, however, the only place where Wittgenstein uses the word 'grammar'. For other occurrences of 'logical syntax' see 3.327, 3.33, 3.334, 3.344, and 6.124.) Since the adjective, 'logical', is italicized in the text, a contrast is plainly intended with traditional school grammar. For the purposes of this discussion, 'logical syntax' can usually be treated as shorthand for 'the rules of logical syntax' (cf. 3.334 and 3.344 for further references to such rules).

The notion of logical syntax is at once linked by Wittgenstein with that of an ideal sign-language (*Zeichensprache*) to cure philosophical confusions engendered by ordinary language. An artificial language of this sort would constitute the well-formed ideography (*Begriffsschrift*) recommended at 3.325 (2) and mentioned again at 4.1272 (2), 4.1273a, 4.431c, 5.533 and 5.534. However, rules of logical syntax do not apply solely to the signs of a hypothetical improved language; ordinary language, like every language, has its own logical syntax.

The notion of a philosophically adequate language, free from the irregularities and misleading suggestions of ordinary language, has often attracted philosophers and inventors of international languages (see E. Cassirer, *Symbolic Forms*, vol. 1, pp. 128–32, for further details). Descartes, for instance, envisaged a universal language for the representation of simple ideas that would so aid the judgement as to make error almost impossible and allow peasants to be better judges of the truth than his own philosophical contemporaries (Letter to Mersenne, 20 November 1629, *Correspondance*, vol. 1, p. 93).

A good modern example of this kind of programme is Edmund Husserl's 'pure logico-grammatical doctrine of forms' (*rein logisch-grammatische Formenlehre*) expounded in his *Logische Untersuchungen*. Husserl calls for an elaborated science of meanings that will reveal the essential laws of their construction and their constitutive laws of combination and modification (p. 328). He says it would be necessary to treat first of the general categories of meaning, 'or, in a sense quite analogous to mathematics, of variables' (*ibid.*). The resulting formal laws of meaning, intended to demarcate the domain of the sensible from that of the senseless, will rank as formal laws of logic. He construes the laws as forbidding 'formal senselessness' (*Gesetze der zu vermeidenden Widersinn*, p. 335). The 'pure theory of forms' establishes 'an ideal scaffolding (*Gerüst*), which every actual language...fills in and dresses up in various ways with empirical material' (p. 338). The analogy with Wittgenstein's conception of the *Begriffsschrift* is striking.

An interesting attempt to provide a philosophical grammar is made by Adolf Stöhr, in his *Grammatik*. His aim is to free thought from the spell (*Bann*) of the inessential and accidental in given speech forms (p. 140). Taking unanalysed units of meaning (morphemes) as given, Stöhr concentrates upon the modes of derivation of complex expressions, and the appropriate algebraic symbolization of the numerous types of operations he brings to light. Having obtained, as he thinks, a systematic way of symbolizing the thought expressed in any sentence, he introduces abbreviations which allow him to re-introduce the patterns of the surface grammars of languages actually in use. Stöhr's linguistic erudition contrasts strikingly with the *naïveté* of his philosophical semantics (which allows him, for example, to treat a sentence as a complex name). His construction, elaborate and ingenious as it is, illustrates the limitations of any attempt to remodel grammar on would-be necessary foundations in the absence of any thorough effort to answer the basic questions of philosophical semantics. The most that results is a certain reorganization and simplification of superficial ideas about meaning and logical structures—while the basic task of philosophical analysis remains undone.

The misleading features of ordinary language that Wittgenstein's *Begriffsschrift* is intended to correct are the following: (i) 'the same word signifies in different ways and so belongs to different symbols' (3.323 a); and (ii) 'two words that signify in different ways are employed in propositions in what is superficially the same way' (3.323 a). An instance of the first fault is the occurrence of 'is' as a copula as well as a sign of identity (3.323 b); an instance of the second is the occurrence of 'to exist', as if it were an intransitive verb on a par with 'to go' (*ibid.*).

Commentary

The first type of imperfection arises from the presence in ordinary language of an enormous number of words that logical analysis shows to be *homonyms* (Wittgenstein does not have parallel objections to the use of synonyms). Inattention to ambiguities that are masked by physical similarities of sign-vehicles leads to fallacious inferences and to the promulgation of 'pseudo-propositions', that seem to make sense but are really nonsensical. (For an instance of an important error of this kind, see Wittgenstein's remarks about the ambiguities of 'relation' at 4.122 (3, 4).) The second kind of imperfection in ordinary language is a complement to the first: words which look different and in fact play different logical roles are treated as analogous because they seem to be used alike in the sentences in which they occur—that is to say, superficial similarities of linguistic arrangement blur the underlying differences of logical form. In the *Notes on Logic*, Wittgenstein says that 'Ordinary language conceals the structure of the proposition: in it, relations look like predicates, and predicates like names', etc. (96 (3), end). In the *Tractatus* he says, in the same vein, that ordinary language 'disguises thought' (4.002 (4)) and he contrasts the 'apparent logical form' of a proposition with its 'real' form (4.0031 *b*). A reformed sign-language is needed because the hidden complexities of ordinary language render it 'not humanly possible' to grasp immediately 'what the logic of language is' (4.002 (3)). Such failure to understand the logic of our language leads philosophers to construct nonsensical sentences that satisfy the pliable standards of conventional grammar (4.003*a–c*). Ordinary grammar is capriciously severe in matters of no logical importance, yet insufficiently strict for logical accuracy.

Wittgenstein's animadversions on ordinary language must be balanced against his emphatic contention that ordinary language is quite free from logical defects. (The contradiction is only apparent.) There is perfect logical order in the propositions of ordinary language, just as they stand (*so wie sie sind*) (5.5563*a*): 'We cannot give a sign the wrong sense' (5.4732) and 'we cannot make mistakes in logic' (5.473 (3)). Language, like logic, 'takes care of itself' (5.473*a*), when used for its proper purposes. (Here we may recall Wittgenstein's remarks in the *Investigations* about philosophical puzzles arising when language goes on holiday.) 'Nonsensical pseudo-propositions' are generated by confusions and illusions that arise from our reflections upon language—we take the wrong turnings in our thoughts and in our theories *about* the words we use.

The passage in which Wittgenstein introduces the notion of logical syntax shows what the rules of logical syntax in the *Begriffsschrift* will be like. To correct the weaknesses of ordinary language, the improved ideography must be constructed with two aims in view: (i) it must conform to the maxim of 'different symbols, perceptibly different signs', and (ii) it must obey strict rules for combining signs. As Wittgenstein said in *Logical Form*, 'The idea is to express in an appropriate symbolism what in ordinary language leads to endless misunderstanding. That is to say, where ordinary language disguises logical structure, where it allows the formation of pseudo-propositions, where it uses one term in an infinity of different meanings, we must replace it by a symbolism which gives a clear picture of the logical structure, excludes pseudo-propositions, and uses its terms unambiguously' (p. 163).

Rules for distinguishing the meanings of homonyms in ordinary language would presumably have to be what are nowadays called 'semantical rules'. If this is so, there is reason to think that Wittgenstein would have to say it was impossible to formulate such rules (cf. 3.263 on the 'elucidation' of names). The position is less clear with regard to the possibility of rules facilitating 'a clear picture of the logical structure'. Wittgenstein's discussion of logical syntax in the *Tractatus* is almost wholly concerned with the second type of rule ('syntactical rules' in modern terminology).

About such rules Wittgenstein makes the following assertions:

(*a*) They make no reference to the meanings of signs, but presuppose only the 'descriptions' of expressions (3.33).

(*b*) The rules of logical syntax must be self-evident once we know how each individual sign signifies (3.334).

(*c*) Logical syntax includes rules for the mutual replaceability of signs, i.e. rules of synonymy (3.343).

(*d*) The logical syntax of any sign-language generates all the propositions of logic (6.124*h*).

Commentary

That is to say, logic may be considered to be a part of logical syntax: the rules for the proper combinations of signs suffice to establish the implications and equivalences that are the subject-matter of logic. If this does not seem immediately obvious, we may consider that the syntactical rules will determine *inter alia* which combinations of signs are tautological and which contradictory. From these results in turn the logical properties of the component expressions can be read off—cf. 6.121–6.1221.

(*e*) The rules of logical syntax are not arbitrary, do not express conventions freely adopted.

In speaking of matters connected with logical syntax, Wittgenstein frequently uses words such as 'correct' and 'incorrect', 'right' and 'wrong'. At 3.343*b*, he speaks of a 'correct sign-language'; at 4.1273*c*, Frege and Russell's expression for a general proposition is condemned as 'false'; at the opening of 5.46 he speaks of the 'right' introduction of logical signs; in 4.1213, he speaks of having the 'right logical conception' once everything is all right in our sign-language (*wenn alles stimmt*). It is an important part of his conception of logical syntax that the arbitrary co-ordination of objects with words implies a non-arbitrary network of logical commitments—cf. the very important section 3.342. The rules of logical syntax, we may say, render manifest the 'essence of the notation' (3.342*b*). This feature of Wittgenstein's conception of logical syntax sets it off sharply from such later developments as those of Carnap in his book *Logical Syntax*.

I will add some critical comments.

(1) Some readers, impressed by the difficulties of making coherent sense of Wittgenstein's remarks about logical syntax, might be tempted to treat his references to 'rules' as no more than a figure of speech. But this lazy exegesis cannot survive an examination of a passage such as 3.33, with its clear implication that the rules of logical syntax can be explicitly formulated. When Wittgenstein says that logical syntax must be 'established' (*muss sich aufstellen lassen*) in a certain way, he means that the subject can be expounded in detail, and the references that follow to 'description of expressions' puts the matter beyond doubt. This passage and the others discussed

earlier in these notes show him to have been contending that determinate rules of logical syntax can be adequately expressed in a suitable notation. It is not easy to understand offhand how this is to be done, but it should be borne in mind that qualms about the possibility, on Wittgenstein's principles, of formally expressing the rules of logical syntax apply equally to the expression of principles of logic. For these principles, according to his conception, are themselves to be regarded as being rules of logical syntax or at least equivalent to such rules. Now Wittgenstein certainly held that the principles of logic could be correctly formulated, even though they must be regarded as 'showing' rather than 'saying', and the same must hold for the rules of logical syntax.

(2) The rules of logical syntax cannot be 'pictures' in Wittgenstein's sense. What he says about logical propositions must apply equally to them, namely that their 'correct explanation' ought to assign them 'a unique status among all propositions' (6.112). We are therefore left with the delicate task of reconciling the possibility of formulating the rules of logical syntax with the theory of the essence of language expounded earlier in the book.

(3) Using terminology that has come into use since the *Tractatus* was written, we may classify the rules of logical syntax into 'formation rules' and 'transformation rules'. If we say, provisionally, that both kinds of rules concern signs, we may say that formation rules prescribe the combinations of signs that count as 'well-formed' (i.e. capable of expressing a sense), while transformation rules prescribe the permissible replacements of signs (i.e. those leaving the sense unchanged). Since rules of entailment can be replaced by rules of logical equivalence (so that instead of saying that A entails B we say that $A.B$ is equivalent to A), we can without loss of generality treat all the transformation rules as consisting of logical equivalences or logical identities.

(4) But is it correct to say that a rule of logical syntax is about a *sign* and not about a *symbol*, i.e. solely about classes of marks and sounds, and not about such marks and sounds *together with their meanings*? Wittgenstein's own remarks encourage this interpretation and later writers on 'logical syntax' like Carnap take this to be the correct foundation for logical syntax.

Consider, however, the following plausible example of a rule of logical syntax (suggested by 6.231 *b*):

(*a*) '1 + 1 + 1 + 1' is synonymous with '(1 + 1) + (1 + 1)'. If this were treated as a rule for the mutual replacement of two complex signs, it would seem to make covert reference to some particular language, say English. It would then be proper to expand it into the following, more adequate, form:

(*b*) In the English language, '1 + 1 + 1 + 1' is synonymous with '(1 + 1) + (1 + 1)'. But (*b*) is plainly a *contingent* statement about one feature of the use of numerals in English, and is certainly not what Wittgenstein envisaged as a rule of logical syntax. The following formulation comes closer to his intentions:

(*c*) '1 + 1 + 1 + 1' (*when used in the particular way that is familiar to us*) is synonymous with '(1 + 1) + (1 + 1)' (*used in the same way*). If (*c*) is an adequate rendering of (*a*), the latter rule can be properly understood only by someone who knows *how* the numerals are used, whereas of course (*b*) might be understood by somebody who was quite ignorant of this use. In Wittgenstein's terminology, one would have to say that (*a*) or (*c*) are about symbols, not merely about signs. So interpreted, both (*a*) and (*c*) must count as *necessary* statements if they are held to be statements at all. (Cf. the rule, 'A pawn can be replaced by a queen on reaching the eighth rank', which is not a contingent statement about what is actually done to pieces of wood by chess-players, but a statement about an aspect of the roles of the pawn and the queen.)

(5) If the rules of logical syntax are necessary, in some sense, it can hardly make sense to speak of 'obeying' them, as Wittgenstein does in the German text of 3.325 *a*. A rule that cannot be violated cannot be respected either, since we have no choice in the matter— and now the word 'rule' begins to seem inappropriate. Did Wittgenstein perhaps confuse what might be called *principles* of logical syntax (with regard to which it makes no sense to speak of violation, obedience, and so on) with the corresponding mechanical rules for the manipulation of *signs*? But if such mechanical rules are to be regarded as 'correct' they must be framed in accordance with previous insight into what I have called the 'principles' of logical

syntax. For instance, if I am to frame a mechanical rule forbidding a certain invented sign in the ideography to be used in a certain way (cf. 3.325 a), I must first be able to see that the old word which the new sign will replace *already* functions as a homonym. I must be able to grasp a definite principle of logical syntax (a principle of non-synonymity) governing the symbols I now employ, if I am to be justified in setting up rules for new signs.

(6) If the principles of logical syntax are necessary, they must be discovered, not stipulated: their correctness ought to *show itself*, we ought to be able to *see* that we have hit upon their correct formulation. But how is this to be done?

(7) Consider first a case in which we have to establish that a certain combination of signs (as we now use them) makes no sense. The reason, according to Wittgenstein, is that we have failed to attach a meaning to a sign or signs occurring as part of a certain combination (cf. 5.473 e, 5.4733 (3) a). It is, however, a contingent fact that we have or have not co-ordinated an object with a given sign. So there is no mystery here: we can establish by ordinary observation, or by recalling our own practice, that the necessary assignment of meaning has in fact not been made.

(8) Consider next a case in which we need to establish that two signs, as we now use them, are synonyms. The situation now seems to be about as follows: We cannot use two synonymous signs, A and B, say, unless we know that one can be substituted for the other (cf. 6.2322 *ad fin.*, also 6.23 b and 6.232 *ad fin.*). In direct or un-reflective uses of language, we simply use A and B interchangeably, without formulating any rule. Only when our attention shifts to a question about A and B (a question *about* language) do we need to record that, according to our given usages of these signs, we do treat them as mutually replaceable. (Whenever we use language we have to distinguish between the significant and the irrelevant features of signs, so that we are in a sense constantly making judgements of synonymy.) Formulation of the syntactical rule merely requires us to make explicit what we are already committed to by our antecedent practice.

(9) One way of recognizing identity of meaning is to consider the corresponding truth-conditions of propositions in which the relevant

expressions, *A* and *B*, occur. This is a process of translation—we show that $p(A)$ is synonymous with $p(B)$ by translating both into one and the same proposition, q, expressing the truth-conditions shared in common.

(10) Another way of establishing the desired identity of meaning is by direct observation of the ways in which *we* actually use the two signs. (It is a contingent fact that we use the signs 'swiftly' and 'rapidly' as synonyms, for instance.) In neither of the two modes of establishing synonymy do we have to assume some instantaneous flash of insight allowing us to 'see' at once that two expressions have the same meaning. 'Seeing' may very well be a discursive procedure.

(11) From the standpoint here sketched, the formulation and subsequent use of syntactical rules must be regarded as a quite special use of language, to be sharply distinguished from the use of language to make empirical assertions. When we use words to make statements about the world, we do not talk about the words. (When we shoot arrows at a target, we do not shoot at the arrows themselves.) For the purposes of philosophical clarification, however, it is essential to reflect upon the facts of our linguistic usages. Abstracting from the senses and meanings of the expressions we use, we produce a rule that can be followed blindly or mechanically (like the rule for replacing a double negative by the affirmative proposition)—we proceed to play a new game, as it were, with meaningless marks. This is what Wittgenstein calls 'calculation'—*the* procedure characteristic of the so-called formal disciplines of logic, mathematics, and logical syntax (cf. 6.2331 and 6.126a). What makes this game of calculation interesting and important (in a way that the meaningless game of chess is not) is its provenance and ultimate application. The rules we formulate are not chosen wilfully, but arise in a determinate way from our pre-existing linguistic practices, reflecting in their own fashion the logical form of reality. And we do not calculate out of pure interest in exploring the consequences of the rules (as a logician might) but with a view to that clarification of thought and language which is the *raison d'être* of philosophical activity.

(12) According to the conception of logical syntax that I have sketched above (trying to remain faithful to Wittgenstein's intentions),

the crucial step is the grasp of our linguistic routines that allows us to record that certain words or expressions are synonyms, that some sentences are well-formed, others not, and so on. The codification of these insights about our language by means of a special ideography (*Begriffsschrift*) may have practical value as a way of forestalling conceptual confusion, but it is at best a useful expedient of no theoretical importance. For the ideography, like every language, relies upon arbitrary conventions (e.g. that certain visible differences in sign-tokens shall count as assigning them to different symbols) which can be misunderstood and abused, like every other convention. No artificial language is immune from the resurgence of nonsensical constructions, and the price of philosophical clarity is constant vigilance.

XXI

REJECTION OF THE THEORY OF TYPES

(3.331–3.333)

These remarks constitute a digression, though a highly interesting one. Wittgenstein makes short work of Russell's theory of types, commonly held to have been one of his main contributions to the modern renaissance of formal logic. But Wittgenstein's reason for dismissing the theory—that its formulation requires Russell to speak about the meanings of signs (3.331)—will not survive examination. The principle to which Wittgenstein is implicitly appealing, that reference to meanings must be absent from logical syntax (3.33), requires more defence than he supplies; but in any case, he quite overlooked the possibility of a purely syntactical version of the theory of types (for which see, for instance, Church's 'Formulation'). It is a travesty of Russell's theory to identify the 'whole' of it, as Wittgenstein does, with the idea that a propositional sign cannot contain itself (3.332). This idea and the related idea that a function cannot be a function of itself (cannot be 'its own argument', 3.333*a*)

Wittgenstein accepts. But Wittgenstein's summary disposal of the paradoxes that provoked the theory of types is as unsatisfying as its brevity would lead one to expect.

It is hard to account for Wittgenstein's evident animus in this digression. For Wittgenstein's own programme for 'logical syntax' can properly be viewed as an attempt to accomplish what Russell was reaching for in his theory of types. Wittgenstein himself once said that philosophical grammar or logical syntax was 'a theory of logical types' (*Phil. Bem.* 3, 2). An improved version of Russell's theory of types might well be a part of logical syntax in Wittgenstein's conception.

3.331 a　**turn to**: rather, 'get a comprehensive view of'.
b　**must be wrong**: the original refers only to Russell's 'mistake' (*Irrtum*).

'[A] theory of types must be rendered superfluous by a proper theory of symbolism' (*Letters*, 121 (1)).

'A THEORY of *types* is impossible. It tries to say something about the types, when you can only talk about the symbols. But *what* you say about the symbols is not that this symbol has that type, which would be nonsense for [the] same reason: but you say simply: *This* is the symbol, to prevent a misunderstanding. E.g. in "*aRb*", "*R*" is *not* a symbol, but *that* "*R*" is between one name and another symbolizes [Cf. 3.1432]. Here we have *not* said: this symbol is not of this type but of that, but only: *This* symbolizes and not that' (*Moore Notes*, 108 (10)).

THE THEORY OF TYPES

This can be regarded as a set of restrictions, superimposed upon the symbolism of *Principia Mathematica,* designed to prevent the construction of expressions of the form $f(f)$ that occur in the symbolic expression of the logical paradoxes. The basic idea is that 'the functions to which a given object a can be an argument are incapable of being arguments to each other' (*Principia*, vol. 1, p. 48). This leads to the stipulation that every propositional function shall be counted as a member of exactly one of a series of so-called types, with the understanding that only members of consecutive types may be conjoined in meaningful formulas. (Thus in a well-formed expression of the form

$\phi(f)$, f must belong to some type n, and ϕ to the next type, $n+1$. I omit the complications of the so-called 'ramified theory of types').

In his original versions of the theory of types, Russell speaks of objects, functions, properties, etc., so Wittgenstein's comment in 3.331 *b* has a target. But it is possible to formulate such a theory without mentioning 'meanings' of the signs concerned (see, for instance, Church's 'Formulation'). Russell himself has said: 'The theory of types is really a theory of symbols, not of things' (*Logic and Knowledge*, p. 267).

3.332 Cf. the special case at 4.442 (2)—the impossibility of a proposition asserting its own truth.

In this remark *Satz* is properly translated, as in P.–McG., by 'proposition', rather than by 'sentence', for W. is implying that the *Satz* does say something (*aussagt*), though not about itself: it is what he has called a *significant* proposition (*sinnvoller Satz*) at 3.13*d*. And when W. denies that a proposition can say anything 'about itself' he means to exclude only a statement about anything that makes the proposition in question significant: he is not denying that a proposition might mean something true about the very sentence (considered as a physical object) that is used to express that proposition (cf. the quotation from Goodstein below). W.'s reason for excluding self-reference is not immediately convincing: it is not clear why the propositional sign must 'include itself' in order to be the expression of a proposition about its own meaning. If I can talk about a man without using a name, why should I be unable to talk about a proposition's meaning by using some description which is part of the propositional sign? (Cf. article on self-reference of propositions, below, for further discussion.)

This section was discussed by McTaggart ('Propositions'). See also, Popper, *Society*, p. 710.

'A proposition cannot occur in itself. This is the fundamental truth of the theory of types' (*Notes on Logic*, 106 (2)—a similar statement occurs at 105 (5)).

'This is not to say that a proposition cannot significantly affirm something of the physical signs by which it is expressed, but that a proposition can say nothing about its own meaning' (Goodstein, *Formalism*, p. 50).

'To me it looks fishy. If I write "this is in haste" in a letter "this" refers to all the writing on the note-paper. Of course a proposition cannot be a proposition *with regard* to itself, i.e. cannot be an element of itself' (Wisdom, 'Constructions', p. 209, f.n. 2).

THE SELF-REFERENCE OF PROPOSITIONS

Can a proposition affirm anything about its own meaning? And if not, why not? The first step in answering these questions had better be an effort to render the expression, 'affirm anything about its own meaning', sufficiently precise to be worth using. Consider the following preliminary example: somebody says 'I mean what I say' (*a*) in a tone of voice which goes with a reference to what he is saying at the time (and not, for example, a reference to what he usually or always says); the sentence (*a*) so used certainly purports to be the expression of a proposition about the meaning of the proposition expressed by that same sentence. The same purported meaning might be otherwise expressed by the sentence 'The meaning of the sentence I am now using is intended by me' (*a'*). This in turn suggests, as one possible form for a putative proposition having self-reference in the relevant sense: 'The sense of *x* has *Y*' (*a''*). In order to get such a self-referring proposition, we have to imagine that 'has *Y*' in (*a''*) has been replaced by the expression of some property (e.g. 'is contingent', 'contains *redness*', 'is not elementary', and so on) and '*x*' has been replaced either by a name or a definite description of the sentence which results after both substitutions have been made. An example would be: 'The sense of this sentence is not the same as that of "Man is a mammal"' (*b*) or, more simply, 'This sentence does not mean the same as "Man is a mammal"' (*b'*). Bluff common-sense is inclined to say that (*b'*) does express an authentic proposition, indeed one that is plainly true (for several arguments of this sort, see Popper, 'Self-reference'). But (*b'*) is intended to imply that (*b'*) itself has some definite meaning: it says that a certain sentence (i.e. (*b'*) itself) has a meaning which is not the same as the meaning of 'Man is a mammal'. But what *is* that meaning? It is identified only as being the meaning of (*b'*), while (*b'*) itself contains a reference to the meaning of (*b'*) again: here there really is a vicious circle. The very same circle would arise if a man were to say 'What I now say is true' and nothing else (cf. 4.442 (2)), for on asking ourselves what it *is* that the speaker says, we get nothing but the same form of words: if we try expanding the original sentence we get 'What I now say (namely "What I now say is true") is true' and at the next try 'What I now say (namely "What I now say [namely 'What I now say is true'] is true") is true' and so on, without being any nearer to understanding *what* the speaker claims to be saying. This type of circularity will obviously arise in every instance of the form (a'') obtained according to the prescription given above. For a sentence containing an expression of the form 'The sense of sentence...' where the gap is filled in such a way as to identify the whole sentence of which that expression is a part will obviously be one whose sense cannot be determined at all. *This* kind of alleged self-reference is certainly impossible and Wittgenstein was quite right in saying so.

3.333 (1) A parallel to 3.332. Echoed at 5.251.

prototype: see 3.315*e* for the meaning of this. To determine the prototype, or equivalently, to determine the use made of the individual variable in $f(x)$, we must specify the range of values of the function (cf. 3.316*b*). This precludes circularity.

(2) W.'s symbolism would have been easier to follow if he had omitted the *x* throughout this paragraph, writing $F(f)$ in place of $F(fx)$, $F(F(f))$ in place of $F(F(fx))$, and so on. (He probably used *fx* rather than the simple variable *f* to indicate that *F* is supposed to be a function of a function; if it were not, the question of its self-application could not even arise.)

'ϕ cannot possibly stand to the left of (or in any other relation to) the symbol of a property. For the symbol of a property, e.g. Ψx, is *that* Ψ stands to the left of a name form, and another symbol ϕ cannot possibly stand to the left of such a *fact*' (*Moore Notes*, 115 (5)).

b An instance of 3.327.

(3) Here *u* takes the place of the variable *fx* in **(2)**. The first formula of this paragraph seems to contain a misprint and should read $F(F(u))$, i.e. with the *f* deleted. In supplying the expanded formula on the second line of **(3)**, W. apparently wishes to show that the outer *F* obeys different laws of transformation from those of the inner *F* (and hence they must signify different functions). $F(u)$ cannot be expanded in a way analogous to the expansion W. gives for $F(F(u))$.

(4) **Russell's paradox**: presumably the variant concerning functions (rather than classes) that are not themselves included in the set of their own values.

XXII

ESSENTIAL AND ACCIDENTAL
FEATURES OF SYMBOLS

(3.334–3.3442)

This instalment may be read with XIX (on the contrast between a sign and a symbol). Throughout the book, Wittgenstein is trying to get clear about the *essence* of language, or any equivalent symbolism. Now, any sign by which a given symbol is manifested will have 'accidental' features that are not unconditionally needed for the expression of *that* symbol. (It will be remembered that symbols are individuated by their respective 'modes of signification' and not by their signs.) Where, then, are we to find the essence of the symbol? Wittgenstein suggests that the essence manifests itself in the necessary consequences of any arbitrary choice of a notation (3.342). Or, again, in the mutual translatability of all equivalent notations (3.343). The essence is what is 'common' to all equivalent signs or systems of signs (3.344). And the *possibility* of a particular notation has the importance for philosophy of revealing something about the nature, the essence, of the world (3.3421). All three—the necessary consequences of the arbitrary choice of a sign, translatability into another notation, the possibility of a given notation—are ways in which is shown the logical form of language, i.e. the logical form of the world.

3.334 obvious: rather, 'self-intelligible', 'self-evident' (*von selbst verstehen*).

how [the sign] **signifies**: not *what* it signifies, e.g. not the simple for which it stands if it is a name, but, rather, how it combines with other signs to produce sentence-facts.

This section is a corollary of 3.327. Each sign determines its 'logico-syntactical employment', i.e. the syntactical rules governing its use in sentences. If we know *how* a sign signifies (not *what* it signifies) we *ipso facto* know the corresponding grammatical rules. The signs in question need not be those of an artificial language.

each individual sign (*ein jedes Zeichen*): an unusual German construction. Does it mean 'each and every sign, taken singly' or '*any* single sign'? In view of 3.42, I am inclined to adopt the latter reading. The rules for the use of even a single sign require reference to its possibilities of connexion with all other signs. Thus, a full account of the logical syntax of even a single sign will require a full account of the whole of logical syntax.

3.34 (1)   essential: see 3.31 (3) for a similar use.

W. is, of course, preoccupied with the essential features of a proposition, i.e. those which cannot be altered without alteration of its sense (cf. 3.34*c* and 4.465*c*). The general contrast between 'essential' and 'accidental' is spelled out in 3.34–3.3441.

'There must be something in the proposition that is identical with its reference [or, meaning (*Bedeutung*)], but the proposition cannot be identical with its reference, and so there must be something in it that is *not* identical with its reference. (The proposition is a formation [or, structure (*Gebilde*)] with the logical features of what it represents (*des Dargestellten*) and with other features besides, but these will be arbitrary and different in different sign-languages)' (*Notebooks*, 17 (2)).

c   Cf. 4.465*c* (on the connexion between essence and sense).

3.341 (1)   what all propositions ... have in common: explained at 3.343*b*. See also 3.344 for elaboration of the idea.

(2)   the same purpose: not in a psychological sense, of course. Approximately equivalent to 'the same use'.

'Each time I say such and such a representation could be replaced by this other one, we take a further step towards the goal of grasping the essence of what is represented' (*Phil. Bem.* 1). Immediately afterwards, W. speaks of the inessential parts of our language as 'idling wheels' (*leerläufende Räder*), an image which he later used in *Investigations*.

3.3411*a*   real: or, 'actual' (*eigentliche*).
signified: or, 'designated' (*bezeichnen*).

'When W. says that the symbol, say a name, is that which its perceptible signs have in common, what he clearly means, in my reading of him, is not some perceptible feature of the signs but their way of signifying' (Hall, *Value*, p. 205).

b   For the 'purpose' of a name (cf. 3.202, 3.203) *can* be served without using a composite sign. Notice that relational signs, as we now use them (e.g., to indicate the sense of a relationship holding *from a to b*) are not arbitrarily replaceable. Cf. Anscombe, *Introduction*, p. 36, for this point.

all kinds of composition . . . unessential: rather, 'no sort of composition at all would turn out to be essential'.

3.342 'What is unarbitrary about our symbols is not them, nor the rules we give; but the fact that, having given certain rules, others are fixed = follow logically' (*Moore Notes*, 113 (3)). An example given later in the same *Notes* is that in arbitrarily determining that a symbol of a certain description shall be a tautology, we necessarily determine whether any other given symbol is or is not a tautology (113 (6)).

3.3421a For an example, see 3.3441 (a possible choice of logical primitives).

In view of the earlier link between form and possibility (2.033), the present statement may be taken to indicate the importance of the *form* of the mode of signification in question.

b Here W. seems to be taking a positive view of the function of philosophy. It can give us insight (*Aufschluss*, commonly used in the sense of 'information') into the essence (*Wesen*) of the world.

generally: or, 'regularly'.

individual case: or, 'detail'.

essence of the world: the same phrase occurs at 5.4711.

3.343a Cf. 4.241 and especially (3) *b* on W.'s conception of definition.

It should be noticed that 'rules' here is being contrasted with 'propositions'. 'The definition is only possible if it is itself not a proposition' (*Notebooks*, 71 (14)).

translating: the translation in question must be adequate or correct—must preserve the *sense* of each translated proposition. Consequently, it will also leave invariant the truth-values of propositions and the logical relations between them.

Rules of translation must presumably make no reference to meanings (cf. 4.242). Since W. treats statements of identity of meaning as mere 'expedients in presentation' (*Behelfe der Darstellung*, 4.242) he may be assumed to attach little philosophical importance to the syntactical rules of synonymy. The *possibility* of mutual conversion of alternative notations can, however, be an important clue to the essence of a symbolism, cf. 3.3421 and 3.3441 *b*.

3.344 According to this section, definitions are among the rules of logical syntax.

'What symbolizes in a symbol, is that which is common to all the symbols which could in accordance with the rules of logic = syntactical rules for manipulation of symbols, be substituted for it' (*Moore Notes*, 116 (5)).

Here and in the immediately preceding sections, one might have expected to find 'sign' instead of 'symbol' (as at 4.241).

3.3441 *a* **notation**: same as 'mode of signification' (*Bezeichnungsweise*) in 3.3421 *a*.

For what is shown by the notation for negation, see 4.0621 *a*, 5.44 (4).

NOTATIONS FOR TRUTH-FUNCTIONS

Wittgenstein first represents truth-functions by means of truth-tables, as in 4.442 *a*, then by means of a row of truth-values (4.442 (3)), and eventually as terms of a certain formal series generated by a single operation upon the elementary propositions (6 *a*). Consider the first kind of representation. Instead of the table reproduced at 4.442 *a*, we can write $\sim p \vee q$. Given the customary rules for calculating the truth-values of the symbol thus introduced, this symbol and the original truth-table will have the same truth-conditions, i.e. the same sense. By the 'notations that use $\sim p$ and $p \vee q$', Wittgenstein must mean these symbols together with their standard meanings (their definitions in terms of the truth and falsity of their components). If replaceability were taken in some weaker sense, it would not be true that the truth-functions and they alone are replaceable by the curl–wedge notation. For interpretations can be given to the formulas of the propositional calculus that are incompatible with their being representations of truth-functions in Wittgenstein's sense. Cf. pp. 331–6 below.

There is a peculiarity of Wittgenstein's notion of 'replaceability' that should be noted. If the truth-table notation is 'replaced' by formulas containing the curl ($\sim$) and the wedge ($\vee$), one and the same truth-table is made to correspond to indefinitely many formulas. The truth-table shown at 4.442 *a*, for instance, corresponds to $\sim p \vee q$, to $\sim p \vee q \vee q$, and to infinitely many others. (Formulas that are logically equivalent in the curl–wedge notation answer to the same truth-table.) The relation, *can be replaced by*, is 'one–many'. Hence, it would be inappropriate to say that the truth-table notation is a *translation* of the curl–wedge notation: distinctions between certain formulas in the latter cannot be represented at all in the former.

Consider now the sense in which the 'stroke' notation can 'be replaced' by the curl–wedge notation. If we define p/q to mean the same as $\sim p \vee \sim q$, the truth-conditions for every formula expressed by the stroke notation remain invariant (and, in particular, tautologies remain tautologies, and contradictions remain contradictions). But, on this correlation, while every well-formed formula in the stroke notation will have a unique definition in the curl–wedge notation, the converse will not be true: no stroke formula will correspond to $p \vee q$, for example, though of course plenty of stroke formulas will correspond to expressions logically equivalent to the disjunction in question. (The stroke notation is 'mapped' upon a proper sub-set of the curl–wedge notation, as mathematicians would say.) Here, too, it would be a mistake to think of the one notation as a translation of the other in the sense in which French is a translation of English.

3.3442   resolve: or, 'analyse'.
   proposition: or, 'propositional structure' (*Satzgefüge*).

● 'The analysis of a sign determines once and for all how *all* occurrences of that sign may be transformed.'
   Cf. 3.25 on the uniqueness of analysis.

XXIII

THE PROPOSITION AS A POINT IN LOGICAL SPACE

(3.4–3.42)

These four sections are dominated by the metaphor of 'logical space', already briefly encountered at 2.11. The basic ideas are suggested by the systems of representation used in 'co-ordinate geometry'. Any material particle, occupying a point in physical space, can be located, in a way that has become commonplace since Descartes introduced the technique, by means of a set of three numerical 'co-ordinates' (e.g. by the distances of the point from three fixed lines, the 'axes of reference'). Wittgenstein thinks of each point in physical space as a possibility—the possibility of the existence of a material particle at that position. Similarly, he conceives of an elementary proposition as an atomic possibility—a 'point' or 'position' or 'place' (*ein Ort*) in *logical* space: the proposition is the possibility of the corresponding atomic fact. According to this conception, logical space is the ordered system of all atomic situations. The 'logical co-ordinates' of a proposition ought therefore to be a set of specifications sufficient to determine the proposition's sense. A natural choice for such co-ordinates would be the set of names of which the proposition is composed. Each name in the language would then be regarded as a distinct 'axis of reference' and the number of 'dimensions' in logical space would be the same as the number of names—or, what is the same thing, the number of different objects in the world. According to this analogy, a complex proposition would correspond to a 'volume', rather than to a 'point', in logical space—cf. 4.463 on the 'range' of a proposition.

An important implication is the inseparability of a proposition from the 'logical space' in which it is located (3.42). The proposition's logical relations partially determine its sense and are not something superadded when the proposition combines with other propositions in truth-functions.

3.4a **place** (*Ort*): Stenius prefers the translation 'position' (*Exposition*, p. 55).

logical space: for an earlier occurrence of this notion, see 2.11. Cf. also 2.013.

b **constituents** (*Bestandteile*): the expressions (3.31a) of which the proposition is composed. Probably, 'ultimate constituent' is meant. Notice that there are not two things here—the existence of the constituents of the proposition and in addition the existence of the proposition as a configuration of its constituents. The existence of the constituents already guarantees the existence of the proposition uniquely determined by them.

'The analogy which induced the use of the expression "logical space" is with the use of co-ordinates in geometry. These are used to name or mark places in space (or it may be on a line or surface) relative to a co-ordinate system of reference. A change of the co-ordinate system will give new names to the places by assigning different co-ordinates: the rules for the translation of names from one system to another can be given depending on the geometrical properties of the space and system of reference. But, of course, the analogy breaks down in this respect, that a logical space is not necessarily a space in any geometrical sense' (Watson, *Physics*, p. 15).

3.41 logical co-ordinates: the word 'co-ordinate' can be viewed as a synonym of *Zuordnung* ('correlation' or 'co-ordination') in 2.1514, 2.1515. The 'co-ordinates' of the propositional sign are, then, the links between the elements of the sign and the objects for which they stand. Accordingly, 3.41 can be read as:

● 'The propositional sign, together with the meanings assigned to its constituents—that is what we mean by a "logical place".'

Notice that on this view the notion of 'logical place' is very close to that of the sense of a propositional sign.

CO-ORDINATES

Wittgenstein certainly had in mind the analogy of geometrical co-ordinates (cf. *Notebooks*, 20 (12, 13)). The basic ideas underlying the use of the latter are the following: (*a*) A number of points, say *a*, *b*, *c*, are arbitrarily selected and designated as *reference points*. (*b*) A set of rules (or a 'co-ordinate system') is adopted, in virtue of which the geometrical relations between an arbitrary point *p* and the reference points, *a*, *b*, *c* (e.g its distances from the latter) uniquely determine the assignment of an ordered set of numbers. These are the (numerical) 'co-ordinates' of *p*. (*c*) Given the reference points, and the adopted set of rules, a given set of determinate co-ordinates uniquely determines the corresponding point *p*. (*d*) Geometrical relations between the members of a *set* of *p*'s (e.g. their all lying on a single straight line) are reflected in arithmetical relations between their co-ordinates. (*e*) Rules can be formulated for transforming the co-ordinates of a point in a given co-ordinate system into its co-ordinates in any other given system.

The Proposition as a Point in Logical Space

In order to apply these ideas to language, we might think of taking an arbitrary number of propositional signs (*Satzzeichen*) as a basis for expressing all other propositions. Since all elementary propositions are logically independent, we would need as many 'reference points' as there are such elementary propositions. The 'co-ordinates' of any proposition would then be given by its representation as a truth-function of the elementary propositions. (We could even present these 'co-ordinates' as classes of binary decimals.)

An alternative way of using the analogy would be to take *names* as co-ordinates; the 'logical place' would then be conceived as a possible state of affairs; and the co-ordinates of a given proposition would be the names of which it is composed (possibly arranged as an ordered set, if we admit that the same names can be combined in various orders).

3.411 Literally: 'A geometrical and a logical place agree in being a possibility of an existence.'

something can exist in it: i.e. some state of affairs.

'This could be interpreted thus: just as the "geometrical position" [= "place"] is a position that a body might occupy and in this sense means a possibility for the existence of a body, the logical position means a "possibility for the existence of worlds"' (Stenius, *Exposition*, p. 55).

3.42 (1) A very important remark. Cf. 2.0131 a (spatial objects must lie in infinite space).

'Logical space' is the totality of the 'logical places', i.e. the totality of all significant propositional signs (in the light of 3.41). If the 'whole of logical space' were not already 'given' by the significance of a proposition sign, *p*, this would mean that the sense of *p* failed to determine the relation of *p* to some of the truth-functions of which it is a component. But that could only be if *p* had different meanings when occurring in isolation and as part of a complex.

● 'Although a proposition expresses a single state of affairs, the conventions determining its sense also provide for the senses of all the complex propositions in which it is a truth-functional component.'

(2) negation: cf. 4.0641 for the effect of negation on the 'logical place'.

elements: objects.

● 'If the sense of p did not already determine the sense of $\sim p$, that could only be because the latter involved reference to additional objects. Similarly for $p.q$. But just because these complex propositions are in logical relations with their constituents, these "additional" objects would have to be logically connected with ("in co-ordination with") the original objects—and so definable in terms of them.'

Notice that the above line of thought would not hold if there were some propositions that had no logical relations with others; but this is excluded by all propositions having the *same* logical form.

Cf. 5.123b (the truth of p as requiring the existence of objects).

(3) **logical scaffolding** (*das logische Gerüst*): cf. 4.023 (5) and 6.124a for other uses of this expression.

The force of: delete (not in the original).

reaches through the whole of logical space: cf. Anscombe, *Introduction*, p. 76.

For comment on this section, see Stenius, *Exposition*, p. 56.

XXIV

ORDINARY LANGUAGE DISGUISES THOUGHT; PHILOSOPHY AS 'CRITIQUE OF LANGUAGE'

(3.5–4.0031)

This may be read as an elaboration of xx (on the confusions fostered by ordinary language). At 3.323 Wittgenstein has already stressed the philosophical importance of the mode of signification (*Bezeichnungsweise*) of a word and its relative independence of the word's physical character (its phonemic constitution) and also of its superficial grammatical category (the 'part of speech' to which it belongs): in order to get clear about the sense of a word, and the sense of the propositions to which it belongs, we must attend to its '*logico-syntactical employment*' (3.327), the hidden rules that allow it to be used correctly, in conformity to the 'logic of the world'. When we are misled by the '*apparent* logical form' (4.0031 b), by the superficial grammatical analogies between words in ordinary language, the kind of nonsense that typically disfigures philosophy can easily result (3.324). Now he hammers these points home. As before, his main emphasis is upon the contrast between the superficial simplicity of language and the 'enormously complicated' understandings (4.002 (5)) which that simplicity conceals. The complexity is there, however, just because ordinary language is 'capable of expressing every sense' (4.002*a*) and because, we might add, there is no limit to the complexity of what we *actually* must be meaning when we produce deceitfully simple-looking sentences. We know *how* to use the linguistic medium, in innocent ignorance of what we are doing (4.002*a*). Now it is a chief philosophical task to render this hidden complexity manifest (inferred from 4.0031)—to transform logical innocence into logical awareness, one might say. This important and highly influential conception of philosophical method Wittgenstein never abandoned in his later work, though he came to regard the conception of the *unique* logical form (the form of reality *reflected* in language) as a profound error.

xxxi can be read as an immediate sequel.

3.5 applied: or, 'used'. Cf. 3.262 for the same usage.
thought out: simply, 'thought' (cf. 3.11*b*).
This section serves as a supplement to 3.4.

4 proposition with a sense: or, 'significant proposition' (*der sinnvolle Satz*). Combined with 3, this yields the equations: 'logical picture' = 'significant proposition' = 'thought'. For the expression 'significant proposition', see 3.13*d*.

4.001 Cf. 1.1 (the ontological counterpart: the world is the totality of facts).
propositions: signs capable of having sense, not actual assertions. Since the totality of propositions, in this sense of the word, is determined by the totality of 'expressions', Wittgenstein might also have said that the language is the totality of its vocabulary (with the grammatical rules for using that vocabulary presupposed).
'Is it a tautology to say: *Language* consists of *sentences* [or, propositions (*Sätzen*)]? It seems it *is*' (*Notebooks*, 52 (4)).

4.002 Cf. 3.323 on the deficiencies of ordinary language.

(**1**) **every sense**: cf. 4.027 on the possibility of communicating a new sense with old words, also 4.02, 4.021, 4.024*c*. An important point, to which W. reverted in his later work.

The variant version in *Notes on Logic* is: 'Man possesses an innate capacity for constructing symbols with which *some* sense can be expressed, without having the slightest idea what each word signifies' (95 (4)). There follows an interesting illustration: 'The best example of this is mathematics, for man has until recently used the symbols for numbers without knowing what they signify or that they signify nothing' (96 (1)).

(**3**) **logic of language** *(Sprachlogik)*: occurs again at 4.003*c*.

'The conventions *(Abmachungen)* of our language are extraordinarily complicated. There is enormously much added in thought to each proposition and not said' *(Notebooks,* 70 (1)). He goes on to say that his aim is that of justifying *(rechtfertigen)* the vagueness *(Vagheit)* of ordinary propositions, and adds 'for it *can* be justified' (70 (2)).

The context shows that by the 'vagueness' of a proposition, he means the *generality* of a proposition such as 'The watch is on the table' (a favourite example in the *Notebooks*).

'These adjustments are all parts of language; whatever their interest for psychologists as phenomena, and whatever theories are put forward to account for them, their status in language must remain a matter of logic' (Watson, *Physics*, pp. 31–2).

4.003 An elaboration of 3.324.

(**1**)*a* **propositions**: here 'sentences' is preferable.

nonsensical *(unsinnig)*: the notion of the nonsensical *(unsinnig)* should always be carefully distinguished from that of the senseless *(sinnlos)*. Logical propositions are 'senseless' (4.461 *c*), but they are not 'nonsensical' (4.4611), involve no violation of the rules of logical syntax.

Husserl *(Untersuchungen,* vol. II, p. 326) makes a distinction between *Unsinn* and *Widersinn* (or, as we might say, the 'contrasensical'). An example of the former would be 'A man and is', of the latter, 'A round square'. The cases of 'nonsense' that concern W. are like the second example, in which no rules of school grammar are broken, but the destruction of sense arises from violation of the 'deeper' rules of logical syntax.

'The question whether philosophers have always so far spoken nonsense might be answered: No, but they have not noticed that they use a word in quite different meanings. In this sense it is not unconditionally nonsense to say that one thing is as identical as another, for somebody who has this conviction means something by the word "identical" at the moment (perhaps "large"). But he does not know that he is here using the word in a meaning other than that in which it is used in $2+2 = 4$' (*Phil. Bem.* 3, 8).

'He said that for any sign whatever there *could* be a method of projection such that it made sense, but that when he said of any particular expression "That means nothing" or "is nonsense", what he meant was "*With the common method of projection* that means nothing", giving as an instance that when he called the sentence "It is due to human weakness that we can't write down all the cardinal numbers" "meaningless", he meant that it is meaningless if the person who says it is using "due to human weakness" as in "It's due to human weakness that we can't write down a billion cardinal numbers"' (Moore, *Papers*, p. 265).

'[He] implied that where we say "This makes no sense" we always mean "This makes nonsense *in this particular game*"; and in answer to the question "Why do we call it 'nonsense'? what does it mean to call it so?" said that when we call a sentence "nonsense", it is "because of some similarity to sentences which have sense", and that "nonsense always arises from forming symbols analogous to certain uses, where they have no use"' (Moore, *op. cit.* pp. 273–4).

4.0031*a*   a critique: delete the indefinite article.

critique of language: the expression *Sprachkritik* was much used by Mauthner, for whom see Weiler, 'Mauthner', pp. 80–7. Commenting on 4.0031, Weiler says: 'The idea, that there is a true logical form (e.g. the one represented in the symbolism of *Principia*) is just the one M. [Mauthner] rejected. The idea of a "perfect" language seemed ridiculous to M. *a fortiori* if it was supposed to picture reality' (*op. cit.* p. 83).

b   The reference is no doubt to Russell's theory of descriptions.

XXV

PROPOSITIONS AS PICTURES

(4.01–4.021)

With this instalment and the two that follow, Wittgenstein resumes and concludes his account (suspended at XI above) of propositions as logical pictures. A proposition is a *logical* picture, which portrays reality as we *think* it to be (*wie wir sie uns denken*—4.01*b*). So the stress, as in previous instalments, is upon the *invisible* logical form (the rules of use, we might say): it is there we must look for the essence of the picture and not in any physical resemblance between picture and what is pictured. Some symbols may strike us as obvious likenesses of what they mean (4.012*b*), but the essence of pictoriality is un-impaired by apparent physical irregularities of notation (4.013): the essence is revealed in the *general rule* for the mutual transformation of equivalent notations (4.0141, cf. XXII). A new point, further elabor-ated in XXVII, is our power to understand propositions without prior explanation of their senses (4.02).

Our capacity to understand sentences that have never been uttered before (say 'It would have taken a brave man to publish this *Companion* in Wittgenstein's own lifetime') has often puzzled those who have reflected on the nature of language. This mysterious capacity neatly illustrates Wittgenstein's basic principle that a pro-position's sense is a unique function of the meanings of its con-stituents (cf. XVIII): to know what words mean *is* to know how to combine them, in *any possible* way, to produce sense (cf. 4.024*c*). The possibility, always open, of genuinely novel utterances shows once again how propositions differ essentially from names; names must be explained to us (4.026*a*), but propositions are as it were self-explanatory (once we understand their constituents)—we *use* them to communicate (4.026*b*, 4.027).

4.01 (1) At 2.12, the proposition was said to be a 'model' of reality. Thus, here and in the next sentence, 'model' = 'picture'.

(2) as we imagine it: rather, 'as we think it is'. These words should be stressed. Cf. 3 on a picture as a *thought*.

'Wittgenstein says that sentences picture facts. But hardly any, if any, sentences in ordinary language do picture facts. Wittgenstein does not want to assert that they do. He is trying to point out an ideal to which some sentences try to attain. He should, I think, have drawn our attention to the fact that some sentences do not try to attain to this ideal' (Wisdom, 'Constructions', p. 202).

'In connection with the *Tractatus* statement that propositions ... are "pictures", he said that he had not at that time noticed that the word "picture" was vague; but he still . . . thought it "useful to say 'A proposition is a picture *or something like one*'" although . . . he was willing to admit that to call a proposition a "picture" was misleading; that propositions are not pictures "in any ordinary sense"; and that to say that they are, "merely stresses a certain aspect of the grammar of the word 'proposition'—merely stresses that our uses of the words 'proposition' and 'picture' follow similar rules'" (Moore, *Papers*, p. 263).

4.011 (1) *a* **with which it is concerned**: or, 'of which it treats', 'which it is about'.

(2) pictures, even in the ordinary sense: this important remark can hardly be defended. It is a metaphor to speak of a musical score as a picture of the music. In this passage, W. seems to be aware that he has stretched the ordinary meaning of 'picture'.

4.012 *aRb*: cf. 3.1432 for the proper interpretation of this expression.

4.013 (1) pictorial character: or, 'pictoriality' (*Bildhaftigkeit*).

4.014 (1) It is important that the picturing relation is taken to be *internal* (because it depends upon identity of logical structure). Notice that the gramophone record, etc., are here treated as *facts*.

(2) logical plan: or, 'logical structure' (*logische Bau*): the only occurrence of this expression. For what is intended, see 3.344. In view of W.'s contrast between 'form' and 'structure', 'logical form' would be more appropriate here.

'Even the best sentences are identical in form with a fact in only a rather unexciting way—not like a map and a country. A sentence is identical with a fact if and only if they contain the same number of elements' (Wisdom, 'Construction', p. 205).

4.0141 Important, as showing that identity of structure is a matter of the possibility of mutual translation. Cf. 3.344, 6.24*b* (the use of equations to express rules of translation).

c **law of projection**: cf. 3.11 for the notion of 'projection'.

4.015 imagery: or, 'pictoriality' (*Bildhaftigkeit*)—cf. the use of this word at 4.013*a*.

is contained in: literally, 'rests upon' (*ruht in*).

4.016 'Let us think of hieroglyphic writing in which each word is a representation of what it stands for [or: presents its meaning (*seine*

Commentary

Bedeutung darstellt)]. Let us think also of the fact that *actual* [or, *real* (*wirkliche*)] pictures of situations [[(*Sachverhalten*)]] can be *right* and *wrong*' (*Notebooks*, 7 (5)).

4.02 Cf. 4.024*c* (to understand a proposition, it suffices to understand its constituents).

this: may refer to what was said in 4.016*b*, but can also be taken as a link with 4.01 (Stenius, *Exposition*, p. 11). What is 'essential' to the use of a proposition is that once the references of its constituents are known, their combination necessarily expresses a sense, without further stipulations; our capacity to understand complicated propositions on first acquaintance dramatically illustrates this. This, again, is why *we* can make a 'model' (4.01*b*) before we know whether anything answers to it in reality.

the fact: not in the original.

4.021*b* Cf. 4.026*a* (the meanings of *words* must be explained).

XXVI

PROPOSITIONS AS SHOWING AND SAYING

(4.022–4.023)

This instalment is notable for its introduction of the crucial notion of *showing*, which will become increasingly important as Wittgenstein's exposition continues (cf. the discussion of this notion in the notes on 4.1211 below). It is a distinctive feature of his conception of language to insist upon two radically different modes of signification, 'showing' and 'saying': to signify, to have meaning, is either to *show* something or to *say* something, but what can be shown cannot be said (4.1212). Only a proposition can *say* anything: what is liable to puzzle a reader (as it has already perplexed previous commentators) is that a proposition also *shows* something, its sense (4.022*a*). The point has already been made, in other words, at 2.221, where Wittgenstein has said that a picture (including a logical picture, a proposition, we are entitled to add) presents (*darstellt*) its sense. We might reasonably infer from 4.022*a* that *darstellt* (presents) is a synonym for *zeigt* (shows). But the sense agrees or disagrees with reality (2.222), and so what is presented or shown already has a truth-value (2.222): what function is left over for *saying*? One might be inclined to equate 'saying' with 'affirming' or 'asserting'—but for remarks such as 4.064*ab* and the like which tell conclusively against this view. The answer is to be found at 4.461*a* (a proposition shows what it says) which I take to imply that the 'saying' is *part* of—or rather, an aspect of—the sense, not something superadded to it.

Section 4.023 is no less troublesome (reference to the *Notebooks* shows Wittgenstein often reverting to the ideas expressed in it), if only because Wittgenstein here speaks of a proposition describing an atomic fact where previously he spoke of its presenting or being a picture of one. So the question arises whether Wittgenstein meant 'description' here emphatically, in Russell's sense (cf. article on the description of facts below), or was using the word loosely.

Wittgenstein's striking reference to the 'logical scaffolding' that goes with a proposition underlines a point by now familiar, that every proposition is located in logical space.

4.022 (1)   Echoed at 4.461*a*. Cf. also 2.202 + 2.221 (a picture presents a sense = a possible state of affairs).

(2)   Cf. 4.064*a* (assertion cannot supply a sense).

Anscombe (*Introduction*, p. 65) says that this is just the difference between a proposition and a picture.

'The proposition takes one of the possibilities admitted by the language and says "reality is like this pictured possibility"' (Watson, *Physics*, p. 30).

Stenius says, 'This [i.e. 4.022] is true of semantical elementary sentences [positive sentences depicting *Sachverhalte*]. Of *negated* semantical elementary sentences we ought rather to say: The sentence *shows* how things stand, *if* it is false. And it says that they do *not* so stand' (*Exposition*, p. 148). For further remarks on this section, see Stenius, *op. cit.* p. 166.

Wisdom calls 4.022 (2) a mistake ('Constructions', p. 209, f.n. 1).

4.023 (1)   Cf. Rhees, 'Anscombe', p. 31. Literally: 'Reality must be fixed (determined) by a proposition—except for a yes or no.'

Commentary

'The reference [*Bedeutung*] of a proposition must be fixed, as confirming or contradicting it, through it *together with its mode of presentation (Darstellungsweise)*' (*Notebooks*, 22 (1)).

● 'A given proposition must either precisely agree with reality (the actual states-of-affairs) or precisely *dis*agree with reality—it is a matter of all or nothing ("yes" or "no").'

(2) **describe reality completely**: i.e. precisely or exactly describe.

(3) **state of affairs**: here one would expect *Sachlage* rather than *Sachverhalt* to occur. Cf. 3.144 *a*, where *Sachlagen* are said to be described.

In the *Notebooks*, the entry which became 4.023 (3) is preceded by the remarks: 'The proposition is correlated (*zugeordnet*) with a hypothetical situation (*hypothetischen Sachverhalt*). This situation is given by means of its description' (38 (5, 6)).

(4) **by giving**: or, 'according to' (*nach*).

a proposition describes reality by its internal properties: in view of the immediately preceding remark, 'reality' should here be taken to mean the same as a 'fact' (i.e. a portion of 'reality'). Suppose the proposition in question consists of the concatenation of two names, *a* and *b*, standing respectively for the things, *A* and *B*. The idea is that just as 'the King of France' describes a person who may or may not exist, so the proposition '*ab*' describes a fact that may or may not be the case. (But notice the awkwardness of speaking of 'a fact that may not be the case'.) If some person is the King of France, the definite description describes an 'external' property of that person—one that *he* might not have had, while still remaining the same person. But a fact consisting of the concatenation of *A* and *B* could not have been *that* fact if it were composed of other constituents. Thus the proposition *ab* describes an 'internal' property of the fact.

The idea that a proposition is a definite description (in Russell's sense) of a fact will hardly do—if only because a definite description is supposed to have 'no meaning in isolation' while a proposition can stand alone and is therefore not an 'incomplete symbol'. Here, as elsewhere in the book, W. was probably using 'description' quite loosely (cf. the article below on whether facts can be described).

(5) *a* **scaffolding**: cf. 3.42 (3), 6.124 *a*, for other occurrences of this word.

b At the corresponding place in the *Notebooks* (16 (3)), W. adds as an example: 'Thus I can see that if "$(x, \phi) . \phi (x)$" were true, this proposition would contradict a proposition, "$\sim \Psi (a)$" [negation-sign inserted].'

Propositions as Showing and Saying

CAN FACTS BE DESCRIBED?

Since Wittgenstein accepted Russell's theory of descriptions, it is worth considering whether that theory could accommodate descriptions of facts. Various philosophers have supposed this to be possible: Moore, for instance, once said, 'I should say that phrases of the form "the fact that aRb" *are* descriptions' ('Facts', p. 198).

I shall discuss the following questions: (*a*) Can a 'that'-clause, such as 'that the sun is larger than the earth', be treated as a definite description in Russell's sense? (*b*) If the answer to the previous question is in the affirmative, is it proper to say that a 'that'-clause is a definite description, in Russell's sense, of a fact?

Let us call the expression 'that the sun is larger than the earth' C. In order to find an analogous expression that is undoubtedly a definite description in Russell's sense, we ought to choose some such example as 'Alexander mounted on Bucephalus' (D, say), rather than one like 'The present Queen of England'. For if we regard Alexander-mounted-on-Bucephalus as a complex object, we shall have to say that it is essential to that object that it answers to D, since anything that failed to answer to that description would be a different object. But although Elizabeth II is the present Queen of England, we should not say she would necessarily have been a different person had she not been the Queen. D might be said to describe the object answering to it 'according to one of its internal properties' (to echo Wittgenstein at 4.023 (4)), namely, the internal property of being composed of Alexander and Bucephalus in a certain relationship. Now if C is to count as a definite description to which something answers, we shall need to say that the description is based upon an internal property of that thing, namely, the property of being composed of the sun and earth in a certain relationship.

So far as I can see, D might properly count as a definite description in Russell's sense. If we write a for 'Alexander', b for 'Bucephalus', m for 'mounted on', and use K to stand for a certain relation of composition, so that $K(x, y, z, w)$ means that x is composed of y and

z (in that order), related by w, we can analyse any assertion about Alexander-mounted-on-Bucephalus, e.g. that it was a beautiful sight, as follows:

(1) $(\exists x) (K(x, a, b, m) . B(x) . K(y, a, b, m) \supset_y y = x)$, where $B(x)$ means 'x was a beautiful sight'. (Or in words: 'There is precisely one beautiful sight composed of Alexander, Bucephalus, and *mounted on*'.)

An analogous analysis of such a statement as 'that the sun is larger than the earth has been established' might run:

(2) $(\exists x) (K'(x, s, e, l) . E(x) . K'(y, s, e, l) \supset_y y = x)$. Here s is an abbreviation for 'the sun', e for 'the earth', l for 'larger than', $E(x)$ for 'x has been established' and K' for some supposed relation of composition such that $K'(x, y, z, w)$ holds when and only when x answers to the 'that'-clause, $\ulcorner$that y has w to $z\urcorner$. (In words: 'Precisely one thing obtains that is composed of the sun, the earth, and *larger than*'.)

Any attempt to maintain an affirmative answer to my first question must be committed to asserting the intelligibility of an expression such as (2). There is, however, a serious difficulty in making sense of such an expression as

(3) $(\exists x) (K'(x, s, e, l))$, or, 'At least one thing is composed of the sun, the earth, and *larger than*'. Consider the parallel expression,

(4) $(\exists x) (K(x, a, b, m))$, which might be rendered in words as: 'There exists at least one thing composed of Alexander, Bucephalus, and *mounted on*.' We find little or no trouble in thinking of Alexander-mounted-on-Bucephalus as a compound material thing that might be pointed out or named. For we have plausible uses for '*That* is Alexander-mounted-on-Bucephalus' and even 'Alephalus is Alexander-mounted-on-Bucephalus' (where 'Alephalus' is a name introduced to stand for the complex object in question). That is to say, we think we know how to verify statements of the form '$K(c, a, b, m)$' where c is a constant, and therefore can admit, at least provisionally, a sense for the corresponding quantified formula (4). If parallel considerations were held to apply to (3), we should have to allow as sensible the following forms:

(5) *That* is composed of the sun, the earth, and *larger than*.

(6) That is that-the-sun-is-larger-than-the-earth.

(7) Solerth is that-the-sun-is-larger-than-the-earth (where 'Solerth' is supposedly a name introduced to stand for whatever answers to the 'that'-clause in question). I find each of these sentences, as they stand, unintelligible.

A defender of the view that C ('that the sun is larger than the earth') is a definite description might argue as follows:

'That the sun is larger than the earth is a fact. *That fact* is composed of the sun, the earth, and *larger than*. In other words, that fact is (the fact) that-the-sun-is-larger-than-the-earth. Since there is such a fact, we can name it, e.g. by calling it "Solerth". Then it will be correct to say "Solerth is the fact that-the-sun-is-larger-than-the-earth".'

In some such way as this, I imagine, a case might be made for treating as sensible an expression of the form $K'(c, s, e, l)$, where c is a constant, and hence for treating (3) and also (2) as sensible.

Of course, Wittgenstein, denying as he does that facts can be named (3.144a), could not accept this defence. Nevertheless, I will now assume, for the sake of argument, that the defence is acceptable, and that C might be taken to be a definite description in Russell's sense. So I proceed to the second question: Of what kind of thing will C then be a description?

If we ask the corresponding question of 'The present Queen of England' or 'The present Queen of France', the correct answer will obviously be 'a person'. (Of course to say '"The present Queen of France" is a description of a person' is not to say that there is some person answering to the description in question but rather to say that anything that answers to the description *would have to be* a person: we so understand the description that *only* a person could answer to it.) Again, if we feel no qualms about calling Alexander-mounted-on Bucephalus a material thing, we may say that D is a description of a material thing (whether or not some material thing answers to D).

If, finally, we ask what kind of thing C describes (on the supposition that C is a description), the only plausible answer would seem to be 'a fact'. For when 'something answers' to a 'that'-clause, we say,

'That is a fact', and when nothing answers, we say, 'That is not a fact'. Once again, in saying e.g. 'that the sun is larger than the earth' describes a fact, we are not saying that there *is* a fact which that clause describes, but merely that the only kind of thing that could answer to it would have to be a fact.

A difficulty I find in accepting this answer is that of understanding how the expression 'a fact' is supposed to function in the answer. Consider:

(8) That the sun is larger than the earth is a fact. I take this to mean (ōn the view here under examination) that something 'answers' to *C*. That is to say, I take (8) to be synonymous with:

(9) That-the-sun-is-larger-than-the-earth exists. I cannot see that (8) adds anything to (9) or *vice versa*. But if so, the statement '*C* describes a fact' would be analogous to:

(10) 'The present Queen of France' describes an existent, which is exponible as: 'Anything which answered to "The present Queen of France" would have to exist', which is a trivial tautology. The statement, '*E* describes a *person*', may be informative, since a person *is* a kind of thing: but 'an existent' is not a *kind* of thing—nor, so far as I can see, can a fact be a kind of thing.

The point may be made as follows: It is not absurd to say 'The poet Ossian never existed', for in using the general term 'poet' we leave it open for investigation whether anything to which the word is applied has the property connoted by that word. But there is a manifest absurdity in saying 'The fact that Ossian composed the Iliad does not exist' or, more plausibly, 'is not the case' or 'is not a fact'. This is like saying 'The actually existing poet Ossian never existed'. Or like saying: 'There are facts that *are* facts—and facts that are not.' In saying that something is a fact we are saying that something exists (to use the language of the view I have been examining) and nothing more.

No matter how much leeway we allow advocates of the view that facts can be described (in Russell's sense of description) it seems impossible to elaborate that view consistently. If we are to accept Wittgenstein's view that facts can be described (4.023*c*), we must divorce that view from Russell's theory of descriptions. Wittgenstein's use of 'description' at 4.023*c* must be taken as shorthand for the full view of the relation between a proposition and its sense which he has explained previously (names as proxies for objects, with identity of logical form between the proposition and what it depicts).

XXVII

THE SENSE OF A PROPOSITION AS A RESULTANT OF THE MEANINGS OF ITS CONSTITUENTS

(4.024–4.0312(1))

We have already seen what a central position the principle of sense as a function of reference occupies in Wittgenstein's exploration of the essence of language. The essence of a proposition *is* to be an 'articulated' configuration of constituents, each of which deputizes for an object. Once we see this, we can easily grasp why only constituents need to be translated in passing from one language to another (4.025*a*) or why a proposition can convey a new sense with old words (4.03*a*). The main themes of Wittgenstein's analysis of propositions are vividly recapitulated in this instalment.

4.024 (1) Knowledge of the sense of a proposition is here identified with knowledge of the proposition's truth-conditions. This is the nearest that W. comes to a 'principle of verifiability' in the book. There is evidence (e.g. in *Phil. Bem.* and in the quotation from Moore below) that W. did come to attach some importance for a time to the principle of verifiability. But the specific forms of the principle advocated by Schlick and other members of the Vienna Circle do not follow from W.'s basic insights.

'Near the beginning . . . he made the famous statement, "The sense of a proposition is the way in which it is verified"; but [later] he said this only meant "You can determine the meaning of a proposition by asking how it is verified" and went on to say, "This is necessarily a mere rule of thumb, because 'verification' means different things, and because in some cases the question 'How is it verified?' makes no sense"' (Moore, *Papers*, p. 266).

'Where one can ask, one can also seek, and where one cannot seek, one cannot ask, and cannot answer either' (*Math. MS.* 638).

(3) Important. Cf. 4.02, for the same idea.

constituents: same as 'expressions', for which see 3.31*a*.

4.025

● 'The grammatical differences between adjectives, adverbs, and other parts of speech correspond to nothing fundamental in the logic of our language. At the superficial level at which ordinary grammar operates, all parts of speech, conjunctions not excluded, must be treated as constituents of statements.'

4.026 (1) Can be read as following 4.025*a*: in translating the constituents of statements, the meanings of the simple signs must be explained.

● 'The meanings of words have to be explained *for* us, have to be shown, but once this has been done, *we* use propositions to make ourselves understood, to communicate thoughts.'

For the explanations of names by means of 'elucidations', see 3.263.

4.027 May be read as following on 4.025*a*. Cf. 4.002*a* (every sense can be expressed in language) and 4.03*a*.

Since the proposition's sense is internal to it (and so belongs to its essence), we can produce propositional signs composed of 'old' words in a new structure. Thus arranged, the words can embody a new sense, e.g. by depicting a situation we may never have encountered.

4.03 (2) Because *we* do not make the connexion: it is no accident.

(3) **logical picture**: cf. 2.181 (condition for a picture to be a logical picture).

(4) Cf. the following passages:

'It all depends on settling what distinguishes the proposition from a mere picture' (*Notebooks*, 34 (9)).

'Can one negate a *picture*? No. And in this lies the difference between picture and proposition. The picture can serve as a proposition. But in that case something gets added to it which brings it about that now it *says* something. In short: I can only deny that the picture is right, but the *picture* I cannot deny' (*Notebooks*, 33 (11)).

4.031 (1) **situation**: or, 'state of affairs' (*Sachlage*): may be read here as '*possible* state of affairs'.

'In the proposition a world is as it were put together experimentally (*probeweise*). (As when in the law-court in Paris a motor-car accident is represented by means of dolls, etc.)' (*Notebooks*, 7 (3)).

(**2**)   **represents**: or, 'presents' (*darstellt*). In the *Notebooks* W. adds: 'It [the proposition] portrays it logically (*Er bildet ihn logisch ab*)' (8 (5)).

4.0311*b*   **tableau vivant**: 'silent & motionless group of persons &c. arranged to represent a scene' *O.E.D.* Literally, 'living picture' (*lebendes Bild*). Cf. the colloquial expression, 'living image'. The *O.E.D.* equates this usage with 'lively', 'vivid', 'brilliant'.

4.0312 (1)   **representatives**: or, 'surrogates'.
    In the *Notebooks* W. adds the remarks: 'Thus in the proposition something has *something else* as its proxy. But there is also the *common* cement [literally, the common bond (*gemeinsame Bindemittel*)]' (37 (9, 10)).

XXVIII

'LOGICAL CONSTANTS' DO NOT STAND FOR OBJECTS

(4.0312 (2))

The logical connectives, 'and', 'if...then', 'every', etc. (or their symbolic substitutes, ' . ', '⊃', '(*x*)', etc.), are not *names*, do not stand for, do not represent, objects. (It follows that the logical propositions, in which only 'logical constants' occur essentially—'tautologies' in Wittgenstein's terminology—must have a connexion with reality that is altogether different from that of empirical propositions. Wittgenstein will claim that they show, but do not *say*.) This idea is at the heart of Wittgenstein's philosophy of logic and will reappear in many forms (e.g. at 4.041, 4.12, 4.441*b*, 4.462*a*, 5.4). Wittgenstein calls it his 'basic idea' (*Grundgedanke*), an expression that occurs nowhere else in the text. In the *Notebooks* the word '*Grundgedanke*' occurs more frequently, to stand for a flash of insight that illuminates a tangle of philosophical problems. Here, the *Grundgedanke* is merely announced. Later, Wittgenstein will argue for it on the basis of the interdefinability of the logical connectives (which proves that they

173

cannot be names in his sense). But the deeper ground is the impossibility of depicting the form of representation, already discussed at VIII.

4.0312 (2) A remark of crucial importance. It is odd to find this 'fundamental thought' appearing without preparation in such a subordinate position in the text. Cf. 2.172, 4.041, 4.12, 4.441 *b*, 4.462 *a*, 5.4, for similar or related remarks. Compare also the similar statement at 5.44(3). The view W. is attacking is expressed in an extreme form in the following passage:

'The discussion of indefinables—which forms the chief part of philosophical logic—is the endeavour to see clearly, and to make others see clearly, the entities concerned, in order that the mind may have that kind of acquaintance with them which it has with redness or the taste of pineapple' (Russell, *Principles*, preface, p. v). W. is denying that there are any such 'entities'. For a thoroughly realistic view of logical constants, see J. A. Chadwick's paper, 'Logical constants'.

XXIX

MULTIPLICITY OF A PROPOSITION
(4.032–4.0412)

A proposition is a fact having a definite structure (XIII above), it is 'articulated' (4.032). A proposition and the state of affairs it depicts have the same logical form (2.18, etc.). Wittgenstein now rephrases this basic point in terms of what he calls 'multiplicity'. A proposition and its sense have the 'same logical multiplicity'—there must be 'just as much distinguishable in the one as in the other' (4.04). Upon reflection, this proves to be just another way of repeating that the specific logical form of a proposition is identical with the specific logical form of the fact it purports to represent. Thus, the idea of the multiplicity of a proposition is closely connected with that of the essence of the proposition (cf. XXII). The impossibility of depicting 'multiplicity' (4.041) is an aspect of the impossibility of depicting 'form of representation' (already discussed in VIII above). Section 4.0411 is an interesting attempt to reveal the essential features of a given notation (the notation for generality).

This instalment substantially completes Wittgenstein's discussion of the essence of symbolism. From now on, he will be increasingly occupied with logical form and its expression (XXII–XXVII, and subsequently). Another central topic will be that of the relations between complex propositions and elementary propositions. This takes the form, in Wittgenstein's exposition, of an analysis of what is involved in truth-functional composition (XL–XLIV).

4.032 (1)   segmented: or, 'articulated' (O.). Is divided into distinct parts in mutual relation, like the jointed segments of a limb. Cf. 3.141 *b* and 3.251, in each of which 'articulated' (*artikuliert*) occurs.

'"Complex sign" and "proposition" are *equivalent* [or, *synonymous* (*gleichbedeutend*)]' (*Notebooks*, 52 (3)).

'He said ... that he had made a mistake (I think he meant in the *Tractatus*) in supposing that a proposition must be complex. He said the truth was that we can replace a proposition by a simple sign, but that the simple sign must be "part of a system"' (Moore, *Papers*, p. 261).

(2)   composite: cf. the use of this word at 5.5261 *a*.

4.04   Cf. notes on 2.161 above.

(2)   dynamical models: 'A material system is said to be a dynamical model of a second system when the connections of the first can be expressed by such co-ordinates as to satisfy the following conditions: (1) That the number of co-ordinates of the first system is equal to the number of the second. (2) That with a suitable arrangement of the co-ordinates for both systems the same equations of condition exist. (3) That by this arrangement of the co-ordinates the expression for the magnitude of a displacement agrees in both systems' (Hertz, *Principles*, § 418).

W. may have had 4.04*b* in mind when (in *Investigations*, § 23, p. 12) he contrasted 'the multiplicity of the tools in language ... the multiplicity of kinds of word and sentence' with 'what logicians have said about the structure of language. (Including the author of the *Tractatus Logico-Philosophicus*)'.

multiplicity: suppose we have two facts, F_1 and F_2, that are concatenations of the sets of objects $(a_1, a_2, ..., a_n)$ and $(b_1, b_2, ..., b_n)$, respectively. F_1 and F_2 may be said to 'have the same logical multiplicity' when the following conditions are satisfied: (i) there are exactly as many a's as b's, (ii) there is a one–one correlation between the a's and the b's $(a_i \leftrightarrow b_i)$ such that the correlated objects are in the same logical category (replacement of a name of a_i by a name of b_i, and *vice versa*, never converts sense into nonsense).

A mathematician might say that F_1 and F_2 are 'isomorphic'. The notion of 'same multiplicity' seems identical with W.'s notion of same (specific) logical form.

The following examples of the use of the idea of 'multiplicity' occur in W.'s later writings: (1) He imagines a calculating machine that replaces the beads on an abacus (or the fingers on a hand) by colour bands. We would then need some colour sign for 0, 'otherwise I would not have the necessary multiplicity'. (This could be done for instance by using black to stand for 0.) 'Here we see how the multiplicity of beads [on an abacus] is projected into the multiplicity of colours on a surface' (*Maths. MS.* 576). (2) In establishing arithmetical equalities by regrouping strokes on paper, the construction used 'has exactly the same multiplicity of every other proof of the theorem' (*op. cit.* 592). (3) If somebody were to object that p/p did not say the same as not-p, the answer would be that the stroke system has the necessary multiplicity. 'So Sheffer found a symbolic system having the necessary multiplicity' (*op. cit.* 618). (4) In order to see how misleading the verbal expression of mathematical proof is, we must pay attention to the 'multiplicity' of the mathematical proof (*op. cit.* 635).

4.041   Cf. 4.0312 b.

a **be the subject of depiction**: literally, 'be pictured' (or 'represented'). Notice that the 'multiplicity' *can* be shown, though not 'depicted' or represented.

4.0411 (1) *a* **for example**: this section is a comment on 4.04, rather than on 4.041, as its number suggests. W. is illustrating, in a specially important case, how the 'multiplicity' of the sense is needed.

   index: cf. notes on 5.02 and introduction to instalment XLV for the meaning of this word.

b **signalize**: or, 'indicate' (*anzeigen*), 'mark'.

   scope: suppose we tried replacing the quantifier in '$(x)(hx \supset p)$' by some device, such as that suggested by W., for showing that the variable is bound: $h(x_g) \supset p$, for instance, would fail to show that p was intended to be governed by the quantifier.

(2)   Here again W. is testing a device for showing a variable as bound. The original formula was probably $(x, y) F(x, y)$. The idea is to replace the variable by the special sign G (for 'generality'). This yields W.'s

$(G, G) F(G, G)$ (though, strictly speaking, the initial symbol (G, G) would now be superfluous). The objection is that the proposed notation would obliterate distinctions between variables: $F(G, G)$ would result from $(x) F(x, x)$ as well as from the formula cited at the beginning of this note. Cf. also 5.5261 *b*. Cf. also Anscombe, *Introduction*, pp. 139–40, for a paraphrase of W.'s point.

(3) In the corresponding passage of the *Notebooks* (18 (7)), W. has 'logical properties' in place of 'mathematical multiplicity' and adds that all of the proposed sign-combinations lack the power to portray (*abzubilden*) the requisite sense.

4.0412 'The categories of Kant are the coloured spectacles of the mind; truths *a priori* are the false appearances produced by these spectacles' (Russell, 'Philosophical Importance', p. 491). W. may have intended a reference to Meinong or Husserl.

● 'Blue spectacles might lead us to see everything blue. But we cannot imagine "spectacles" that would impose spatial relations where none had previously been perceived. No ubiquitous distortion of visual experience can explain the logical properties of visual space.'

XXX

TRUTH-VALUE AND SENSE; NEGATION

(4.05–4.0641)

In this difficult, but important, instalment Wittgenstein begins to wrestle with what in the *Notebooks* he called 'the mystery of negation'. He is here engaged in the first part of the ambitious task of showing how all complex propositions (truth-functional propositions, general propositions, etc.) are related to the 'world' *via* elementary propositions. His chief concern is to refute the idea that affirmation and negation (expressible as 'is true' or 'is false') are co-ordinate relations between propositions and the world (4.061 *a*). Truth and falsity are not different and parallel modes of signification (as say the modes of signification of 'Mr' and 'Mrs' might be regarded);

negation is a way of altering the 'direction' as it were of the positive proposition (4.0621 (3)) *without introducing new objects*; affirmation or negation is an aspect *of* the sense of a proposition (determining which facts shall count for and which against its truth), not something superadded to the sense (4.064). Wittgenstein's argument at 4.0621*a* confirms his 'fundamental thought' (4.0312*b*) that logical constants do not stand for objects.

4.05 Like 2.223, except that there the proposition is compared with reality.

'A picture cannot be compared with reality, unless it can be placed against it *(anlegen)* like a ruler' *(Phil. Bem.* 16, 9).

4.06 Can be read in conjunction with 2.21.

● 'Propositions are true or false because they are pictures, and therefore because they have sense. Not *vice versa*—they do not have sense because they have truth-values.'

Cf.: 'To have meaning *means* to be true or false: the being true or false actually constitutes the relation of the proposition to reality, which we mean by saying that it has meaning *(Sinn)*' *(Moore Notes,* 112 (1)).

4.061 (1) sense that is independent of the facts: for propositions have sense by presenting *possibilities* (cf. 2.201, 2.203, and 4.063 (2)). A point of basic importance in W.'s philosophy of language.

of equal status: in the corresponding passage of *Notes on Logic* (95 (1)), W. uses the expression, 'equally justified relations'.

One might be tempted to think of a true proposition, and the corresponding false proposition, its negation, as having equally good claims to be considered as directly linked with reality. If the true proposition were like an ordinary mirror reflection of a scene, and its negation like an inverted reflection of the same scene, the link between the false proposition and the real scene would be just as primary and direct as that between the true proposition and the scene. If my book is on the table (fact *F*, say), one might be inclined to say that the proposition, 'My book is on the table' (*p*) signifies *F* 'in the true way', while 'My book is not on the table' (∼ *p*) signifies *F* 'in the false way'. W.'s conclusive reason for rejecting this conception is that it would make the sense of every proposition depend upon a question of fact. We would not know *how* a given proposition was to be understood until we had established its truth-value, and a proposition of unknown truth-value would be hopelessly ambiguous. The absurdity is obvious: we have to know the sense of a proposition *before* we set out to verify it; the way a proposition signifies is independent of its truth-value. It should be noted, however, that Wittgenstein's objections do not apply to the view, not to be confused with the one he has refuted, that a positive (not: true) proposition and the corresponding *negative* (not: false) proposition signify 'in different ways'. For here the imputed difference in mode of signification might be expressed in the proposition itself by the absence or presence of a negative sign.

4.062   In this section, W. is elaborating the consequences of considering true and false propositions as signifying in different but co-ordinate modes (the view rejected in the previous section).

● 'It might appear that we could invariably use false propositions, with a prior understanding that they always "signify in the false way" (so that we say the opposite of what we mean, as it were). But if, with this understanding, we say "The book is on the table" (p), meaning that the book is not on the table, and if the book is in fact not on the table, what we mean is true. Thus, on the plan proposed, the words "The book is on the table" mean what is normally meant by the words "The book is not on the table". The connexion between p and the world is still the normal one; the accord between p and the facts still consists in p being *true*.'

4.062 is discussed by Stenius (*Exposition*, pp. 173–4).

c   **we use it to say**: rather, 'we say'.

4.0621 (1)   The reference here to the importance of the *possibility* that p and $\sim p$ might mean the same should be compared with W.'s dictum at 3.3421 on the general importance of the possibility of a given mode of signification.

the signs p and $\sim p$ *can* say the same thing: W. cannot mean here by 'the sign $\sim p$' merely a propositional sign p to which a curl has been attached without any prior understanding about its meaning. If the curl in $\sim p$ were taken to be a mere curlicue, obeying no syntactical or semantical rules, it would be a trivial observation that p and $\sim p$ can say the same thing, no more interesting than the remark that an underlined propositional sign can have the same sense as the original sign. No doubt, W.'s thought was that the role of the negation sign in our present language might be reversed, so that its presence would mean affirmation and its absence negation. This more interesting interpretation of his remark presupposes that the curl is a sign of *negation* and is therefore governed by such rules as those of the cancelling of double negation that partially determine its meaning.

Commentary

To test this idea, let us suppose that we find some documents containing (i) positive propositions expressed in English words, obeying the customary grammatical rules of English, (ii) a special angle sign '$\urcorner$' attached to propositions, somewhat as we attach 'not' to our own propositional signs. Let us call a language in which we use English in the customary way to represent positive propositions and also use the curl sign '$\sim$' (but no verbal equivalent) to express negation, the language E. Let us also call the hypothetical language, containing the angle sign '$\urcorner$', E'.

W.'s thought now seems to be that we might discover the following semantical correlations:

p (in E') is true when and only when $\sim p$ (in E) is true.

$\urcorner p$ (in E') is true when and only when p (in E) is true. If this were so, we might certainly be inclined to say that the role of '$\urcorner$' in E' is exactly the reverse of the role of '$\sim$' in E. Just as the presence of '$\sim$' in E means negation, so the absence of '$\urcorner$' in E' means negation—and correspondingly for affirmation.

But let us pursue the matter further. It is a characteristic of the use of '$\sim$' in E that $\sim \sim p$ has the same truth-conditions as p (cf. 4.0621 b) while '$\sim p$' does not. But, according to the second of our semantical correlations between E' and E, $\urcorner p$ in E' has the same truth-value as p in E and $\urcorner \urcorner p$ therefore has the same truth-value as $\urcorner (p)$, i.e. the same truth-value as p again. In other words, repeated applications of the angle sign '$\urcorner$' in E' reduce to a single application of it. On the other hand, nothing answers in E' to the repeated applications of the curl, '$\sim$', with alternate changes of truth-value in E. Since the correlate in E' of $\sim p$ in E is simply p, in which there is no operator sign present, it is impossible to show in E' anything answering to the repeated application of the curl sign in E, and there is no correlate in E' for the distinction in sense between $\sim \sim p$ and $\sim p$.

All this being so, we would have no right to say that the angle sign in E' constituted a negation sign used in reverse. The proper verdict would be that its use in E' constituted a special device for negating or affirming a *single* proposition, with no provision for the possibilities of repeated application that define the formal properties of the curl operator in E, or of the verbal negative 'not' in ordinary English. Exactly similar conclusions would apply if we tried replacing the curl by some such device as writing the propositional sign upside down. Here, too, there would be no way of indicating the formal properties of the curl.

My conclusion is that there is an important sense in which W. was wrong in saying that p and $\sim p$ 'can say the same thing' (though also a trivial sense in which he was right). Given our present meaning for '$\sim$', we cannot 'reverse its role', in the manner supposed.

180

nothing in reality corresponds: this means simply that the negation sign is not a *name*—that negation is not an object. It does not mean that the negation sign does no work and could be dispensed with. Nor does it mean that there are no negative facts.

The argument that the possibility of dispensing with the curl in representing the negative proposition $\sim p$ shows that to the sign 'nothing in reality corresponds' seems rather weak. Consider the following analogy. Imagine that the objects of the world (the logical simples) consist of two individuals, a and b, and a single predicate, P, which can be attached to them singly, or to both at once (without the order of the arguments counting). The elementary propositions would then be: Pa, Pb, and Pab. Now consider an alternative mode of representation in which reference to a is shown by the *absence* of a sign k and reference to b by the *absence* of a sign l. In this system the three elementary propositions become: Pl, Pk, and P, respectively. Now, this new mode of representation has exactly the same 'logical multiplicity' as the old one. (And in general, if the list of logical simples were known, it would be possible to refer to *some* of them by suitable conventions concerning the *absence* of signs.) This possibility would not show that a stood for no genuine object in the original symbolism. By parity of reasoning, no conclusion about the ontological status of negation ought to follow from the possibility (if it *is* a genuine possibility) of representing negation by means of a sign's absence.

For further statements of the view that the negation sign does not refer to anything in the world, see 4.431 (3) b and 5.44e. (The contention with regard to the negation sign is, of course, a special case of the view that the 'logical constants' do not represent, cf. 4.0312b.)

(2) **is not enough to**: rather, 'does not yet'. The mere occurrence of the negation sign somewhere in the expression of a proposition does not yet show anything definite about the sense: for instance, $\sim \sim p$ is the very same proposition as p. (But this does not mean that the presence of a negation sign makes *no* difference to the sense of the whole. A world in which p is true is different from one in which $\sim p$ is true, and this difference is reflected in the difference between the two propositional signs.)

If the curl of negation were the name of an object, $\sim \sim p$ would have to be a different proposition from p (because it would involve reference to more constituents than p does). We might say that the power of the negation sign to cancel itself shows that its form is not that of a name. (It is characteristic of an operation sign that it can cancel out (5.253b), and negation will later be said to be an operation (5.2341b).)

Commentary

(3)   one and the same reality: according to 2.06a, reality consists of negative as well as positive facts. Suppose p is 'My book is on the table'; then the 'reality' to which both p and ~ p corresponds will be the fact that my book is on the table (if that is a fact)—or, alternatively, the fact that my book is not on the table (if *that* is a fact). Rhees takes this remark to mean that if either of p and ~ p has sense the other must have sense ('Anscombe', p. 28) and he adds that the sense in which W. is using 'corresponds' is not that in which some people talk of a true proposition corresponding to the facts. For what makes p true is not what makes ~ p true (*ibid.*).

opposite sense: oppositely *directed* senses, we might say—cf. 3.144b on propositions as resembling arrows. Both p and ~ p lead us to the *same* state of affairs (e.g. my book's being on the table), but whereas p is verified if that state of affairs occurs and is falsified otherwise, the situation is exactly reversed with ~ p. (So there is a specific internal relation between the two senses—they are not mutually independent.)

● 'There is an internal relation between the senses of p and ~ p, for whatever makes the first proposition true *must* make the second false, and whatever makes the second true *must* make the first false. (This can be stated metaphorically as: "The two senses are *opposed* to one another.") But it must not be supposed that the two propositions refer to different states of affairs; the *very same* procedure that tests the first will also test the second—only the allocation of truth-values in the two cases will be different.'

4.063 (1) ● 'Think of an elementary positive fact as if it were the fact that a particular point on a white sheet of paper were black. The corresponding negative fact would then consist of the absence of pigment at the corresponding point, i.e. in the point's being white. (So the entire world—the totality of elementary facts—could be imagined as a set of black patches against the empty white background.) To pick out a point on the paper, without saying whether it is white or black, would then be like formulating a proposition, without yet indicating whether it was to be affirmed or denied.'

b   negative fact: one of the rare instances of the occurrence of this expression (cf. 2.06b).

c   supposition (*Annahme*): an unasserted proposition (cf. Frege, *Translations*, p. 34). The reference to Frege may be *via* Russell's discussion in *Principles* (§ 477, p. 502), as Anscombe suggests (*Introduction*, p. 105 f.n.). But Russell's account of the matter is mistaken (cf. Anscombe, *loc. cit.*).

Frege seldom uses *Annahme* and never in a technical sense. According

to him, an unasserted proposition expresses a *thought* (the sense of the unasserted proposition) and refers to a *truth-value* (either the True or the
False). A *judgement* is 'the acknowledgement of the truth of a thought'
(*Translations*, p. 156). Thus the form of words 'Venus is larger than Mars'
is, according to Frege, an 'acknowledgement' that the expression 'that
Venus is larger than Mars' refers to the True. This acknowledgement or
assertion is symbolized in Frege's ideography by 'ㅏ (that Venus is larger
than Mars)'. See also notes on 4.442 (1) below.

For further remarks on 'assumption' (*Annahme*), see *Investigations*, § 22,
pp. 10–11.

a truth-value according to Frege: rather, 'in Frege's sense'. This
seems to be a mistake. For Frege, the truth-value of a proposition was
'the circumstance that it is true or false' (*Translations*, p. 63). But there
are, for Frege, just *two* truth-values ('the True' and 'the False'). A point
on the sheet of paper in W.'s analogy would probably be taken by Frege
to correspond to the sense of the proposition in question.

The procedure imagined in this paragraph bears some resemblance to
the application of a 'network' in 6.341.

(2) ● 'I cannot *say* whether a point is black or white unless there is
a prior convention as to what states of affairs shall count as showing that
the point is black or white; and so, in general, the sense of a proposition
must be determined, prior to assertion, by conventions determining which
states of affairs shall count as verifying and which as falsifying it.'

(3) *b* **The verb**, etc.: W. means that it would be wrong to analyse a
proposition such as 'Venus is greater than Mars' as having the form '*A* is
true', with '*A*' regarded as the name of a *thing* (perhaps a thing that could
also be designated by the clause 'Venus being greater than Mars'), and
the 'verb', 'is true', regarded as expressing a property of that thing; the
link with reality (that would be expressed by the words 'is true') is already
part of the sense of the proposition.

● 'The analogy breaks down because I can indicate a point on a sheet
of paper without using the words "white" or "black" (it is not essential
that the point should have one of those two colours), but there is no such
thing as a proposition that is neither true nor false: if it were not true or
false it would have no sense and would correspond to *nothing*.' (Cf.
Anscombe's rendering at *Introduction*, p. 58.)

4.064 Cf. 4.022*c* for the same idea.

This remark can be read as a summary of the main point in the preceding section. Anscombe treats it as an attack on Frege (*Introduction*, p. 58).

For comment, see Stenius, *Exposition*, pp. 171–3.

Commentary

4.0641 (1) **be related to**: or, 'have reference to', or 'concern'. In the *Notebooks*, W. compares p and $\sim p$, respectively, to a picture and the infinite plane outside the picture (28 (6)).

If the proposition considered is not elementary, it would 'determine' a region in logical space (rather than a 'place', i.e. a point). The positive and the corresponding negative proposition might then be thought of as drawing a boundary around the *same* region of logical space. (For the notions of 'logical space' and 'logical place' see instalment XXIII above.)

(2) This remark might suggest that W. intended to say that the meaning of $\sim p$ was the same as 'something *other than p* is the case'. But the general trend of W.'s remarks concerning negation tells against this interpretation. (This passage, and the one that immediately follows, may have been written at a time when W. thought that 'logical space' consisted of both positive and negative possibilities.)

(4) **preliminary to a proposition** (*Vorbereitung*): the same as *Annahme* in 4.063 above.

'In not-p, p is exactly the same as if it stands alone; this point is absolutely fundamental' (*Notes on Logic*, 97 (3)g). Cf.: 'Assertion is merely psychological. There are only unasserted propositions' (96 (2)de). Cf. 4.442 bc.

what is negated is already a proposition: this section is probably still directed against Frege, as W. understood him. Let what is negated be expressed by the expression 'that today is Monday' (or E, say); since W. does not count assertion as part of the proposition, the negated proposition can be expressed by the clause 'that today is not Monday' (or F, say). (It would make no difference to the argument if we used indicative sentences in place of 'that'-clauses each time.) W. is insisting that E expresses a full proposition, just as F does, and that F is obtained by a transformation of nothing less than E. The view he is attacking is that E does not yet express a full proposition (and would do so only if equated with the True, in Frege's terminology): on this rejected view, a certain complex description is first transformed into a corresponding negative description, and only then is a proposition constructed by saying that the resulting description is a description of the True.

The negated proposition can be negated again: when you have obtained $\sim p$ you have certainly arrived at a full proposition. But you can go right ahead and negate it, so *sometimes* a full proposition is the subject of negation. But negation always works in the same way. Hence negation is always negation of a complete proposition.

XXXI

THE NATURE OF PHILOSOPHY;
PHILOSOPHY IS NOT A SCIENCE

(4.1–4.116)

This instalment can be read as a sequel to xxiv. Wittgenstein made a sharp break with Russell's conception of a scientific philosophy and, in later life, had no sympathy for the efforts of the Vienna Circle to carry forward Russell's programme. The task of philosophy, as Wittgenstein sees it, has nothing in common with that of the natural sciences. Philosophy has nothing to *say*: it is an activity (not a theory) directed towards the clarification of thoughts. We are not told here how this task is to be performed. Presumably, the exhibition of logical form with the help of improved notations is an important part of philosophical method. It is noteworthy that in this part Wittgenstein allows philosophy a positive function (cf. 6.53–7).

4.1 existence and non-existence of states of affairs: according to 2.06*a*, this is the same as 'reality' (*die Wirklichkeit*), and according to 2.11 (which expresses much the same thought as 4.1) the same as the state of affairs (*Sachlage*) in logical space.

represent: or, 'present' (*darstellt*). Here means 'show'. What is presented by a proposition is its sense, i.e. a certain affirmed possibility (a possible state of affairs). Thus at 2.201 above, a picture has been said to present a possibility (of actualization and non-actualization of atomic situations), and similarly, at 4.2 and 4.4 below, there will be references to possibilities. In order to bring 4.1 in line with these other entries, some reference to 'possibility' should be added.

● 'A proposition presents its sense, which is a possible state of affairs, i.e. a possibility of the actualization and non-actualization of atomic situations.'

The reader may turn immediately to 4.2, since the intervening sections mostly deal with other matters.

4.11 This identification of science with the totality of contingent truths obliterates any distinction between science and common sense, does not square with the more sophisticated account of scientific language supplied later (e.g. at 6.341), and is therefore unacceptable. Science is more than a thesaurus of contingent truths and its intricate web of mutually dependent observations, manipulations, calculations and theories is remote from the simplicities of the picture theory. But W. is here drawing a rough boundary between *philosophy* and the realm of what can be 'said' (i.e. 'science' in the present broad sense). It may be noticed that 6.53*a* implies that 'science' consists of what *can* be said.

Popper objects that 4.11 requires hypotheses that are not true to be excluded from the domain of science: 'And since we can never know of a hypothesis whether or not it is true, we can never know whether or not it belongs to the sphere of natural science' (*Open Society*, p. 634). He also complains that 4.11 itself cannot belong to science, 'but, rather, to a metascience, i.e. a theory that speaks about science' (*ibid.* p. 710), and so, if true, must assert its own untruth. The answer is that 4.11 is intended to be an 'elucidation' (4.112*c*) belonging to philosophy (i.e. not to science), and is not itself to be regarded as a proposition having truth-value.

For further criticism of 4.11 in the same vein, see Popper's 'Philosophy', p. 164.

4.111 (1) 'Philosophy gives no pictures of reality, and can neither confirm nor confute scientific investigations' (*Notes on Logic*, 93 (2)*c*). Philosophy does not bother with the truth or falsity of propositions—indeed methodically considers propositions (such as that I feel a pain in another's tooth) which are physically impossible (*Phil. Bem.* 23, 8). For a similar attitude towards the relations between philosophy and mathematics, see *Foundations*, § 52, p. 157.

4.112 Cf. *Investigations*, § 109, for W.'s later conception of philosophy as 'a battle against the bewitchment of our reason' by language.

'Philosophy is the doctrine of the logical form of scientific propositions (not primitive propositions only)' (*Notes on Logic*, 93 (2)*g*).

'The function of philosophy ... is to clear up our understanding of the use of symbolism, and to remove the discomfort sometimes caused by our notation' (Watson, *Physics*, p. 21).

This section is criticized by Carnap (*Logical Syntax*, pp. 283 ff.).

(1) clarification: 'I think that a written sentence is "clear" in so far as it has *visible* properties correlated with or "showing" the internal properties of its sense' (Ramsey, *Foundations*, p. 283). This emphasis upon visible properties is a mistake, in my judgement. A symbol is clear when the rules for its use are followed correctly and without fumbling or hesitation. Ramsey goes on to say that in a 'perfect language' the sentences will be 'clear' though in our present language the internal properties are in general 'complicated ones involving the notion of meaning' (*ibid.*).

It would perhaps be adequate to say that the 'clarity' W. is aiming at is correct apprehension of logical form. How this is to be achieved remains one of the book's largest unanswered questions.

(3) **elucidations**: for another sense of this word, see 3.263.

4.1121 (1) 'It is uninteresting whether the pupil knows a rule for the certain solution of $\int \sin^2 x dx$—but not whether the *calculus* which is before us (and which he accidentally employs) contains such a rule. Our interest is not in whether the pupil can do it, but whether the calculus can, and *how it does it*' (*Math. MS.* 641).

4.113 Literally: 'Philosophy sets the boundary of (or: demarcates) the controversial domain of natural science' (an obscure remark).

● 'By clarifying thoughts, philosophy demarcates the boundary of the realm where disputes are possible, i.e. the realm of states of affairs.'

4.114 (2) working outwards: literally, 'from within' (*von innen*). There is no way of getting outside language to mark its boundaries. Cf. 5.6, 5.61 (on the limits of language and limits of the world).

4.115 what cannot be said: literally, 'the unspeakable', or 'the unsayable' (*das Unsagbare*).

signify: or, 'mean' (*bedeuten*). Only in some loose sense: one cannot refer to what cannot be said, or use propositions whose sense is the unspeakable.

● 'By removing the obstacles to speaking clearly, philosophy allows us to *see* what can only be shown.'

4.116a It might be objected that there is a sense in which everything that is thought *is* already thought clearly. See 5.5563a (ordinary language is perfectly in order), 5.4733b (every proposition is correctly constructed).

b **put into words**: 'expressed', 'said'. Cf. Preface (2)*b*, 3.251 (a proposition's sense can be given *clearly*), 4.112a (philosophy as logical clarification).

XXXII

THE IMPOSSIBILITY OF
REPRESENTING LOGICAL FORM
(4.12–4.1213)

In the preface, Wittgenstein has said that he wishes to demarcate the boundaries of the expression of thought (cf. 4.114). He is doing so whenever, as in this instalment, he condemns certain types of would-be assertions as logically improper (logically impossible). The present topic has already been introduced in instalment VIII (cf. also XXVIII), and the main argument, that a proposition cannot get 'outside' logic, is reminiscent of what has already been said at 2.174.

Compared with the earlier discussions, a more positive tone is noticeable here. Although logical form is unsayable, it does 'mirror itself' ('shows itself') (4.121). Although what can be shown cannot be said (4.1212), we are encouraged to hope that, with the aid of a well-constructed notation or ideography (4.1213), much that is philosophically important may yet reveal itself to us through clarification of the essence of language. Cf. instalment XXXIV on the expression of formal features.

4.12 'The main point is the theory of what can be expressed (*gesagt*) by propositions—i.e. by language—(And, which comes to the same, what can be *thought*) and what can not be expressed by propositions, but only shown (*gezeigt*): which, I believe, is the cardinal problem of philosophy' (*Letters*, Cassino 19.8.19. This passage is omitted from the *Notebooks*, p. 129).

We can take as a rule of thumb that for W. whatever can be shown but not said would commonly be held to be *a priori*—and *vice versa*.

(1)   the whole of reality: according to 2.063 = 'the world'.

Cf. 2.172, 2.174, 4.0312*c* for similar statements about impossibility of representation.

(2)   propositions: might well be in the singular, as in the German.

Cf. 5.61 on the boundaries of logic coinciding with the boundaries of the world.

   outside: cf. 2.173 and 2.174.

represent: since logical form *can* be shown, this is a passage where, by way of exception, *darstellen* has to be taken in the sense of 'say' (= 'represent'). Similarly in 4.121.

● 'In order to *refer to* (talk about) logical form, we should need a form of presentation (symbolization) which would have not the logical form but something else—something which logical form had, *per impossibile*, in common with our purported statements. But every fact has the logical form, so our statements would have to be embodied in something that was not a fact—and so would be "outside the world", i.e. would be nothing at all.'

4.121 (1) **Propositions**, here again, might well be in the singular (and so throughout the section).

represent: see note under 4.12 (2) above.

is mirrored: a synonym for 'shows itself'. The image of a mirror occurs also at 5.511, 6.13a.

'Thus a language which *can* express everything *mirrors* certain properties of the world by these properties which it must have; and logical so-called propositions show *in a systematic way* those properties' (*Moore Notes*, 107 (6)).

For criticism of 4.121 see Carnap (*Logical Syntax*, p. 282): 'Syntax is exactly formulable in the same way as geometry is . . . .'

(2) 'In saying that we cannot represent or speak about the logical form of representation, no more [would be said] than that we cannot talk about what makes a fact a fact, nor ultimately *about* facts at all, because every statement apparently about facts is really about their constituents. These things he certainly believes, but it seems to me unlikely that his complicated propositions about the form of representation amount to no more than this' (Ramsey, *Foundations*, p. 273).

(3) Notice the emphasis on '*itself*'. W. consistently speaks of logical form as showing itself. Cf. 6.124g (in logic the essence expresses itself) and 5.473a (logic must take care of itself).

'In order that you should have a language which can express or *say* everything that *can* be said, this language must have certain properties; and when this is the case, *that* it has them can no longer be said in that language or *any* language' (*Moore Notes*, 107 (4)).

(5) **display**: or, 'show forth' (as in 2.172), or 'exhibit'. All these are synonyms for 'show'.

4.1211 (1) **the object *a* occurs in its sense**: or, simply, 'the proposition is about *a*'. (Since the sense is a possible state of affairs, *a* 'occurs' as a constituent of this possible state of affairs—a *Sachverhalt* or *Sachlage*.)

Cf. 5.13, 5.2, for similar remarks.

THE NOTION OF 'SHOWING'

Wittgenstein uses the verb 'to show' (*zeigen*), or its cognates, very often—there are some forty occurrences in his special sense, to which must be added occasional uses of the near synonyms, *aufweisen* (show forth) and *spiegeln* (mirror). The word *darstellen*, when used in the sense of 'to present', also expresses the same idea. Unfortunately, this crucial concept is most elusive.

We can be sure that Wittgenstein intended a sharp contrast between 'showing' and 'saying' or asserting. 'What *can* be shown *cannot* be said' (4.1212) and, we may safely add, what can be said cannot be shown. Showing, however we understand it, has to be conceived as quite unlike assertion by means of configurations of objects standing as proxies for objects. The intended opposition comes out neatly in a point of diction: it is we, the users of the language, who 'say' things, make assertions, by means of the arbitrary co-ordinations we have assigned to words; but whatever is shown *shows itself* (*zeigt sich*, as Wittgenstein often says), independently of any arbitrary conventions we may have adopted—what is shown is not something that '*we* express' (cf. 6.124*g*). (Unhappily, Wittgenstein does once or twice use the expression '*we* show', in the sense of 'we prove or demonstrate'—as at 6.126 (4). We can usually see whether Wittgenstein uses, or might as well have used, the reflexive form. For example, the important remark that a proposition shows its sense, 4.022*a*, can be legitimately transformed into: 'A proposition's sense shows itself in the proposition'.)

Examination of Wittgenstein's usage will confirm that whatever shows itself does so in some feature of a *symbol*, whether it be a full proposition or a propositional component. The standard form characteristic of Wittgenstein's usage is: '*X* shows itself in a feature of the symbol *Y*.'

Among the things that are said by Wittgenstein to show themselves are: the sense of a proposition (4.022*a*), that a proposition is about a certain object (4.1211*a*), that two propositions are about the same object (*ibid.*), that a given symbol signifies an object (4.126 (3)*c*), that a given sign signifies a number (*ibid.*), that the sign ' ∼ ' corresponds to nothing in reality (4.0621 *b*), that logical propositions (tautologies and contradictions) say nothing (4.461 *a*), that there is no such thing as a soul (5.5421 *a*), that two given propositions contradict one another (6.1201 *a*), that a given proposition follows from another (6.1221), that two expressions have the same meaning (6.23 *b*). (Also the 'limit of empirical reality' shows itself, 5.5561 *b*; so does 'what solipsism intends', namely, that 'the world is my world', 5.62 *c*; and 'the mystical' shows itself, 6.522.) Leaving the last three examples aside as doubtful, we may summarize Wittgenstein's usage by saying that what shows itself is either (i) something material about the reference or the sense of a given expression (e.g. that it stands for a certain object, for no object, or the same object as some other given expression) or (ii) something about the logical form of the reference or sense (e.g. that it is a number, or a significant proposition, or the contradiction of a given proposition, or a consequence of another proposition.) (If we used 'meaning' to cover both sense and reference, we could say more briefly that what is shown is some feature of either the content or the form of the meaning of a given expression.) The second type of case is the more prominent in Wittgenstein's exposition.

I said above that what shows itself is manifested in a feature of the corresponding symbol. If what shows itself is a 'material' feature of the meaning, this presumably appears in some feature of the *use* of the symbol (though Wittgenstein does not explicitly say so). For example, that 'Eisenhower' stands for some one living person presumably 'shows itself' in the situations in which we correctly use sentences containing that name. Knowing *whom* the name stands for is knowing *when* to use the name. In the case of a name whose reference we do not know, we can discover when to use it correctly by observing the linguistic practices in which it has a role. (So it is possible to learn, and to teach, the reference. What shows itself is not wholly incommunicable.) If Wittgenstein spoke like many contemporary logicians, he would say that the reference can be stated in the form of a 'semantical rule', but we have seen that he regards such rules as impossible.

In the second type of case, where what shows itself is something about the form of the meaning, this manifests itself in a corresponding 'formal' or 'logical' feature of the corresponding symbol. For example, that '$p \vee q$' follows from 'p' manifests itself in '$p \supset p \vee q$' being a tautology. Wittgenstein says that some formal features of propositions are 'shown' by their structure (4.1211*b*). Such formal features may be expressed by means of what Wittgenstein calls 'rules of syntax', but these do not 'say' anything, are not assertions having truth-values.

In ordinary language, we sometimes find *showing* opposed to *describing* or *talking about*. ('Don't describe the President to me— show him, point him out'—i.e. put me in a position to see him for myself. Similarly, when I show somebody the crawl, by swimming it, I provide him with an instance of the movement—put him in a position to see for himself what it is like.) One is consequently tempted to think that what is shown must somehow be 'seen' in some single non-discursive act: just as we see the visual pattern of some design 'in a flash', so, we should be able to 'see', by immediate inspection, that a given proposition is a tautology or a contradiction, that it is a consequence of another proposition, and so on. This suggestion must be rejected: Wittgenstein's conception does not require us to apprehend logical form in a single act of insight. On the contrary, the 'logical form' of a symbol is, in general, revealed discursively by appeal to the relevant rules of syntax that govern its use. Logical form is discovered by calculation with signs—not by intuition.

THE LIMITS OF LANGUAGE

Among the most important remarks in the text are a number of what might be called 'principles of linguistic impotence', statements about what *cannot* be expressed in language. (It will be recalled that in his preface Wittgenstein said that the aim of the book was to 'set a limit' to 'the expression of thoughts' [para. 3].) At 2.17–2.174 Wittgenstein has said that a picture (and hence a proposition, *qua* logical picture) cannot represent its form of representation which it has 'in common with reality'; at 3.26–3.263 he has implied that the meanings of names (= simple signs) cannot be stated (see the discussion of this in the notes on 3.263 above); according to 4.041 the logical 'multiplicity' of a proposition cannot be represented; and now at 4.12 these limitations are brought together under the formula that logical form cannot be represented (cf. Wittgenstein's 'fundamental idea' that 'the *logic* of facts' cannot be represented, 4.0312).

Sometimes these principles of impotence are connected with the impossibility of self-reference (for which see the discussion under 3.332 and at pp. 148–9 above), but Wittgenstein's idea is that certain aspects of linguistic representation cannot be represented *at all*. Here, 'representation' must be taken in the special sense of 'picturing' (*Abbildung*) which Wittgenstein has introduced: it is not his intention to claim ineffability for logical form or the other things that cannot be pictured—the meanings of names e.g. *can* be 'explained' (3.263 a) and logical form *does* show itself. His point might be made by saying that when language reveals the '*logic* of the world' it is used in a way radically different from its use in constructing logical *pictures* (= significant propositions).

The aspects of representation which language is impotent to represent are all the *internal* features of the representation (i.e. all those features that can only be shown by 'formal concepts' or by necessary truths). It is, for instance, internal to the *symbol* 'red' that it means red and not something else; similarly, the specific logical form of a proposition is internal to that proposition (so that a symbol having another specific logical form would necessarily be a different symbol).

The reasons why the specific logical form, say f, of a given proposition (say an elementary concatenation ab of a and b) cannot be pictured are easy to see. Suppose, *per impossibile*, that some proposition did picture f. Then in order to allow for the requisite complexity of such a proposition we should have to conceive it as uv, say, with u standing for ϕ_1 (the form of a) and v for ϕ_2 (the form of b). To this the following objections might be made from the standpoint of Wittgenstein's theory of symbolism: (i) ϕ_1 and ϕ_2 are not objects (variables for 'formal concepts' are used quite differently from names), (ii) f is not generated from ϕ_1 and ϕ_2 by a contingent concatenation, (iii) if uv meant what was assumed, it would be necessarily true, (iv) if uv were a picture of the complex form, f, the two would have to possess a form in common and so we should have to admit the manifest absurdity of a form of f, i.e. a form of a form (or a possibility of a possibility). But it is hardly necessary to elaborate such details, since it is plain enough that Wittgenstein's rigid stipulations concerning the nature of 'picturing' make the idea of a *picture* of the 'method of picturing' a patent monstrosity. (It is instructive to consider whether a photograph could show what some other photograph 'has in common' with the scene it depicts. Suppose I hung a faithful photograph by an open window through which the very scene depicted in the former could be plainly seen and then took another photograph of the whole wall—with the original photograph beside its landscape; would I then have succeeded in *photographing* the 'method of representation'?)

It is more troublesome to decide whether Wittgenstein was justified in drawing so sharp a line between the use of language in contingent propositions (i.e. in 'saying') and its use in necessary propositions (i.e. in 'showing'). The author of the *Investigations*, one might speculate, would have treated this sharp dichotomy with scant respect.

4.1212 By contraposition, this is equivalent to: 'What can be said cannot be shown.'

'In any ordinary proposition, e.g. "Moore good", this *shews* and does not say that "*Moore*" is to the left of "good"; and *here what* is shewn can be *said* by another proposition. But this only applies to that *part* of what is shewn which is arbitrary. The *logical* properties which it shews are not arbitrary, and that it has these cannot be said in any proposition' (*Moore Notes*, 110 (4)).

4.1213 **in which everything is all right**: having devised a notation for rendering logical form (the internal relations between propositions) obvious. To have accomplished this *is* to have 'the right logical conception'. For, since logic 'takes care of itself' there remains nothing for *us* to do apart from the practical task of improving logical notation.

already: delete.

XXXIII

FORMAL PROPERTIES AND
FORMAL RELATIONS

(4.122–4.123)

Wittgenstein now introduces the adjective 'formal' and its synonym 'internal' to refer to 'features' of logical form. For Wittgenstein, 'formal properties' and 'formal relations' are sharply distinct from genuine properties and relations: he would have been ready to call them 'pseudo-properties' and 'pseudo-relations' (cf. his use of 'pseudo-concept' at 4.1272). In 4.1271, he will argue that 'formal properties' must be expressed in a distinctive way by the use of variables.

4.122 (1) **In a certain sense**: because, strictly speaking, 'formal properties' are not properties at all (cf. (3), where 'internal' relations are contrasted with 'proper' relations), and cannot be talked about (cf. (4)). The sentence should be put into apposition with 4.12a, where we are told that logical form belongs to the unspeakable.

formal properties: in the light of the statements that follow at once, 'formal' can almost always be equated with 'internal'. In the *Notebooks* (6 (2)), W. says that a property of a *Sachverhalt* must be internal. This fits neatly with the idea that it is logically impossible to *say* anything about a *Sachverhalt* (or, for that matter, about any fact).

or, in the case of facts: the implication, in P.–McG., that facts do not have formal properties is misleading.

(2) '... he immediately went on to add that the expression "internal relation" is misleading and that he used it "only because others had used it".' [Perhaps the reference here is to Moore's well-known essay on external and internal relations.] [He explained it as] 'a relation which holds if the terms are what they are, and which cannot therefore be imagined not to hold' (Moore, *Papers*, p. 294). 'Finally, he introduced a new phrase, in explanation of his view that the expression "internal relation" is misleading, saying that internal and external relations are "categorically" different; and ... [spoke later of] "an internal *or* grammatical relation"' (*ibid.* p. 295). See also *Foundations*, where he says that the 'characteristic mark' of 'internal properties' is that they persist unalterably (§ 102, p. 30) and attributes this to a 'connexion' in language between 'paradigms' and 'names' (§ 105, p. 31).

(3) The expression 'internal relation' has already occurred once before at 3.24*a*. In the *Math. MS.* (758), W. traces mistakes in the philosophy of mathematics (e.g. treating π as comparable with rational numbers) to a confusion between the property of a form (*Eigenschaft einer Form*) and the usual sense of 'property' in which a book has the property of being read.

(4) Cf. 4.124*b* on the nonsensicality of ascribing formal properties.

make themselves manifest: literally, 'it shows itself' (*es zeigt sich*). This is one of several places at which W. says that something unsayable nevertheless shows itself in features of propositional symbols. There is, however, a serious difficulty in trying to say that some specific such and such cannot be said. Consider the following statement: 'That "Socrates" means Socrates cannot be said, but shows itself in our use of propositions containing "Socrates"' (cf. 3.262, 3.263). Of *what* is it said that *it* shows itself? What can only be shown has already been identified by the words, 'That "Socrates" means Socrates', i.e. by purporting to say what cannot be said. And there is no way to identify what cannot be said, except by 'saying' it. But if it cannot be said, it cannot be said, and we deceive ourselves if we think otherwise. (Cf. 5.5422 on the impossibility of 'judging' a nonsense.) Thus we do not succeed in saying or otherwise making plain what it is that we allege to be unsayable. It is nonsensical (here in a pejorative sense) to use a form of words intended to say of something that it cannot be said.

Consider (1) '"Socrates" means Socrates', and (2) 'That "Socrates" means Socrates cannot be said but shows itself'. We might say that (1) is the kind of nonsense that tries to express something that *can* be shown; while (2) is the kind of nonsense that cannot even be shown—nonsense on stilts, as it were.

4.1221 feature: for other occurrences of this word, see 3.34, 4.126 (6).

4.123 (1) unthinkable: cf. 4.114 for other occurrences of this word. 'Unthinkable' in the sense of its being logically impossible that there should be such a thought: any form of words by means of which we attempted to say that an object had a formal property would be nonsensical (*unsinnig*). But: '... taken literally such expressions as "The unthinkable" are without meaning' (Gasking, 'Anderson', p. 2).

(2) **objects**: here, *not* logical simples. For the impossibility of colours as constituents in elementary propositions, see 6.3751.

(3) **shifting use**: as between 'internal' and 'external' properties or relations. Similarly, by 'object' we may mean a tree, a man, etc., whose existence is contingent—or an object that is a logical simple, and whose existence (= subsistence) is necessary.

● 'Just as there is a sense of "property" in which it is a necessary truth that something has the property in question, so there is a sense of "object" in which it is a necessary truth that the object in question exists.'

XXXIV

HOW FORMAL FEATURES ARE EXPRESSED

(4.124–4.126)

Formal (= internal) properties or relations are 'features' of facts (4.1221), as we have just seen. Although such features cannot be 'said' or stated in propositions, they can be 'shown', as Wittgenstein now proceeds to argue, with further details to come in the next few instalments. How, then, are such formal features expressed, how do they show themselves? The answer given in this instalment is that formal features (aspects of logical form) are shown by formal features of propositions (4.124). Wittgenstein says that symbols (propositional components) show the logical category of the objects with which they are co-ordinated (4.126 (3)), although how this is done is unclear.

The idea of a 'formal series', here introduced for the first time (4.1252), will be prominent in Wittgenstein's subsequent analysis of mathematics (e.g. at 6.02–6.03).

4.124 (1) There is a parallel statement about internal relations at 4.125.
The existence of: or, 'That there is . . .'.
expresses itself: with stress on '*itself*', cf. 4.121 (3), 4.126 (3).

4.125 Compare the parallel statement 4.124 (1).

4.1251 the vexed question: possibly a reference to Moore's essay, 'Relations', directed against 'the dogma of internal relations' held by Bradley and other idealist logicians.

How is the dispute about the alleged internality of all relations settled? Perhaps by understanding the distinction made in the previous sections. 'Internal relations' are essentially different from 'external relations'. Internal and external relations are not species of a genus; to ask whether all relations are external or internal (and so to treat both adjectives on a par) is as absurd as asking whether a man's name is to count as one of his properties.

4.1252 (1) series of forms: or, 'formal series' (*Formenreihe*). Also simply called 'series', e.g. at 5.232.

(2) order of the number-series: rather, 'number-series' simply. **number-series**: for details, see 6.02.

(3) The same series is discussed at 4.1273 (1).

(4) successor: used again only at 4.1273a.

4.126 (1) formal concepts: occurs only in sections 4.126–4.1274. W. has introduced the expression, 'formal property', at 4.122a. He now wants to make a distinction between a 'formal concept' or 'pseudo-concept' (4.1272a) and a 'proper concept' that parallels the earlier one between a 'formal' or 'internal' property and a 'proper' or genuine property (cf. 4.122 (3)). W. seems to have little need to introduce the expression, 'formal concept', since 'formal property' would have served his purpose sufficiently well. No doubt, he wished to connect his remarks with what Frege and others had said about 'concepts'. (Frege says: '"the number −1 has the property that its square is 1" can be equivalently expressed as "−1 falls under the concept: square root of 1"' (*Translations*, p. 30).) For Frege, as for W., the word 'concept' does not have a psychological sense, having a 'purely logical use' (*op. cit.* p. 42). A concept, for Frege, is 'a function whose value is always a truth-value' (*op. cit.* p. 30).

(2) traditional logic: literally, 'old logic'. No doubt, W. meant to include the logic of Frege and Russell.

(3) As pointed out in Anscombe, *Introduction*, p. 122, the view expressed in this paragraph is very close to a puzzling doctrine of Frege's. Frege held that it is impossible to say of a concept that it is a concept (see, for instance, *Translations*, pp. 45–7). W. is saying that it is impossible to assert that something is a concept; the presence of a concept in a proposition is, however, *shown* by the occurrence of a predicative symbol (a symbol for a function).

a **falls under a formal concept as one of its objects**: more simply, 'is an instance of the formal concept' as 2 is an instance of the formal concept, *number*. Of course, 'object' must not be taken here in the sense of 'logical simple', a *Gegenstand* or *Ding* in W.'s technical sense of those terms. Anscombe makes this point (*Introduction*, p. 122, f.n. 1) and thinks that W. resorted to the 'misleading terminology' in question because it is 'less loaded with philosophical doctrine' in the German. (But I suspect an echo of Frege's language.)

b Cf. 4.12721 *a* (a formal concept given with the object that falls under it).

c **sign for a number**: = 'numeral'.

(4) Cf. 4.1272 (8) (formal concepts presented by variables).

(5) This remark and the instances of formal concepts given in 4.1272 suggest that W. thought of formal concepts as typically expressed in ordinary language by such very general predicates as 'object', 'fact', 'number', i.e. by what are sometimes called 'category-words'. Formal *properties* and *relations* might then be understood to be the distinctive 'marks' of formal concepts, for which see below. Formal concepts are expressed by propositional variables, as in (8), but formal properties are expressed by *features* of symbols, as in (6). For 'feature', see 4.1221 above.

characteristics: rather, 'marks' (*Merkmale*), in the sense of 'criteria' or defining properties. (If 'man' means the same as 'rational animal', a *Merkmal* of the concept of man is rationality.) The *O.E.D.* has for 'mark' the entry 'A characteristic property; a criterion'.

(6) In the light of 4.1221, this can be expanded into: 'The expression of a formal property is an internal property of certain symbol-facts.' Notice that at 4.1221 an internal property is called a feature, whereas here the *expression* of a formal or internal property is called a feature.

(7) **the characteristics**: rather, 'the marks'. In view of 4.1221, this remark can be read as:

● 'A mark of a formal concept is symbolized by a distinctive internal property of all sentence-facts that include instances of the concept.'

(8) An important remark. For the notion of a 'variable', cf. 3.312. For examples of the expression of formal concepts with the aid of variables, see 4.1273 (1), 5.2522, 6.022 (2), 6.03.

A comparison of what is said at 4.126 (8) about the use of a propositional variable with what was said earlier at 3.313, apparently about the same topic, may raise puzzles. At 3.313 *a*, Wittgenstein said that a propositional variable presents an expression, while now he says that a propositional variable expresses a formal concept. It would be wrong to infer that Wittgenstein somehow equated 'expression' and 'sign for a formal concept'; on the contrary, he is insisting in 4.126 that a formal concept cannot be properly symbolized by an expression.

In order to understand what Wittgenstein has in mind, consider as examples the expression 'is red' and the formal concept 'is a colour predicate'. With regard to the first, Wittgenstein has implied that it is presented by the general form of the propositions which it characterizes (3.312 a), and its proper expression is:

$$x \text{ is red}, \tag{1}$$

where, as stipulated by W., 'the expression is constant and everything else variable' (3.312 b). In a correct ideography, there must be some way of showing that the values of x in (1) are such as to make the whole propositional symbol significant. Imagine this to be done in the following way,

$$x_k \text{ is red}_c, \tag{2}$$

that is to say, the suffix k, attached to a name or a corresponding variable, shows that the objects in question can sensibly be said to be coloured, while the suffix c attached to a predicate or the corresponding predicate variable shows that the property in question is a colour. These suffixes might now be regarded as expressing the 'features' of symbols, to which Wittgenstein refers in 4.126 (6, 7). (For example, all symbols referring to colours will have the feature of including the suffix c.)

It now seems impossible to do as Wittgenstein demands in 4.126 (8) and produce a propositional variable 'in which only this characteristic feature' is constant. Consider the following symbol:

$$\Upsilon_c(x_k). \tag{3}$$

Here, the only 'constants' are the suffixes, and the whole symbol may be said to express the formal concept 'singular colour proposition' (let us say). So this formal concept can be symbolized according to Wittgenstein's specifications. But how are we to symbolize 'colour predicate' by itself?

The nearest we can come to expressing the formal concept *in isolation* is by some such symbolism as:

$$(\ )_c(\ ), \tag{4}$$

which is, after all, only a blurred version of (3).

But we have no occasion to refer to formal concepts in isolation. When we want to make some general remark about things that can sensibly be said to be coloured (for example), the correct symbolic representation will involve the quantifiers $(x_k) \ (\ldots)$ or $(\exists x_k) \ (\ldots)$ where the character of the variable (marked by the presence of the distinctive suffix) will answer our purpose (cf. 4.1272 (2, 3)). And this is enough for Wittgenstein, whose main point is that 'formal concepts', however they are used, are symbolized in a way quite different from that in which 'proper' concepts are symbolized. The correct symbol for a proper concept is a propositional function (an expression); the correct symbol for a formal concept is an auxiliary mark (a suffix, say—a 'feature' of a symbol).

My suggestion, therefore, is that Wittgenstein's view requires variables to serve two distinct but compatible purposes, according to the occasions of their use. In such a context as (1) or (2), our attention is drawn to the range of values—the set of propositions in which 'is red' functions. While in such a case as $(\exists x_k)$ (...) our attention is directed rather to the logical category of the entities involved.

XXXV

VARIABLES AS SIGNS FOR FORMAL CONCEPTS

(4.127–4.12721)

This instalment should be read together with XVII and XVIII, where variables are discussed. It is worth noting that in 4.1271 (2) the notion of formal feature is linked with that of logical form. The rejection of statements *about* formal concepts is especially emphatic in this instalment (4.1272). Interpretation of 'number' as a formal concept (4.1272 (7, 8)) will eventually lead Wittgenstein to reject the view of mathematics defended by Russell and by Frege.

4.127 signify the objects: this is not strictly correct, unless W. means 'refer to the objects in combination'. At 3.313 the values of a propositional variable were said to be propositions; here and at 4.1272 *a*, however, Wittgenstein talks loosely as if the values were names or other referring expressions.

4.1271 This adds to 4.127 the idea that the variable presents a form, and so explicitly links the idea of form with that of formal or internal property. Strictly speaking, it is wrong to say that the form *is* a formal property, as W. seems to imply.

Commentary

'When a child learns "Blue is a colour, red is a colour, green, yellow are colours" he learns nothing new about the colours but learns the meaning (*Bedeutung*) of a variable in statements like "The picture has pretty colours", etc. The former statement gives him the values of a variable' (*Phil. Bem.* 2, 2).

4.1272 This section is criticized by Carnap (*Syntax*, p. 295) on the ground that W.'s method for construing what Carnap calls 'universal words', though acceptable, need not prevent these words from also being regarded as 'proper concept-words'.

(**1**) **proper**: or, 'actual', 'real' (*eigentliche*).

pseudo-concept (*Scheinbegriff*): the only occurrence of this word. It should not be read pejoratively. In the light of 4.1271 *a*, the 'pseudo-concept' is the same as the formal concept: 'pseudo-' here stresses the contrast with 'proper'.

(**3**) Here the variables are subject to the identity conventions discussed at 5.53 ff.

(**4**) The use of 'pseudo-proposition' at 6.2 *b* shows that the term is not necessarily pejorative. In the *Notebooks*, W. says that all combinations of signs that seem to say something about their own form are pseudo-propositions 'like all propositions of logic' (12 (9)). 'Pseudo-propositions are such as, when analysed, turn out only to *shew* what they were supposed to *say*' (16 (1)).

(**5**) See the similar remark at 4.1274.

'That M is a *thing*, can't be *said*; it is nonsense: but *something* is *shewn* by the symbol "M". In [the] same way, that a *proposition* is a subject–predicate proposition can't be said: but it is *shown* by the symbol' (*Moore Notes*, 108 (9)).

(**8**) **in conceptual notation**: in the ideography of 3.325.

not by functions: cf. 4.126 (4).

4.12721 *a* Cf. 4.126 (3) for a similar remark.

● 'A formal concept is defined by explaining the use of a certain variable, which in turn calls for a specification of the possible values of that variable. So, in defining the formal concept we necessarily identify its instances.'

The reference to Russell's conception of function may be tied to *Principia* ∗1 (p. 92) where both the notion of 'elementary propositional function' and 'negation' (a special case of the former) are presented as 'primitive ideas'. W. seems to object also to Russell's procedure in giving independent definitions of *cardinal number* and the special cardinal numbers, such as 0, 1, etc.

XXXVI

HOW TO EXPRESS THE GENERAL TERM
OF A FORMAL SERIES

(4.1273)

This instalment is important, because Wittgenstein bases his philosophy of arithmetic upon it (cf. 6.02). Wittgenstein's main point is that the general term of a 'formal series' (one in which each term is generated by an internal relation to its predecessor) *must* be symbolized by means of a variable, i.e. a symbol for a 'formal concept' (cf. 4.1271). Here, Wittgenstein insists upon the logical *necessity* of a feature of symbolic notation: as always when discussing a question about a mode of signification, he is concerned only with the 'essence' of the notation. His thought is that it would be logically impossible to represent the general term of a formal series except by a variable (in his special sense of a sign for a formal concept). Since Wittgenstein correctly takes the series of integers to be 'formal' in his sense, he accuses Frege and Russell of logical fallacy in their definition of 'successor' (= next higher integer). In the notes that follow, I examine whether the indictment of vicious circularity is correct. The difficulty turns upon Frege and Russell's use of the concept of '*all* properties' in defining a particular property or relation: Wittgenstein's criticism points to a weakness that is central in the 'logicist' reduction of arithmetic to logic. His attack is intended to be mortal.

4.1273 (1)*a* **series of forms**: or, 'formal series'. Cf. 4.1252*a* for a definition and 4.126 (3) for a parallel remark.

b *formal* **concept**: for the meaning of this see 4.126.

c **incorrect**: rather, 'false' (*falsch*).

   vicious circle: W.'s objection seems to be directed against Frege and Russell's definition of the so-called 'ancestral' of a relation, which they use in their definitions of a natural number (cf. Anscombe, *Introduction*, p. 128). The idea of the 'ancestral' may be illustrated as follows: Suppose

F is the relation, *father of*. Consider the relation, G say, which holds between x and y when x is the father of y or x is the father of the father of y or...or x is the father of the father of...of the father of y (i.e. when x is a *direct male ancestor of y*). Then G is the *indefinite* relative product of F: it may be called the *ancestral* of F and is written as F_*. (A further illustration may be helpful: let Mxy mean that x, a number, is *twice y*; then M_*xy will mean that $x = y.2^n$, for some value of n greater than or equal to 1. So we have $M_*10, 5$ and also $M_*8, 1$, etc.).

It is not easy to see how to define F_* in terms of F. Let us begin by noticing that whenever x and y are related by the ancestral of F (so that we have F_*xy) the possession of *some* properties by x will ensure the possession by y of the *same* properties. Let us call a property, P, *transmissible with respect to F*, or 'trans_F' for short, if P is such that $Px.Fxy$ always entails Py (i.e. if the holding of F between x and y guarantees that the latter will have the property P if the former does). It is obvious that if two things, u and v, are related by the *ancestral* of F (i.e. by F_*), v must have every trans_F property of u. (For we shall have $Fux_1, Fx_1x_2, ..., Fx_nv$ and P will be successively transmitted from u to $x_1, x_2, ..., x_n$, and so at last to v.) We can reach a definition, now, by taking this idea in reverse. Suppose we were told only that v had every trans_F property of u, but were not told what the relation between them was. What would the situation be? Well, (i) v might be identical with u, or (ii) v might be related to u by F_* (in the light of what was said above). It looks obvious that no *other* case could arise. (One is inclined to say that nothing excluded from the series $x, \overline{F}'x, \overline{F}'\overline{F}'x, ...$, etc., could have *all* the trans_F properties of x. For *one* such property is that of being connected with any other member of the series by a finite number of applications of F.) Following Frege and Russell, we might then define F_* as follows:

$$F_*xy =_{Df} x \neq y . y \text{ has all the } \text{trans}_F \text{ properties of } x.$$

(This account deviates in minor details from the original, for which see, for instance, Quine, *Methods*, pp. 228–9, Quine, *Mathematical Logic*, pp. 215–16 and Russell, *Mathematical Philosophy*, pp. 25–6.)

The construction is clearly quite general and may be used to generate from any given relation, R, the corresponding ancestral R_*.

This ingenious idea, originally due to Frege (*Begriffsschrift*, p. 60), plays a crucial role in the reduction of arithmetic to logic attempted in *Principia*. Suppose we have succeeded in defining a single cardinal number, say 0 (which is easy), and also the successor relation, S. We can then proceed to define the ancestral of S, S_*, and thereafter define the 'natural numbers' (i.e. those having the form $S'0, S'S'0$, and so on) as the class of all things having the relation S_* to 0. In effect, the notion of the ancestral of the successor relation is a substitute for the vague notion of 'and so on', and permits the application of 'mathematical induction' to the series of natural numbers defined by means of it.

However, a danger of circularity enters through the presence in our definition of a reference to '*all* trans$_F$ properties': shall we count having all trans$_F$ properties in common with x as itself a property or not? The danger becomes serious when it is necessary to prove certain general properties of the ancestral (e.g. $S_{**} = S_*$) or of the number series defined by using that relation. The danger is overcome in the first edition of *Principia* by using the axiom of reducibility to avoid reference to 'all classes' or 'all properties'.

(2) **operation**: see 5.21 ff. for further discussion.

XXXVII

THE IMPOSSIBILITY OF COUNTING LOGICAL FORMS

(4.1274–4.128)

Wittgenstein now brings his important account of formal concepts to a close. The first remark (4.1274a) of this instalment is crucial. No question about the 'existence' of a formal concept is proper (as he has already argued, with illustrations, at 4.1272). (We might add that what philosophers might want to express by the unfortunate expression 'the existence of a concept' will *show* itself in the resources of language, e.g. in the word 'man' having a meaning.) It immediately follows that would-be numerical statements about formal concepts (e.g. that there are more than two objects in the universe—cf. 4.1272e) must be nonsensical; and this brands as nonsense the traditional disputes between monists and pluralists (4.128b). But this standpoint also spells ruin for the programme which Wittgenstein still defended in *Logical Form* of bringing to light the logical forms of the elementary propositions (cf. 4.1274b). (One is still inclined to wonder whether such forms might not be *shown*? Wittgenstein's slide from 'cannot be said' to 'nonsensical' and then to 'illegitimate' is often unconvincing.)

4.1274 (1) In view of the example that immediately follows, a question about the existence of a formal concept has to be identified with a question about the existence of *instances* of that concept (cf. 4.12721*b*). Hence, 4.1272 (5) provides examples of such nonsensical questions. Since what cannot sensibly be asked can nevertheless be shown, 'nonsensical' may be too strong here.

(2) Yet W. was much concerned with similar questions in the *Notebooks* (e.g. at 3 (4)), where he asks whether 'A is good' is a subject–predicate proposition).

4.128 (1) *without* **number**: or, 'anumerical' (*zahllos*). It is nonsense to speak of counting logical forms. It is not clear what W. had in mind here: certainly in a universe containing a finite set of objects and a finite set of their combinations, a list could be made of distinct logical forms, which might then be counted. (Compare the example of a model universe given at p. 128 above.) Perhaps W. wanted to stress that 'is a logical form' is not an authentic predicate such as 'is a star'.

(2) **no privileged numbers**: or, 'no pre-eminent numbers'; echoed at 5.553 (2).
possibility of: delete (not in original).

XXXVIII

PROPOSITIONS CAN BE ANALYSED
(4.2–4.24)

Although there is a marked break between this instalment and its predecessor, continuity can be restored by a consecutive reading of 4.1, 4.11, 4.12, 4.2, 4.21, 4.22, 4.23, 4.24. Wittgenstein here recapitulates some of the chief points in his account of language and its relation to the universe (see, for example, XIV and XV above)— the link between a proposition's sense and the existence of atomic facts (4.2), the elementary proposition's function of affirming a single atomic fact (4.21), its independence of other elementary propositions (4.211), and its being composed of names in direct combination (4.22). The main principle of Wittgenstein's version of logical atomism, that there must be such elementary propositions, is stated emphatically in the last two sections of the instalment. It is of great interest that Wittgenstein holds this position to be compatible with a universe that is 'infinitely complex' (4.2211) because it contains atomic facts with infinitely many constituents or complex facts constructed of infinitely many atomic ones. He does not appear to have been troubled by the obvious difficulty of how such infinite complexity could be adequately mirrored in language. Possibly his reference to the possibility of such complexity is only a roundabout way of conveying how inescapable he took logical atomism to be.

4.2 This section should be compared with 4.1 (propositions present the existence and non-existence of atomic facts) and 4.4 (propositions express agreement and disagreement with truth-possibilities of elementary propositions).

agreement and disagreement: not to be confused with the sense in which a proposition agrees or disagrees with reality (for which see 2.222). Agreement or disagreement with reality determines the truth-value of a proposition, for to agree with reality is to be true, and to disagree is to be false; but agreement or disagreement with various combinations of atomic situations determines the *sense* of the proposition. 'Proposition p agrees with the existence of state of affairs S' means the same as 'If S is actualized, p is true'; 'p disagrees with S' means the same as 'If S is actualized, p is false'.

possibilities of existence and non-existence of states of affairs: these are *complex* possibilities, each of which can be expressed by a conjunction of elementary propositions or their negations. Cf. the discussion of 'truth-possibilities' at 4.28 and 4.3 below.

4.21 **simplest**: in the sense of not being analysable into component propositions.

elementary proposition: the first use of this expression. Cf. also 4.25, where there is additional reference to the falsity of elementary propositions.

[Speaking of views in the *Tractatus* that were definitely wrong] 'He said ... that it was with regard to "elementary" propositions and their connection with truth-functions or "molecular" propositions that he had had to change his opinions most; and that this subject was connected with the use of the words "thing" and "name"' (Moore, *Papers*, p. 296).

Commentary

4.211 A linguistic analogue of 2.061 (atomic facts are mutually independent). See also 5.134 (no elementary proposition inferrible from an elementary proposition), 4.27 (2) (mutual independence of combinations of atomic facts), 6.3751 (3) *a* (an apparent exception to 4.211).

Later, W. revised this statement: 'Atomic propositions, though they cannot contradict, may exclude one another' (*Logical Form*, p. 168). The reasons for this shift are explained in the notes on 6.3751 below.

sign: in the sense of criterion, distinguishing mark. A somewhat useless one, since it presupposes that elementary propositions can already be recognized.

4.22 a Cf. 3.202 (simple signs are names).
Echoed at 5.55 *b*, 4.24 *a*.

b **concatenation**: like links in a chain. Cf. 2.03 for the same image.

4.221(1) The postulate of analysis. Cf. 3.25 and 3.26 for further remarks about analysis.

'Our analysis, if carried far enough, must come to the point where it reaches propositional forms which are not themselves composed of simpler propositional forms. We must eventually reach the ultimate connection of the terms, the immediate connection which cannot be broken without destroying the propositional form as such' (*Logical Form*, pp. 162–3).

'His present view was that it was senseless to talk of a "final" analysis, and he said that he would now treat as atomic all propositions in the expression of which neither "and", "or", nor "not" occurred, nor any expression of generality, provided we had not expressly given an exact definition, such as we might give of "It's rotten weather", if we said we were going to use the expression "rotten" to mean "both cold and damp"' (Moore, *Papers*, p. 296).

'... the false concept that Russell, Ramsey, and I had. So that one awaits a logical analysis of facts, as if for a chemical analysis of compounds. An analysis by which one really finds a 7-place relation, like an element that actually has a specific weight of 7' (*Math. MS*. 557).

(2) ● 'How can names combine to form a sentence? How can objects combine to form a state of affairs?'

The questions are nowhere answered and it is hard to see how any answers, in W.'s view, could be expected. Here perhaps we have instances of irredeemable nonsense.

4.2211 Something seems to be wrong with the supposition that every *Tatsache* might consist of infinitely many *Sachverhalte*. For an aggregate of any *two* of the latter already constitutes one of the former.

208

It is worth noting that simplicity of objects is compatible with infinite divisibility of complex facts (and so with the non-existence of atomic facts), as the following construction may show.

Suppose that a fact F is composed of the infinitely many constituents $(c_1, c_2, c_3, ...)$. Then we can imagine F to have the following parts:

$$F_1: \quad (c_1, c_3, c_5, ...)$$
$$F_2: \quad (c_2, c_4, c_6, ...)$$
$$F_{11}: \quad (c_1, c_5, c_9, ...)$$
$$F_{12}: \quad (c_3, c_7, c_{11}, ...)$$
$$F_{21}: \quad (c_2, c_6, c_8, ...)$$

....

(The method of construction is the following: If F_i is a given fact in the series, F_{i1} consists of the odd-ranked members of F_i, while F_{i2} consists of the even-ranked members.) In this construction, every part of F is further divisible. The objection to this, on Wittgenstein's principles, is that the c_i would not really 'hang together'. Whenever we thought we had found some of the constituents combined in one of the parts of F, further analysis would require us to abandon the supposition, since the part in question would separate into distinct and independent facts.

4.23 nexus: or, 'context' (*Zusammenhang*).
  An elaboration of 3.3 (in the light of 4.221 *a*).
  'A name cannot only occur in two different propositions, but can occur in the same way in both' (*Notes on Logic*, 98 (3) *c*).

4.24 (1) Seems to conflict with 3.202 and 3.26, where names are called signs.
  For the use of variables, cf. 4.1272.

(2) Cf. 3.318 (a proposition as a function of its constituent expressions).
  It must not be supposed that W. is here suggesting that elementary propositions may contain only a single name (and so have the form *fx*) or only two names (and so have the form $\phi(x, y)$). We are unable to provide any examples of elementary propositions and cannot determine their logical forms *a priori* (cf. 5.553 and 5.5571).

  How is 4.24(2) to be reconciled with 4.22 (the proposition as a concatenation of names)? Suppose an elementary proposition consists of the combination of three names, *a*, *b*, and *c*. Then the elementary proposition can be symbolized as $K(a, b, c)$, where K stands for concatenation. So W.'s *fx* might be taken to be the same as $K(x, b, c)$; and his $\phi(x, y)$ as say $K(x, y, c)$. For a defence of this interpretation, see Anscombe, *Introduction*, pp. 100–1.

XXXIX

DEFINITIONS AND IDENTITIES

(4.241–4.243)

'his instalment provides only a preliminary glimpse of Wittgenstein's
iews concerning the proper interpretation of identities and should be
ead in conjunction with LXIII, where the same topics are discussed
1ore fully. It is already clear from 4.242 that Wittgenstein regards
lentities as dispensable—as mere aids to representation, having no
ntological significance. This follows immediately from his conten-
ion (4.242 b) that an identity makes no reference to the meanings of
ts component signs. In the last section of this instalment, Wittgen-
tein argues against the view that identities convey genuine informa-
ion. But what he says at 4.243 (1, 2) is compatible with identities
)eing logical propositions that 'show', although they do not 'say';
ndeed his later remarks about the use of equations (= identities)
n mathematics (e.g. at 6.2 b) suggest that he would have been
)repared to regard *some* identities as not trivially certifiable by
.nspection. His rejection of identities of the form $a = a$ at 4.243
.s more solidly grounded, although even these might be assigned
the function of simplifying the rules of the system to which they
belong.

4.241 In this section and the next two, W. apparently has in mind only
equations connecting genuine names. This is perhaps implied by the
reference in the first sentence of the present section to the *Bedeutung* of each
sign (3.24 (2) suggests that complex signs do not have a *Bedeutung*).
However, W. elsewhere wishes to introduce abbreviatory definitions,
which will allow complex signs to be replaced by signs that are apparently
simple (cf. 3.261 (2)). The specific definitions that W. uses in the
Tractatus (e.g. at 5.502) are all of this character.

(2) substituted: replaceable without alteration of the sense of the
sentences (or other full contexts) in which the respective signs occur—not
merely replaceable *salva veritate* (as in Leibniz's theory of identity).

means (*heisst*): it would be a mistake to read this as meaning that an equation of the form $a = b$ is supposed to be taken as an assertion *about* the signs a and b. It is important to stress that the equation, on W.'s view, is the expression of a *rule* (cf. (3) b and also 3.343 a).

(3) **rule dealing with signs**: or, 'rule about signs'. Cf. 4.242 on absence of reference to meanings.

It is curious that W. never uses the notation he introduces here. Possibly he projected a more systematic presentation of the foundations of logic and mathematics than the *Tractatus* contains.

4.242 devices: or, 'expedients' (*Behelfe*) or 'resources' (the word is not pejorative). For a similar use of this word (the only other case of its occurrence), see 5.452 (1, 3). We could get along without identities—say everything sayable even if they were banned. (On W.'s views, we could similarly dispense with all necessary propositions. Apparently, he did not envisage the possibility of identities expressing contingent truths.)

b **state nothing**, etc.: this is the case for *all* rules concerning signs (cf. 3.33).

4.243 The questions are, of course, rhetorical (cf. 5.5303).

There is some danger here of the introduction of 'irrelevant psychological considerations', suggested by the apparent reference of the section to what 'we' can or cannot 'know'. W.'s thought is that the supposed empirical use of an equation of the form $a = b$, where both a and b are names, in his sense, is logically impossible.

● 'No place is left for verification in an equation of the form $a = b$, in which both a and b are names. For a and b determine either the same or different objects, as the case may be, *prior* to verification.'

Here, as elsewhere, W. does not admit the possibility of identities that might be contingently true or false. But such identities do occur.

(3) **nor is there any other way in which they have sense**: notice that W. is here altogether rejecting identities in which the *same* name appears on both sides of the sign of identity. Such degenerate identities cannot even be regarded as *showing* something. This follows from his view that equations express rules for the mutual substitutability of signs. For clearly a rule to the effect that a sign can be substituted for itself would not make sense.

will become evident: or, 'will be shown': presumably at 5.531–5.533.

XL

COMBINATIONS OF ATOMIC TRUTH-POSSIBILITIES AND THEIR EXPRESSION IN TRUTH-TABLES

(4.25–4.31)

From this point onwards, Wittgenstein is increasingly concerned with the nature of logic (see XL–XLVI, XLVIII, L–LX, LXVI, LXXI–LXXVII). Wittgenstein's elaborate discussion can be conveniently divided into four parts: (i) views about elementary propositions (notably: that there must be elementary propositions, 4.221 a, composed of concatenations of names, 4.22 b, and mutually independent, 4.211, 5.134); (ii) the 'principle of extensionality', that all propositions are truth-functions of elementary propositions (5 a, also 4.4, 4.2, 5.54); (iii) the characterization of logical truths as tautologies (6.1), i.e. as 'limiting cases' of truth-functions; and (iv) consequences of the foregoing (notably: that there are no 'logical objects', 4.0312 b, 4.441 b, 5.4, that logical truths can be shown but not said, 6.11 a, 5.43 c, that logical symbols belong to a system (are all given together), 3.42, 5.47 (3), that all logical propositions have the same status, 6.127 a, that logical truth is perceivable 'in the symbol alone', 6.113, that logical propositions show the form of the world, 6.12, the nature of proof and calculation in logic, 6.126, and the dispensability of logical propositions, 6.122).

In the present instalment, Wittgenstein begins to prepare the ground for his analysis of propositions as truth-functions of elementary propositions (for which see the next instalment). The schematic arrangement of the truth-conditions of molecular propositions in the form of 'truth-tables', as illustrated in 4.31, has become a standard procedure in elementary symbolic logic.

4.25 Might be read as an elaboration of 4.21.

This entry shows that all elementary propositions are to be regarded as positive. Cf. Anscombe, *Introduction*, p. 33.

Atomic Truth-possibilities

I have argued previously (see notes on *negative facts*, on pp. 70–2) that Wittgenstein is required to hold that the universe consists wholly of atomic facts, which are essentially negation-free. It must be possible, therefore, to analyse the complex situation consisting of the successful verification of some elementary proposition in wholly positive terms. Suppose, for simplicity, that the sentence-fact, *lm* (with *l* standing for object *a*, *m* for object *b*), is itself atomic. Then if *P* (= *lm*) is true, the verification situation can be analysed into the two atomic facts, *lm* and *ab*, together with all such other facts (presumably positive) as ensure that *l* and *m* shall stand for *a* and *b*, respectively. But now suppose, instead, that *P* is false: we no longer have a fact composed of *a* and *b* for *P* to correspond with, and the verification situation must be somehow analysed in terms of *P*'s relation to the atomic facts actually to be found in the universe. I shall now consider some plausible attempts to provide such an analysis.

Imagine the atomic facts to be inspected in falsifying *P* to be constituted by a number of cards each divided into two squares of different colours and suppose *l* and *m* stand for the presence in a card of red and blue respectively. Then the falsification might proceed in the following stages: (i) we put a check sign on every card having a red square; (ii) we do the same for every card having a blue square; and (iii) we confirm finally that every checked card has one and no more than one check mark. (I am assuming that at least one card will have a red square and at least one a blue one: if this were not so, *l* and *m* could not be used by anybody.) Now it seems as if the falsification of *P* has been expressed in wholly positive terms: *P* is falsified by something that *is* the case about the set of cards selected from the original pack, namely all of them having a single added mark, not by something that is *not* the case.

Discarding the illustration, we get the following schema: *l* selects a class *A* of atomic facts, namely all the two-termed ones of which *a* is a constituent, and *m* a corresponding class *B* (and we assume that neither class is null). What falsifies *P* is the fact (if we are to count it such) that *A* and *B* have *no common members*. But is this a positive fact? Surely not. (It is plain that the absence of a common member cannot be expressed as a truth-function of the atomic facts.) We are reduced to saying once again that *P* is falsified by something's *not* being the case and our attempt to construe the falsification of *P* in wholly positive terms has misfired.

There seems to be no good alternative to construing the verification of an elementary proposition as follows: the proposition is successively compared (cf. 2.223, 4.05) with each atomic fact (or with the subsets *A* and *B* above); when we encounter a 'match', i.e. a fact *ab*, we count *P* as true, and we count *P* as false if this never happens. This means that *P*'s truth is established directly, by confrontation with a fact; but its falsity is established *by default*. Since we can never be in a position to know that every atomic fact has been inspected, the best we can say of even a false elementary proposition is that it has not been found to be true *so far*, and disconfirmation will be provisional in a way in which confirmation is not. (Some philosophers would be inclined to say that whereas a true elementary proposition is verified by a single atomic fact, a false one is verified by the whole universe, since we must inspect all reality to establish its truth-value.) This radical asymmetry between confirmation and disconfirmation is disagreeable, but so far as I can see it is unavoidable in the *Tractatus*.

4.26 *b* listed: or, 'provided' (*Angabe*). A language that permitted all elementary propositions to be formulated, while containing no provision for complex propositions (molecular or general propositions) would be able to express the whole truth about the world (and indeed, we might add, would be able to describe completely every possible world).

There is evidence that W. had some qualms about this remark. The original entry in the *Notebooks* corresponds precisely to 4.26*b*. But the revised version printed in Anscombe's edition of the *Notebooks* (98 (1), and see the footnote on the same page) begins with the words, 'It may be doubted whether . . .' and includes a reference to Russell. In spite of Russell's objection it seems clear that W. must affirm 4.26, if the character of his conception of the relation of language to the universe is not to be radically altered.

The first and second remarks of this section seem to be in conflict, inasmuch as the latter demands the additional provision of indications of falsehood. In the light of 1.12 (the totality of facts also determines everything that is not the case), we may conclude that the supplementary information about the false elementary propositions is superfluous.

To provide a proposition with an indication that it is true is equivalent to asserting that proposition: '"*p*" is true says nothing else but p' (*Notebooks*, 9 (7)). Thus the thought of 4.26 can be alternatively rendered as:

● 'The world is completely described by asserting a certain number of elementary propositions—or by asserting the conjunction of those propositions.'

4.27   states of affairs: i.e. 'atomic facts' (*Sachverhalte*).

(**1**) K_n: has the value 2^n.

(**2**)   **combination**: same as 'set' or 'selection'.

This remark is connected with earlier remarks about the independence of *Sachverhalte*, e.g. 2.061. See also 4.211 (mutual independence of elementary propositions) and 5.134 (absence of inferential connexions between elementary propositions).

4.28   correspond: this implies that W. is distinguishing a 'combination of the existence and non-existence of atomic facts' from the corresponding 'combination of the truth and falsity of elementary propositions'. The latter is what he calls a 'truth-possibility' in 4.3. Suppose there are only the three elementary propositions, p_1, p_2, and p_3. Then one combination of actualization and non-actualization of the atomic situations would be expressed by the following set of propositions:

$$p_1, \quad p_2, \quad \sim p_3, \tag{1}$$

while the corresponding combination of truth and falsity of the elementary propositions would be expressed by:

$$p_1 \text{ true}, \quad p_2 \text{ true}, \quad p_3 \text{ false}. \tag{2}$$

As already explained in the notes to 4.26 above, these two forms of expression may be taken as equivalent (e.g. 'p_1 true' may be taken to mean the same as 'p_1').

When the three components of (1) are united in a conjunction, we have what Carnap calls a 'state-description' (*Probability*, p. 70). Leibniz might have said that a state-description describes a 'possible world'.

4.3   Truth-possibilities: same as 'possibilities of truth and falsity' in 4.28, and exemplified by line (2) in the notes on that section above. Notice that every such 'possibility' is complex.

mean: stand for, or refer to. Here again, W. seems to be making the distinction discussed in the notes on the last section.

This section should be compared with 4.1 and 4.4.

4.31 Here *p*, *q*, *r* are supposed to be *elementary* propositions. A modified representation is described at 4.43.

Truth-tables, such as the ones shown in this section, had been used earlier by Frege and others (cf. Church, *Logic*, p. 161, for further details).

THE INTERPRETATION OF TRUTH-TABLES

Although Wittgenstein says he is using 'an easily intelligible symbolism', it is worth while spelling out his intentions in detail. Consider the second figure contained in 4.31, which is used at 4.442 as part of a representation of *p* ⊃ *q*, or, let us say, *r* for short—where *p* and *q* are supposed to be elementary propositions.

Then, in accordance with our previous discussion at 4.28, the table for *r* may be supposed to include a presentation of the four 'truth-possibilities':

p true and *q* true
p false and *q* true
p true and *q* false
p false and *q* false

respectively symbolized in Wittgenstein's diagram at 4.31 by the four rows of *T*s and *F*s. The last column of the figure in 4.442 assigns truth-values to each of these four complex possibilities.

Accordingly, the whole of the figure in 4.442 may be translated into the following verbal formulation of the sense of *p* ⊃ *q* or *r*:

(*a*)   true in case '*p*' is true and '*q*' is true; and true in case '*p*' is false and '*q*' is true; and false in case '*p*' is true and '*q*' is false; and true in case '*p*' is false and '*q*' is false.

According to this interpretation, which seems to answer to Wittgenstein's intentions, the truth-table expresses the sense of *r* by spelling out the conditions in which *r* will be true or false—it is, as Wittgenstein says, an 'expression of the truth-conditions' of *r* (cf. 4.431 *b*). In reading the figure the *T*'s and *F*'s in the truth-table must then be understood to stand for truth and falsehood respectively (cf. 4.31 *b*): if *T* were read as a meaningless mark, we should not know what the truth-table was intended to say. I shall call this the 'new-level'

216

interpretation of the truth-table, because it treats that table as saying something *about p* and *q*. If the table is a correct expression of the sense of *r*, that proposition will be *about* the elementary propositions and consequently at a 'new level'. (Our verbal translation (*a*), is in a 'meta-language'.)

There is, however, another way of understanding the truth-table. Let us now suppose that the four lines of the middle figure in 4.31 are supposed to symbolize four 'combinations of existence and non-existence of atomic facts' or 'combinations of actualization and non-actualization of atomic situations', i.e. four different states-of-affairs. Then the verbal forms of the four lines in the figure will not be as we stated them before but rather:

p and q
not-p and q
p and not-q
not-p and not-q

and the full table for *r* will be equivalent to the following verbal expression of the sense of *r*:

(*b*) p and q; or not-p and q; or not-p and not-q; but not (p and not-q).

On this interpretation, there is no reference *to p* and *q* in the table, and no reference to truth-values. The *T* and *F* serve merely as indicators of the positive or negative quality of the propositional signs to which they are attached and might be replaced by plus and minus signs, or by ticks and crosses. I shall call this the 'same-level' interpretation of the truth-table, because it regards that table as not being about *p* and *q*, but rather about the very same objects in the world that those propositions are about. On this interpretation, the sense of *r* as presented by the table is on the 'same level' as the senses of *p* and of *q*. (Our verbal translation (*b*) is in the 'object-language' to which *p* and *q* belong.)

As stated previously, Wittgenstein's discussion of truth-tables seems to have been intended to be understood according to what I have called the 'new-level' interpretation. Yet, from the stand-point of Wittgenstein's philosophy of language, there are decisive reasons for rejecting this interpretation in favour of the 'same-level' interpretation.

According to Wittgenstein's conception, the proposition expressed by the sign '*p* is true' has exactly the same truth-conditions as the proposition expressed by '*p*', and is therefore identically the same proposition (cf. 5.141). There is no way of interpreting '*p* is true' as a truth-function of '*p*' that does not identify it with '*p*'. As he says in the *Notebooks* (9 (7)), '"*p*" is true' says (*aussagt*) nothing else but '*p*'. (He goes on to say that '"*p*" is true' is a pseudo-proposition, like all combinations of signs that apparently say something that can only be shown.) Similarly, '"*p*" is false' says the same, is exactly the same proposition as, 'not-*p*'. Thus the supposed difference between our verbal forms, (*a*) and (*b*) above, is an illusion: both express exactly the same.

Yet this does not mean that both are equally acceptable: (*a*) must be regarded as misleading and to be excluded from formulation in 'a correct ideography'. For there is no place in Wittgenstein's conception of language for talk *about* propositions, as seems to occur in (*a*). All significant propositions refer to the world by having their components stand proxy for objects in the world, but a proposition is not an object, and any method of symbolization that suggests the contrary must be incorrect. There is no room for a 'meta-language' in Wittgenstein's theory. (We might add that even elementary propositions can be represented by truth-tables, so the 'new-level' interpretation would lead us to treat a proposition as referring to itself, which Wittgenstein has explicitly forbidden at 3.332.)

For these reasons, I henceforward assume that the 'same-level' interpretation, formulated at (*b*) above, is correct and I assume that all of Wittgenstein's remarks about truth-tables should be understood in the light of this interpretation.

XLI

PROPOSITIONS AS TRUTH-FUNCTIONS OF ELEMENTARY PROPOSITIONS

(4.4–4.431)

With what has since come to be called the 'thesis of extensionality', that propositions enter into the make-up of complex propositions only as arguments to truth-functions (also stated at 5, 5.54) we arrive at a point of decisive importance for Wittgenstein's philosophy of language. By comparing 4.2, 4.3, and 4.4, we see that Wittgenstein takes the *sense* of any proposition to be 'agreement and disagreement' with the atomic possibilities (the atomic situations) expressed in elementary propositions. Thus, every proposition signifies *via* the elementary propositions that can be uncovered by analysis. A truth-table is, therefore, a perspicuous rendering of the sense of a complex proposition (cf. 4.4). The great stumbling-block for this conception is the existence of general propositions (for which see LXI, LXII, below).

4.4 This is what came to be called the 'principle of extensionality', also stated more concisely at 5. See Carnap, *Syntax*, p. 245 (with further references, and criticism of the principle of extensionality).

Cf. 4.2 (sense of proposition as agreement with truth-possibilities), 5.54 (propositions result from truth-operations).

W. later abandoned this 'thesis': 'The grammatical rules for "and", "not", "or", etc. are not exhausted by what I said in the *Tractatus*, for there are rules about truth-functions that also treat of the elementary constituents of the proposition' (*Phil. Bem.* p. 34).

agreement: not in the same sense in which a proposition may 'agree' with reality (e.g. at 2.21, 2.222, 5.512). A proposition agrees with reality when it is true; a molecular proposition, *r*, 'agrees with' certain 'truth-possibilities' of the elementary propositions *p* and *q* if e.g. *r* is true when both *p* and *q* are true, or when *p* is false and *q* true, etc.

truth-possibilities: the reference to possibility here, which has troubled some commentators, is not essential. By collation with 4.3 and

4.2, we can see that W. means in 4.4 that the sense of any proposition is a determinate function of the senses of the elementary propositions. 4.4 expresses the very same thought as 5a (propositions are truth-functions of elementary propositions).

COMPLEX PROPOSITIONS AND THE PICTURE THEORY

Suppose we treat each of two naturalistic paintings as analogous respectively to each of two propositions p and q; what would then be an analogue for the disjunctive proposition, $p \vee q$? The two original paintings must be united into a whole, perhaps by having a single picture-frame around them, and there must be some definite indication of the intended truth-functional connexion. Two paintings set side by side with a superimposed 'V' or 'OR' obviously do not constitute a picture in any straightforward sense. The connective mark, 'V', does not represent in the way that patches of paint do, and the arrangement of all the elements in the composite 'painting' taken together no longer means the existence of a corresponding spatial arrangement in reality. The 'picture theory' therefore needs to be supplemented by an account of the function of logical signs, which Wittgenstein's discussion of truth-functions will attempt to provide.

4.41 Cf. 4.431 a for a similar statement.

Each truth-possibility with which a compound proposition 'agrees' constitutes a sufficient condition for that proposition to be true. For instance, since $p \supset q$ agrees with the truth-possibility, 'p false and q true', a sufficient condition for the implicative proposition to be true is that p is false and q true. (In terms of the 'same-level' interpretation, for which see pp. 216–18 above, the sufficient condition in question would be expressed by $\sim p . q$.) Similarly, each truth-possibility with which a proposition 'disagrees' generates a sufficient condition for the proposition to be false.

If we took 4.431 a to be correctly formulated, we would have to amend this section to read '*Agreement and disagreement with* the truth-possibilities', etc.

4.411 It immediately strikes one as probable: an odd expression. Instead of 'probable' one might try 'likely' or 'plausible'. The corresponding passage in the *Notes on Logic* (100 (1)*d*) starts: 'It is *a priori* likely that . . . .'

introduction: in the sense of 'consideration'.

b **palpably**: or, 'obviously', as in *Notes on Logic* (*loc. cit.*). Cf. 4.52*b* (all propositions as generalizations of elementary ones).

HOW COMPLEX PROPOSITIONS DEPEND ON ELEMENTARY ONES

Consider an idealized 'language-game' in which provision is made only for negation-free propositions referring to definite states-of-affairs, and in which no logical operators occur. For example, a child might be offered one picture at a time from a pack of picture-cards, with the understanding that he scores a point in the game if the depicted object is on the mantelpiece, and loses a point otherwise. (This could be played as a kind of memory and observation game.) Each card might plausibly be looked upon as an elementary proposition. Now let the game be modified by introducing a detachable marker (say a red tab) that can be clipped on to a picture-card, with the supplementary convention that the marker converts a 'win' into a 'loss', and *vice versa*. If any number of the red tabs may be attached to the same card, with the understanding that two markers 'cancel out', we shall have a close analogue to the way in which the logical operator, ' $\sim$ ', normally functions. We should be justified in saying that *negation* had been introduced into the game.

The following comments seem to apply:

(i) The new language is derivative from the old, for in order to understand how to use a card with an attached marker (i.e. the equivalent of $\sim p$), the player must first understand how to use the primitive negation-free language. The new language is, as it were, grafted upon the old.

(ii) In teaching the new language, no reference is made to new objects—as would have been the case had a new set of *pictures* been added to the original pack.

(iii) The verification situations for the new game are the same as before: the player must still go to the mantelpiece and 'look for the same state of affairs', the only change being in the definition of a win.

Commentary

This model can easily be made to provide analogues for the use of the other logical operators. Thus we can imagine a further game in which two cards are clipped together in a distinctive way, with the convention that a winning point shall be scored if either picture represents something on the mantelpiece. The new 'marker' that would be needed for this purpose might be thought of as playing the part of the sign of alternation, '∨', as ordinarily used. And just as the 'negation-marker' appears as a mode of transforming the conditions in which a win is scored, without the introduction of any reference to new objects, so the further marker required for combining two pictures in the disjunctive way might be said to indicate a new way of scoring points, and not to involve the examination of new objects.

Here, I believe, we have an accurate picture of how Wittgenstein took the understanding of elementary propositions to be 'a basis' for understanding *all* propositions. Elementary propositions express what might be called the atomic verification situations to which *all* propositions must refer, however indirectly, in virtue of the rules for assignment of truth-values that govern them. But although the truth-conditions (cf. 4.41) of a given proposition must be a determinate function of the truth-conditions of elementary propositions, it does not follow that every proposition is expressible as an explicit function of elementary propositions.

4.42 L_n: has the value 2^{2^n} (cf. 4.27a for 'K_n').
Echoed at 4.45a.
ways: or, 'possibilities', as in the original.

4.43 (2) It is more usual to show 'disagreement' by using the letter F. For an example of W.'s notation, see 4.442.
For reasons for regarding W.'s use of the T's and F's as ill-advised, see pp. 216–18 above.

4.431 (1) **truth-conditions**: the same as 'conditions of truth and falsehood' (4.41).
We were told at 4.41 that the truth-conditions of a proposition *are* the truth-possibilities of elementary propositions with which it agrees. Accordingly, the correct form for this entry should be: 'Formulation of the truth-possibilities of the elementary propositions expresses the truth-conditions of the proposition.'

(**2**) A proposition expresses its sense (3.1431*b*, 3.34*c*, 3.341*a*, 4.5*a*, etc.). So we now get a new conception of the sense of a proposition as being identical with the proposition's truth-conditions.

(**3**) For example, in the *Begriffsschrift*, § 5, Frege defines the sign that means *if p then q* in his notation by a truth-table (in effect) (see Frege, *Translations*, p. 5). In the *Grundgesetze* (vol. 1, § 32), Frege says that every well-formed designation in his symbolism receives a sense as well as a reference, and every name of a truth-value (i.e. a proposition) expresses a sense, a thought. 'For our conventions indeed determine the conditions in which it [the proposition] refers to the True. The sense of the name, the *thought*, is that these conditions are satisfied.'

absolutely undetermined: the German is less emphatic and has the sense of 'by no means determined'.

b 'We are therefore driven into accepting the *truth value* of a sentence as constituting its reference. By the truth value of a sentence I understand the circumstance that it is true or false. . . . For brevity I call the one the True, the other the False' (Frege, *Translations*, p. 63—see also p. 154). For Frege's conception of negation, see *op. cit.* p. 157.

W.'s point here may be that Frege fails to tell us what 'the True' and 'the False' are (indeed any two arbitrary objects would serve in his system). Cf. 5.44 (3, 4) for related remarks about negation.

Of ~ *p*, Frege tells us only that its *reference* is the truth-value other than the truth-value to which *p* refers. But this does not determine the *sense* of ~ *p*. Cf. Anscombe, *Introduction*, p. 107, for further discussion.

XLII

TRUTH-TABLES AS PROPOSITIONAL SIGNS; THERE ARE NO 'LOGICAL OBJECTS'; ASSERTION
(4.44–4.442)

Viewing a truth-table as a propositional sign (4.44), Wittgenstein is now able to reinforce his 'fundamental thought' (4.0312*b*) that 'logical constants' stand for no objects (are not names). For the 'logical constants' appear now to be no more substantial than devices for grouping complex truth-possibilities, which are expressed by lines drawn around these sets of possibilities, by 'brackets' (4.441 *a*). The rejection of assertion as something psychological (4.442 (2)) is also noteworthy.

4.44 Follows from 4.431 *b* as interpreted above. If the sense of a proposition is its truth-conditions, the symbolic expression of these conditions by means of a truth-table is a propositional sign.

We might say that a truth-table *is* a declarative sentence.

4.441 (1) *a* The *T*'s and *F*'s are a means of showing a partition of the elementary truth-possibilities—as could also be done by drawing lines (or 'brackets') round the sets of truth-possibilities.

It is clear: if challenged, W. might say 'Try to use names and see what happens!' But the truth-tables *can* be replaced by complex statements containing logical connectives (cf. discussion at pp. 216–18) so W. seems to be begging the question.

horizontal and vertical lines: i.e. of the figures in 4.31.

brackets: cf. 5.461 for another reference to them.

b **There are no 'logical objects'**: an important statement. Cf. 4.0312 *b* and 5.4 for similar remarks.

HOW LOGICAL SIGNS SYMBOLIZE

Wittgenstein's important conclusion that there are no 'logical objects' follows immediately from his principle that objects are represented by genuine names, while the logical signs are 'interdefinable' (cf. 5.42 *b*). The negation sign cannot stand for anything if its application to itself 'cancels' out. But this is not to say that such symbols as 'v' and '⊃' are otiose, for these and the other logical symbols contribute to the sense of the compounds in which they occur, and $p \vee q$ has quite a sense distinct from that of $p \supset q$. How does Wittgenstein regard the contributions to sense made by the logical symbols?

Consider the role of the negation-symbol, ' ∼ '. In the simple 'mantelpiece' game discussed above at pp. 221–2, it was natural to think of the 'red marker' (the sign of negation) as demanding a reversed sense of the picture card (proposition) to which it was clipped. A player who already knows how to play with the unmarked card (how to confirm and disconfirm a proposition) is instructed by the red tab to interchange verification with falsification. If the world is conceived as an aggregate of negation-free atomic facts, the 'red marker' (or, normally, the sign of negation) might plausibly be held to show only *how we take* a proposition. Negation, from such a standpoint, is merely a feature of our mode of representation and is no more substantial than the difference between linear and polar co-ordinates. Since the world could be completely described in a language containing only primitive negation-free propositions, the presence of negation in any language we use merely shows that *we* have chosen a more indirect form of representation. This path leads straight on to conventionalism. The Wittgenstein of the *Investigations* would have said that we are free to use the 'markers' as we please; a decision to introduce a device for reversing the sense of propositions in the original game does not prejudge any rule of 'double negation' and we are free, for instance, to count a double occurrence of the negation sign as simply illegitimate. All manner of 'language games' might be played with the curl and the other logical signs and it is up to us to decide how we shall assign truth-values to the compounds in which they occur.

Such a view was quite alien to Wittgenstein's thought in the *Tractatus*. Although he would have agreed that the 'curl' might be arbitrarily introduced in a variety of ways, some of them only remotely analogous to what we now mean by negation, he would have insisted that any such choice involved necessary commitments: 'Although there is something arbitrary in our notations, this much is not arbitrary—that when we have determined something arbitrarily, then something else is necessarily the case. (This derives from the *essence* of the notation)' (3.342). But *what* is non-arbitrary about our notation for negation? According to Wittgenstein, this must be revealed in the use of any symbol 'that can serve the same purpose' (3.341). Everything now turns upon what we shall count as 'the purpose' or the use of negation. Suppose we say that nothing shall count as a sign of negation unless it has *all* the semantical and syntactical features of the curl, ' ∼ '. Then a 'red marker' which may not be duplicated on the same picture card cannot count as a sign of negation, and similarly for other deviations from our present pattern of usage of the curl. But then the insistence that we are not free to introduce a negation sign obeying whatever rules we please reduces to a triviality: if we have made up our minds in advance that nothing shall count as a sign of negation unless it obeys the same laws as the curl, it follows at once that every sign of negation (whether expressed by a red tab, by turning words upside down, or in some other way) must commit us, for example, to the rule of double negation. But what requires us to say that no other sign shall count as a sign of negation? If Wittgenstein thought that the *syntactical* rules controlling the use of ' $\sim$ ' sufficed to determine its role in truth-functional compounds (as I suspect he did) he was mistaken. Only when $\sim p$ is spelled out to *mean* the same as 'It is not the case that p' does the desired invariance of function emerge.

4.441 (2) On the principle that the essence of a symbol is unchanged by translation.

4.442 (1) An example of 4.44 for the case of $p \supset q$.

The figure is a complete sentence—no further assertion sign is needed.

'Frege's assertion sign marks the *beginning of the sentence*. Thus its function is like that of the full-stop' (*Investigations*, § 22).

'Assertion is merely psychological. There are only unasserted propositions' (*Notes on Logic*, 96 (2) *ef*).

In a great many contexts of the *Tractatus*, W. can be taken to mean by a proposition what could be expressed by a 'that'-clause (e.g. 'that snow is white'), i.e. what he called a 'proposition-radical' (*Satzradikal*) in *Investigations* (p. 11, foot).

For Frege's use of the assertion sign, see *Translations*, pp. 33–4, 156–7. For Russell's different use, see *Principia*, vol. 1, pp. 8, 92.

ASSERTION

Russell introduces the assertion sign 'for distinguishing a complete proposition, which we assert, from any subordinate propositions contained in it but not asserted' (*Principia*, vol. 1, p. 8). The distinction between a complex proposition and its components is sufficiently marked without the use of a 'sign-post', so its function really is, as Wittgenstein says, to indicate that the authors of *Principia* are putting forward some propositions as true. Even so, the sign is unnecessary.

Frege needs the sign-post (or, strictly speaking, the vertical part of the sign, which he calls the 'judgement stroke') in order to pass from a sentence that *designates* the True or the False to a 'recognition of the truth of a thought' (*Thought*, p. 294)—i.e. from a designation to what he calls a 'judgement' (*Urteil*). In Frege's conception, 'judgement' might be taken to have the same relation to an act of judging that a 'thought' has to an act of thinking. That is to say, Frege is not required to say, *pace* Wittgenstein, that the presence of his sign-post in his text means that *Frege* judges the proposition in question to be true. But on the other hand, it is hard to make sense of this supposedly 'objective' judgement, which cannot, on Frege's principles, be a thought. Frege's sign-post serves no purpose. If certain sentences did designate the True, it would be sufficient to list them in a treatise purporting to contain only the truth and their presence in the treatise would suffice to show that their truth was intended. Frege's formal arguments would be unimpaired if his 'judgement-stroke' were simply deleted. Frege's introduction of the assertion-sign may be viewed as an unsuccessful attempt to restore to the propositional sign, which he had degraded to a mere designation, its truth-claiming aspect. Wittgenstein's account of the proposition does justice to this aspect from the start.

See also notes on 'supposition' at 4.063 (1)*c* above.

4.442 (2)*c*   Echo of 3.332.

However, Frege's view of assertion did not require him to say a proposition asserts its own truth.

(3)*b*   Illustrates 4.441 (2). The notation is used in 5.101.

(4)   The number is $K_n (= 2^n)$, where n is the number of terms in the right-hand pair of brackets.

XLIII

TAUTOLOGY AND CONTRADICTION AS LIMITING CASES OF TRUTH-FUNCTIONS

(4.45–4.4661)

This instalment is of decisive importance for Wittgenstein's philosophy of logic, for he will proceed to say that logical truths are tautologies (LXXI). Wittgenstein's conception of the 'limiting cases' of truth-functions is original and illuminating, even for those who cannot accept his analysis of the essence of representation and symbolism. The present instalment might well be read together with XLVIII.

The notion of 'range' (*Spielraum*) introduced at 4.463 will later prove important for Wittgenstein's theory of probability (XLIX).

4.45 (1) L_n has already occurred at 4.42, of which this is a repetition.

(2)   They are so ordered at 5.101. The series is what W. calls a 'formal' series.

4.46 (1)   **extreme cases**: also called 'limiting cases' at 4.466 (4).

TAUTOLOGIES AND CONTRADICTIONS AS 'DEGENERATE CASES'

A tautology and a contradiction are 'extreme' in having respectively the largest possible number of independent 'truth-conditions' (all of them), and the smallest number of them (none). But Wittgenstein's use of the expressions 'limiting case' and 'degenerate case' shows that he means more than this. When mathematicians call a circle a 'limiting' or a 'degenerate' case of a regular polygon, they wish to emphasize (i) that the circle can be treated as a 'limit', in the mathematical sense, of a certain infinite series of regular polygons with constantly increasing numbers of sides (i.e. as a figure which the members of the series of regular polygons 'approach' as closely as desired), (ii) that the circle *lacks* certain properties possessed by each member of the series (e.g. the property of having a finite number of sides), (iii) that it is a convenient linguistic fiction to speak of a circle *as being* a regular polygon. (Cf. the sense in which a pair of lines is called by mathematicians a 'degenerate' conic.)

Analogues of all three features of the mathematical uses of the expressions 'limiting case' and 'degenerate case' mark Wittgenstein's conception of tautology and contradiction: (i) All truth-functions can be arranged in a series of propositions with steadily increasing ranges (cf. 5.101) in such a way that tautology appears as the limit (or, strictly speaking, the upper bound) of the series, (ii) a tautology, unlike each member of the series of significant propositions that it bounds, says nothing (4.461 *a*), has no truth-conditions (4.461 *b*), is senseless (4.461 *c*), is not a picture of reality (4.462 *a*), etc., (iii) a tautology, lacking as it does the essential property of being true-or-false (the bi-polarity of a genuine proposition), is only by courtesy called a proposition (4.466 *c*), and the signs in it separate or 'disintegrate' (4.466 *e*). This assimilation of a tautology (and of a contradiction) to 'degenerate cases', in the mathematical sense of that expression, lends itself to sustained elaboration and is genuinely illuminating.

Wittgenstein uses another, closely related image, when he says in the *Moore Notes* that in a tautology 'all its simple parts have meaning, but it is such that the connexions between these paralyse or destroy one another, so that they are all connected only in some irrelevant manner' (117 (4)). In his 1939 lectures, he compared a tautology to a wheel running idly in a mechanism of cog-wheels, and contradiction to a wheel that jams and cannot turn at all (*Math. Notes*, p. 38). There is an obvious affinity between these ideas and the account given at 4.462 (2) of the 'conditions of agreement with the world' as 'cancelling one another' in a tautology.

We can make Wittgenstein's conception plainer by returning to our illustration of the 'mantelpiece games' for which see p. 221 above. Suppose the player has been taught a game in which a 'move' consists of checking two picture cards, connected by a green band (which functions like the logical sign ' $\equiv$ ' of equivalence), against objects on the mantelpiece, with the understanding that he wins if *both* pictures represent objects to be found there or if *neither* does, but not otherwise. Suppose the player is now handed two cards, connected in this way, that are duplicates (i.e. that he is asked to 'verify' a proposition of the form $p \equiv p$). A dull-witted child might proceed to check each card separately, in order to compare the two outcomes, exactly as in the other cases. He can first check one card, as he did when given a set of two different pictures ($p \equiv q$), and then check the second (the duplicate) and finally 'compare' the two results. This will be a case of a 'degenerate' verification—a 'mock' verification, as it were. For one is inclined to say that the rules of the game *already* determine the correct verdict in the case of two duplicate cards. Any moderately intelligent and alert player will see at once that he need not look at the mantelpiece at all, because inspection of the move itself (the two duplicate cards) suffices to determine that he *must* 'win'. (A *very* intelligent child, however, might simply refuse to play, on the ground that the 'degenerate case' had not been covered in the rules previously explained to him.) The defining rules of the game are such as to sever the connexion between the instruction (the two duplicate cards combined by the bond of equivalence) and the contingent state of affairs on the mantelpiece.

It is easy to construct other illustrations of Wittgenstein's conception of tautologies. I will mention two more: (i) A game played by drawing a line around a half, a quarter, a fifth, or some other assigned fraction of a given sheet of paper. (The outcome might depend on the skill with which the player approximated the desired fraction.) In this game, an instruction to surround the *whole* of the sheet of paper, and an instruction to surround *no* part of it, would both be 'degenerate': we may say, as we choose, either that the player *cannot* satisfy these orders—or, alternatively, that he is bound to 'satisfy' them by doing nothing: the rules of the game guarantee that he will 'win' ('Logic takes care of itself'). (ii) A maze-tracing game, in which, given a plan of a maze, a player has to draw a path leading from an entry to an exit. An 'extreme' case is one in which only one path is possible, so that the player is bound to get the right answer (like a chess problem for morons in which there is only one legal move)—or, again, one in which no path connects the entry with any exit, so that the player is bound to fail. In such a game recognition of the extreme cases is not necessarily immediate—a parallel to the cases of complex tautologies and complex contradictions, for which Wittgenstein envisages a decision procedure.

4.46 (2) *tautological*: W. seems to have been the first to use this word and the corresponding noun in this sense. 'Tautology' has since become a permanent item in the philosopher's vocabulary.

There is an interesting anticipation of W.'s idea in W. E. Johnson's 1892 paper on 'The Logical Calculus'. Johnson's 'truism' and 'falsism'—or 'formal truth' and 'formal falsity' (*Calculus*, p. 343) seem to correspond exactly to W.'s 'tautology' and 'contradiction'. Many of the ideas expressed in Johnson's paper, such as the distinction he makes between *universal* and *formal* truths (*op. cit.* p. 3) and his interpretation of general propositions as infinite conjunctions or disjunctions (*op. cit.* p. 240), are close to W.'s ideas. I do not know whether W. had read Johnson's paper.

(4) **tautology**: among the important statements in which this concept occurs are 6.1 (all the propositions of logic are tautologies) and 6.113 (existence of an effective decision procedure for tautologies—cf. also 6.122, 6.126a, etc.). It plays a central part in W.'s attempt to clarify the notion of logical truth.

4.461 (1) **show what they say**: i.e. their senses (cf. 4.022a).

For tautologies as saying nothing, cf. 5.142. For tautologies as showing that they are tautologies, cf. 6.127b.

W. held that a tautology could show at least three different things: (i) each tautology shows that it is a tautology; (ii) that a symbol having a definite structure is a tautology shows something about the logical forms of its constituent expressions (cf. 6.12d); (iii) that the entire set of tautologies consists of expressions having a certain determinate character shows something about the world (cf. 6.124d). Only the first of these three aspects of what is shown by tautologies will be considered here.

Consider the tautology $p \vee \sim p$ as an illustration. What does it mean to say that this tautology shows that it 'says nothing', that it is a tautology? The answer might run as follows: In order to understand the expression $p \vee \sim p$, we must understand that p is a proposition, and that '$\vee$' and '$\sim$' have the rules of use specified in their respective truth-tables. If we understand these definitions for the wedge and the curl, we must see that the complex expression $p \vee \sim p$ provides no possibility for its own falsification (its truth-table ends in a column of *T*'s). If we have any doubt about this, we have not yet grasped the definitions of the operators: it is a criterion for our understanding the definitions of the operators involved that we regard it as absurd to 'try to see' whether $p \vee {\sim}p$ accords or disaccords with contingent facts. (Of course, in the case of a sufficiently complex tautology, we are permitted to establish its modality by calculation, as in 6.1203.) The rules for the use of the wedge and the curl guarantee that $p \vee {\sim}p$ shall be the kind of 'degenerate case' that W. calls a tautology. '*E* shows that it is a tautology' means: 'The rules for the use of the constituents of *E* determine, without reference to any facts, that *E* is true, no matter what truth-values its constituents have.'

(2) 'The supposed truth-conditions of tautologies and contradictions are in no literal sense truth-conditions of them, such as logically to *condition* their truth-values—if it makes sense to ascribe truth-values to them. The supposed function of such truth-conditions in matrix definitions [= truth-table definitions] . . . is a fiction' (Lazerowitz, 'Tautologies', p. 201).

(3) **lack sense**: i.e. are senseless (*sinnlos*), but not nonsensical (cf. 4.4611). See note on 4.003 above.

'So far as I can see, if we use "make sense" in any way in which it is ordinarily used, "Either it's raining or it's not" *does* make sense, since we should certainly say that the meaning of this sentence is different from that of "Either it's snowing or it's not", thus implying that since they have different meanings, both of them have *some* meaning' (Moore, *Papers*, pp. 272–3).

(4) The two arrows conflict—an image that fits the case of contradiction. For tautology we might perhaps imagine a re-entrant arrow sending us nowhere.

4.4611 Although 'o' is not a numeral, it is convenient to have the symbol and to treat it for the most part like a numeral. Similarly, it is convenient to admit as well-formed the degenerate cases of the truth-table in which the last column consists entirely of *T*'s or entirely of *F*'s.

Compare the following remark from the *Notebooks*: 'We cannot say that both tautology and contradiction say *nothing* in the sense that they are both, say, zero points (*Nullpunkte*) in a scale of propositions. For at least they are *opposite* (*entgegengesetzte*) poles' (45 (1)).

In the paragraph of the *Notebooks* at which the entry corresponding to 4.4611 occurs (58 (8)), W. says that the roles played by 'pseudo-propositions' which are tautologies or contradictions 'must be clearly set forth'. Unless their use in logical symbolism can be explained and defended, the presence of logical propositions must be regarded simply as a nuisance. W. assigns a certain philosophical role to logical propositions as presenting the 'scaffolding' of the world (6.124 a), but they ought also to have some more mundane employment. W. assigns useful roles to some logical propositions when he says, with some exaggeration, that every logical proposition 'is the form of a proof' (6.1264 b) and is 'a *modus ponens* presented in signs' (6.1264 c), but the function of expressing inferential connexions between contingent propositions can at best belong to tautologies involving implication. This account does not fit the case of as simple a tautology as $p \vee \sim p$ and says nothing about the uses of contradictions. Indeed W.'s view that all tautologies 'say the same' leaves their function in language and thought a mystery. The reason for this may be that W.'s conception of sense as a partition of logical space into regions respectively composed of verifying and falsifying conditions compels him in the end to treat all tautologies as synonymous, and so leaves him with no resources for explaining their differential functions. (Something like Frege's distinction between reference and sense might have helped at this point.) All logical propositions, from this standpoint, have the same limiting function of 'saying nothing'—or, as we might reasonably say, no function at all.

4.462 (1) If they were 'pictures of reality' they would have sense and would be propositions. Tautology and contradiction are *not* propositions: 'Logical propositions are neither true nor false' (*Moore Notes*, 108 (6) b).

'Tautologies and contradictions are not true and false respectively in *any* sense in which contingent propositions are true or false' (Lazerowitz, 'Tautologies', p. 197).

4.463 (1) range: or, 'freedom'. The word, *Spielraum* (literally, 'play space'), suggests room in which to move (as we speak of some part of a machine having a certain 'play', having a certain space in which it can move freely, although connected with the other parts of the machine). The next paragraph makes plain the idea behind the metaphor: a solid body can be conceived as occupying a portion of space, whose use it denies to any other body; in this way it 'restricts the freedom of movement of others' (4.463 b).

For the analogy with logical space, we must think, first, of each 'point' as consisting of what W. has called a 'truth-possibility of the elementary propositions' at 4.4 above. If there were only the three elementary propositions, p, q, and r, one such 'point' would correspond to the 'possibility' $p.q.r$, another to the possibility, $p. \sim q.r$, and there would be eight such 'points' in all. (In general, a point corresponds to a conjunction in which each elementary proposition or its negation occurs.) A proposition may be said, by analogy, to 'occupy' the region of logical space consisting of all the 'points' answering to elementary truth-possibilities that *falsify* the given proposition. (Thus, in our simplified illustration of a world with three elementary propositions, the proposition $p \vee q$ has a range consisting of the two points, $\sim p . \sim q . r$ and $\sim p . \sim q . \sim r$.) An alternative way of working the analogy is to conceive of the range of a given proposition as consisting of all the points answering to truth-possibilities with which the given proposition is compatible, i.e. the truth-possibilities that *verify* it. (On this interpretation, the proposition $p \vee q$ would have a range consisting of the six points, $p . q . r$, $\sim p . q . r$, $p . \sim q . r$, etc.) See also Stenius, *Exposition*, p. 57.

W.'s use of the notion of *Spielraum* in connexion with his discussion of probability (cf. 5.15 below) may have been derived from von Kries, who uses the idea frequently in his book on probability.

The term 'range' was adopted by Carnap, with acknowledgement to W. (*Syntax*, p. 199). In *Meaning and Necessity*, Carnap defines the range of a sentence as 'the class of all those state-descriptions' in which it holds (p. 9)—i.e. he adopts the second of the two interpretations mentioned above.

(2) **in the negative sense**: the elementary truth-possibilities denied by a given proposition leave the rest of logical space (the remaining possibilities) for further determination by another proposition.

in the positive sense: the elementary truth-possibilities allowed by (compatible with) a given proposition constitute a bounded portion of logical space.

● 'Think of logical space as the totality of elementary truth-possibilities (answering to conjunctions of affirmed and negated elementary propositions). Then a given proposition can be thought of as *occupying* all the positions corresponding to the elementary truth-possibilities it denies.'

(3) A tautology is compatible with every state of affairs, hence it 'occupies' no part of logical space; similarly, a contradiction 'occupies' all positions in logical space—renders everything impossible.

4.464a Cf. 5.525*ab* (on how the modality of a proposition is shown).

(2) Cf. 5.152 (3) (certainty as a limiting case of probability).
first: not in the original.

4.465 Further develops the point that a tautology says nothing. (In the light of 4.4611 we might compare the truth that $n + 0 = n$ for all n.)

'The essence of a "logical law" is that its product with any proposition yields this proposition' (*Math. MS.* p. 541).
c Cf. 3.34*c* (essential features of a proposition as enabling the expression of its sense).

For: the 'product' referred to in *a* and *b* must be *essentially* the same as the original proposition, because it says the same, has the same sense.

4.466 (1) 'The combination of symbols in a tautology cannot possibly correspond to any one particular combination of their meanings—it corresponds to every possible combination; and therefore what symbolizes can't be the connexion of the symbols' (*Moore Notes*, 117 (7)).

● 'Tautology corresponds to every state of affairs—if we allow ourselves to speak of correspondence for the moment—i.e. to an "arbitrary combination of objects". But every particular combination of signs must determine a particular combination of the objects named by the signs. So, if *every* combination of the objects is permitted, their names cannot really be logically connected in the tautological sentence. The relations between the signs depict nothing.'

Anscombe, at *Introduction*, p. 76, happily compares a tautology to the Bellman's map in the *Hunting of the Snark* that was 'A perfect and absolute blank'. See also her reference to 4.466 at p. 77.

their meanings: the co-ordinated objects.

(4) **limiting cases**: cf. 4.46*a* on 'extreme cases'. Tautology and contradiction are 'limiting cases' of combinations in the sense of not being combinations at all. (Similarly we might say that parallel lines are limiting cases of intersecting lines inasmuch as they do not intersect at all.)

'Ramsey very rightly called tautologies and contradictions degenerate propositions' (*Math. MS.* 565).

4.4661 The 'combinations' in question here can be no more than physical relations of the sign-vehicles. Strictly speaking, there is no 'symbol' in the logical proposition, since no sense emerges.

In the *Notebooks*, W. says that $p \vee \sim p$ is only apparently (*scheinbar*) a sign, but really the dissolution (*Auflösung*) of a proposition (54 (11)).

have no meaning: are insignificant, immaterial.

XLIV

THE GENERAL PROPOSITIONAL FORM
(4.5–5.01)

The 'general form of a proposition' is the same as the essence of a proposition (4.5 (2), cf. 5.471). So, much that has already been said about propositions bears upon the present topic. Wittgenstein is always seeking the essence, and is uninterested in the accidental features of a particular mode of representation. Since we know what we mean by a proposition in general, it must be possible to express this formal concept definitively (4.5 (3)). What is this 'general form'? Wittgenstein first says it can be expressed as 'This is how things stand' (4.5 (3) *b*). (We might try saying, more ponderously: The essence of a proposition is its capacity to say something about how matters are in reality.) This cryptic and unsatisfactory answer is later replaced by the conception of any proposition whatever as resulting from a single logical operation of joint negation upon elementary propositions (see 6). Wittgenstein's considered answer to our question is that the essence of a proposition—its 'most general form'—is the character of being a truth-function of elementary propositions. (But does this not leave the essence of elementary propositions in the dark? Perhaps we might say that the essence of an elementary proposition is to be a picture of a concatenation of objects? If so, we are back to something like the original answer that Wittgenstein gives in 4.5 (3) *b*.)

Instalment LVI may be read immediately.

4.5 (1) **now**: a link with 4.4. It will be seen that the expression of propositions as truth-functions of elementary propositions shows the general propositional form (*allgemeine Satzform*).

'In giving the general form of a proposition you are explaining what kind of ways of putting together the symbols of things and relations will correspond to (be analogous to) the things having those relations in reality' (*Moore Notes*, 112 (2) *c*).

general propositional form: discussed again at 5.47–5.472, 5.54.

Notice that the rule of construction envisaged will not require reference to the meanings of names (in accordance with previous prescriptions for logical syntax, cf. 3.33).

(3) *a* In the *Notebooks*, W. adds that if we ever encountered a propositional form that could not have been 'foreseen', this would mean that a *new experience* first made this propositional form possible. But all propositional forms must be *a priori* (89 (7–10)).

b **This is how things stand**: or, 'things are thus and thus' or 'this is how things are'.

This is not an adequate solution of the problem set at the beginning of the section: indeed, the form of words offered is cryptic to the point of unintelligibility. A better discussion of the general propositional form is given at 6.

'That [referring to 4.5 (3) *b*] is the kind of proposition one repeats to oneself countless times. One thinks that one is tracing the outline of the thing's nature over and over again, and one is merely tracing round the frame through which we look at it' (*Investigations*, § 114, p. 48).

'At bottom, giving "This is how things are" as the general form of propositions is the same as giving the definition: a proposition is whatever can be true or false. For instead of "This is how things are" I could have said "This is true" (or again "This is false")' (*op. cit.* § 136). See also § 134 for further criticism.

4.51 *b* **there I have**: or, 'those are' (*das sind*).

fixes their limits: or, 'demarcates them'. For a similar use of *begrenzen*, see 5.5262 *b*. See also 5.5561 *ab*. That *all* propositions are truth-functions of elementary propositions shows the 'limits' of the world. To anything that is not thus constructed out of elementary propositions, there can correspond nothing in the world.

4.52 *a* Cf. 1.11, 5.524 (2).

its being the *totality* of them all: I do not think that W. needs any 'super-fact'. Cf. notes to 5.524 *a* below.

b **in a certain sense**: they are 'generalizations' in the sense of being truth-functions that are less determinate than elementary propositions—not in the narrower sense in which generalization involves quantification.

4.53 Strictly speaking, we ought to say that the form is expressed by or presented by a variable (cf. 4.1271 *b*).

5 truth-function: first introduction of this expression.

This is a concise statement of the 'thesis of extensionality'. See notes on 4.4 above.

b The identity function—the one having the same truth-value as its argument.

5.01 Another way of stating 5.

XLV

THE DISTINCTION BETWEEN 'ARGUMENT' AND 'INDEX'

(5.02)

This instalment contains an interesting example of the way in which Wittgenstein sometimes introduces a technical term to mark a distinction in logical grammar. (For other examples of this procedure the reader may refer back to Wittgenstein's use of the adjective 'formal' in connexion with concepts, and his distinction between 'sign' and 'symbol'.)

Wittgenstein has just said, at 5.01, that elementary propositions are arguments of (all) propositions, which is, of course, the same as saying that the latter are functions of the former. (Thus, 5.01 means exactly the same as the preceding remark 5*a*.) Now, according to Wittgenstein's conception of a function, to say that a complex proposition is a function of elementary propositions is to imply that grasping the sense of the former requires grasping the senses of its components (cf. the discussion of $\sim p$ in 5.02 (2)*b*). (This is why, later on, at 5.25*c*, he will distinguish an operation from a function; and why, at 5.251, he will say that a function cannot be its own argument.) We might say that, for Wittgenstein, the sign for a value of a genuine function is *essentially* complex. A good example of this is the propositional sign, which *must* be complex, because the proposition is a function of its component expressions (3.318). We might replace a whole sentence, in some code, by a single symbol that *looked* simple; but in order to understand that apparently simple symbol, we should have to be able to translate it into an articulate sentence.

Wittgenstein now accuses Frege of having confused argument and 'index' (5.02 (3) *a*), in treating propositions as designations of truth-values. By an 'index' of a name, Wittgenstein means an expression forming part of the name, though its meaning is irrelevant to the meaning of the whole (as the meaning of 'cock' is irrelevant today to the meaning of the complex 'cock and bull story' of which it is a part—cf. notes on 5.02 (2) *b* below). But Wittgenstein's allegation is incorrect. Had Frege really thought of the names composing a proposition as 'indices' in Wittgenstein's sense, he must have conceded that the meaning of any proposition could just as well have been conveyed by a simple symbol—say *T* for a true proposition, and *F* for a false one. Now, Frege would have agreed that the reference (*Bedeutung*) of a proposition could be identified by a name; but he also held that the *sense* of a proposition was a function of the senses of its components (as Wittgenstein himself seems to recognize at 3.318 in his allusion to Frege). The weaknesses of Frege's semantics lie elsewhere.

5.02 (1) *a* **indices**: the word 'index' occurs again in the text only at 4.0411 *a*, where W. considers the possibility (which he rejects) of using an index to replace the notation '(*x*).*fx*' by, say, 'Gen. *fx*'.

(2) *b* **the sense of** '∼ *p*': see notes on 5.5151 below.

For Russell's use of ' +$_c$', see *Principia*, vol. II, p. 73.

In the *Blue Book*, W. gives the illustration of 'Bright's disease'—where 'Bright' does not designate a particular person, but is merely part of a name for a disease (p. 21).

W.'s thought is that an essentially complex symbol is readily confused with one that seems to be complex, while actually replaceable by a simple symbol. An example might be the expression 'Venn diagrams'. A novice might take this as an abbreviation for 'the diagrams invented by Venn', in which case the expression would be essentially complex. But in fact the expression is so used that statements containing it would remain true even if it were discovered that John Venn never used the diagrams in question. The word 'Venn', as it occurs in 'Venn diagram', is merely a distinguishing tag: to use it correctly, all one has to do is to be able to recognize cases of 'Venn diagrams' and to distinguish them from, say, 'Boole's diagrams'. The whole expression functions as a name, and merely 'alludes' to Venn. (See the quotation below.) W. would call 'Venn' an *index* in such a case. An index, in this sense, is a supplementary mark, not itself a name, attached to another sign in order to obviate ambiguity. Its presence is shown by the possibility of replacing the ostensibly complex name in which it occurs by a simple symbol (cf. W.'s remarks about ' $+_c$ ' in 5.02 (2) *b*).

'One may say that an index *alludes* to something, and such an allusion may be justified in all sorts of ways. Thus calling a sensation "the expectation that *B* will come" is giving it a complex name and "*B*" possibly alludes to the man whose coming had regularly been preceded by the sensation' (*Blue Book*, p. 21).

d **is always part of a description**: this seems an unnecessary condition, that does not fit some of W.'s own examples.

(3) *b* I think Frege would have maintained, however, that the proposition's truth-value is a function of the references of its names—and would therefore have dismissed W.'s objection.

XLVI

THE CONSEQUENCE RELATION
(5.1–5.134)

Wittgenstein orders all the truth-functions of two variables into a single formal series (cf. the definition of 'formal series' at 4.1252 *a*), which he uses later in his discussion of probability (XLIX). The remainder of this instalment is devoted to the consequence relation between propositions—the relation that holds between *p* and *q* when the first follows from the second. Wittgenstein leans heavily on a number of metaphors, none of them notably illuminating. He describes the situation usually expressed by '*p* follows from *q*' (or, '*q* entails *p*') in the following alternative ways: (i) the 'truth-grounds of *p* contain the truth-grounds of *q*', i.e. every state of affairs that verifies *q* also verifies *p* (5.101 (2) + 5.12), (ii) the sense of *p* is 'contained' in the sense of q (5.122), (iii) p is affirmed (*bejaht*) by q (5.124). To these might have been added that the 'range' of p has the 'range' of q as a part. I believe the notion of one proposition 'containing' another in Wittgenstein's sense is an impediment to clarity. Wittgenstein's main point, however, is that the consequence relation is internal (5.131). This in turn connects with his important contention that 'laws of inference' cannot serve to justify or validate inferences (5.132 (3, 4)).

5.1 (1)   See the similar statements at 4.45 b.

series: note the plural form here. There are alternative ways of arranging truth-functions in a formal series. An example follows at 5.101.

(2)   This will be elaborated in sections 5.15 ff.

5.101 (1)   The rows of T's and F's between parentheses are the last columns of the corresponding truth-tables, as explained in 4.442 (3).

The sixteen truth-functions have been so arranged by W. that if r entails s it appears lower on the page: one ordering principle is that the stronger truth-function appears below the weaker one. Where this principle fails to determine the order of appearance, W. has used a supplementary lexicographical order. The latter is arbitrary, of course; there are many other ways in which the truth-functions might have been arranged with the weaker preceding the stronger.

(2)   truth-possibilities: have been defined at 4.3. The definition of 'truth-grounds' here given means that, for instance, $p \supset q$ has the three truth-grounds *p-and-q*, *not-p-and-q*, and *not-p-and-not-q* (see the corresponding truth-table at 4.442 (1)).

5.11   As an illustration, suppose we have four propositions expressed as follows in the notation of 5.101:

$$(T \ \ T \ F \ T \ \ T \ F \ F \ \ T) \quad (p, q, r) \qquad (s_1)$$
$$(F \ T \ \ T \ F \ F \ F \ \ T \ \ T) \quad (p, q, r) \qquad (s_2)$$
$$(T \ \ T \ F \ F \ \ T \ F \ \ T \ \ T) \quad (p, q, r) \qquad (s_3)$$
$$(F \ \ T \ F \ \ T \ F \ F \ F \ \ T) \quad (p, q, r) \qquad (t)$$

The 'common truth-grounds' of s_1, s_2, s_3 will be shown by vertical columns containing nothing but T's in the first three lines of the above figure. Inspection shows this to be the case in columns 2 and 8 but in no others. Since t has a T in the 2nd and 8th place of its entry, we can conclude that t does follow from $s_1 . s_2 . s_3$.

5.12   A special case of 5.11 when there is only a single premise.

5.121   A brief restatement of 5.12.
See the similar remark at 5.14.

5.122   **contained**: a peculiar (and possibly unfortunate) use of this word, that does not occur elsewhere, in this sense, except at 5.121.

5.123 *a*   come true: rather, 'are true' (*stimmen*).
***b*   its**: refers to the proposition, not to the 'world'. In the corresponding passage of *Notes on Logic*, W. says 'No world can be created in which a proposition is true, unless the constituents of the proposition are created also' (98 (2)).
similarly: because in both cases the other things are *necessarily* connected with the proposition.

5.124   affirms: for a similar use of '*bejahen*' see 5.513, 5.514.

5.1241 *b*   proposition with a sense: i.e. 'significant proposition', one that is not a contradiction.
c   It is hard to see the point of this remark.

5.13   can be read as a sequel to 5.12. Cf. 4.1211 *b* (logical relations shown by structure), 5.2 (structures stand in internal relations to one another).
structure: one might have expected 'form' instead.

5.131   Cf. 5.132 *b* (nature of an inference gathered from the propositions alone), 5.2 (propositional structures have internal relations).
Notice that W. has slid into talking about 'forms', rather than 'structures' as in 5.13.

5.1311 (1) *b*   the inner connexion becomes obvious: the inference is from $(p|q.|.p|q)$ and $(p|p)$ to $(q|q.|.q|q)$.
One can only guess why W. thought the connexion between conclusion and premises more 'obvious' in this form than in the alternative notation. My best conjecture is that he thought the presence of the stroke function in both premises showed an 'internal connexion' which is not so plain when two different logical connectives are used.
This section is interesting as showing the value that W. attached to a suggestive notation (to a suitable 'geometry of signs' we might say) as displaying internal relations, though one might hope for a more persuasive illustration.

(2)   generality: cf. 4.52 *b* (all propositions are generalizations in a certain sense).

5.132 (2) Cf. 5.13, 5.131, above. The intended sense is, probably, 'gathered from the two propositions alone'. W. admits other ways of perceiving the consequence relation.

nature: or, 'manner', 'mode'.

(4) **have no sense** (*sinnlos*): one might have expected 'nonsensical' (*unsinnig*) here.

'Deductions only proceed according to the laws of deduction, but these laws cannot justify the deduction' (*Notes on Logic*, apparently omitted from Anscombe's edition, but see 100 (4) for a similar statement).

For the primitive principles of inference used by Russell, see *Principia*, vol. 1, pp. 94–5 (principles *1.1 and *1.11). See also his *Principles*, §§ 17, 18, pp. 15–17, for 'principles of deduction'.

5.134 Follows from 4.21 and 2.062.

XLVII

THERE IS NO CAUSAL NEXUS

(5.135–5.1362)

Wittgenstein denies that there is any 'internal' necessary connexion between states of affairs involving different occasions: thus, future events cannot be inferred from present events (5.1361). This standpoint has been familiar since Hume's presentation of it (see, for instance, the *Enquiry*, § IV, part II), and Wittgenstein's description of 'belief in the causal nexus' as 'superstition' (5.1361 *b*) is quite in the spirit of Hume. Like Hume, too, Wittgenstein lays down rigorous conditions for what he is prepared to count as genuine knowledge. 'The connexion between knowledge and what is known is that of logical necessity' (5.1362*c*): If q is the proposition that p is known, the conditional, $q \supset p$, according to Wittgenstein, must be a tautology.

5.135 Cf. 4.21 + 4.27 *b* (elementary propositions assert the holding of atomic facts; mutual independence of the latter).

entirely different: having no *Sachverhalt* as a (non-vacuous) component in common with the first. Cf. Stenius, *Exposition*, p. 59.

5.136   causal nexus: 'It is clear that the causal nexus is not a nexus at all' (*Notebooks*, 84 (19)).

'By "causal nexus" he obviously means the aprioristic *certainty* of causal connections' (Stenius, *Exposition*, p. 60). W. does not mean to deny the existence of causal regularities: he does deny that they are *a priori*.

5.1361 (1)   Cf. 6.31 (the law of induction not *a priori*), 6.36311 (not known that the sun will rise), 6.37*a* (no necessary connexion between events).

(2)   A remark primarily about belief in the causal bond, rather than about superstition. The play on the words *Glaube–Aberglaube* is necessarily lost in the English.

5.1362 (1)*a*   The idea that there is a connexion between freedom of the will and ignorance of relevant circumstances is common in philosophical discussion. For example, in the following well-known passage: '[Men's] idea of liberty therefore is this—that they know no cause for their own actions; for as to saying that their actions depend upon their will, these are words to which no idea is attached' (Spinoza, *Ethic*, part 2, prop. xxxv, schol., p. 81).

***b   inner* necessity like that of logical inference**: Anscombe ('Aristotle', p. 13) thinks that W. recognized a necessity which 'is not just truth-table necessariness'. She continues: 'It is the unfamiliar necessariness of which Aristotle also speaks. "*A* knows that *p*" make sense for any *p* that describes a fact about the past or present; so it comes out in Wittgenstein, and in Aristotle; past and present facts are necessary. (In more detail, by the *Tractatus* account: if *A* knows that *p*, for some *q* ($q \supset p$) is a tautology, and *q* expresses a fact that *A* is "acquainted" with)'. But cf. 6.37*b*.

c   ●   '*A knows p to be the case* entails that *p* is the case—it is no accident that what I know turns out to be the case. So I cannot assert knowledge of an effect on the ground that I know the cause—this would be possible only if the existence of the cause entailed existence of the effect.'

(2)   no sense (*sinnlos*): possibly 'nonsensical' was intended. (But Anscombe, *Introduction*, p. 158, thinks not.)

XLVIII

TAUTOLOGY AND CONTRADICTION
'SAY NOTHING'

(5.1363–5.143)

The ideas in this instalment are connected with the earlier discussion of logical propositions as 'limiting cases' of significant propositions (XLIII) and of the nature of the 'consequence relation' (XLVI). In XLIII, Wittgenstein arrived at the notion of a tautology as a 'limiting case' by considering its truth-table representation. Since the last line of the truth-table for a tautology consists of an unbroken series of T's, the tautology is 'unconditionally true' (4.461 b), i.e. does not have a sense depending in any way upon the actual condition of the universe. This is why Wittgenstein spoke at 4.466 (4) of the connexion of symbols in a tautology as 'dissolving': the purported connexion of the symbols no longer reflects a possible mode of connexion of objects—we have reached a kind of 'degenerate case' of symbolization, where the symbolism breaks loose from any dependence upon anything external to it. Similar remarks apply to the case of a contradiction.

In the present instalment, Wittgenstein presents substantially the same idea in another setting. If two propositions are such that p follows from each of them, it is natural to say that they have p 'in common'. Since *everything* that follows from both a and b must follow also from their disjunction, $a \lor b$, and since that disjunction also follows from a and from b separately, it is natural to think of that disjunction as *the* 'common part' (the greatest common part, as it were) of a and b. This leads to the idea that all propositions have a tautology in common since, on Wittgenstein's views, a tautology is entailed by any proposition. However, consideration of the *ranges* of propositions (the sets of their 'truth-conditions') leads just as naturally to the different idea that what is common to two propositions, a and b, say, is their logical conjunction, $a.b$. A tendency to confuse these two possible senses of 'having in common', also present in the

245

corresponding passages of the *Notebooks* (cf. 55 (10)), aggravates the difficulty of understanding the cryptic section, 5.143 (but see the paraphrase offered in the notes below). It is doubtful whether the difficulty of understanding the metaphor of 'having something in common' is compensated by any illumination it furnishes. Wittgenstein's earlier account of logical propositions as limiting cases of truth-functions is more perspicuous and less liable to create confusion.

5.1363 self-evident (*einleuchtet*): or, 'obvious'.
Cf. 5.4731 *a*, for this use of the word.

5.14 An alternative formulation of 5.121 or 5.122.

5.141 Propositions that mutually entail one another are identical. This conception will force Wittgenstein to hold that all tautologies are identical.

5.142 Cf. 4.461 *a* (a tautology shows that it says nothing).
Since everything 'follows from' a contradiction, W.'s principles might require him to hold that a contradiction 'says everything'. But according to 4.461 *a*, a contradiction 'says nothing'.

5.143 the common factor: literally, 'what is common' (*das Gemeinsame*). For comments on this expression, cf. notes on 5.513 (1) *infra*.
The basic idea is that the two conjuncts $p.q$ and $p.r$ have the proposition p 'in common'. In general, we can define 'a and b have c in common' as 'c follows from both a and b'—or, what comes to the same thing, 'c follows from $a \vee b$'. That l follows from k, W. expresses as: k 'says more' than l; we might also say that k is 'stronger than' l. Then every proposition p has itself 'in common' with any 'stronger' proposition $p.q$ since p is equivalent to $p \vee pq$. In order to get a proposition 'which *no* proposition has in common with another' we would have to take successively stronger propositions. The limit, if it existed, would be the strongest of all propositions, i.e. the logical product of all propositions, positive and negative. This, however, is not a significant proposition but a contradiction.
To have 'nothing in common', a and b must be such that anything entailed by $a \vee b$ must be as 'weak' as possible, must say nothing, must be a tautology. Thus, epigrammatically, propositions that 'have nothing in common' have tautology (i.e. 'nothing') in common.

● 'Contradiction is the limit we approach as we try to find propositions that are not simultaneously entailed by all propositions—the limiting case of progressively stronger propositions. Tautology is the limit we approach as we try to find propositions simultaneously entailed by all propositions—the limiting case of progressively weaker propositions. If we think of the stronger proposition as occupying more of logical space (cf. 4.463c), contradiction would have to fill the whole of logical space—and so would be an external boundary, as it were—while tautology would fill no logical space, and so might be conceived as an internal boundary. Neither tautology nor contradiction draw a line around truth-possibilities *within* logical space.'

XLIX

PROBABILITY

(5.15–5.156)

Wittgenstein's discussion of probability (4.464, 5.1, 5.15–5.156) has to be taken as an attempted 'elucidation' or 'logical clarification' (cf. 4.112) of a concept. Intended to be *a priori*, his remarks must belong to the realm of 'the unspeakable' (4.115). Here, as elsewhere, Wittgenstein is necessarily in the awkward position of trying to say what could at best be shown. He is concerned throughout with the 'internal' properties of probability.

Wittgenstein's theory of probability is of the type commonly called 'logical', of which other well-known instances are the theories of Laplace, Keynes, and Carnap. Such theories characteristically construe probability as a logical relation depending solely on the *meanings* of the propositions concerned. Whereas Laplace took as a measure of probability the ratio of the number of 'favourable cases' to the total number of 'cases', Wittgenstein substitutes the notion of the relative size of 'ranges' (see discussion under 4.463 (1)).

A critical problem for all 'logical' theories of probability is that of the relation of probability assertions to the contingent results of observation. This is particularly acute for Wittgenstein, because his basic conception of the mutual independence of elementary propositions requires the probability of any elementary proposition, relative to any conjunction of elementary propositions by which it is not entailed, to be 1/2. This means that no knowledge of the past can confer upon any prediction a probability greater than it would have had in the absence of such knowledge (cf. 5.1361*a* on the impossibility of inference from present to future). It is therefore hard to see how probability statements, as Wittgenstein construes them, can have any empirical significance.

5.15   In terms of the notion of range (*Spielraum*, see discussion of this notion in the notes to 4.463 (1)), the definition becomes: the measure of the probability of *s* relative to *r* is the ratio of the size of the range of *r-and-s* to the size of the range of *r*. The size of a range is here taken to be the number of truth-grounds it contains. (For the definition of 'truth-ground', see 5.101 (2).)

This basic idea is at least as old as Bolzano, whose *Wissenschaftslehre* (§ 161) contains a similar definition. The idea of a 'Spielraum' appears prominently in the probability theory of von Kries: see his *Wahrschein-lichkeitsrechnung*, especially ch. 2. W.'s conception is well expounded in Waismann's 'Wahrscheinlichkeitsbegriff'. (It should be noted, however, Waismann does not follow W. in taking an absolute size for the range of a proposition, equal to the number of *T*'s that appear in the last column of its expression, as a truth-function of elementary propositions. For Waismann, the choice of 'the metric' is partly conventional, and made in the light of experience.) A similar idea is used by Carnap (for whose relation to W. and Waismann see Carnap's *Probability*, p. 299).

5.1511   no special object in probability statements: they are all *a priori*, as can easily be seen from the definition of 5.15. So 'it is probable that' must be regarded as a logical constant, i.e. as something that does not stand for anything in the world (cf. 4.0312*b*—the logic of the facts cannot be represented).

5.152 (1)   According to 5.01, the 'truth-arguments' are the elementary propositions. Here, 'in common' must be taken literally and does not mean the same as at 5.143*a*.

   we call: Anscombe says, 'This is not an author's "we"' (*Introduction*, p. 156), and thinks that W. intends to report common usage.

● 'Two propositions are called independent if the sets of elementary propositions of which they are truth-functions need have no common members.'

   It follows that any two elementary propositions, *p* and *q*, are independent. For although *p* can be expressed as a function of *q* in the form *p*.(*q*v ∼ *q*) it *need not* be so expressed.

(2) This follows directly from the definition of probability measure in
5.15, on the assumption that elementary propositions are independent
(4.211, 5.134). For every truth-ground of p in which q appears, there will
be another truth-ground differing from the first only in the appearance of
not-q in place of q. Thus the range of $p.q$ will have exactly one-half the
size of the range of p.

(3) *b* Cf. 4.464 (2) on connexions between modality and probability.

5.153a This is necessitated by 5.15, which defines probability as a
relation between propositions. Nevertheless, there is room in W.'s conception for the *a priori* probability of a given proposition, *s*, which might be
defined as its probability with respect to a tautology, i.e. as the ratio of
the size of the range of *s* to the size of the greatest possible range. (This
notion is used in Carnap's theory of probability.)

b **middle way**: literally, 'intermediate thing' (*Mittelding*), thing that
neither happens nor does not happen.

5.154 (2) *this*: the fact that a prolonged series of drawings from the urn
manifests approximate equality of the numbers of balls of the two kinds.
This cannot be something that is assertible on mathematical (or, we
may add, logical) grounds, since observation is needed to show that it is
a fact.

(3) **the circumstances that I know**: all that I know about the defining
conditions of the trials, the composition of the balls in the urn, and so
on—but *excluding* the approximate convergence mentioned in (1).

the laws of nature assumed as hypotheses: generalizations, based
upon previous experience in similar cases, about what happens when balls
are drawn at random from urns. ('Laws of nature' seems needlessly
portentous—'empirical generalizations' would have served.) They are
'hypotheses' because the observer has to assume that they hold, and
cannot know their exact character; he proceeds on the assumption that
the natural laws, whatever they are, render the selection of a white and of
a black ball equally likely. Notice that if W. is not to commit the fallacy
of arguing from frequencies to probabilities, he must assume that the
supposed 'laws of nature' include statistical generalizations about relative
frequencies.

b **definitions**: rather, 'explanations' (*Erklärungen*).

(4) **confirm**: the outcome of the experiment (the series of drawings)
can only be rendered highly probable by the assumptions mentioned
in (3). The observed frequencies cannot verify the antecedent, but may be
said to confirm or support it. W.'s views about scientific laws (6.341 ff.)

demand that the requisite rules for accepting or rejecting hypotheses in the light of observational evidence shall be partly arbitrary.

It should be noted that no observations could show the propositions about the occurrence of a white or of a black ball to be mutually independent; for this must be a necessary truth. The observer assumes the truth of some relevant hypothesis, *h*, that would render *a* and *b* equally probable. Observation can only confirm the truth of *h* (a contingent proposition): the equal probabilities of *a* and *b* then follow by strict inference. It is misleading to say, as W. does, that observation confirms the independence of *a* and *b* relative to *h*.

circumstances of which I have no more detailed knowledge: I have only schematic knowledge of the relevant circumstances (the number of balls in the urn, the manner in which the draws are made, etc.). This is connected with what W. says in 5.156 about probability assertions involving generality.

'The fact that a die is homogeneous and exactly cubical and that the laws of nature that I know say nothing about the result of a throw does not suffice for a conclusion about the approximately equal distribution of the numbers 1 to 6 in the throws. The prediction that such a distribution will be the case conceals an assumption, rather, about those laws of nature which I do *not* know exactly. That is, the assumption that *they* will produce such a distribution' (*Phil. Bem.* 135, 3).

● 'When I assert that the probabilities of drawing a white and a black ball from an urn containing equal numbers of balls of the two colours are equal, I assume that certain relevant generalizations (whose exact character is unknown to me) are true of the situation. If these generalizations are of such a character that, in relation to them and the propositions expressing the conditions under which balls are drawn, the two kinds of drawings are equally probable, it follows (by mathematical calculation) that in a prolonged series of drawings it will be highly probable that the number of white balls drawn will be close to the number of black balls drawn. When I find by trial that the numbers of balls drawn of the two colours approximate to equality, I count the hypothesis as being supported. Since I demanded that the hypothesis should be one rendering the two kinds of drawings equally probable, I may therefore be said, also, to have *confirmed* the equality of the two probabilities.'

5.155 A new sense of 'probability' is being defined here, in terms of the original sense explained in 5.151.

minimal: delete (not in the original).

unit: in the sense of the simplest probability assertion having some (indirect) connexion with experience.

circumstances: as in the preceding section, W. stresses that these are partly unknown to me. If I knew enough about the situation, a probability assertion would be pointless—only when I am uncertain about the details must I fall back upon probability connexions, cf. 5.156 (3).

5.156 (1) **It is in this way**: or, simply, 'Thus' (*so*). It follows from what has been said in 5.155 that the antecedent of the probability statement is a general statement.

(2) **general description**: we assume just as much about the logical form of the antecedent as will suffice to give the consequent in question the asserted degree of probability.

(3) **about its form**: in a loose sense of 'form' as 'make-up'.

(4) **of *something***: delete. The text has, simply, '*a* complete picture'.
'The proposition must describe its reference [or, meaning (*Bedeutung*)] completely' (*Notebooks*, 40 (5)).
'Every proposition that has a sense has a COMPLETE (*kompletten*) sense, and it is a picture of reality in such a way that what is not yet said in it simply cannot belong to its sense' (*Notebooks*, 61 (7)).
'His idea was that definiteness of sense consists in this: a proposition may indeed leave a great deal open, but it is clear *what* it leaves open' (Anscombe, *Introduction*, p. 73).
This paragraph is directed against the idea that because a probability assertion (or, for that matter, any generalization) is a partial description of a given situation, there is something wanting or lacking in the description. We might say that the probability statement is intended to draw a boundary around a number of situations that would verify it, but the line is sharp: the statement is general, but not therefore vague or defective. (Still, the idea of the sharp boundary is hard to reconcile with what was said in the notes on 5.154 (4) above about the arbitrary factor involved in counting a given observation as supporting a given hypothesis.)

(5) 'The Galtonian (composite) photograph is the picture of a probability. A probability law is a natural law seen while blinking' (*Phil. Bem.* 136). We might say that probability assertions express a myopic view of nature.

THE NATURE OF PROBABILITY

According to Wittgenstein, the simplest probability statement expresses a relation between two contingent propositions; it has the form, *r gives s the probability p* (5.151). It will be noted that such a

251

statement refers to two propositions that are its constituents; if Wittgenstein admitted the concept of levels of language, he would have to say that probability statements belong to a meta-language. I shall sometimes write the standard probability statement as the equation, $pr(r, s) = p$; r will be called the 'antecedent'.

Most contemporary writers on probability would agree with Wittgenstein in saying that probability is a relation; or, as they might put it, that 'probability varies with the datum'. Wittgenstein's second contention, however, would be emphatically rejected by many theorists. For he asserts that the probability relation is a *logical* relation, so that all probability statements are *a priori*. Hence, 'probability' might be regarded as a 'logical constant' that stands for nothing in the world: 'There is no special object peculiar to probability propositions' (5.1511). Wittgenstein's definition of 'probability' will be found to use none but 'formal' concepts; his programme is that of fitting probability statements into their proper positions in 'logical space'.

Suppose there are altogether n 'elementary propositions' in Wittgenstein's sense of that expression; form a conjunction composed of each elementary proposition or its negation: such a proposition might be called a 'description of a possible universe' (it corresponds closely to Carnap's notion of a 'state description', for which see his *Probability*, pp. 70, 582) or a '*U*-proposition' for short. If there were three elementary propositions, a, b, and c, in all, there would be eight *U*-propositions, among them $a.b.c$, $a.\sim b.c$, $\sim a.\sim b.\sim c$, etc. In general, if there are n elementary propositions, there must be 2^n *U*-propositions, all of them mutually exclusive. The single *U*-proposition that is true of the actual universe is the most specific and determinate contingent proposition that can be truly asserted; it expresses the whole truth and nothing but the truth about the universe.

Consider next the relation between a given proposition p (that may be either elementary or not) and the set of all *U*-propositions. Clearly, p must be compatible with a sub-set of *U*-propositions: if a tautology it is compatible with all of them; if a contradiction, with none; if contingent, it is compatible with some but not all of them. Let U_p be the largest set of *U*-propositions with each of which p is compatible; then U_p is what Wittgenstein calls the 'range' or '*Spielraum*' of p (4.463 a). Clearly, p is logically equivalent to the disjunction of all the U-propositions contained in its range (they are the components in the expansion of p as a 'complete disjunctive' truth-function of the elementary propositions). It is natural to think of the range of a proposition as its extension.

An example or two may be welcome. Preserving the simplified assumption of three elementary propositions introduced above, let r be logically equivalent to the truth-function $a \vee b$; then its range, U_r, consists of six of the eight U-propositions, i.e. all of them except $\sim a. \sim b.c$ and $\sim a. \sim b. \sim c$; and r is logically equivalent to the disjunction of these six propositions. Again, if s is logically equivalent to the truth-function $a.b$ its range consists of the two U-propositions $a.b.c$ and $a.b. \sim c$; and s is logically equivalent to the disjunction of these two propositions.

Only a short step is now needed to reach Wittgenstein's definition of the probability of one proposition with respect to another. Let r's range have μ members, of which ν also belongs to the range of s; then $pr(r, s)$, the probability of s relative to r, is simply the ratio ν/μ. Alternatively, we may reach the same result by counting the number of members of the range of r, and the number in the range of the conjunction, $r.s$, taking the ratio of the second number to the first. If we call μ and ν the *sizes* of the corresponding ranges, Wittgenstein may be said to define the probability measure ('*Mass der Wahrscheinlichkeit*', 5.15) as the ratio of the sizes of the ranges in question.

In the example used two paragraphs ago, r has a range of size 6 and $s.r$ has a range of size 2, so $pr(r, s) = 2/6$.

The following are almost immediate consequences of the definition:

(i) If r and s are logically incompatible, $pr(r, s) = pr(s, r) = 0$.

(ii) If s follows from r, $pr(r, s) = 1$ (5.152 (3)).

(iii) If s is a tautology, then for all non-contradictory r, $pr(r, s) = 1$.

(iv) If s is a contradiction, then for all non-contradictory r, $pr(r, s) = 0$.

(v) If neither s nor $\sim s$ follows from r, $pr (r, s)$ is between 0 and 1.

(vi) If r and s are elementary propositions, $pr(r, s) = pr(s, r) = 1/2$ (see 5.152 (2)).

The first five of these results make it natural to say, as Wittgenstein does, that certainty is 'a limiting case of probability' (5.152 (3), see also 4.464 (2)). The same idea is expressed when Waismann speaks of probability as a measure of the logical proximity (*logische Nähe*) of two propositions ('Wahrscheinlichkeitsbegriff', p. 237) or when Carnap refers to the probability relation as one of 'partial *L*-implication' (*Probability*, p. 297).

It is easy to verify that Wittgenstein's definition generates the usual principles of the elementary mathematics of probability, except those depending upon some variant of the 'principle of in-difference'—i.e. all except those calling for determinate non-limiting values for given probabilities. (In a sense, however, the doctrine of logically independent elementary propositions serves the same function as the 'principle of indifference'). This is not sur-prising, since Wittgenstein's definition is in direct descent from the classical Laplacean conception in terms of the ratio of the number of 'favourable' to the total number of cases. Wittgenstein's choice of propositions, rather than events, as the terms of the basic probability relation is unimportant. The essential novelty of his position, upon which its philosophical adequacy depends, is the absence of anything equivalent to the 'principle of indifference'. By counting the 'possible states of the universe' (or the number of *U*-propositions) he avails himself of an absolute measure of the extension of a proposi-tion; the notorious embarrassments arising from the principle of indifference seem to have been obviated from the beginning.

Let us now consider a case in which we seem to be able to make probability assertions absolutely, without reference to a designated antecedent. Drawing from an urn containing white and black balls in equal numbers (5.154a) we sometimes claim categorically that the probability of drawing a white ball is 1/2. Wittgenstein's answer postulates a suppressed antecedent describing the relevant 'circum-stances' (*Umstände*). The 'circumstances' consist of all the known facts about the situation, such as the composition of the urn and the manner in which the drawings are made, plus some 'natural laws assumed as hypotheses' (5.154 (3)). We shall see that these 'natural laws' must entail some generalizations about the frequencies of occurrence of black and white balls under the specified conditions for drawing.

Imagine the totality of the relevant 'circumstances' (initial conditions and generalizations) to be expressed as a single proposition, h; the proposition that the probability of drawing a white ball is $1/2$ is to be interpreted as having h as its antecedent; and the sense of probability involved remains unchanged. In this way, Wittgenstein is able to accommodate ostensibly non-relational probability assertions in his relational conception.

Consider next how the observation of an approximate equality of the numbers of white and black balls in a prolonged series of trials can, on Wittgenstein's principles, support the antecedent hypothesis h. Let the supposedly confirming evidence be expressed in the form of a proposition e; and let a_i be the proposition that a given drawing will result in a white ball being chosen. The following points should be noticed:

(i) If $pr(h, a_i) = 1/2$ *for every* i, then $pr(h, e)$ is close to 1. This special case of 'The Law of Large Numbers' is provable in the usual way by the principles of mathematical probability. (The italicized clause, equivalent to the assumption that all the propositions a_i have ranges of equal size, is essential.)

(ii) In the absence of some *rule of confirmation*, as I shall call it (some principle of inverse probability), no inference to r from s and $pr(r, s) \simeq 1$ is justifiable. (This is the familiar difficulty, thoroughly discussed in the standard treatises on probability, of the indeterminacy of inversions of probability assertions.)

The situation with regard to Wittgenstein's example is, accordingly, the following. If he had justified the step from e to h (i.e. if he had presented and defended what I have called a 'rule of confirmation'), and if he had further justified the assumption that all propositions expressing the possible results of individual drawings have ranges of equal sizes, he would then have shown how observation could support antecedent empirical hypotheses. In the absence of any justification or discussion of these missing links, Wittgenstein's discussion must be held to be unsatisfactory. (Opinions may well differ on this.)

Commentary

The chief defect of Wittgenstein's definition of probability is its failure to apply to any given language. Ironically, its one claim to novelty ensures its lack of relevance to concrete examples. The idea of computing the ratio of favourable to total possible cases is as old as Laplace, and has remained the common starting-point of all mathematical discussions of probability. Even the terminology of the '*Spielraum*', with its encouragement to thought about the extensions of propositions rather than their senses, appears in von Kries, and is in any case inessential to Wittgenstein's thought. The one new move that Wittgenstein makes is the conception of the proposition as following from a determinate but unknown number of mutually exclusive, maximally specific, 'descriptions of possible states of the universe'. This postulates a unique and objective measure of a proposition's content and so allows us to contemplate an objective probability, defined in terms of the relative overlap of ranges. Only we have no way of analysing the propositions of ordinary life or of science, and so no way of calculating the degree of probability between given propositions. Should we wish to know the degree of probability conferred by the proposition, *This book contains printed pages* (*a*) upon the proposition, *The number of printed pages this book contains is even* (*b*), Wittgenstein's definition would require us to ascertain the sizes of the 'ranges' of a and $a.b$, i.e. the number of possible states of the universe compatible with each. Were the propositions 'fully analysed' in Wittgenstein's sense, they would be exhibited as truth-functions of the elementary propositions, and the necessary information about the ranges could be read off or obtained by a simple calculation. But 'complete analysis' is a metaphysical mirage, whose hypothetical existence leaves the problem of handling the propositions with which we are acquainted, in all their remoteness from the canons of an 'ideal language', stubbornly insoluble. Wittgenstein's definition may tell us how probability might be computed in a language that does not exist; applied to any language actually available, it would compel us to treat all probability measures as unknown.

The only plausible way out of this impasse would be to suppose it possible to establish identity of form by comparisons between propositions incompletely analysed. If the alternative to the proposition *b* of the last paragraph—i.e. the proposition, *The number of printed pages in this book is odd* (*c*)—were somehow certifiable as *isomorphic* with *b*, we could conclude that the two ranges had equal, though unknown, sizes. Then it would follow at once that $pr(a, b) = pr(a, c) = 1/2$. Now there certainly is a strong inclination to suppose that *b* and *c* are isomorphic, i.e. that the fully analysed expression of the one could be transformed into the complete analysis of the other by a simple renaming of the ultimate 'logical simples'. Similarly, we are strongly inclined to believe we can 'see' that the propositions describing the various drawings from Wittgenstein's urn have the same logical form. If such inclinations could be supported by sound argument, Wittgenstein's view would be saved, at least in a large class of cases where numerical calculation of probabilities is required in practice.

The trouble is that the problem of showing propositions to be iso-morphic is simply the ancient puzzle of how to choose 'equiprobable alternatives' or 'equally likely cases' in disguise. It is to be expected that the devastating battery of objections directed against the traditional Principle of Indifference by Keynes and others can be readily adapted to apply against the proposed remedy.

It may be worth recalling how some other theorists sympathetic with Wittgenstein's general approach try to cope with this fundamental difficulty: Bolzano, in effect, claims to be able to intuit identity of logical form (not that he uses that terminology) in the cases that interest him; Waismann abandons the idea of ranges with sizes objectively determined by the structure of logical space, and proposes to let the 'choice of a metric' be determined partly by statistical observation and partly by considerations of what we find it convenient to regard as 'chance events'; Kneale takes refuge in the notion of 'natural units' (*Probability*, p. 171); Carnap makes the notion of the size of ranges relative both to the choice of an artificial language and to the choice of some one confirmation function. Whatever the defects of Wittgenstein's original theory, it must be recognized to have had a stimulating effect.

As for Wittgenstein's essay at connecting his hypothetical probability measures with statistical experiment, we have already seen how that is crippled by the impossibility of assigning the requisite probabilities to the propositions needing consideration. Were this lacuna filled, perhaps by one of the expedients mentioned above, there would still remain the need for a theory of *confirmation*, whose absence is not even noticed in Wittgenstein's account. Inferences from samples to 'populations' are among the most common instances of the application of probability concepts. A theory that is silent about the logic of sampling cannot be regarded as adequate.

L

OPERATIONS AS EXPRESSING INTERNAL RELATIONS

(5.2–5.254)

From the prominence that Wittgenstein gives to the notion of an 'operation', we may suppose that he attached great importance to it. (He will be found using it in his attack upon Russell and Frege's conception of the nature of mathematics, see LXX and especially 6.031 *a*.) Yet the sharp contrast he wished to enforce between 'operation' and 'function' (5.25*c*) is hard to accept (for the reasons explained in the notes on 5.23 below). As distinctive features of operations, Wittgenstein presents the following: (i) operations are shown by variables (5.24*a*), (ii) they indicate differences between forms, not the forms themselves (5.241), (iii) their occurrence is not a feature of a proposition's sense (5.25*a*), (iv) operations, unlike functions, are self-applicable (5.242*a*), (v) operations may 'cancel' one another (5.253). None of these considerations seems decisive (see the detailed discussion below).

On the whole, Wittgenstein's emphasis upon operations seems best viewed as a way of rendering prominent the associated *rules* for the construction of complex symbols (cf. notes on 5.23 below). Wittgenstein's introduction of operations can also be regarded as an alternative way of expressing ideas for which he has already introduced the terms 'formal' and 'internal' (cf. xxxiii). For, as he uses 'operation', the relation between the operand and its transform is always 'internal' (5.22–5.231).

The notations for expressing the general term of a formal series, introduced at 5.2521–5.2522, will be used later by Wittgenstein in his discussion of the general form of a proposition (6).

5.2   Cf. 5.13 and 5.131 on internal relations and deductive connexions.

'Propositions can have many different internal relations to one another. *The* one which entitles us to deduce one from another is that if, say, they are ϕa and $\phi a \supset \Psi a$, then $\phi a . \phi a \supset \Psi a : \supset \Psi a$ is a tautology' (*Moore Notes*, 116 (2)).

5.21   **operation**: defined at 5.23.

5.22   **relation**: i.e. an *internal* relation.

5.23   **operation**: 'An operation is the transition (*Übergang*) from one term to the next in a series of forms (*Formen-Reihe*). Operation and form-series are equivalents' (*Notebooks*, 81 (12, 13)).

'The concept "and so on" and the concept of operation are equivalent' (*Notebooks*, 90 (2)). Cf. 5.2523.

'The concept of the operation is quite generally that according to which signs can be constructed according to a rule' (*Notebooks*, 90 (4)).

W. wishes to make a distinction between an operation and a function (5.251), yet the difference between the two seems at first nothing more substantial than a difference in point of view (and consequently in terminology). Mathematicians commonly use the terms 'function' and 'operation' interchangeably. For example: 'A function is an operation which may be applied to one thing (the argument) to yield another thing (the value of the function)' (Church, *Calculi*, p. 1). It should be noted that for Church a function is a 'rule of correspondence' for obtaining the value of the function whenever an argument is provided. It is accurate to say: 'As most commonly used [i.e. by mathematicians] an operation in a set S is nothing but a single-valued function $f(x, y)$' [x and y being arbitrary members of S] (Wilder, *Foundations*, p. 159). W. himself consistently calls $\sim p$ a truth-function of p; if we say alternatively that $\sim p$ results from p by the operation of negation (5.2341 *b*), we focus attention upon the character of the *rule* for deriving $\sim p$ from p. And so in general: we can say indifferently that x^2 is a certain function of x—or, alternatively, that x^2 is derived from x by the *operation* of 'squaring'. The language of 'operations' serves merely to 'give prominence to' (5.21), to emphasize, the rule for expressing one symbol as a function of another—or, what comes to the same, the 'internal relations' of the things correlated by means of the function.

The important point is that W. restricts 'operation' to the case where the 'bases' and the 'result' (5.22) of the operation are *internally* related. (He could have made all his points by introducing the expression '*internal* function' by analogy with 'internal property' and 'internal relation'.)

what has to be done: cf. the expressions 'how we can get' (5.24*a*) and 'the way in which [the result] is produced' (5.3*b*). All three are figurative: nothing is literally done to the propositions that are the 'bases' of the operation. We do, however, literally operate on the corresponding signs, converting some into others by attaching operation signs.

5.232 by which a series is ordered: cf. 4.1252 for the way in which a formal series arises.

equivalent: the internal relation uniquely determines the operation and *vice versa*.

5.233 logical construction: i.e. as a truth-function of other propositions. The idea is rather cryptically expressed. W. wishes simply to deny that there can be other than truth-functional operations.

5.234 Cf. 5.3*b* for definition of 'truth-operation'. For difference between 'operation' and 'function' see 5.25*c*, 5.251.

***a* Truth-functions**: this expression can be used in two ways which need to be carefully distinguished. Suppose c is the proposition $a \vee b$. Then (i), it is proper to say that c is a *truth-function of* the propositions a and b, and, more specifically, that it is the disjunction of a and b. In this sense, a truth-function of anything is always a proposition. (Compare saying that 6 is *a function of* 2 and 3, namely their product; in this sense, a numerical function of anything is a number.) But (ii) it is also proper to speak of *the* truth-function of disjunction, which might be represented in Frege's manner by leaving appropriate blanks, thus: ( ) $\vee$ ( ). In the passage in question, and also in 5.2341, it is sense (i) that is relevant. Cf. 5.251, where sense (ii) is probably in point.

On 5.234, Anscombe comments: 'To say this is to make a radical distinction between a truth-function and an ordinary function like "ϕx"' (*Introduction*, p. 118).

5.24 (1) Compare remarks on formal concepts, 4.126 (4, 8), 4.127, 4.1272 (8).

(2) Cf. 5.241.

(3) have in common: of course, not in the sense of 5.143. We might perhaps say that the *signs* for the 'bases' must occur in the signs for the 'result'.

5.241 Echo of 5.24 *b*.

5.25 (1) Cf. 5.254.

(2) But notice that this reason would apply just as well to a function.

On the face of it, there seems a conflict between this section and 5.2341 *a*. For there it was implied that a truth-function (say a proposition *r*, which is a disjunction, *p* v *q*) has its sense determined by the sense of its constituents. We can also say, in the language of operations, that *r* is the result of the *operation* of disjunction upon *p* and *q*, and so be led to conclude that the sense of *r is* determined by the operation (and, of course, also by the identity of the operands). Perhaps what W. wanted to say was that the sense of *r* is determined jointly by the operation *and* the identity of the operands. No doubt he also wanted to stress that a given proposition can be analysed in all sorts of ways as the result of different operations upon different operands. But the same is true of things which are functions of other things: $9 = 7+2 = 10-1 = 3^2$, etc. In this respect, however, a truth-function is markedly different from the 'concatenation function' which unites objects into elementary propositions. For an elementary proposition does not admit of alternative analyses into concatenations of simples.

(3) Cf. 5.234 *a* (truth-functions as results of operations).

5.251 Cf. beginning of 3.333 *a* (a function cannot be its own argument). Of course a *value* of a function can sometimes be an argument of that function—3^2 can itself be squared.

its: = 'that operation's'.

5.252 b W.'s criticism can properly be levelled against the use of 'typical ambiguity' in *Principia* (for which see vol. 1, p. 65, and the 'prefatory statement' to vol. 2). It has often been pointed out that Russell needs, for example, not a single axiom of reducibility, but an indefinite number of such axioms, applicable to entities of different types. For a specific criticism of this sort, see Anscombe, *Introduction*, p. 130.

5.2521 (1) This notation is used at 6.02. The use of the apostrophe after the operation sign is reminiscent of Russell's notation for 'descriptive functions' (e.g. *R'a*). Since operators are typographically distinct from names and name variables, the apostrophe is actually redundant. Anscombe makes this point at *Introduction*, p. 124, f.n. 1.

(**2**)   This idea is used at 5.32.

5.2522   Cf. 4.1273*ab* for the expression of the general term of a formal series. It might be noticed that the presence of the *x*'s in W.'s notation is unnecessary: all he needs to supply is the first term of the series (*a*), and the generating operation (*O*).

The notation is used at 6.

5.2523   the concept 'and so on': W. means what is shown when we write a few terms of a series and append some dots, i.e. the sign '...'. In the section of the *Notebooks* from which 5.2523 was taken, W. says about 'the concept "and so on"' [that] it alone justifies us in constructing logic and mathematics' from their principles and primitive signs (89 (15)). See also notes on 5.23 above.

(For extensive discussion of the notion of a rule, see *Investigations*, pp. 26, 27, 38, 39 and *passim*.)

5.253*b*   In the *Notebooks* (39 (16)), W. says that only operations can vanish (*verschwinden*).

5.254   An example of what is asserted in 5.253.

LI

PROPOSITIONS AS RESULTING FROM TRUTH-OPERATIONS ON ELEMENTARY PROPOSITIONS

(5.3–5.32)

Here Wittgenstein recapitulates the main point established by his discussion of truth-functions: All propositions can be generated from elementary propositions by means of a single 'truth-operation'. At 5.5, Wittgenstein will define the operation he chooses: it is the operation of forming the conjunction of the negations of each of a given set of selected propositions. Wittgenstein's assertion is a form of the 'principle of extensionality': he denies that a proposition can be constructed out of others except 'extensionally', i.e. as a truth-function.

5.3*a* Elaborated at 5.5*a*.

b Cf. similar remark at 5.234.
  the way: cf. 'how we can get' in 5.24*a*.

(3)*a* It is of the essence of an operation to be capable of iteration (cf. 5.251).

(4) Repetition of (1). Cf. also 5.32 below.

5.31*a* Cf. 5.3 (3).

5.32 This has already been said (e.g. at 5.234). The only addition here is the explicit reference to the number of the truth-operations being finite.

LII

THERE ARE NO 'LOGICAL OBJECTS'; NEGATION

(5.4–5.442)

Wittgenstein reaffirms, as on previous occasions (XXVIII, XLII), that logical connectives—'or', 'not', etc., or the signs replacing these words in a calculus—do not stand for objects in the world. He rests the conclusion upon the interdefinability of the logical connectives (5.42*b*). If the logical connectives deputized for objects like genuine names, one and the same proposition would admit of different ultimate analyses, which we already know to be impossible (3.25). The point is illustrated by the case of negation (5.44): If ' $\sim$ ' stood for an object, $\sim \sim p$ would have to be a different proposition from p. The identity of the truth-conditions for $\sim \sim p$ and p shows them to be the same proposition, however (cf. 5.141 above).

It should be noticed that Wittgenstein's argument against regarding the logical connectives as names is independent of his detailed views about the ways in which propositions represent. Indeed, it is present in his early manuscript, *Notes on Logic*, where the 'picture theory of meaning' has not yet been formulated.

The rejection of 'logical objects' marks a climax in Wittgenstein's inquiry. It is, as he puts it, a 'fundamental thought' for him that the so-called 'logical constants' do not stand for anything in the world (4.0312 *b*). His entire conception of logic turns on this.

5.4 Cf. 4.441 (1) *b* for a similar remark.
becomes manifest: literally, 'shows itself' (*zeigt sich*).

5.41 **The reason is**: over-emphatic—the text has 'For' (*Denn*).
According to 5.141, propositions that follow from one another are identical. Thus two different combinations of truth-operations on the same bases (e.g. $p \supset \sim q$ and $\sim (p.q)$) can yield identically the same result. This is here offered as a ground for denying that the operation signs stand for 'objects'. Cf. 5.42 (2), 5.43 (1).
'All that is essential about molecular functions is their T–F (true–false) schema (i.e. the statement of the cases where they are true and cases where they are false)' (*Notes on Logic*, 100 (1) *c*).

5.42 (1) **self-evident**: or, 'obvious' (*leuchtet ein*). Why so? Perhaps because they can 'cancel one another' (5.253) and 'vanish' (5.254). Again 'right and left' are relations between objects, which when so related constitute a fact; but '$\supset$' would have to express a 'relation' between propositions or states of affairs, which is impossible.

(2) 'The logical constants seem to be complex symbols, but on the other hand, they can be interchanged with one another. They are not therefore really complex; what symbolizes is simply the general way in which they are combined' (*Moore Notes*, 117 (6)).
'Alternative indefinability shows the indefinables have not yet been reached' (*Notes on Logic*, 104 (3)).

(3) **obvious**: because the truth-tables are the same in both cases.

5.43 (1) *a* 'If p = not-not-p etc., this shows that the traditional method of symbolism is wrong, since it allows a plurality of symbols with the same sense; and thence it follows that, in analysing such propositions, we must not be guided by Russell's method of symbolizing' (*Notes on Logic*, 100 (2)*d*).

at first sight: rather, 'in advance' (*von vornherein*).

(2) Cf. 4.461*a* (logical propositions show that they say nothing), 6.11*a* (logical propositions say nothing).

5.44(1) material functions: these would presumably have values depending contingently upon the values of their arguments. An example might be, 'the first proposition to occur after *p* in the *Tractatus*'. The expression 'material function' does not occur again in the text: it means what W. normally expresses by 'function' (e.g. at 4.126 (4)).

(3) **written into**: literally, 'prejudged' (*präjudiziert*) or 'presupposed'. Cf. 5.5151 (3) for an occurrence of the last word (*voraussetzen*).

5.441 For the second example, cf. 5.47 (2)*b*.
apparent: or, 'pseudo-'.

5.442 If we are given a proposition: = 'If we understand it' = 'When the sense of a proposition has been explained to us'. Cf. 5.47 (2)*a* (all logical operations are contained in the elementary propositions).

LIII

THE PRIMITIVE NOTIONS OF LOGIC

(5.45–5.452)

Wittgenstein states conditions to be satisfied by any acceptable answer to the question, What are the 'primitive ideas' (5.451), the indefinables, of logic? The primitive ideas must be independent of one another (5.451*a*)—otherwise we should not have reached bedrock. (One might say that it is part of our idea of an 'indefinable' that it should not be capable of further definition.) Secondly, the rules for using the signs expressing the primitive ideas must cover all contexts in which they can occur. It will not do to engage in piecemeal definition (as sometimes happens in *Principia*, or in the practice of contemporary logicians) for then a question would remain about the mutual consistency of the partial definitions (and so, after all, a comprehensive discussion of all the cases would be needed). Wittgenstein's later account of the single 'primitive logical sign' or 'logical indefinable' (5.472) satisfies his own reasonable stipulations. See also LV below.

5.45*a* The idea is expressed positively in the original.

primitive logical signs: = 'indefinables of logic'.

how they are placed relatively to one another: or, simply, 'their relative status'. Cf. 5.452 (3).

existence: *Dasein*—one might say *raison d'être*. It is not enough simply to introduce the indefinables of logic; it is necessary to show how they are to be used, e.g. in the construction of complex signs.

5.451 (1)*a* For if not, they would not be indefinables.

ideas: or, 'concepts' (*Grundbegriffe*).

d 'If the form *xRy* has been introduced, it must henceforth be understood in propositions of the form *aRb* just in the same way as in propositions such as $(\exists x, y).xRy$ and others' (*Notes on Logic*, 104 (3) *d*).

'Russell and Whitehead did introduce " $\sim$ " and " v " all over again for uses with quantifiers (*see* Sections *9 and *10 of *Principia Mathematica*). Modern logicians mostly introduce them with a merely truth-functional explanation, and then go on using them "with innocent faces" in the predicate calculus' (Anscombe, *Introduction*, p. 145).

(**2**) For Frege's views, see *Grundgesetze*, vol. 1, § 33; vol. 2, §§ 56–67, 139–44.

'A definition of a concept (of a possible predicate) must be complete; it must unambiguously determine, as regards any object, whether or not it falls under the concept (whether or not the predicate is truly assertible of it).... Now from this it follows that the mathematicians' favourite procedure, piecemeal definition, is inadmissible' (Frege, *Translations*, p. 159).

5.452 (1)*a* **device**: or, 'expedient' (*Behelf*); definitions have been called 'devices' at 4.242.

is necessarily: literally, 'must always be'.

b **in brackets**: phenomenologists like to talk of 'bracketing'—taking up an assumption without commitment.

(**2**) An example of what W. has in mind is the 'primitive proposition' *1.1: 'Anything implied by a true elementary proposition is true' (*Principia*, vol. 1, p. 94).

c What would need justification would be the consistency of the verbal definitions and the verbal propositions with the propositions expressed by means of special symbols.

(3) In the *Math. MS.* (749), W. proposes (following a similar idea of Frege's) to replace the word 'infinite' and its cognates by meaningless expressions, in order to see what the mathematician really *does* with the signs. Similarly, if we thought that chess gave us information about kings and rooks, W. would propose to change the shapes and names of the pieces to facilitate the insight that everything relevant to the game must lie in the rules.

LIV

THE NATURE OF LOGIC

(5·453–5·4541)

The remarks in this instalment are of great interest as revealing Wittgenstein's attitude towards logic, and so to his entire inquiry. Here we get a glimpse of what Wittgenstein means when in later life he criticized the *Tractatus* by saying, 'A *picture* held us captive' (*Investigations*, § 115). Wittgenstein's picture of logic, in the *Tractatus*, is of something unified, harmonious, as clear and as hard as a crystal, and with something of a crystal's cold beauty.

Wittgenstein said in the *Notebooks*: 'The great problem round which everything that I write turns is: Is there an order in the world *a priori*—and, if so, what does it consist in?' (53 (11)). It would be intolerable for Wittgenstein that the '*a priori* order' should be infected by imprecision or lack of organic unity—as intolerable as it is for a certain type of pure mathematician to think of his subject as concerned with the 'more or less', or as falling apart into branches having only an accidental connexion with one another. The *Tractatus* cannot be fully understood unless we sympathize with this demand for an unchanging order and harmony. (It is a demand, not a discovery.)

Commentary

The pattern of thought is beautifully expressed in Wittgenstein's posthumous book: 'Thought is surrounded by a halo.—Its essence, logic, presents an order, in fact the *a priori* order of the world: that is, the order of *possibilities*, which must be common to both world and thought. But this order, it seems, must be *utterly simple*. It is *prior* to all experience, must run through all experience; no empirical cloudiness or uncertainty can be allowed to affect it—It must rather be of the purest crystal' (*Investigations*, § 97). Compare also notes on 5.5563 (2) below. He rejected these demands in his later teachings.

5.453 This section and the next are directed against any inclination to suppose that logic handles objects that can be counted or classified. (But surely the truth-conditions can be counted?)

(2) Cf. 4.128*a* (the logical forms are anumerical).

(3) Repeated at 4.128*b*, 5.553 (2). Cf. also 5.474 (the number of primitive operations varies with notation).
privileged: special, exceptional.

5.454 Cf. 6.127 (1) (all logical propositions are on the same level).
no co-ordinate status: literally, 'no side-by-side' (*Nebeneinander*).

5.4541 (1) Cf. 5.551 on the summary disposition of logical problems.
With what is 'simplicity' here intended to be contrasted? No doubt with the tentative, unsystematic ways in which *empirical* investigations proceed.

(2) *a priori*: qualifies 'answers'.
self-contained system: literally, 'closed, regular, structure' (as in O.).
Simplex sigillum veri: 'simplicity is the hallmark of truth', a motto of the celebrated physician, Herman Boerhaave (1668–1738), of Leyden, who may have invented it. Translations of this dictum are well known in Europe.

LV

LOGICAL SIGNS AS PUNCTUATIONS
(5.46–5.4611)

This instalment can be read as a continuation of the discussion of the primitive logical signs (*Urzeichen*) in LIII above. There Wittgenstein said that the primitive signs must be so introduced as to provide for a definite interpretation of their occurrences in all contexts (5.451 *b*). Now, he draws an interesting corollary from this principle: The logical connectives, such as ' ∼ ' and 'v', have to be accompanied by brackets, whose positions influence the total meaning of the complexes in which the connectives occur; hence, a correct explanation of the logical connectives must refer to the logical signs, such as ' ∼ ' and 'v', and at the same time to the brackets that accompany them. But this line of thought leads still further: since all logical signs can occur together, we need to explain all of them (or, at least, all of those we treat as 'primitive') in one fell swoop. This is why Wittgenstein will speak a little later (at 5.472) of the 'one and only' primitive sign of logic: his line of thought has led him to the conclusion that the sole indefinable of logic is the general propositional form. (For his method of representing this form, see sections 6 ff.).

The concluding remark that logical operation signs are punctuation signs (5.4611) may be taken to be a hyperbolic way of stressing the grammatical roles of logical operators. (See also the further notes on this remark below.)

5.46 An application of 5.451 *b* (the use of a sign must be defined for all the combinations in which it occurs).

c **real general primitive signs**: or, 'the real indefinable signs of logic'.
general form of their combinations: what is shown by giving a completely general description of a truth-function = 'general form of a proposition'. Cf. 5.472 on the unique indefinable of logic.

5.461 (1) It is odd to find *Tatsache* used here: it is, of course, no contingent *fact* that brackets are needed.

In the *Moore Notes* there is the additional sentence: 'This fact has been overlooked, because it is so universal—the very thing which makes it so important' (115 (6)).

(2) *a* 'It's obvious that the dots and brackets are symbols, and obvious also that they haven't any *independent* meaning. You must, therefore, in order to introduce so-called "logical constants" properly, introduce the general notion of *all possible* combinations of them = the general form of a proposition' (*Moore Notes*, 116 (7)).

5.4611 ● 'Consider a complex sentence minus punctuation-marks; then the subject-matter (the objects and relations to which reference is made) is determined, but the structuring of the sense remains to be settled (just as " $7 - 2 + 1$ " might be read as " $7 - 2, + 1$ ", i.e. 6—or as " $7 -, 2 + 1$ ", i.e. 4). Punctuation-marks serve to select one of the possible complex senses (they eliminate amphiboly). Similarly, the logical operator (the part of the $(TFFT)(p, q)$ sign before (p, q)) shows how the elementary propositions (the subject-matter of *every* proposition) are to be structured.'

Notice that on this line of thought there is little if any difference between 'punctuation-marks' and 'brackets'.

LVI

THE GENERAL FORM OF A PROPOSITION

(5.47–5.472)

Wittgenstein has already had one unsatisfactory try at expressing the general form of a proposition (XLIV). He will try later to express this general form more adequately (LXIX). For the time being, he reminds us of some important general points concerning 'general propositional form': (i) it must be possible to provide, *a priori*, a definitive expression of this form (5.47 *a*), (ii) expression of the general form will be equivalent to providing the *single* logical primitive (5.47 (4), 5.472), (iii) the general propositional form is the same as the essence of a proposition, (iv) and hence the same as the essence of the world (5.4711). We see here how some of Wittgenstein's main preoccupations in the *Tractatus* focus upon the problem of clarifying the general form of a proposition.

5.47 (1) *in advance*: *a priori*. Cf. 4.5 (3).

'If the most general form of proposition could not be given, then there would have to come a moment where we suddenly had a new experience, so to speak a logical one. That is, of course, impossible' (*Notebooks*, 75 (12, 13)).

Cf. 5.551 (1) (all logical questions decidable forthwith), 6.125 (possibility of a single *a priori* characterization of logical truths).

(2) **contain**: in the sense that even the elementary propositions can be expressed in terms of them. Cf. 5.515*b* for a similar idea. To the example given in the text might be added the expansion of *p* (an elementary proposition) as *p*.(*q* ∨ ∼*q*), in which three logical operators appear. The expansion of *fa* was used in 5.441 to illustrate the *disappearance* of the 'logical constants'.

(3) It is, of course, assumed here that an elementary proposition (like all propositions, cf. 5.5261 *a*) is composite. Cf. note to 4.24 (2) above.

(4) **sole logical constant**: cf. 5.472.

nature: a synonym for 'essence'—cf. the next two sections.

had in common: cf. 3.343 *b*, 3.344.

(5) Cf. 4.5 on the 'general propositional form'.

5.471 For the **essence of a proposition** see 3.341 *a*.

5.4711 **essence of the world**: for the proposition has its form in common with the world (cf. 2.17).

This section formulates the heart of Wittgenstein's task. 'My *whole* task consists in explaining the nature [or, essence (*Wesen*)] of the proposition. That is, in giving the nature of all facts (*Tatsachen*), whose picture the proposition *is*. In giving the nature of all being (*Sein*). (And here being does not stand for existence—in that case it would be nonsensical)' (*Notebooks*, 39 (7–10)).

'It is clear that it comes to the same thing to ask what a sentence [or, proposition (*Satz*)] is, and to ask what a fact (*Tatsache*) is—or a complex' (*op. cit.* 52 (12)).

5.472 Restatement of 5.47 (4, 5).

LVII

THE AUTONOMY OF LOGIC;
SELF-EVIDENCE;
HOW NONSENSE ARISES

(5.473–5.4733)

'Logic must take care of itself' (5.473*a*). Logic, as Wittgenstein conceives it, is not amenable to human control or manipulation; it would be the height of absurdity to speak of our making logical propositions come true. So, although he has emphatically rejected the idea that there are 'logical objects' (xxviii, xlii, lii), he is not subscribing to a 'conventionalistic' view of logic. To be sure, any selected logical notation will have arbitrary features, but the essence of the notation (the same in every notation) expresses something that is not arbitrary (6.124*fg*).

Wittgenstein has no patience with 'self-evidence' as a way of reaching logical truth (5.4731), his chief objection being that 'obviousness' is no guarantee of validity (cf. 5.1363). The correct method for recognizing the validity of complex logical propositions is calculation (6.233, 6.2331). The construction of tautologies by means of a systematic truth-table procedure can be regarded as an instance of such 'calculation'—an instance of the way in which a well-designed notation renders superfluous any supposed need to appeal to a psychological criterion like self-evidence.

If logic is self-sufficing, 'we cannot make logical mistakes' (5.473 (3)). Nonsense arises because *we* have failed to do something which is in our power, by not attaching some arbitrary meaning to a given sign (5.4733*ab*).

5.473 (1) The opening remark of the *Notebooks*. Soon after, W. calls this an extremely profound and important insight (2 (3)*c*). The sense of the remark is elaborated by the rest of the present section: cf. also 4.121 (3) (we cannot express what expresses itself), 6.124*g* (the essence of symbolism expresses itself).

● 'It would be absurd to speak of an "illogical language" (cf. 5.4731 *b*): every language necessarily exemplifies the web of logical connexions. The logic of the language shows *itself*: it would be nonsensical to speak of our "doing anything" to logic—even in the sense of making mistakes about it (cf. (3))—or making discoveries about it (cf. 5.47 *a*).'

The idea that logic 'takes care of itself', i.e. that logical validity is independent of human choice, decision, or convention, constantly re-appears in one form or another in the text (as it does in the *Notebooks*).

(2) *ab* Cf. 2.0121 (3) on logic as concerned with possibilities.

c **no property**: cf. 5.5301 *a*. One might perhaps say that 'Socrates is identical' is not strictly nonsensical but rather incomplete, because a reference is missing for one of the words it contains.

d Cf. 5.4733 (3).

we have failed to make an arbitrary determination: W. is here speaking of '*possible* propositions,' i.e. those not involving collisions between incompatible logical forms. There is only one way in which *such* a pro-position can be nonsensical (*unsinnig*), namely as a result of having no meaning assigned to one or more of its component expressions. (Thus he treats 'Socrates is identical' as if it were 'Socrates is *X*'.) This kind of nonsense, for him, is always incompleteness of sense (cf. 5.4733 (3) *a* and 6.53 *b ad fin.*). He may have been led to this view by his insistence upon the word–thing co-ordinations as the sole determinants of the sense of the proposition in which the words occur. The structure of the sentence-fact in which the words occur will ensure that the right categories of things are correlated with the words, if we succeed in making those correla-tions. (Notice that he treats 'identical' as an adjective, even though he says it has no meaning.) Because our freedom to assign meanings exhausts what *we* can do, the only way in which we can go wrong is by failing to assign such meanings. We cannot produce an erroneous logical form—there is, as it were, only semantical nonsense, not syntactical nonsense.

This way of looking at nonsense seems artificial, however: for example, it treats 'Socrates is identical' and 'Socrates is and' as infected with exactly the same kind of mistake. It is at least equally plausible to say that the first sentence violates a syntactical rule for the use of 'identical'. This does not require us to say that in the nonsensical sentence 'identical' has its regular meaning. We can say that it has no meaning *because* the syntactical rule has been violated. So far as I can see, this would still be in harmony with W.'s general position.

(3) Cf. 5.4731 *b*.

5.4731 a Self-evidence: cf. 5.1363 for strictures against appeal to this. In the *Notebooks*, W. adds that 'self-evidence' is and always has been wholly deceptive (4 (9)).

'If one calls the proposition [that every region in the visual field is coloured] self-evident, one actually intends (*meint*) what is expressed by a grammatical rule that describes, for example, the form of propositions about visual space' (*Math. MS.* p. 555).

'In order that such a knowledge [i.e. of logical truths] be possible, it is necessary that there should be self-evident truths, truths which are known without demonstration' (Russell, 'Philosophical importance', p. 490). In the same article (dated 1913), Russell calls self-evidence a 'psychological property' and calls it 'subjective and variable' (*op. cit.* p. 492). He says that the 'ultimate premises' of logic and mathematics are not self-evident, but appear only probable.

Elsewhere, however, he says of logical principles: 'Their truth is evident to us, and we employ them in constructing demonstrations; but they themselves, or at least some of them, are incapable of demonstration' (*Problems*, p. 176).

b The notion of an 'illogical thought' is self-contradictory.

5.4732 Cf. 5.5563a (ordinary language is quite in order).

sense: here one might have expected 'meaning' (*Bedeutung*)—in accordance with 3.202 + 3.203.

● 'If a sign has meaning, the form of a sentence in which it occurs will necessarily be identical with the form of any fact depicted (we cannot go wrong about the logical form of the sign); our choice of the *particular* meaning of the sign is arbitrary and therefore cannot be mistaken.'

5.47321 (1) Occam's maxim: see the similar statement at 3.328a.

'The form usually given, "Entities must not be multiplied without necessity" (*Entia non sunt multiplicanda sine necessitate*) does not seem to have been used by Ockham. What Ockham demands in his maxim is that everyone who makes a statement must have a sufficient reason for its truth' (Boehner, *Ockham*, p. xxi).

Russell once called the 'razor' (in its traditional form) 'the maxim which inspires all scientific philosophizing' (*External World*, p. 112).

unnecessary units: = those elements not actually *used* (cf. 3.328a).

(2) purpose (*Zweck*): for a similar use of this word, cf. 3.341b.

5.4733 (1) Frege says: cf. *Grundgesetze*, vol. 1, § 32 and vol. 2, § 92.

legitimately constructed: or, 'well-formed'.

'What W. means by "Every possible proposition is well-formed" is that the relations that must hold between the elements if a sentence is to be a sentence at all must be there also in any nonsensical sentence, if you could make this have a perfectly good sense just by changing the kind of reference that some part of the sentence had' (Anscombe, *Introduction*, p. 68).

(3) *a* Cf. 5.473 (2) *c*.

b Cf. 3.321 on different symbols having the same sign in common.

LVIII

RELATIVITY OF THE PRIMITIVE LOGICAL OPERATIONS

(5.474–5.476)

Once again Wittgenstein attacks the idea that logic has a distinctive subject-matter, analysable into basic elements as the world is analysable into objects. His conception, we might say, is that there is no logical *substance*. The way in which we choose to develop a logical notation as a construction out of 'primitive notions' is partly arbitrary, a matter of our choice. However, the systematic internal connexions of the elements of our preferred notation (expressed by means of rules of transformation, 5.476) are not arbitrary: they manifest the indivisible essence of logic.

5.474 Connects with the absence of numbers in logic (5.453 *bc*).
necessary: or, 'needed'.
fundamental operations: the undefined operations needed for the systematic construction of formal logic.

5.475 **multiplicity**: cf. 4.04 for this notion.

5.476 **a rule**: for transforming signs of the system into one another. W. may intend 'a *single* rule'. Cf. 5.512 (3) for an illustration and 5.514 for further details about the kind of rule in question.

LIX

JOINT NEGATION AS THE BASIC LOGICAL OPERATION

(5.5–5.511)

Wittgenstein now chooses for his basic logical operation the simultaneous negation of each of a set of propositions, that set being determined as the range of values of a variable. (This operation corresponds to one of the so-called 'stroke-functions' discovered by Nicod and Sheffer.) He will proceed to show how this single operation suffices for the expression of all truth-functions and hence for the expression of the general propositional form (6).

5.5 (1) a A further specification of 5.3a (all propositions result from truth-operations on elementary propositions).

The notation here introduced is somewhat puzzling at first sight. In $(\ldots T)(\xi, \ldots)$, the second pair of brackets enclose a set of propositions, while the first contains a column of a truth-table, with blanks taking the places of F's. (W. used this device at 4.442 (3).) Upon reinserting the F's, the notation, for the special case of two propositions, p, q, would become $(FFFT)(p, q)$. According to the conventions of 4.442, this means $\sim p. \sim q$. Thus the operation singled out by W. is that of 'joint negation'. The symbolism is subsequently abbreviated at 5.502a. (For the history of attempts to use a single primitive connective in the propositional calculus, see Church, *Logic*, p. 133, f.n. 207.)

5.501 (1) a The bar notation is peculiar to W. It is used later at 5.502, 5.52, 6, 6.01. The line over the Greek letter must not be confused with the universal quantifier: 'I suppose you don't understand the notation "ξ". It does not mean "for all values of ξ . . ."' (*Letters*, 130 (7)). As W. uses the bar, it means that all the values of the variable beneath it are to be considered together.

(3) **stipulated**: or, 'prescribed'. Cf. 3.316a for a similar statement.

(4) Cf. 3.317ab on the determination of values of a variable.

(5) **not essential**: i.e. for the meaning of the variable. Cf. 3.317 (5).

(6) values for all values of *x*: not values in the sense of truth-values. An example would be all propositions of the form '*x* is human'. Thus the function in question is a formal one.

formal law: this expression occurs nowhere else in the text. What W. has in mind is explained at 4.1273 (2). Nowadays, the procedure in question would probably be called 'recursive definition'.

5.502 (1) So: since the values of ξ will in general not be enumerated but rather given by procedures 2 and 3 of 5.501 (6).

N: like the 'stroke-function' of Nicod and Sheffer.

5.503 exact expression: see 5.51 and 5.52 for explanation of logical operations in terms of *N*.

5.51 Since all truth-functions can be expressed in terms of negation and conjunction, it follows that every truth-function can be expressed solely by using *N* (a well-known result).

5.511 which mirrors the world: or, 'world-reflecting'.
world-use: rather, 'world, use'.
peculiar: rather, 'special'.
crotchets: or, 'hooks' (*Haken*).

b The **infinitely fine network** *is* 'the great mirror'. For the image of the mirror, cf. 4.121 (1). Anscombe takes 'the great mirror' to be language (*Introduction*, p. 164).

● 'What can logic, that embraces everything, reflects the world, and "takes care of itself", have to do with special tricks and devices like the *N*-operation? Well, every such device is connected in *its* way with the network of formal relations which is what we mean by "logic".'

(All logical dodges, we might say, are equal—and none are more equal than others.)

LX

ESSENTIAL ASPECTS OF A LOGICAL NOTATION, ILLUSTRATED BY THE CASE OF NEGATION

(5.512–5.5151)

Here, Wittgenstein makes plainer for us what he meant by saying that in constructing an adequate logical notation we are concerned with 'the expression of a rule' (5.476). In order to introduce the negation sign, ' ~ ', correctly into a logical notation, it is necessary to provide rules for determining the senses of all propositional signs in which the logical connective can occur. Useful details are provided.

5.512 (1) If *p* is false, it 'disagrees' with reality (cf. 2.222 for this way of talking). That is to say, the configuration of signs in the sentence expressing *p* shows how the corresponding objects are *not* combined. How, then, can the mere addition of a curl change this situation (so drastically, as it were) into one in which the proposition now *agrees* with reality?

(2) **what is common**: according to 3.343 and 3.344, what is 'common' to all symbols for negation should be a possibility of mutual translatability. For example, it seems that negation could be satisfactorily expressed by inverting the propositional sign, so that instead of ~ *p* we would have *q̇*: let us call this the 'inverse' notation. Then what the 'inverse' and the customary 'curl' notation have in common is that each can be converted into the other according to a simple syntactical rule. Perhaps we can go a step further and say that the essential feature of negation here made prominent is its self-cancelling power. What is 'essential' to negation is that it reverses a sense (cf. 4.0621*d* above).

In the present entry, W. is attending to what ' ~ *p*' has 'in common' with all its equivalent signs in the *same* notational system.

(3) *b* **factor**: not in the original, which runs simply 'that which is common', etc.

mirrors negation: 'I cannot understand how it mirrors denial [= negation]. It certainly does not do so in the simple way in which the conjunction of two propositions mirrors the conjunction of their senses. This difference between conjunction and the other truth-functions can be seen in the fact that to believe *p* and *q* is to believe *p* and to believe *q*; but to believe *p* or *q* is not the same as to believe *p* or to believe *q*, nor to believe not-*p* as not to believe *p*' (Ramsey, *Foundations*, p. 279).

5.513 (1) what is common: in 3.341–3.3441 this expression has been used in the sense of that which is essential in equivalent symbols (3.341*b*) —i.e. the possibility of mutual translation. Here, however, the expression occurs in the same sense as in 5.143 (see notes on that section).

A proposition which 'affirms' both *p* and *q* is one from which both *p* and *q* follow (5.124). Thus (as explained in the notes on 5.143), 'what is common' to all propositions affirming both *p* and *q* is the disjunction of all propositions from which both *p* and *q* follow, which is easily seen to be *p.q*, as stated in the text. A similar argument applies to the second part of (1). Cf. Anscombe, *Introduction*, pp. 61–2.

(2) nothing in common: their disjunction is a tautology (= the limiting case of a proposition having *no* sense).

every proposition has only one negative: cf. Anscombe, *Introduction*, pp. 62–3, for an attempted proof of this assertion. Her argument (corrected) runs as follows: Suppose there were some other negative than $\sim p$, say $\approx p$. Since these are assumed different, we must suppose either that (i) $\approx p$ can be true when $\sim p$ is false, or (ii) that $\sim p$ can be true when $\approx p$ is false. Take supposition (i) and let $\approx p$ be true. Then *p* is false, because $\approx p$ is a negative, and $\sim p$ is false, too, according to the supposition. Hence, $p \vee \sim p$ would have to be false and so could not be a tautology. Similarly, on supposition (ii), $p \vee \approx p$ could not be a tautology. One of these consequences will fail to square with what we demand of negation.

(3) is manifest: or, 'shows itself' (*zeigt sich*).

5.514*b* Cf. 5.555*b* on the importance of the system of rules.

'The sign for a rule is a sign in a calculus, like every other sign: its task is not to have a suggestive influence, but to be used systematically (according to rules) in the calculus. Therefore its external form, like that of an arrow, is incidental—the system, however, in which the rule-sign is used, is essential' (*Math. MS.* p. 706).

5.515 (1) be manifest: literally, 'show itself'.

There seems to be a misprint in the German text ('ist' for 'sind').

(2)*a* The German text is puzzling and may have been printed incorrectly. I suggest (as an alternative to P.–McG.) that the remark might read: 'And this is so, for the symbol *p* in *p* v *q* itself presupposes "v", "$\sim$"', etc.

presupposes: in the sense of belonging to a system containing these signs. Cf. 5.44 (3) for an occurrence of *präjudiziert* and 5.47 (2)*a* (all logical operations are contained in the elementary propositions) for a related idea.

5.5151 It might seem agreeable to the picture theory to try representing the sense of a negative proposition by a 'negative fact'—so that the fact verifying the proposition would agree with the sentence-fact in being negative. But this would not work. Suppose we tried to represent the fact that Tom is not happy by the absence of the sentence, 'Tom is happy', from the page: we should still have to indicate *what* was absent (e.g. by writing the sentence with a line through it), otherwise the mere blank would fail to express any determinate sense. This is what W. has in mind when he says, in (2), that the negative proposition is (or: must be) constructed *via* the positive. Cf. also 5.02 (2) above, where, in denying that ' $\sim$ ' is an index, W. is denying that we could use a simple letter, say q, for the negative of p. (We might say that something is here shown about the essence of negation: a language in which there was no provision for converting 'p' into its opposite, for repeated application of that operation, for its self-cancellation, etc., *could not* contain negation.)

We notice that, in (3), W. regards it as an essential feature of *affirmation* that positive propositions should be able to arise from negative propositions. Affirmation and negation belong to one and the same system: the roles of p and $\sim p$ may be compared to the roles of $+x$ and $-x$ in a system of directed numbers.

(1)*a* **with**: or, 'by means of'.

(2) **by**: or, '*via*', 'by means of' (*durch*).

(3) Cf. 5.44 (2), where the same point is made by a rhetorical question. For the emphasis on **proposition**, see 4.0641 (4).

LXI

GENERALITY

(5.52–5.525)

A satisfactory account of general propositions is of vital importance for Wittgenstein's philosophy of language. He has said that the essence of a proposition is manifested in its being a truth-function of elementary propositions. This principle of extensionality obviously fits the case of any molecular propositions that are *given* as truth-functions of elementary propositions. But since we cannot produce even a single elementary proposition, we cannot produce any proposition that is an explicit truth-function of elementary propositions. All the propositions that we can supply are 'general' in Wittgenstein's sense of that word, i.e. their symbolic expression in an adequate ideography would require the use of bound variables. So Wittgenstein must try to reconcile the existence of general propositions and their use of bound variables with the principle of extensionality, if his account is to be satisfactory. His philosophy of language must fit the languages we know, if it is to reveal the essence of all language.

Wittgenstein's conception of the relation of general propositions to elementary propositions is hard to grasp. It seems certain that he wanted to construe general propositions as conjunctions and disjunctions of elementary propositions. Whereas a finite conjunction of elementary propositions, such as $p.q.r$, determines its conjuncts by enumeration, a general proposition, such as $(x).fx$, according to Wittgenstein, selects the elementary propositions to be jointly asserted by using a propositional function. On this view, $(x).fx$ is assimilated to '$fa.fb.fc...$', i.e. to an indefinitely continued conjunction of all propositions having the form fx. But it is easy to see that the dots in the indefinite conjunction function just like a quantifier, though less perspicuously. If the difference between giving a set of elementary propositions by enumeration and giving them as the values of a propositional function is regarded as unimportant, it becomes possible to represent both general and molecular propositions in the same symbolism (for which see 5.52). (Cf. Ramsey's construction of 'predicative functions' in *Foundations*, pp. 37–42, adopted in the introduction to the 2nd edition of *Principia* as the principle that 'functions occur only through their values'.) This way of looking at general propositions leads Wittgenstein to distinguish two aspects of such propositions (5.521*a*): *qua* truth-functions of elementary propositions, they resemble all propositions; their generality, however, consists in the range of relevant propositions being specified as being *all* the values of a given propositional variable. Hence, Wittgenstein links the essence of generality with the notion of a variable, rather than with that of a quantifier. This is a marked departure from Russell's earlier views (though it is accepted in the second edition of *Principia*) and leads Wittgenstein to reject, with reason, Russell's early conceptions of certainty, possibility, and impossibility (5.525 *b*).

A second reason for Wittgenstein's great interest in the analysis of general propositions is his desire to improve upon Russell's unsatisfactory conception of logical propositions as being completely general. It is easy to see that this view is unsatisfactory—for some propositions belonging to logic (at any rate, on Wittgenstein's broad conception of that subject) are not wholly general; and some wholly general propositions, expressible by means of variables and logical operators exclusively, are not *a priori*. It is a serious problem for Wittgenstein how general propositions can be contingent, even though they employ no names. This will be the principal theme of LXII.

5.52 The notation has been explained in 5.502, which refers back to 5.501 *a*. The present section continues 5.51.

The notation Wittgenstein is here introducing can be illustrated by the following example: (i) Abbreviate '*x* has mass' by writing in its place *Mx*; (ii) next, introduce a variable, defined by the equation, $(\bar{\xi}_1) = (Mx)$, (where the Greek letter reminds us we are using the notation introduced at 5.501 *a*, while the attached subscript indicates that the variable now has a definite range of values); (iii) then the symbol $N(\bar{\xi}_1)$, for which provision has already been made at 5.51, will mean the same as $\sim (\exists x)(Mx)$ in the more conventional notation, i.e., the same as 'Nothing has mass'.

If we had started with the two singular propositions, 'The earth has mass', and 'Jupiter has mass', respectively abbreviated as *Me* and *Mj*, we might have introduced a variable defined by $(\bar{\xi}_2) = (Me.Mj)$, and thus have obtained $N(\bar{\xi}_2)$, with the same meaning as $\sim Me. \sim Mj$ or 'Neither the earth nor Jupiter has mass'.

W.'s proposed notation treats generalization as a truth-function (cf. 4.52—all propositions are generalizations of elementary propositions). Thus $N(\bar{\xi}_2)$ and $N(\bar{\xi}_1)$ are presented in the suggested symbolism as having the same form, the first denying the application of the property, *having mass*, to the earth and Jupiter; while the second makes the same denial for each and every thing in the world.

'What is novel about general propositions is simply the specification of the truth-arguments by a propositional function instead of by enumeration. Thus general propositions, just like molecular ones, express agreement and disagreement with the truth-possibilities of atomic propositions, but they do this in a different and more complicated way' (Ramsey, *Foundations*, p. 153).

'He said that there was a temptation, to which he had yielded in the *Tractatus*, to say that $(x).fx$ is identical with the logical product

$$\text{``}fa.fb.fc\ldots\text{''},$$

and $(\exists x).fx$ identical with the logical sum "$fa \vee fb \vee fc \ldots$"; but that this was in both cases a mistake' (Moore, *Papers*, p. 297).

'He said that, when he wrote the *Tractatus*, he had supposed that *all* such general propositions were "truth-functions"; but he said now that in supposing this he was committing a fallacy' (*op. cit.* p. 298).

'He said that, when he wrote the *Tractatus*, he would have defended the mistaken view which he then took by asking the question: How can $(x).fx$ possibly entail fa, if $(x).fx$ is not a logical product? And he said that the answer to this question is that where $(x).fx$ is not a logical product, the proposition "$(x).fx$ entails fa" is "taken as a primary proposition"' (*ibid.*). (Cf. 5.521*c*.)

5.521 (1) dissociate: or, 'separate' (as in O.).

We can consider *all* the values of a variable, without yet considering any truth-function of those values. Thus in the notation '$(\bar{\xi})$', introduced at 5.501*a*, the bar can be regarded as symbolizing the concept of generality (*der Begriff 'Alle'*). $\sim (\exists x).fx$ agrees with $\sim fa . \sim fb$ in involving the *same* operator, N (or, alternatively, the same truth-function, 'simultaneous negation'); the general proposition differs from the finite one in involving generality, *not* in being a special sort of truth-function.

'I suppose you didn't understand the way how I separate in the old notation of generality what is in it truth-function and what is purely generality. A general proposition is *a* truth-function of *all propositions* of a certain form' (*Letters*, 130 (6)).

'We can distinguish [in the cases of universal and existential propositions] first the element of generality, which comes in specifying the truth-arguments, which are not, as before, enumerated, but determined as all values of a certain propositional function; and secondly the truth-function element which is the logical product in the first case and the logical sum in the second' (Ramsey, *Foundations*, p. 153).

(2) in association with: or, 'as tied up with'. Russell introduces the universal and existential quantifiers as 'two new primitive ideas'

(Introduction to *Principia*, vol. 1, p. 15), and seems to have no independent account of generality except 'in association with' general statements. For Frege's introduction of the quantifiers, see *Translations*, p. 35. See also Anscombe, *Introduction*, p. 142.

b **in which both ideas are embedded**: or, 'which cover both ideas'. In order to understand the quantified propositions, we must understand what is meant by 'all' *and also* what is meant by 'joint negation'—or some other truth-function.

● 'If we do not understand what generality is, and do not separate it from the concept of truth-functions, we shall be unable to see what there is *in common* between a universal proposition and the corresponding existential proposition.'

5.522 indicates: or, 'points to' (*hinweist*).

logical prototype: for the meaning of 'prototype', see notes on 3.315*e* above. At 3.24 (3)*c*, the notation for generality (*Allgemeinheitsbezeichnung*), as in the present section, is said to 'contain' a prototype. A 'logical proto-type' (*Urbild*) is the proper symbol for a completely general logical form (cf. 3.315 *ad fin.*). Thus the notation $(x) Mx$, used above in the notes on 5.52, and W.'s own notation, may both be said to contain the *Urbild* ϕx.

● 'One distinctive thing about a general proposition, or any symbol replacing such a proposition, is that it exhibits a general logical form.'

(It is worth noting that this seems to be true of *all* propositions. Thus the singular proposition *Me* also 'contains' the *Urbild*, ϕx. Perhaps W.'s thought is that the quantifiers, or their symbolic equivalents, are *attached to* an *Urbild*? Alternatively, we might say that in the case of a general proposition the operation, N, has an *Urbild* as its basis.)

gives prominence to constants: or, 'draws attention to' (*hervorhebt*) them. I think the 'constants' in question must be the names that could be substituted for the variable in the propositional function to which the quantifier is attached (not the constant formal features of the generalized proposition, i.e. those that show its form).

● 'The symbol for a general proposition draws attention to each of the *values* of the corresponding propositional function. Thus $(x).fx$ emphasizes (*hervorhebt*) the constant singular propositions, fa, fb, etc.'

An alternative account is given by Anscombe (*Introduction*, p. 144): '"$(x)x$ moves slower than light", for example, *lays emphasis on* "moves slower than light" as an expression which collects together a class of propositions, and *points to* a "logical proto-picture" xRy, where (taking R as variable) all the constants have been turned into variables.'

Generality

5.523 For comment on this section and the next, see Anscombe, *Introduction*, p. 144.

'That arbitrary correlation of sign and thing signified which is a condition of the possibility of the propositions, and which I found lacking in the completely general propositions, occurs there by means of the generality notation [or: sign], just as in the elementary proposition it occurs by means of names. (For the generality notation does not belong to the *picture*.) Hence the constant feeling that generality makes its appearance quite like an argument' (*Notebooks*, 25 (8)).

The generality symbol (the quantifier with its attached variable, $(x)(...x...)$) is conceived here as analogous to a proper name. Inserting the proper name a into the argument place of the propositional function, fx, produces a definite proposition which is linked with the world because a stands for a thing; similarly, binding the variable, x, in fx, by adjoining a quantifier, produces a definite proposition which is linked with the world by its reference to *all* things. Instead of fa, we have as it were '$f(\text{everything})$'. In the *Notebooks*, 90 (14), W. suggests that the analogy between quantification and instantiation could be stressed by treating a name as a kind of quantifier, so that instead of fa we could write $(ax).fx$.

● 'The quantifier in a general proposition refers to the *things* that satisfy the propositional function in question, and does not symbolize a property of the function itself.'

In view of the present section, one might be tempted to treat the quantifier explicitly as a peculiar sort of name, and so replace $(x)fx$ by, say, $f(g)$. This would not work, for the reasons already explained at 4.0411. (So, after all, the quantifier does not 'occur as an argument' in the way that a name does—it would be misleading to treat a quantifier as a peculiar sort of name.)

5.524 Cf. 1.11 (reference to '*all* the facts'), 1.12 (the totality of facts as determining what is not the case).

'Each thing modifies [or, conditions (*bedingt*)] the whole logical world (*die ganze logische Welt*), the whole of logical space, so to speak' (*Notebooks*, 83 (10)).

(1) This remark, and the next, are directed against the inclination to regard a 'general fact' as a 'super-fact', in addition to the atomic facts. There is not something properly referred to as 'all objects', over and above each individual object; talk about '*all* objects' is just talk about each *individual* object. (There is no universal class.) But cf. 4.52a *ad fin*. See also 1.11 and 1.12.

Another way of considering the matter: the symbol for a singular proposition must contain the proto-picture (*Urbild*) that is needed in the notation for generality. Thus, in being 'given' an object (i.e. in the light of 3.3, in understanding a single proposition in which a name of that object occurs), I have all that is needed for giving sense to the corresponding general propositional sign—no further experience is needed, and no such further experience is conceivable.

at the same time: or, 'thereby' (*damit*).

(**2**) '"It is necessary also to be given the proposition that all elementary propositions are given" [apparently quoting from a letter from Russell]. This is not necessary because it is even impossible. There is no such proposition! That all elementary propositions are given is *shown* by there being none having an elementary sense which is not given' (*Letters*, 130 (5)).

5.525 (1) A characteristic statement of the position here under attack is: 'One may call a propositional function *necessary*, when it is always true; *possible*, when it is sometimes true; *impossible*, when it is never true' (Russell, 'Philosophy of Logical Atomism', lecture V, in *Logic and Knowledge*, p. 231).

On this early view of Russell's the proposition, 'It is possible for a man to know *Principia* by heart' is taken to have the same meaning as 'There exists at least one man who knows *Principia* by heart', i.e. as having the form $(\exists x).fx$. The weakness of this contention is obvious—the proposition about possibility may well be true even if no man ever in fact performs the feat in question. So Russell does not begin to do justice to the notion of empirical possibility. (More generally, it is well known that Russell's logical symbolism is inadequate for the representation of modal operators.)

But in any case, W. is here concerned with 'essential' generality (for which see 6.1232 *a*) and so with 'essential' certainty, possibility, and impossibility—i.e. with logical features of logical forms, not with anything that is in fact the case.

(**2**) An interesting interpretation is given by Anscombe (*Introduction*, p. 157). Suppose *s* is a significant proposition and *r* expresses something known. Then the situation expressed by *s* will be 'certain' if $r \supset s$ is a tautology (with similar interpretations for the other two cases). But this reading seems forced and contrary to W.'s intentions.

For a connexion between the modal notions and probability, see 4.464.

Anscombe calls the views expressed by W. in this paragraph a 'pure exigency' of the picture theory (*Introduction*, p. 80).

(3) **The precedent**: the ground for an assertion of possibility, etc.

'He held, therefore, that in many cases the "linguistic expression" of "It is possible that p should be true" or "should have been true" is "The sentence 'p' has sense". And I think there is no doubt that he here meant by "possible" what is commonly called, and was called by him on a later occasion, "logically possible"' (Moore, *Papers*, p. 275).

● 'In establishing a contention with respect to possibility (certainty, impossibility), one must always inspect a symbol (*sc.* a proposition). That the symbol makes sense *shows* that the corresponding situation is *possible*.'

Cf. 3.13*bc*—a proposition as 'containing' the possibility of what it represents.

LXII

DESCRIPTION OF THE WORLD BY COMPLETELY GENERAL PROPOSITIONS

(5.526–5.5262)

Discussion of general propositions is now continued. How are completely general propositions, containing no names, connected with the world? Wittgenstein makes the striking claim that the world can be 'completely' described by such propositions, i.e. that proper names are theoretically unnecessary in a complete record of what is contingently the case. It might reasonably be objected that the general propositions would have no meaning unless there were names to identify the objects belonging to the ranges of the variables (cf. 3.316*b*), so even a description of the universe in completely general terms might be said to presuppose the existence of names in the language used. But in any case, Wittgenstein's claim seems to be mistaken. For more than one world might satisfy even the most complete general description. One such world might consist of the single atomic fact Ma, and another of the single atomic fact, Nb (where M, N, a, and b are supposed to be four different objects). The completely general proposition, $(\exists x, \phi) . \phi x$, fits both worlds equally well, and no other *general* propositions can express the difference between the two worlds. *Pace* Wittgenstein, the completely general propositions state only the contingent *pattern* of the actual world, and an exhaustive description of the world must necessarily employ names.

5.526 describe the world completely: for a similar use of this expression see 4.023 *b*. With that other passage in mind, we might say that Wittgenstein is here stressing the *definiteness* of the sense of general and even of wholly general propositions.

without first correlating any name, etc.: this suggests a language not containing names at all.

W. does not mean that names are theoretically superfluous: as he explains in the *Notebooks*, 'Names are necessary for an assertion that *this* thing possesses *that* property and so on. They link the propositional form with quite definite objects' (53 (8, 9)). W.'s point is that general propositions describe, without any imprecision, the general structural features—the make-up or constitution—of the actual universe. However, such a description cannot express the respects in which the actual universe differs from an isomorphic one that might have existed in its place.

Suppose, for example, that the logical simples consist of the individuals, a and b, and the single property, f (an illustration used by W. himself in the *Notebooks*, 14 (4)). Now consider two possible worlds, W_1 and W_2, respectively defined by the following state-descriptions:

$$(W_1): \quad fa. \sim fb$$
$$(W_2): \quad \sim fa.fb$$

and also consider a 'completely general proposition', g, expressed as follows:
$$(\exists x, y, \phi)(\phi x. \sim \phi y).$$

Then 'g' would constitute the 'complete description' of the universe to which W. is referring in 5.526 *a*.

(I am here using W.'s suggested convention about identity (5.53), which requires the two variables, x and y, to refer to different objects.)

It is clear that the truth of g is compatible with the universe being *either* W_1 *or* W_2. The general proposition determines the contingent structure or general constitution of the universe of which it is true: such a universe might be either W_1 or W_2, but it could not be represented, say, by $fa.fb$.

In order now to introduce names, in the way indicated at 5.526 *b*, we need only convert g into:

$$(\exists x, y, \phi)(\phi x. \sim \phi y.x = a.y = b.\phi = f). \tag{h}$$

Description of the World by Completely General Propositions

In view of W.'s reference to the additional clause as running 'there is one *and only one* x, which . . .', one might suppose that the correct form should be, not (h), but rather the following:

$$(\exists x, y, \phi)\, (z, \Psi)\, (\phi x . \sim \phi y . x = a . y = b . \phi = f . \sim \Psi z). \qquad (k)$$

Anscombe points out (*Introduction*, p. 148) that a form such as (k) would require the employment of '*more* variables than there are names of distinct objects'. I think the answer must be that upon our supposition of only three objects (a, b, f), a form such as (k) must be nonsensical. Consider the simpler proposition:

$$(\exists x, y, z, \phi)\, (\phi x). \qquad (l)$$

On W.'s view, we ought to think of this as meaning something like

$$fa \vee fb \vee f*,$$

where the asterisk in the last term is to be replaced by a name for something *other than a* or *b*. But on our supposition, the expression, 'something other than a or b', must be sheer nonsense. It is nonsensical to imagine that there might be *more* logical simples than there are.

I take (h), accordingly, to be the correct expression of what W. had in mind. It should be noted that although (h) is, on this view, a complete description of the world, it is impossible to *express* that it is complete. This *shows* itself, e.g. in nonsense resulting when we try to construct (k).

In the *Notebooks*, W. calls the representation of the world by means of completely general propositions 'the impersonal representation of the world' (*die unpersönliche Darstellung der Welt* (20 (2)))—perhaps implying that the use of proper names is pre-eminently a convenience to a person who needs to identify particular things.

'And if the general description of the world is like a stencil (*Schablone*) of the world, the names pin it to the world so that the world is wholly covered by it' (*Notebooks*, 53 (10)).

The present section recalls the view, once popular with logical positivists, that scientific assertions deal only with the structure of the world and not with its content. (See, for instance, Carnap, *Aufbau*, § 16.)

5.5261 Propositions have already been characterized as necessarily composite (e.g. at 4.032 (2)). At one time, W. was inclined to regard completely general propositions as simple (because they seemed to involve no designations of objects) and hence to treat them as 'pictures' of logical forms. In the present section, he says that variables in generalized propositions *do* stand in signifying relations to things in the world, and indeed in various ways (they have distinct ranges of values).

Cf. 4.0411 on the 'multiplicity' of general statements.

(1) *c* **just as is the case**: rather, 'as in'.

(2) **mark**: or, 'criterion'.

something in common: of course all symbols have *something* in common, logical form.

5.5262 We have seen in our discussion of 5.526 above that the completely general propositions determine the 'constitution' or general make-up of the actual universe, while leaving its detailed character unsettled. Now the truth-value of *any* contingent proposition changes the 'constitution' of the universe. For example, if *fa* is true, in our former illustration at 5.526, then $(\exists x, \phi)\,(\phi x)$ must be true (the universe has the feature of containing at least one fact of the subject–predicate form); and if another elementary proposition, *fb*, is true, then the general proposition $(\exists x, y, \phi)\,(\phi x \cdot \phi y)$ becomes true (the world has the feature of containing at least two facts of the subject–predicate form).

W.'s purpose here is to emphasize that 'completely general propositions', like all significant propositions, are contingent.

(In the above, I have translated *Bau* as 'constitution' rather than 'construction' as in P.–McG. '*Spielraum*' in this section has the vague sense of 'room' or 'open space' rather than the technical sense of 'range', for which see 4.463).

LXIII

IDENTITY

(5.53–5.534)

Wittgenstein has already said that identities are 'only expedients in presentation' (4.242). He will now try to show that identities are not truth-functions of elementary propositions, as genuine propositions are, but are mere 'pseudo-propositions' (*Scheinsätze*) (5.535a). His procedure is to introduce a possible notation, dispensing with any sign for identity, which will be just as adequate as the customary notation. The basic idea is to show identity of objects, whether identified by names or included in the ranges of given variables, by means of physical similarities in the signs for such names and such variables (5.53, 5.531–5.5321). The possibility of doing this will establish that the identity sign is 'not an essential constituent' of an adequate logical notation (5.533). Construction of a system of formal logic employing Wittgenstein's proposed conventions is feasible, at the cost of certain inconveniences (cf. the references to Hintikka given below).

5.53*a*   As it stands, this remark might easily mislead a reader. Since the word 'identity' does not *stand for* anything on W.'s view, one might be inclined to say there is no such thing as 'identity of the sign', and of course no such thing as 'identity of the object'. Thus there is nothing to be expressed and nothing by means of which it could be expressed. The fact is, as explained below, that W. proposes to use a certain convention for counting sign-tokens as occurrences of the same sign-type as a surrogate for what some philosophers have mistakenly tried to make the sign of identity express.

● 'Instead of using the nonsensical phrase, "identity of the objects", I shall introduce a convention for the mutual replaceability of signs, which might loosely be called a convention about the "identity and difference of signs".'

It may be noticed that 'identity of the object' is already often expressed by 'identity of the sign'. For example, it is usually understood that '*Raa*' expresses a relationship of a thing *to itself*. (Cf. also note on 5.532 below.) Thus W.'s main innovation is his proposal that *different* signs shall be understood to have different meanings.

Of course, W. is not demanding the convention, but merely presenting it as a possible one (as Anscombe points out, *Introduction*, p. 146, f.n. 1).

5.5301 (1) *a*   **a relation between objects**: compare, for instance, the following: '... numerical identity, which is a dyadic relation of a subject to itself of which nothing but an existent individual is capable' (Peirce, *Papers*, 1.461).

self-evident: or, 'obvious'. Because in such a context as $(x):fx. \supset .x = a$, the assertion amounts to saying that a satisfies f and that nothing else does: there is no reference to any relation between a and the things that do not satisfy f. And similarly in other cases where the symbolism for identity makes identity look like a relation.

(2) ● 'If we thought of identity as a certain relation, say R, that objects have to one another, then in analysing the meaning of $(x):fx. \supset .x = a$, we should still have to make it plain that only a has R to a. In order to do this, we should still need to use the identity sign—or else leave the crucial property of R (namely that it relates a thing to itself and to no other thing) unexpressed.'

In the *Moore Notes* (116 (3)), W. spoke of 'the symbol of identity' as expressing an 'internal relation between a function and its argument'. What he may have had in mind was that '$(\exists x):fx.x = a$' is logically equivalent to 'fa'. Thus the identity sign in the former expression is being used as a way of showing how a stands with respect to f (namely that it is one thing satisfying f).

5.5302 Does it really make sense to say that two things have *all* their properties in common, as W. emphatically says it does in *b*? W. does not seem at all troubled here by the need to take account of differences in logical categories of the 'properties' concerned. (Possibly he was thinking only of the 'properties' that are ingredients in *atomic* facts.)

Russell's definition of identity (*Principia*, vol. 1, definition 13.01) is based upon the principle of the identity of indiscernibles, which W. is here rejecting. (For references to various discussions of this principle, see Black, *Problems*, p. 292.)

'The definition makes it self-contradictory for two things to have all their elementary properties in common. Yet this is really perfectly possible, even if, in fact, it never happens. Take two things, a and b. Then there is nothing self-contradictory in a having any self-consistent set of elementary properties, nor in b having them, nor therefore in a and b having all their elementary properties in common. Hence, since this is logically possible, it is essential to have a symbolism which allows us to consider this possibility and does not exclude it by definition' (Ramsey, *Foundations*, p. 31). But Ramsey here seems to commit the fallacy of composition, or something like it. Given any elementary property, it is possible that a and b might both have that property, but it does not follow that a and b might have all elementary properties in common. The inference from $(P)\Diamond(Pa \equiv Pb)$ to $\Diamond(P)(Pa \equiv Pb)$ needs a special defence (cf. the argument from 'For any given ticket in the sweepstake, it is possible that it might win first prize' to 'It is possible that all the tickets in the sweepstake might win first prize'). W.'s own line of thought is untenable, for the reason suggested above (the senselessness of the expression '*all* properties').

5.5303 Cf. 4.243 (1) on understanding identity and difference of names. It follows from this remark that all identities are necessary, not contingent.

5.531 Here, and in the next four sections, W. seems to be thinking of a language in which there are no synonyms for genuine names, and no abbreviations, introduced by definition, in place of complex signs (cf.

Identity

4.241), i.e. a language in which every proposition is uniquely formulated by means of 'primitive' signs. But in any language that admits of various signs with the same reference, the convention proposed in this section will need modification. Thus suppose we are considering a system of signs that refer to integers (i.e. a language for arithmetic), and let H stand for the relation of 'having all factors in common'. Then the sign, $H(4, 2+2)$ which would customarily be taken to express the correct arithmetical assertion that 4 and $2+2$ have the same factors (i.e. that 4 has the same factors as itself) would, with the proposed convention, carry the mistaken implication that 4 and $2+2$ are different integers. W.'s convention seems to imply a ban on synonyms. The point is discussed further in the note on 5.533 below.

5.532 Here, W.'s proposed convention for dispensing with identity is applied to variables. It is worth noticing that the customary conventions governing the use of variables already involve rules for the 'identification of variables'. Thus a formula like $(x).fx \supset gx$ is customarily understood in such a way that the two occurrences of the x after the quantifier are 'identified': from the general formula we are permitted to infer $fa \supset ga$, but not $fa \supset gb$—the two occurrences of the x have to be treated in the same way for the purpose of instantiation. W. modifies the convention by demanding that visibly different variables shall be treated *differently* for the purpose of instantiation—so that, for example, $R(x, y)$ shall not be permitted to have $R(a, a)$ as a substitution instance.

Carnap has pointed out (*Syntax*, p. 50) that W.'s proposed conventions for the use of variables would be difficult to employ unless further symbolic machinery were available. W.'s method forbids us to pass from $R(x, y)$ to $R(a, a)$; yet the substitution could be made in two stages, the first result being the sign $R(x, a)$, in which there is nothing to show the impropriety of proceeding to a further replacement of the remaining free variable, x, by means of a. Unless such piecemeal substitution were to be forbidden (which would require supplementary conventions), it would be necessary to tag such a formula as $R(x, a)$ with an indicator showing which substitutions had already been made. (Carnap suggests some such symbol as $^{x,a}R(x, a)$, *Syntax*, p. 50.)

W.'s proposal would certainly introduce troublesome complications into standard logical notation and it is doubtful whether his innovations would work in practice. Ramsey said, 'the convention is slightly ambiguous, but it can be made definite, and is then workable, although generally inconvenient' (*Foundations*, pp. 31–2). But he also said, 'this rejection of identity may have serious consequences in the theory of aggregates and cardinal number; it is, for example, hardly plausible to say that two classes are only of equal number when there is a one–one relation whose

Commentary

domain is the one and converse domain the other, unless such relations can be constructed by means of identity' (*Foundations*, p. 282). Since W. rejected Russell's definitions of cardinal numbers in terms of classes (cf. 6.031 (1)), he would be untroubled by any complications in the *Principia* system that might result from his proposed identity conventions. In any case, his purpose was the philosophical one of showing that a certain new convention was possible; he was not recommending a technical innovation for the mathematical logician.

Recently, Hintikka ('Identity') has shown how to construct a formal logic embodying W.'s suggested convention. See also his subsequent paper ('Vicious Circle').

5.5321 It is important to notice that W. here attaches sense to propositions of the form '*only* one x satisfies $f(\ )$' (cf. also 5.526 (2)). Compare the discussion of the axiom of infinity in the notes on 5.535 (2, 3) below.

5.533 **conceptual notation**: or, 'ideography' (*Begriffsschrift*), as in 3.325 (2).

W.'s line of thought is not immediately convincing. His new convention for showing identity and difference apparently amounts to using certain relations between signs (similarity and dissimilarity of tokens) in order to *show* what the customary symbolism seems to assert. Where the older symbolism allows $R(a, b).a = b$, with the second clause apparently asserting the identity of a and b, W. has $R(a, a)$ with the similarity between the two tokens of a showing that the relation is holding between a thing, a, and itself. It would seem, however, that a similar device could be employed in the case of relations that are admittedly 'part of the world' in a way in which identity is not. In place of the expression 'greater than', used to refer to a certain relation, we could *show* this relation by means of a symbolic convention involving the relative sizes of tokens. In place of 'The sun is greater than the earth' we might have 'THE SUN the earth' (and similarly in other cases). Or we could *show* facts about colours by having the corresponding sentences in different colours. In these proposals, as in W.'s identity conventions, it might be said that we are making sentences *more iconic* (making sentences exemplify properties or relations to which other sentences previously *referred*). But we would not want to say that properties and relations exemplifiable by signs cannot belong to 'the world'.

The answer, from W.'s standpoint, must turn upon whether the convention adopted uses 'accidental' or 'essential' features of the corresponding signs. That signs should be of different sizes or different colours in a certain system is clearly an 'accidental' feature of those signs, and is not essential to their capacity to mean what they do mean. But W.'s identity conventions are different. If we allow for the presence of synonyms

294

in the language, he may be taken to be saying the following: 'The names of the language fall into mutually exclusive classes, with all the members of any one such class having the same reference (*Bedeutung*). What answers in language to the supposed property of identity in "the world" is just this common reference of synonymous signs. There *must be* conventions or rules to determine when names are, or are not, synonymous; now it is these rules (or the perceptible features in the sign-tokens expressing such rules) that *show* what the older notation pretended to assert.' (The important point here is that W. does not really want to insist upon physical similarity and dissimilarity between tokens as showing identity and difference, but rather upon the membership of the tokens in different synonym classes. Identity is shown by signs belonging to *the same symbol*, difference by signs belonging to *different symbols*.) Now the features which W. is here using to show 'identity' and 'difference' are certainly essential features of the symbolism; that two signs refer to the same or different objects is something that is part of the meaning of *those* signs. W. might say: 'What is confusedly referred to as "identity" or "difference" is *necessarily* shown by the segregation of signs into classes of synonymous members. My proposed conventions are merely a device for making these classes (and the rules that produce them) more perspicuous—and for curbing the temptation to write nonsense like "$a = a$".'

5.534 correct conceptual notation: 'correct ideography' (*Begriffsschrift*) as in the preceding section. The use of 'correct' is interesting here. There is a sense in which all systems of signs having meaning must be 'correct' because they are 'perfectly in order'.

LXIV

THE AXIOM OF INFINITY; PROPOSITIONS ABOUT THE NUMBER OF OBJECTS IN THE UNIVERSE

(5.535–5.5352)

In rejecting Russell's conception of the axiom of infinity as an empirical proposition Wittgenstein makes a decisive criticism of 'logicism' (cf. notes on 5.535 below). In Wittgenstein's system, the number of objects in the universe must be a necessary feature of logical space, shown by the availability of a corresponding number of distinct names (5.535c). On the other hand, Wittgenstein elsewhere (as in 5.5261) seems to assign sense to general propositions, such as $(\exists x, \phi) . \phi x$, that seem to limit the total number of objects. Yet, if such propositions have sense, assertions about the number of objects must be contingent. It is hard to see how this difficulty can be resolved.

5.535 (1) **pseudo-propositions** (*Scheinsätze*): this sounds as if W. wishes to ban formulas such as those listed in the preceding section. At 4.1272 (4) he has talked about 'nonsensical pseudo-propositions' (and see the note on the meaning of *Scheinsatz* at that place), but, on the other hand, he will later claim that mathematics consists entirely of 'pseudo-propositions' (6.2b). So, after all, W. is perhaps not blacklisting identities. (It is worth noticing that negation could be expelled from a *Begriffsschrift*, as W. proposes to expel the identity symbol, for example, by inverting the propositional sign to show negation, as suggested by Ramsey, *Foundations*, p. 146. So any grounds for rejecting identities would tell equally in favour of rejecting formulas containing the negation sign, or more generally, in favour of rejecting any logical formulas.)

(**2, 3**) In *Principia*, the axiom of infinity was intended to guarantee the existence of a sufficient number of objects to permit the definition of infinitely many different integers. But on W.'s analysis, the attempt to *say* that even a single object exists (for instance $(\exists x) (x = x)$) already produces nonsense. Thus the reason for rejecting the axiom of infinity is not that it involves the problematic notion of infinity, but rather that it involves the absurdity of trying to assert the existence of objects (cf. 4.1272ef).

Notice that at this time W. was untroubled by qualms about the sense of the expression 'an infinite number of names'. In his later work, he rejected this phrase as meaningless.

THE AXIOM OF INFINITY

'The axiom of infinity is an assumption which may be enunciated as follows: "If n is any inductive cardinal number, there is at least one class of individuals having n terms"' (Russell, *Mathematical Philosophy*, p. 131).

According to Russell, the axiom is an empirical truth: 'true in some possible worlds and false in others; whether it is true or false in this world, we cannot tell' (*op. cit.* p. 141). Again, 'it seems plain that there is nothing in logic to necessitate its truth or falsehood, and that it can only be legitimately believed or disbelieved on empirical grounds' (*Principia*, vol. 2, p. 183). Wittgenstein seems to have shared this view at one time. He said it was a 'matter of experience' (literally, a question of physics, *Sache der Physik*) to determine the truth of statements about the number of existing things (*Letters*, 127 (4)).

The axiom is needed in the *Principia* system to prevent all cardinal numbers beyond a certain point being identical with the null class, with consequent contradiction. Accordingly, this indispensable axiom has been regarded as a sign that arithmetic cannot be reduced to logic (Schmidt, *Grundlagenforschung*, p. 38). Church agrees that 'the necessity for an axiom of infinity marks the decisive lacuna in the Frege–Russell derivation of arithmetic from logic' ('Review of Schmidt', p. 199).

For Wittgenstein, of course, the number of individuals can only be *shown*, as explained in 5.535c. Compare the detailed remarks on this point in Ramsey, *Foundations*, pp. 59–61, 79.

Ramsey suggests that a proposition of the form, 'There are at least n individuals' is 'always either a tautology or a contradiction, never a genuine proposition' (*op. cit.* p. 60). Cf. Anscombe, *Introduction*, pp. 147–9.

5.535 (3) **infinitely many names**: another way in which the axiom of infinity's truth would be reflected in language would be in the possibility of infinitely many distinct variables (cf. notes on 5.526 above).

5.5351 (1)c 'Every proposition implies itself, and whatever is not a proposition implies nothing. Hence to say "p is a proposition" is equivalent to saying "p implies p"; and this equivalence may be used to define propositions' (Russell, *Principles*, p. 15). In *Principia*, 'elementary proposition' is a primitive notion, and the device that W. is here criticizing has been abandoned.

Shwayder says that W. is here unfair to Russell: 'Following Frege, Russell used it primarily as a device enabling truth-functions to take *any* argument and not just sentences. This is almost the opposite of what W. says' (*Thesis*, p. 89).

(2) **hypothesis**: better, 'antecedent'.

5.5352   W. is attacking the idea of identity as an 'accidental' property that things contingently have.

The proposed symbolism has no sense. For if it did, it would also have to make sense to negate $x = x$ and hence to envisage the possibility of things not being identical with themselves.

● 'If " $\sim(\exists x).x = x$ " made sense, so would " $(\exists x).x = x$ ". Both expressions must allow for the possibility of things *not* being identical with themselves. Thus, the first might be true, even if some things did exist, namely, those not identical with themselves.'

(A last fling at the notion that identity and difference are relations between objects.)

LXV

OSTENSIBLY NON-EXTENSIONAL OCCURRENCES OF PROPOSITIONS (EXPRESSIONS OF BELIEF, JUDGEMENT, ETC.)

(5.54–5.5423)

We have seen how strongly Wittgenstein is committed to the principle of extensionality, that all propositions are truth-functions of elementary propositions—or, what comes to the same thing, that all propositions can be generated by means of truth-operations applied to elementary propositions. The present instalment opens with a reaffirmation of this principle (5.54).

We have also seen how Wittgenstein tries to reconcile the existence of general propositions with the extensionality principle (LXI). Now he wrestles with another kind of proposition that seems to be an exception. A proposition of the form '*A* believes *p*' seems *prima facie* not to be a truth-function of *p*, since its truth in no way depends upon the latter's truth-value. When it is true that *A* believes *p*, it looks as if the proposition, *p*, stands in a genuine relation to the believer (cf. 5.541 *c*). How is this to be reconciled with the principle of extensionality?

Russell's 'multiple theory of judgement' (for which see note on 5.5422*b* below) provides a way out of the difficulty. For, according to that theory, '*A* believes *p*' does not express a relation between *A* and *p*, but rather between *A*'s mind and the *constituents* of *p*. Accordingly, '*A* believes *p*' is not a function of *p* at all, and the difficulty about the function's being non-extensional disappears. Wittgenstein's only stated objection to Russell's theory is that it fails to make it impossible to believe in or judge a 'nonsense' (5.5422*a*). However, this objection and similar ones made by later critics can be met: the real weaknesses of Russell's theory are located elsewhere.

Wittgenstein's own outline of an alternative analysis of belief statements is hardly more than a hint that generates its own perplexities. His idea seems to have been that a rough analysis of '*A* believes *p*' can be taken to be: '*A* utters *S*. *S* says that *p*' (where '*S*' is to be imagined replaced by the quotation of some sentence). The second conjunct in this analysis might take the form: '"London is larger than Paris" says that London is larger than Paris.' This certainly looks like a proposition that is merely contingently true, and that ought therefore to count as significant on Wittgenstein's principles. But it is far from obvious how it could possibly be construed as a truth-function of elementary propositions.

5.54 Connects with 4.4.
general propositional form: cf. 5.47 (5) for another reference to this.

● 'All functions of propositions are truth-functions' (the 'thesis of extensionality', for which see Carnap, *Syntax*, pp. 245–7).

5.541 For the topics of this and the succeeding section, see Appendix C, 'Truth-functions and others' (*Principia*, 2nd edn., vol. 1). Also Carnap, *Meaning and Necessity*, especially § 13 ('Sentences about Beliefs').

(**1**) 'There are *internal* relations between one proposition and another; but a proposition cannot have to another *the* internal relation which a *name* has to the proposition of which it is a constituent, and which ought to be meant by saying that it "occurs" in it. In this sense one proposition can't "occur" in another' (*Moore Notes*, 115 (7)).

(**3**) 'When we say that *A* judges that, etc., then we have to mention a whole proposition which *A* judges. It will not do either to mention only its constituents, or its constituents and form but not in the proper order. This shows that a proposition itself must occur in the statement to the effect that it is judged. For instance, however "not-p" may be explained, the question "What is negated?" must have a meaning' (*Notes on Logic*, 96 (3)).

(4) 'The epistemological questions concerning the nature of judgment and belief cannot be solved without a correct apprehension of the form of the proposition' (*Notes on Logic*, 97 (2) *d*).

5.542 When A (some person) says that today is Monday, he utters the sentence 'Today is Monday' (S) or some synonymous sentence. So part of what we mean by saying 'A said that today is Monday' is: 'A uttered some S and S means that today is Monday.'

Similarly we take A's judging or thinking or believing that today is Monday to require uttering S (or using some equivalent sign, such as one composed of images). In all these cases, p (that today is Monday) occurs in the original statement (A believes p) through the component statement 'S ($= \ulcorner p \urcorner$) means p'.

a fact: the fact consisting of what A did (the fact that he spoke the words he spoke).

an object: A.

'It is perhaps not quite right to say that "A judges p" is of the form "'p' says that p"; what he should have said was that the business part of "A judges that p", the part that relates to something's having as its content a potential representation of the fact that p, was of the form "'p' says that p"' (Anscombe, *Introduction*, p. 88).

correlation of facts by means of the correlation of their objects: i.e. of the elements of a sentence-fact (the fact consisting in the utterance of S) and the objects in the corresponding state-of-affairs (that today is Monday) *via* the references of the names occurring in S.

'p enters into the fact that A believes that p only in so far as the statement that A believes that p is a statement about language' (Ayer, *Thinking*, p. 17).

It should be noticed that on W.'s principles the meaning of a sentence can only be shown (4.022 *a*). So the proper verdict is that p does not occur at all in 'A believes p' (which is *not* a truth-function of p). A cannot *say* that he believes p, but he shows that he does so by uttering a certain sentence; and we show that we take him to be believing p by treating him as asserting p, e.g. by contradicting him or agreeing with him.

[W.] 'explicitly reduces the question as to the analysis of judgement . . . to the question, "What is it for a proposition to have a certain sense?"' (Ramsey, *Foundations*, pp. 274–5).

Anscombe, however, holds that a proposition of the form '"*p*" says that *p*' is a genuine proposition (*Introduction*, p. 89). Her reading can be illustrated as follows: take *p* to be 'London is larger than Paris'; then '"*p*" says that *p*' becomes, on her view: 'That, in "London is larger than Paris"', "London" stands to the left and "Paris" to the right of "is larger than" says that London is larger than Paris.' *This* assertion about the sentence might have been false, if our conventions of meaning had been different, and hence is a genuinely empirical proposition (*op. cit.* p. 90). She does not, however, explain how, on her view, '"*p*" says that *p*' can be construed as a truth-function of its constituents, as it should be in order to be a 'genuine proposition' on W.'s principles. I do not see how it can be so construed.

5.5421 (1) **no such thing**: the German has *Unding* (= non-entity), with the secondary sense of 'chimaera'.

the subject: cf. 5.631 *a*, for a similar remark.

(2) **a composite soul**: on W.'s analysis in 5.542, the supposed 'soul' is as it were replaced by an aggregate of facts.

'The original form of words ["*A* believes *p*"] which *prima facie* is about the person *A* in this way turns out to be about a *proposition* which is somehow connected with *A*. This proposition is taken by W. to be a part of the "subject" *A*; for otherwise the complexity of *p* (or, under an alternative reading, the multiplicity of propositions believed by *A*) would not show that the subject (the soul) is complex' (Hintikka, 'Solipsism', p. 90).

'The relation of "I believe *p*" to *p* can be compared to the relation of "'*p*' says (*besagt*) *p*" to *p*: it is just as impossible that *I* should be a simple as that "*p*" should be' (*Moore Notes*, 118 (2)).

5.5422 'Every right theory of judgement must make it impossible for me to judge that "this table penholders the book" (Russell's theory does not satisfy this requirement)' (*Notes on Logic*, 96 (3) *h*).

b **Russell's theory**: the so-called 'multiple theory of judgement', for which see Russell's 'Truth', or *Principia*, vol. 1, pp. 43–4. (The theory is criticized in Geach, *Mental Acts*, §§ 12–13).

Russell's view was that a judgement has 'several interrelated objects' (*Principia*, vol. 1, p. 43). Judgement requires a relation between the mind and the various constituents of the proposition in question. 'That is, when we judge (say) "this is red", what occurs is a relation of three terms, the mind, and "this", and red' (*ibid.*).

There is nothing in this view to prevent *A* judging that 2 loves 7, for Russell lays down no condition on the corresponding four-termed relation (*J*, say) that would prevent '*J*(*A*, 2, loves, 7)' from making sense. This is W.'s objection in 5.5422 *b*. (Russell might have retorted that it *is* possible to 'judge a nonsense'—or, alternatively, might have sought to satisfy W. by imposing further demands on *J*.)

5.5423 This may be directed against Russell's idea that we perceive a complex by standing in a complex relation to its several constituents. (So in (**1**), 'that' needs emphasis and in (**2**) *b* 'facts'.)

(**2**) The figure of the ambiguous cube is discussed in *Investigations* (p. 193 and subsequently).

(**b**) How could *the fact that* I see a fact *F*, i.e. itself some other fact *G*, be reconciled with the principle of extensionality? Could *G* be a truth-function of *F*? Cf. 5.542.

LXVI

THE FORMS OF ELEMENTARY PROPOSITIONS; LOGIC AND ITS 'APPLICATION'

(5.55–5.5571)

Here, Wittgenstein abandons all hope of specifying the forms of elementary propositions (5.5571). The most we can say about such propositions *a priori* is that they consist of names (5.55 *b*). Elementary propositions will come to light when we succeed in analysing the propositions of ordinary language (5.557), but what the elementary propositions will be like, how many objects they will contain, and so on, we cannot 'anticipate'—cannot know *a priori*. This instalment contains some important remarks about the task of philosophical analysis (5.5563), conceived as dealing with the languages we know, not with some 'ideal language' yet to be constructed.

5.55 (2)*a* Repetition of 4.22 *a*.

b **give** (*angeben*): or, 'supply'.

Notice the shift from 'forms' in (**1**) to 'composition' (*Zusammensetzung*) in (**2**) *b*. It does not seem necessary, at first sight, to know all the names in order to know the forms of the elementary propositions, though we would need those names in order to know their composition. However, forms are expressed by variables (3.315) and in order to use a variable we must know its values (3.316*b*), i.e. a list of names.

'An atomic form cannot be foreseen' (*Logical Form*, p. 163).

5.551 (1) The implication is that the question about the forms of elementary propositions, raised in 5.55 (1), does not belong to logic. But the character of these forms is not a contingent matter; is there then an *a priori* domain outside logic (cf. 6.41)?

(2) It is interesting to notice that W. got on to this 'wrong track' in *Logical Form*. For example, when he said 'We can only substitute a clear symbolism for the unprecise one by inspecting the phenomena which we want to describe. . . . That is to say, we can only arrive at a correct analysis by, what might be called, the logical investigation of the phenomena themselves, i.e. in a certain sense *a posteriori*, and not by conjecturing about *a priori* possibilities' (p. 163). This must be regarded as a temporary aberration, which he later repudiated.

5.552 (1) **something** *is*: i.e. that there 'is' substance (or: that there 'are' objects).

(2) ***prior* to**: cf. 6.1222*b* on impossibility of experiential confirmation or refutation of logical propositions.

(3) For the contrast between 'the How' and 'the What', see 3.221*d*. See also 6.44 on the connexion with the mystical. 'The How' = the contingent, the 'changing' (2.0271); 'the What' is Substance (2.024).

'There seemed to pertain to logic a peculiar depth—a universal significance. Logic lay, it seemed, at the bottom of all the sciences.—For logical investigation explores the nature of all things. . . . It takes its rise . . . from an urge to understand the basis, or essence, of everything empirical' (*Investigations*, § 89).

5.5521*a* **apply**: cf. 5.557 for further remarks about the 'application' of logic.

b **world**: must here be taken to mean the *substance* of the world (in the sense of 2.0211).

If logic were quite independent of what makes it possible to talk, to frame sensible propositions (i.e. the objects comprising the world's substance), it would be impossible to understand how logic could have anything to do with propositions, with the expression of thought. Cf. Rhees, 'Anscombe', pp. 26–7.

For comment on this section and the preceding one, see Anscombe, *Introduction*, p. 165.

5.553 (**1**) 'I see no particular reason to suppose that the simplest relations that occur in the world are (say) of order *n*, but there is no *a priori* reason against it' (Russell, *Logic and Knowledge*, p. 206).

(**2**) Repetition of 5.453 (3).

5.554 arbitrary: in the sense of unjustified. But it is hard to see why. There must be rules for the permissible combinations of names in elementary propositions and such rules ought to express necessities.

5.5541 It is supposed: no doubt by Russell (allegedly). Nowadays it might be added that 2-termed relations will suffice for all logical purposes. But perhaps W. would have regarded this as a mere dodge.

5.5542 The answers to all three questions are clearly intended to be in the negative. But it is ironical to notice that the third question expresses one of the main preoccupations of the *Tractatus*.

(**1**) **form of sign**: sign-form, form which a sign has.

(**2**) **what there must *be***: in the sense of 'be' applicable to substance.
be the case: these words should be hyphenated.

● 'It is nonsensical to ask: What must substance be like if facts are to be possible?'

5.555 (**1**) Cf. 5.55 (2).
some concept: literally, 'a concept'. The concept of their being independent concatenations of names.

(**2**) Cf. 5.514 on the systematic character of a notation.
'"to understand *p*" means to know its system. If *p* apparently moves from one system to another, *p* has really changed its sense' (*Math. MS.* p. 640). He goes on to say that *p*'s belonging to a system *S* must show itself—and cannot be said.

(**3**) *b* **What must be necessary is that I should deal**: rather, 'I must have to deal'.
possible: cf. 2.0121 (3) on the possible as logic's concern.

● 'Logic has nothing to do with what I can invent or construct: it deals with *a priori* possibilities and necessities.'

5.556a hierarchy: or, as we might say, a typology. Cf. 5.252, 5.5561. Whitehead and Russell use the word in another sense in *Principia*.

● 'We cannot provide any *a priori* specifications for the construction of the forms of elementary propositions.'

b It will be remembered that the *general* propositional form *can* be foreseen and constructed (4.5 (3)).

5.5561 (1) ● 'An atomic fact must be a combination of objects: alternatively, whatever *can* be the case is expressible by means of elementary propositions. (So logical space is defined by the totality of objects—or, equivalently, by the totality of elementary propositions.)'

a **reality**: the German word *Realität* also occurs at 5.64*b*. W. usually employs *Wirklichkeit*.

limited: or, 'bounded'. Cf. 2.0124.

(2) Hierarchies: e.g. those indicated at 5.252 (and, indeed, *any* hierarchies).

5.5562 If: with the force of 'since'.

there must be elementary propositions: cf. 4.221*a* on the analysis of propositions. Cf. also 4.411 (understanding general propositions requires understanding elementary ones).

5.5563 (1)*a* Cf. 5.4733*b* (every proposition is legitimately constructed).

'It is clear that every sentence in our language "is in order as it is". That is to say, we are not *striving after* an ideal, as if our ordinary vague sentences had not yet got a quite unexceptionable sense, and a perfect language awaited construction by us' (*Investigations*, § 98).

'But this is surely clear: the propositions which are the only ones that humanity uses will have a sense just as they are and do not wait upon a future analysis in order to acquire a sense' (*Notebooks*, 62 (2)).

'How strange if logic concerned itself with an "ideal" language and not with *ours*. For what should this ideal language express? Surely what we now express in our ordinary language; so this is what logic must investigate. But if something else, how am I to know what this is.—Logical analysis is the analysis of something that we have, not of something that we do not have. So it is the analysis of statements *as they are*' (*Phil. Bem.*, p. 2).

The contexts of the above quotations suggest that 'order' was being contrasted with 'vagueness' by W. Thus, for statements in ordinary language to be 'in order' means, among other things, that they have a *determinate* sense. Cf. 3.251 (propositions express in a definite way).

b **utterly**: rather, 'most'.

simple: there may be an allusion here to the 'simplicity' of logic, as in 5.4541*a*.

image: or, 'likeness'.

(2) [Logic] 'must run through all experience; no empirical cloudiness or uncertainty can be allowed to affect it—It must rather be of the purest crystal. But this crystal does not appear as an abstraction; but as something concrete, indeed, as the most concrete, as it were the *hardest* thing there is (*Tractatus*, no. 5.5563)' (*Investigations*, § 97).

'The crystalline purity of logic was, of course, not a *result of investigation*: it was a requirement' (*op. cit.* § 107).

'The *preconceived idea (Vorurteil)* of crystalline purity . . .' (*op. cit.* § 108).

Cf. also introductory comment to LIV above.

● 'We set out to investigate language and the world just as they are and appear to us, without the aid of abstract mathematical or scientific constructions.'

5.557 (1) *application*: the word *Anwendung* has previously been used by W. either to mean employment (or use), as in 3.262 *a*—or to mean the application of an operation, as in 5.2521. In connexion with logic, it occurs again only at 5.5521.

It will be remembered that the meanings of signs play no part in logical syntax (3.33)—cf. also 6.126 (2) *b*. Thus the 'application' of logic may be thought of as the bringing to bear upon particular, definite, statements of the *a priori* logical principles.

decides what elementary propositions there are: we cannot 'give' the form of the elementary propositions (5.55 (2)) so long as we stay within the realm of logic proper, but analysis of a given proposition will ultimately lead us to elementary propositions (cf. 4.221 *a*).

(2) **anticipate**: = 'foresee', as in 4.5 (3) and 5.556 *b*.

(3) **clash**: literally, 'collide' (*kollidieren*). We might perhaps say: there cannot be any question of a conflict between logical principles and the logical analysis of a given proposition.

(4) **be in contact with**: or, 'touch'. For another use of this image, see 2.15121. For an explanation, see perhaps 6.124 *bc*.

(5) **overlap** (*übergreifen*): or, 'encroach upon'.

The whole section should be compared with 6.124. See also Anscombe, *Introduction*, pp. 156–7.

5.5571 **If**: with the force of 'since'.

the attempt: or, 'to want' (*wollen*).

LXVII

THE LIMITS OF LANGUAGE
(5.6–5.61)

In the *Preface* (para. 3) Wittgenstein said that his aim was 'to set a limit to thought' or rather to 'the expression of thoughts', and made the important point that the demarcation has to be made '*in* language', since anything beyond the limit would 'simply be nonsense' (para. 4). 5.61*b–d* of the present instalment amplifies this dominating thought. Yet Wittgenstein continues to speak, at 5.6 and 5.61*a*, of the 'limits of the *world*' in a way which, on his conception, ought to be irremediably nonsensical. (As will be seen later, at 6.45, his inexpungeable view of the world as a '*limited* whole', as a subject for metaphysical predication, is the root of his mysticism.) This is not unexpected, but the sudden intrusion of the personal pronoun in expressions such as 'my language' and 'my world' (5.6 and later) is startling. One would have supposed that 'the world' in the relevant sense of 'logical space' (= the world's essence) could not admit of such qualification. But Wittgenstein's later writings show that he had a profound and sympathetic understanding of the metaphysical motives that drive men to solipsism. If expressions like 'my language' and 'my world' are 'ladders to be thrown away' (cf. 6.54*b*), they are not wilfully invented. Although he will say that there is no such thing as the 'I' in the metaphysically interesting sense (5.631*a*)—and so no such thing as '*my* language', we might add—he recognises the temptation that lies behind solipsism to be important and not easily dispelled.

5.6 *limits*: or, 'boundaries'. There is a sense in which language has no 'limits'—the 'limits' are not in language or anywhere else.

    mean: better read as 'are' (though *bedeuten* is in the German text). Cf. the second clause of 5.61*a*.

    my language . . . my world: these expressions often recur in the remainder of the book. But W. never speaks of 'my logic'.

    Cf. 5.62 (3), for elaboration of 5.6.

'The boundary of language is not between "what can" and "what cannot be thought", indeed, to speak of the boundary of language is to break the grammatical rules for the word "boundary". A boundary separates two parts of space, whereas there is no logical place in language for nonsense. If we wished a spatial analogy to represent a logical space we should conceive of the logical space as the whole of a space: there is no boundary, for there is no space outside' (Watson, *Physics*, pp. 19–20).

5.61 (1) The boundaries are the boundaries of the *possible*: only the logically impossible (i.e. nothing at all) could be found 'beyond' the boundaries.

(2) **The world has this in it, and this**: such and such objects (*not*: such and such facts). Cf. 4.1272 (5) on the impossibility of speaking about the existence of objects.

(3) Cf. 2.0121 (3) *b* (logic deals with every possibility), also 4.12 *b*.

(4) Cf. 7 (silence about the unsayable). Also 3.03 (impossibility of illogical thought) and 5.4731 *b* (we cannot think illogically).

'What cannot be expressed we do not express—And how try to *ask* whether THAT can be expressed which cannot be EXPRESSED?' (*Notebooks*, 52 (1)).

LXVIII

SOLIPSISM;
THE 'METAPHYSICAL SUBJECT'
(5.62–5.641)

Wittgenstein, like Schopenhauer, entertains the idea of a transcendental 'I', but, unlike him, eventually rejects it. The 'metaphysical subject' cannot be identified with my body, nor with my experience or any part of it (5.631 *b*). Descartes' soliloquizing 'I', which *has* thoughts, is not itself a thought. That which experiences is not itself an experience, is not *part* of the world (5.641 *c*). The metaphysical subject must be looked for in the boundary or 'limit' of the world (5.632, 5.641 *c*): it is, as it were, that *outside* the world on which the existence of everything depends—it might as plausibly be identified with God as with my very self. Wittgenstein might have added that this way of talking is nonsense: there is no sense in talking about a limit of the world, and hence no sense in talking about a 'metaphysical subject' (5.631 a). This is why a consistent solipsism leads to the same result as a consistent realism (5.64). A man who *intends* to be a solipsist can only be brought to see that there is nothing that he really intends to say (cf. 6.53 on correct method in philosophy). But a remark such as 5.62 b with its reference to the correctness of the solipsist's intention is evidence of Wittgenstein's ambivalent attitude towards metaphysics.

5.62 (2) *means:* rather, '*intends*' (*meint*) or '*wants to say*'.

makes itself manifest: or, 'shows itself' (*zeigt sich*).

'Of sense-data, in the sense in which it is unthinkable that the other has them, for that very reason one cannot say that the other does not have them. And for just this reason it is senseless to say it is *I* who *has* them' (*Phil. Bem.* 23, 9).

'[He said] that any one who is at all tempted to hold Idealism or Solipsism knows the temptation to say "The only reality is the present experience" or "The only reality is *my* present experience". Of these two latter statements he said that both were equally absurd, but that, though both were fallacious, "the idea expressed by them is of enormous importance"' (Moore, *Papers*, p. 311).

'W. has never held to solipsism, either in the *Tractatus* or at any other time' (Rhees, *Anscombe*, p. 388).

Cf. also Stenius, *Exposition*, p. 221.

(3) that language which alone I understand: the meaning of the German is uncertain. I take it to mean 'the *only* language which I understand', *my* language, as in 5.6. Cf. Russell's introduction, p. xviii, foot. The correct translation is discussed at length by Hintikka ('Solipsism', p. 88). Both Hintikka and Stenius (*Exposition*, p. 221) accept the rendering, 'the only language which I understand'. Anscombe, however (*Introduction*, p. 167, f.n. 1), reads it as 'the language that only I understand'. I think she must be wrong.

5.621 Immediately followed in the *Notebooks* by the remark: 'Physiological life is of course not "Life". And neither is psychological life. Life is the world' (77 (6)).

5.631 (1) Cf. 5.5421 (1), for a similar remark.

'[He said] "In one sense 'I' and 'conscious' are equivalent, but not in another", and he compared this difference to the difference between what can be said of the pictures on a film in a magic lantern and of the picture on the screen' (Moore, *Papers*, p. 310).

(2) **mentioned**: in the sense of 'discussed', 'talked about'.

5.632 Cf. 5.641 (3), for a similar remark.

5.633 (2)b 'I often feel this: what eye can see itself?' (Stendhal, *Brulard*, ch. 1). 'The eye cannot see itself' (*ibid.* ch. 14).

(3) 'He said that "Just as no [physical] eye is involved in seeing, so no Ego is involved in thinking or in having toothache"; and he quoted, with apparent approval, Lichtenberg's saying "Instead of 'I think' we ought to say 'It thinks'" ("it" being used, as he said, as "Es" is used in "Es blitzet"); and by saying this he meant, I think, something similar to what he said of "the eye of the visual field" when he said that it is not anything which is *in* the visual field' (Moore, *Papers*, p. 309).

5.6331 'In visual space there is not an eye which belongs to me and eyes which belong to others. Only the space itself is unsymmetrical, while the objects in it have the same status (*sind gleichberechtigt*). But in physical space this expresses itself as follows: the eye situated in one of the equal-ranking (*gleichberechtigt*) places becomes pre-eminent (*wird ausgezeichnet*) and is called *mine*' (*Phil. Bem.* 30, 6).

5.634 ● 'That what I experience is *my* experience is not a contingent fact. Hence, if the "metaphysical subject" were detectable within experience, there would be *per impossibile* something *a priori* to be discovered as a part of experience.'

(1) **the fact that**: not in the original.

(4) A dubious remark, unless 'things' is a slip for 'facts'.
  order: or, 'arrangement' (*Ordnung*).
'The great problem around which everything that I write turns is: Is there an order (*Ordnung*) in the world *a priori*, and if so, what does it consist in?' (*Notebooks*, 53 (11)).

5.64 followed out strictly: or, 'thoroughly thought out'.
'Idealism singles men out from the world as unique, solipsism singles me alone out, and at last I see that I too belong with the rest of the world, and so on the one side *nothing* is left over, and on the other side as unique, *the world*. In this way, idealism leads to realism if it is strictly thought out' (*Notebooks*, 85 (11)).

5.641 (1)   there really is a sense: cf. (2).

(2)   Cf. 5.62 (3) (the world is *my* world).

(3)   In the *Notebooks*, W. adds the sentence: 'The human body, however, my body in particular, is a part of the world among others, among animals, plants, stones, etc., etc.' (82 (8)).

'That which knows everything and is known by nothing is the *subject*. It is, accordingly, the bearer (*Träger*) of the world, the universal condition always presupposed for all appearance, all that is object : for whatever is, is only for the subject. Everyone finds himself as this subject, but only insofar as he knows, not insofar as he is an object of knowledge. But his body is already an object... an object among objects...' (Schopenhauer, *Die Welt*, §2, my translation).

'. . . the subject does not lie in space and time . . .' (*ibid.*).

LXIX

THE GENERAL FORM OF A TRUTH-FUNCTION

(6–6.01)

Wittgenstein now resumes his discussion of the general form of a truth-function—i.e. the general form of a proposition (since all propositions are truth-functions, 5). Wittgenstein has already explained what he means by an 'operation' (5.23) and by a 'formal series' (4.1252a); he has introduced a special notation for expressing the general term of a formal series (5.2522); and he has asserted that all truth-functions can be ordered into a single formal series by means of the operation of joint negation, symbolized as $N(\bar{\xi})$. He now makes the claim good by expressing (in 6a) an arbitrary truth-function as a term in a formal series.

In order to understand Wittgenstein's notation in 6a, we must remember (i) that Wittgenstein writes the general term of a formal series as $[a, x, O'x]$ (where a is the first term, x an arbitrary term of the series, and O the generating operation), 5.2522; (ii) $\bar{\xi}$ means all the values of the range of the propositional variable, ξ (5.501ab); and (iii) N stands for joint negation (5.5, 5.502). For the resulting meaning of $[\bar{p}, \bar{\xi}, N(\bar{\xi})]$, see notes on 6 (1) below and the concluding paraphrase.

Commentary

The purpose of introducing this cumbersome symbolic apparatus seems to be to define the operation, $\Omega'(\bar{\eta})$—in effect, the operation that must be performed upon a set of propositions, η, in order to arrive at some proposition by the repeated use of joint negation alone. Wittgenstein bases his theory of arithmetic upon this operation, in the instalment that follows immediately.

---

6 (1) The notation seems to be intended as a special case of the expression for the 'general term of a formal series' explained at 5.2522 (see also 5.501a, 5.502 for further details). However, in that case $\bar{p}$ ought to be the 'beginning of the formal series' (5.2522b) and hence a constant, while the bar notation has been introduced only in connexion with variables (5.501a). Wittgenstein's intention seems to have been that $\bar{p}$ should stand for the set of all elementary propositions. In the formula, then, $\bar{\xi}$ (the 'form of an arbitrary term of the series'—5.2522b) would stand for an arbitrary selection of propositions already considered; and finally $N(\bar{\xi})$ for the joint negation of all the propositions selected by '$\bar{\xi}$'.

● 'The most general truth-function can be obtained as follows: Take any selection of elementary propositions and form the conjunction of the negation of each of them; then add this proposition to the set of elementary propositions; take any selection from the enlarged set, jointly negate them, add the new proposition to the set; and continue in the same way.'

For difficulties that arise if the set of elementary propositions is infinite, see Anscombe, *Introduction*, pp. 136–7.

(2) Cf. 5.3 (1), also 4.5, for further remarks on this topic.

6.001 Even the elementary propositions themselves can be generated, somewhat artificially, by W.'s N-operation. (From p and q, select p, then negate it and add it to the original set; from p, q, and $\sim p$, select the last and negate it.)

6.002 Cf. 5.22 on 'operation'.

are given: may here be read as equivalent to 'understand'.

6.01 (1) The operation $\Omega'(\bar{\eta})$ is: what must be done to any set of propositions, η, in order to obtain a truth-function of them (by using the procedure already explained in the note on 6 (1)).

For the notation used, see 5.2522.

(2) **from one proposition**: actually, from one *set* of propositions.

LXX

NUMBERS

(6.02–6.031)

Wittgenstein now explains how he would introduce integers in connexion with the operation, $\Omega'x$, that has just been defined at 6.01. Wittgenstein's basic idea can be illustrated in connexion with some other operation, say the one expressed in ordinary language by the expression, 'parent of x', which may be abbreviated to $P'x$ for the purpose of this explanation. Consider the following series of expressions: parent of x, parent of parent of x, parent of parent of parent of x, ..., or in the shorter form:

$$P'x, \qquad P'P'x, \qquad P'P'P'x, \qquad \qquad ....$$

Now write these as:

$$P^{1'}x, \qquad P^{1+1'}x, \qquad P^{1+1+1'}x, \qquad \qquad ...,$$

and, finally, as

$$P^{1'}x, \qquad P^{2'}x, \qquad P^{3'}x, \qquad \qquad ....$$

Here, the symbols, 1, $1+1$, $1+1+1$, etc., have been introduced to mark the number of times the phrase 'parent of' occurs in a compound phrase of the form 'parent of parent of...parent of x'; and the symbols '2', '3', etc., have then been introduced as abbreviations for '$1+1$', '$1+1+1$', etc.

This simplified sketch differs from Wittgenstein's own account in choosing the operation $P'x$ rather than his own $\Omega'x$ and in omitting the definition of '0' for the sake of simplicity. But the basic idea of a number as 'the exponent of an operation' (6.021) has been preserved.

It may be possible to construct a formal arithmetic along the lines that Wittgenstein here indicated. But it might reasonably be objected that Wittgenstein's sketch does not begin to do justice to the 'logic' of numbers in ordinary language. Wittgenstein here seems to be adhering to Russell's programme of substituting a constructed concept for the less tidy numerical concepts already in use. It is hard to see how, on his conception, we are to make sense of, say, a proposition like 'Tom was the third man to speak', involving a number but contingently true. Russell, whose analysis Wittgenstein rejects (6.031 a), bore the applications of arithmetic to counting in mind; Wittgenstein seems to have made no provision for such application.

6.02 W.'s idea is hard to grasp. If x stands for a single proposition, $\Omega'x$ should stand for any truth-function of x alone, i.e. for x or $\sim x$. But then $\Omega'\Omega'x$ means the same as $\Omega'x$. The same result holds if x is intended to stand for a *set* of propositions. The self-application of the Ω-operation must result in the same operation, as its definition (for which see 6.01) makes obvious. It would seem that for all m and n greater than zero, we must have $\Omega^{m'}x = \Omega^{n'}x$. Does it follow that $m = n$ for all positive integers?

(**1**) **numbers**: i.e. integers.

(**2**) **which deal with**: rather, 'about'.

6.021 **exponent**: the only occurrence of this word. 'Exponent' is not to be confused with 'index' (for which see notes on 5.02 above).

6.022 (1) **simply**: literally, 'none other than'.
 general form: shown at 6.03.

(**2**) Cf. 4.126 (8) on the proper expression of a formal concept.

6.03 **general form of an integer**: W. is here using the notation for the general term introduced at 5.2522 a. Given the account of integers as 'exponents' in 6.02, it is hard to see how the formula of 6.03 is to be used —or what purpose it serves.

6.031 (1) **theory of classes**: cf. Carnap, *Syntax*, § 38 ('The Elimination of Classes'), pp. 136-9.

(**2**) **the fact that**: not in the original.
 accidental: cf. 6.1232 a on the contrast with 'essential' generality.

THE FOUNDATIONS OF ARITHMETIC
IN 'PRINCIPIA MATHEMATICA'

Whitehead and Russell had Peano's axioms at their disposal. Their task accordingly consisted in finding definitions, using exclusively logical notions, of Peano's primitives, and showing that, with such definitions, all his axioms become truths of logic. Since Peano's axioms include existential statements, the logicist programme must at some point assert the *existence* of certain (presumably logical) entities. This proves to be a matter of crucial importance.

Peano's axioms may be taken to consist of the following five assertions:

(i)   o is a number.

(ii) Each number's successor is a number.

(iii) o is no number's successor.

(iv) Different numbers have different successors.

(v)   Any predicate applying to o and also to the successor of each number to which it applies, applies to every number.

Here, o (zero), *number* (i.e. natural number), and *successor*, are the primitive notions. It is easily verified that the force of these axioms, taken together, is to guarantee the existence of the successor of o (say o′ or 1) as distinct from o, then the existence of its successor (o″ or say 2) as another distinct number, and so on indefinitely. The fifth axiom (the so-called 'principle of mathematical induction') has the effect of restricting the entities thus generated to the smallest class of entities satisfying the other four axioms.

Whitehead and Russell's task accordingly reduces to that of constructing suitable definitions for *zero, number,* and *successor.* By using the notion of a *class* (later shown to be dispensable) this may be done as follows: Two classes may be said to be *equinumerous* when their members can be put into one–one correlation (I omit the technical details). Since equinumerosity, so defined, is a symmetrical and transitive relation, it satisfies the conditions for a 'definition by abstraction'. Accordingly, the *number of members* of a given class can be defined as the class of all classes equinumerous with that class. *Zero* is the number of any null class (i.e. one having no members). Suppose a given class, K, has m members; form a new class, L, composed of the members of K together with a single new member; the number of members of L is said to be the *successor* of m. Call a class *inductive* if o is a member and every successor of any of its members is also a member. *Number* may then be defined as the 'intersection' of all inductive classes, i.e. as the class of classes that are members of every inductive class.

Finally, reference to classes may be removed as follows: designations for classes are treated as 'incomplete symbols', so that all statements ostensibly referring to classes are regarded as abbreviations, in accordance with determinate rules, for statements in which classes are no longer mentioned. There results a chain of definitions parallel to those given in the last paragraph, but now referring to *functions* instead of classes.

A serious objection to this programme is that we have no guarantee that infinitely many distinct numbers will result. Unless we can be sure that the universe contains infinitely many individuals, we must face the risk that all the 'numbers' beyond a certain point will be the null-class and consequently identical (cf. Russell, *Introduction*, p. 132, for a clear discussion of the reasons for this). A further stipulation, the 'axiom of infinity', is needed in order to prevent such an absurdity.

Nothing is achieved by using the alternative formulation in terms of functions: the bogey of an insufficiently populated universe reappears as a doubt concerning the existence of functions having sufficiently extensive ranges. The difficulty is inescapable, given Russell's conception of a class (or, alternatively, of the range of a function) as something whose existence is a matter of empirical fact. Once this is granted, a question about the existence of numbers becomes as contingent as one about the existence of galaxies, and arithmetic is as empirical as astronomy. Russell clearly recognized the empirical character of his axiom of infinity: he says that it 'will be true in some possible worlds and false in others; whether it is true or false in this world, we cannot tell' (*op. cit.* p. 141). This seems an understatement, since it is impossible to see how the existence of infinitely many independent individuals could ever be empirically established. At any rate, if this is the final verdict, the 'logicist' programme of showing mathematics to consist of *a priori* truths stands on shaky ground.

An equally serious difficulty is that of *understanding* Russell's principles. In the official presentation of his system, reference to the *existence* of functions is indispensable. In practice, the only functions he needs or uses are the identity predicate $x = x$ and the identity relation $x = y$. I can attach no good sense to the assertion that these two functions 'exist'. Wittgenstein's attack on Russell's conception of identity is directed against an indispensable component of the 'logicist' construction of mathematics and is consequently of the first importance. Wittgenstein's rejection of the *Principia* system was based, not upon disagreements about technical details, but upon a well-founded conviction that the undertaking was radically misguided.

LXXI

LOGICAL TRUTHS AS TAUTOLOGIES; THE NATURE OF LOGICAL PROPOSITIONS
(6.1–6.113)

Wittgenstein has already made a number of general remarks about the nature of logic (notably in LIV, LVII) and has implied others by his rejection of the idea of substantial logical objects (LII). Now he takes the final step of identifying logical truths with tautologies (6.1). Given the features of tautologies that have already been established (e.g. that they are limiting or degenerate cases of truth-functions, XLIII, and that they 'say nothing', XLVIII) a number of conclusions about the nature of logic follow at once. Among the most important are: logical propositions 'say nothing' (6.11a), are purely formal (6.111a) and can be certified by exclusive attention to symbols, in abstraction from meanings (6.113a).

Discussion of the nature of logic is continued in the next six instalments.

6.1 Echoed at 6.22. A remark of great importance.

'All propositions of logic are generalizations of tautologies and all generalizations of tautologies are propositions of logic. There are no other logical propositions' (*Letters*, 127 (4)). It is interesting to find W. speaking here, as he did not in the final text, of 'generalizations' of tautologies.

According to von Wright, W. made 'a substantial contribution to the clarification of the idea of logical truth' (*Form and Content*, p. 13). He adds that there are severe difficulties in extending the analysis of logical truth in terms of tautology to the functional calculus. The 'concept of a tautology in all possible worlds' is 'far from clear' (*op. cit.* p. 18), so much so 'that it is probably senseless' (*op. cit.* p. 20). The chief difficulty is that there are logical truths good for every finite world, but not holding in an infinite world (*op. cit.* p. 20).

ARE LOGICAL PRINCIPLES TAUTOLOGIES?

Wittgenstein's philosophy of logic culminates in his assertion that logical propositions are tautologies (6.1). Given his conception of tautologies as 'limiting cases' of truth-functions (for which see the discussion under 4.46 (1) above), all his chief contentions about logical propositions follow; for example, that they 'say nothing', that their truth can be established by inspecting the symbols that express them, and so on. Had Wittgenstein made good his identification of logical propositions with tautologies, he would certainly have succeeded in assigning them the desired 'unique status among all propositions' (6.112) and would have solved one of his chief philosophical problems.

As usual, Wittgenstein offers no reasons in support of his important claim about the nature of logic. His line of thought must have been that if all propositions are truth-functions of elementary propositions, as he thought they had to be (cf. 6*b*), necessary propositions could be generated only as 'extreme cases' of such truth-functions, i.e. as tautologies. This view certainly fits any necessary truth such as $p \vee \sim p$ that is explicitly constructed as a truth-function of its constituents, but is quite unsatisfactory as a universal account of the nature of logical truth. Consider even so trivial a principle as $(x)(fx) \supset (\exists x)(fx)$, which is not an explicit truth-function. There is certainly no obvious way of presenting this as a tautology. Wittgenstein's treatment of general propositions (for which see LXI above) tries to overcome the difficulty by thinking of $(x)(fx)$ as a quasi-abbreviation for the indefinite conjunction, $fa.fb.fc...$, where $a, b, c, ...$, are the objects of the universe, and $(\exists x)(fx)$ similarly as a quasi-abbreviation for the indefinite disjunction, $fa \lor fb \lor fc \lor \ldots$ One might try to argue that since $(fa_1 . fa_2 \ldots fa_n) \supset (fa_1 \lor fa_2 \lor \ldots \lor fa_n)$, where n is a definite integer, is a tautology, the same is true when the value of n is not given. But this trick will not do. The dangling dots in $fa.fb.fc\ldots$ are not what Geach called the 'dots of laziness', which might be removed at will: they mean 'and *so on*' which, expanded, amounts to 'and so for *all x*'. The symbolism $fa.fb.fc\ldots$ has what Wittgenstein would call the 'same multiplicity' as the original $(x)(fx)$ and any belief that we have reduced the latter to a formula in the propositional calculus is an illusion. In order to make appeal to an 'indefinite conjunction' respectable, explicit rules would have to be given for passing from formulas in the predicate calculus to derived formulas in the propositional calculus by means of a definite procedure which would establish their tautological character. This would be what is nowadays called a *decision procedure* for the original formulas: the need for known decision procedures for checking on putative logical truths is an integral and indispensable feature of Wittgenstein's philosophy of logic. For he would find it intolerable that we might understand a proposition without knowing in advance how to find out whether it was a tautology or a contradiction; he could never admit that the tautological character of a proposition might reveal itself by accident, as it were, after we had stumbled upon a proof of it. But subsequent research in logic has shown that a universal decision procedure is impossible, even in the relatively simple case of the predicate calculus. This result is fatal to Wittgenstein's philosophy of logic. It shows that any adequate account of the nature of logical truth must be more complex and more sophisticated than that contained in the *Tractatus*.

6.11a Repetition of 5.43 (2). Cf. 4.461a (logical propositions show that they say nothing).

b **analytic**: the only occurrence of this word.

Nowadays, analytic propositions are often defined as those 'which are true by definition or follow from the meanings of terms' (Lewis and Langford, *Logic*, p. 212). This extension of Kant's sense of 'analytic' is probably due to Frege (cf. his *Foundations*, § 3, p. 4). Lewis and Langford say that a logical principle 'is an analytic proposition' and explain their meaning to be that it is 'true by definition . . . it merely explicates, or follows from, a meaning which has been assigned, and requires nothing in particular about the universe or the facts of nature' (*op. cit.* p. 211). It is doubtful whether W. meant anything like this. The context suggests that he was simply using 'analytic propositions' as a synonym for 'propositions that say nothing'.

6.111a to have content: or, 'to be informative'.

d **all the characteristics**: rather, 'quite the character'.

6.112 'A correct explanation of the logical propositions must give them a unique position as against all other propositions' (*Notes on Logic*, 93 (2)*h*).

6.113a fact: W. uses *Tatsache* twice in this section, although what he is pointing out is clearly not a contingent fact.

can recognize that they are true from the symbol alone: but not by direct inspection, necessarily—cf. 6.126 (1) on the calculation involved.

'By merely looking at them [logical propositions] you can *see* these [logical] properties; whereas, in a proposition proper, you cannot see what is true by looking at it' (*Moore Notes*, 107 (2)).

LXXII

TAUTOLOGIES REVEAL THE FORMAL PROPERTIES OF THE UNIVERSE
(6.12–6.1202)

Wittgenstein has previously stressed the autonomy of logical propositions: their validity is determined solely by their symbolic expression, without appeal to anything external. This, he has emphatically said, contains in itself the whole philosophy of logic (6.113*a*). But the autonomy of a logical proposition, its independence of what is the case, does not prevent it from manifesting *logical* features of the universe. Indeed, Wittgenstein now wishes to insist that, for example, the tautological character of a given combination of symbols does show something about the 'formal properties' of the universe (6.12a). For the formal properties of language, rendered manifest in the occurrence of tautologies as limiting cases, are, at the same time, formal properties of the world. As a general principle, whatever is necessarily true of language answers to something necessarily true of 'logical space', i.e. of this world *and* all possible worlds.

We may recall Wittgenstein's earlier remarks about the non-arbitrary aspects of any given symbolism or notation (3.34ff.). An arbitrary sequence of signs, belonging to a given language, will not usually result in a tautology; when a given sequence of symbols does express a tautology, that reveals something about the logical forms of the constituents (6.12 b–d). The logical form of the world that is shown in one way by the contingency of significant propositions (4.121 d) is also shown in another way by tautologies—and, indeed, also by contradictions (6.1202). The logical modality of a proposition (its being a tautology, a contradiction, or a significant proposition, as the case may be) in each case shows something specific about logical form. Each tautology gives us a glimpse of the constitution of logical space.

6.12 (1) **The fact**: not in the German.

that the propositions of logic are tautologies: i.e. that specific, given, propositions are tautologies (in each case shows something, etc.).

shows: cf. 4.461 (1), 6.124 ab, for similar remarks.

(2) 'How, usually, logical propositions do shew these [logical] properties is this: We give a certain description of a kind of symbol; we find that other symbols, combined in certain ways, yield a symbol of this description; and *that* they do shews something about these symbols' (*Moore Notes*, 107 (7)).

Cf. 6.121, for elaboration of the same idea.

(3) **certain**: or, 'determinate' (*bestimmte*), in both occurrences.

structural properties: here, one might have expected 'formal properties' instead.

6.1201 W. has said at 6.12 (2) above that the combination of expressions to produce a tautology 'characterizes the logic' of those expressions, i.e. shows something about their formal properties. His first example in the present section is that the tautological character of $\sim (p . \sim p)$ shows that p and $\sim p$ contradict one another. One proposition 'contradicts' another when the facts verifying the one are precisely those falsifying the other (negation reverses the sense, 5.2341 c). Now, if we understand the truth-table for ' $\sim$ ', as must be the case in order for $\sim (p. \sim p)$ to show anything, we must already understand that $\sim p$ is the contradiction of p. So, what is left for the complex tautology to show? Perhaps W.'s thought went somewhat as follows: 'It follows from the definitions of ' $\sim$ ' and '.' that $\sim (p. \sim p)$ is a tautology; and, conversely, the latter formula's being a tautology is an indication that ' $\sim$ ' really is the sign of negation, and not of some other logical operation.' But of course the formal structure of the tautology does not suffice to fix ' $\sim$ ' as the sign of negation. If α and β are logical operations, $\alpha(p\beta\alpha p)$ can be a tautology, without α being negation or β conjunction. Perhaps we ought to say something like this: 'That negation and conjunction combined in *this* way cancel out—produce tautology— reveals something about these operations that is already sufficiently shown by their definitions' (cf. also 5.131 on the internal relations between propositions as already shown by the forms of those propositions, without our needing to bring them into relation in a complex proposition).

Similar remarks apply to W.'s other examples in this section. Cf. also 5.1311.

LXXIII

CALCULATION OF TAUTOLOGIES; LOGICAL PROPOSITIONS ARE EXPENDABLE

(6.1203–6.1221)

Calculation is assigned an important function in Wittgenstein's philosophy of logic. We have already seen that he has no patience with 'self-evidence' or 'intuition' (5.1363, 5.4731, see also 6.1271 *bc*, below). Wittgenstein expects of 'calculation' what others have expected of intuition (6.2331 *a*). In the present instalment, Wittgenstein offers an ingenious example, his own invention, of the kind of calculation he has in mind—a systematic procedure for establishing, without any reference to sense or meaning (cf. 6.126c), whether a given propositional sign expresses a tautology. The technique, described in 6.1203, proves upon examination to be a graphical way of tracing out the assignments of truth-values to a complex propositional sign, in accordance with the standard definitions of the logical connectives it contains. The method is substantially the same as the more familiar construction and evaluation of truth-tables.

Wittgenstein was mistaken in thinking that 'calculation' of this sort is always applicable to the detection of tautologies. Subsequent developments in mathematical logic have shown that 'decision procedures' in logic are, in general, impossible. Nor can we agree with Wittgenstein that an adequate notation would render logical propositions superfluous (6.122). It is not always possible to recognize formal properties by what Wittgenstein calls 'inspection', and calculation must be acknowledged to be more than a 'mechanical expedient' (6.1262). It would be nearer the mark to say that calculation, in a broad sense of the word, is of the essence of both logic and mathematics.

6.1203   If we follow W.'s instructions for testing a tautology, given at the end of this section, we get the following figure for $\sim (p.\sim p)$ (Fig. 3). Here we get an embarrassing outermost F in the diagram, whereas a tautology should yield only T. W. needs a supplementary convention, forbidding the drawing of lines between the positive and negative poles of the same proposition. With this additional stipulation the diagram would appear as Fig. 4. In more complex cases, it would be tedious to find out

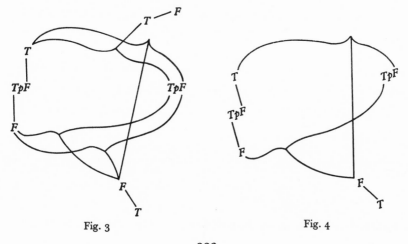

Fig. 3   Fig. 4

which lines in the figure needed to be erased, in accordance with the supplementary convention suggested above, and mistakes in tracing the lines would be likely to occur. W.'s 'intuitive method' is clumsy and impracticable. The tabulation in modern style of W.'s example of $\sim (p . \sim p)$, would appear as follows:

$$\sim (p \; . \; \sim p)$$
$$T \; T \; F \; F \; T$$
$$T \; F \; F \; T \; F$$

This is obviously far superior to W.'s procedure.

It should be noted that W.'s procedure fails to apply to general statements (as acknowledged by W. in the second line of the section).

6.121 (1) Cf. 6.12*b*.

that say nothing: i.e. tautologies.

In the course of lectures given at Cambridge in the spring of 1939, W. said: 'What does it mean to say that a proposition is a tautology, gives no information, says nothing? When I thought about this many years ago, I thought up the *TF* symbolism as a means of transforming Russell's propositions so that they all looked similar. I showed that all Russell's propositions give a column of all T's and said then that Russell's propositions are compatible with any state of affairs and so can't be used to give information. All that I did was to translate his propositions into a different symbolism' (*Math. Notes*, lecture XXVIII, p. 107).

6.122 Cf. 6.126 (4) (tautologies show, without proof, that they are tautologies).

suitable: or, 'corresponding' (*entsprechend*). In a sense, every notation is suitable.

6.1221 (2) 'Take $\phi a, \phi a \supset \Psi a, \Psi a$. By merely looking at these three, I can see that 3 follows from 1 and 2; i.e. I can see what is called the truth of a logical proposition, namely, of [the] proposition $\phi a . \phi a \supset \Psi a : \supset : \Psi a$. But this is *not* a proposition; but by seeing that it is a tautology I can see what I already saw by looking at the three propositions: the difference is that I *now* see THAT it is a tautology' (*Moore Notes*, 107 (10)).

LXXIV

LOGICAL PROPOSITIONS ARE 'A PRIORI'

(6.1222–6.123)

The remarks in this instalment can be treated as corollaries of Wittgenstein's basic principle that the validity of logical propositions is determined solely by their symbolic expression (6.113). It is by now sufficiently clear why, on Wittgenstein's principles, logical propositions are immune from empirical confirmation or confutation (6.1222), and how they are connected with 'the theory of forms and of inference' (6.1224). Our feeling that we must stipulate or postulate 'logical truths' Wittgenstein justifies as a feeling that we are entitled to demand a satisfactory notation (6.1223). It is perhaps less easy to see offhand why he cannot admit that there should be 'further logical laws' to which lower-level tautologies would be subject (6.123). But such laws, if there were any, would have to manifest a kind of 'super-form', for which there is no room in Wittgenstein's account. As he has already said, 'In logic there cannot be a more general and a more special' (5.454b). Since every proposition of logic 'is its own proof' (6.1265), there can be no question of grounding the validity of some given logical truth in a 'higher' law.

6.1222b Cf. 5.552 (2) (logic precedes every experience).

6.1223 *postulate*: or, 'require' or 'demand' (*fordern*).

● 'We call logical principles "postulates" because we *demand* a way of expressing them that will make their character as tautologies obvious.'

   adequate: in a sense, every notation is 'adequate' to express whatever meaning it expresses.

6.1224 Cf. 6.122 for reference to 'formal' properties and 6.1221a for the link with *inference*.

6.123 (1) W. may have been thinking here of the traditional derivation of the valid moods of the syllogism by means of the *dictum de omni et nullo*— or, of the proof of logical principles in *Principia*.

Of course, on W.'s views, 'laws of logic' must be a misnomer in any case.

(2) 'Negation and disjunction and their derivations must have a different meaning when applied to elementary propositions from that which they have when applied to such propositions as $(x).\phi x$ or $(\exists x).\phi x$' (*Principia*, vol. I, p. 127).

'The first difficulty that confronts us [after adopting the "vicious circle principle"] is as to the fundamental principles of logic known under the quaint name of "laws of thought". "All propositions are either true or false", for example, has become meaningless. If it were significant, it would be a proposition, and would come under its own scope' (Russell, *Logic and Knowledge*, p. 63).

LXXV

LOGIC AND 'ESSENTIAL' VALIDITY; THE AXIOM OF REDUCIBILITY

(6.1231–6.1233)

Wittgenstein's target in this instalment, as so often in the book, is Russell's philosophy of logic. Russell at one time held generality to be a distinguishing mark of logical propositions: In *Principles*, for instance, he said that logic 'is distinguished from various special branches of mathematics mainly by its generality' (p. 11) and in *External World* he spoke of logic as consisting of 'self-evident general propositions' (p. 66). Many similar statements could be cited. Wittgenstein finds this unacceptable, and for good reason. Logical propositions need not be general, since a tautology containing names—an 'ungeneralized proposition' (6.1231 c)—may be valid in virtue of its form. And when logical propositions are general, they are not 'accidentally' valid, do not *happen* to be true of everything, but have 'essential validity', because they treat of the 'formal' aspects of the world (6.12 a). A proposition, such as the axiom of reducibility, may be completely general and yet have a contingent truth-value. (Wittgenstein might also have cited at this point the simpler example of an existential proposition such as $(\exists x, \phi)\,(\phi x)$.) Wittgenstein's use of the axiom of reducibility as an example of a general proposition not belonging to logic is particularly interesting, since the status of that axiom is still controversial. It is a pity that Wittgenstein did not amplify his reasons for regarding the axiom as contingent.

6.1231 (1) **general validity**: or, simply 'generality'.

'The ideas and propositions of logic are all *general*: an assertion (for example) which is true of Socrates but not of Plato will not belong to logic, and if a proposition which is true of both is to occur in logic, it must not be made concerning either, but concerning a variable *x*. In order to obtain, in logic, a definite proposition instead of a propositional function, it is necessary to take some propositional function and assert that it is true always or sometimes, i.e. with all possible values of the variable or with some possible value' (*Principia*, vol. 1, p. 93).

(2) **to be accidentally valid**: to hold accidentally.

6.1232a For the contrast between 'essential' and 'accidental', see 3.34.

'This distinction of accidentally and essentially true propositions explains—by the way—the feeling one always had about the infinity axiom and the axiom of reducibility, the feeling that if they were true they would be so by a lucky accident' (*Letters*, 125 (1) end).

b **axiom of reducibility**: this was invoked by Russell in connexion with his hierarchy of *orders*, supplementing the hierarchy of *types* demanded by the 'simple' theory of types.

A propositional function of one individual is called 'predicative' by Russell if its expression shows no quantification over functions. Thus $(y)\phi(\hat{x}, y)$ counts as predicative, while $(\exists y)\,(\exists \Psi)\,(\Psi y \equiv \phi\hat{x})$ does not.

This distinction between predicative and non-predicative functions was introduced to deal with the so-called 'semantical' paradoxes. To obviate the intolerable complications that then threatened to render the construction of arithmetic impossible, Russell assumed that for any given function there always exists a *formally equivalent* predicative function (*Principia*, vol. 1, p. 58). This is the axiom in question. Since only the extensions of functions play a role in the construction of arithmetical notions, the effect of the axiom is to allow us to proceed as if the hierarchy of orders had not been introduced. This device was abandoned in the second edition of *Principia* in favour of the view 'that functions of proposi-tions are always truth-functions, and that a function can only occur in a proposition through its values' (*Principia*, 2nd edn., p. xiv).

Cf. *Principia*, vol. 1, pp. 55–60, 160–7, Quine, 'Reducibility', pp. 498–500, Fraenkel, *Einleitung*, pp. 259–63, Black, *Mathematics*, pp. 111–18.

As early as 1913, W. thought he had found a way of demonstrating that the axiom was a contingent proposition: 'Imagine our living in a world, where there is nothing but *things*, and besides *only one relation*, which holds between infinitely many of these things, but does not hold between every one and every other of them: further, it never holds between a finite number of things. It is clear that the axiom of reducibility would certainly *not* hold in such a world. But it is also clear to me that it is not for logic to decide whether the world we live in is actually like this or not' (*Note-books*, 127 (4) *g*).

I do not know exactly what W. had in mind, but his remark suggests the following argument. Imagine first a model-universe, U_1, in which there are only the two objects a, b, and the two simple functions (not involving logical operators in their definitions) f and g; and suppose the atomic facts are fa, ga, fb, gb. Let U_2 be exactly like U_1 except that the atomic facts are fa, gb (with neither ga nor fb obtaining). In U_1, a and b are indiscernible with respect to f, g and all finite truth-functions of f and g. Thus the 'non-predicative' function, $x = a$ (however defined) which must have different values for a and b, cannot have an equivalent 'predicative' (simple) function, as demanded by the axiom. In U_2, however, a and b are 'discernibles', so the objection does not apply and for all that has been said so far the axiom might be true. Now the difference between U_2 and U_1 is a contingent one (cf. 5.5302): both universes have the same 'logical space' and differ only in what is the case in each. Since indiscernibility with respect to simple function is a logical possibility (cf. 5.5302), the axiom must be rejected.

Attempts have also been made by Ramsey (*Foundations*, p. 57) and Waismann ('Reduzibilitätsaxiom', pp. 143–6) to show that the axiom is a contingent statement. For criticism of these attempts, see Black, *Mathe-matics*, p. 117. According to Church, Ramsey's attempted demonstration does not survive the rejection of W.'s conception of tautology in favour of more adequate conceptions of analyticity such as those proposed by Carnap and Tarski: 'the analyticity of the axiom of reducibility depends on the character of the meta-language and on the choice of the *rules of valuation* (Carnap's terminology)' ('Review of Schmidt', p. 199).

6.1233*a* **is not valid**: or, 'does not hold'.

LXXVI

LOGIC PRESENTS THE 'SCAFFOLDING' OF THE WORLD; THERE ARE NO SURPRISES IN LOGIC

(6.124–6.1251)

The 'scaffolding' of the world (6.124a) is the same as the logical form of the world. In saying that logic exhibits (*darstellt*) this scaffolding, Wittgenstein is reminding us of his point, by now familiar, that logical propositions are concerned only with logical form and so, in a sense, have no subject-matter. Yet he insists that logic nevertheless has a 'connexion' with the world (6.124c), so that although logical propositions are not about the objects of the world, they still 'show something about the world' (6.124d). This is perhaps the most important component of Wittgenstein's philosophy of logic, and as debatable as it is important.

The connexion between logic and the world arises because logical propositions 'presuppose' that names stand for objects and hence that propositions make sense (6.124c). Of course, on Wittgenstein's view, names *must* stand for objects and propositions *must* have sense, but we may regard it as a contingent fact that there are any names at all—that there is any language—and hence a contingent fact that there are any logical propositions. But that there are objects that the names stand for, and senses that the propositions express, is not a matter of fact: it is necessary that there should be substance, whether language exists or not. Given the contingent fact that a language exists, it *must* be linked with the world by having its logical form in common with it. This common form, according to Wittgenstein, will reveal itself in the tautological character of certain definite expressions of the language (6.124d). That just *these* expressions are the tautologies of a given language 'shows something about the world'—namely, that it has the form that it has. Wittgenstein was, therefore, far from taking a 'formalist' or 'conventionalist' view of logic, even though, as we

329

have seen before, he insisted that there are no 'logical objects'. It is fair to say that according to him certain kinds of inference (in a loose sense of that word) from logic to ontology are possible—though it is very hard to see what such inferences would be (see the notes on 6.124*c* and the further discussion on pp. 331–6 below).

The 'connexion' of logic with the world is an identity of logical form, and has nothing to do with the contingent features distinguishing the actual world from the other possible worlds that might have existed in its place. That is why *we* do not express anything by means of logical propositions: the substance of the world shows *itself* through them (6.124*g*). And that is why there can be no surprises in logic (6.1251); for in order to be surprised, we must be able to entertain suppositions that *turn out* to be false. The language of 'surprise' and 'discovery' is appropriate in the natural sciences, where contingent falsifications sometimes clash with reasonable expectations: in logic there is nothing to be expected and nothing to cause disappointment or produce gratification.

6.124 The logical propositions are tautologies (6.1). We have already been told that they say nothing (6.11). The new point contained in the present section occurs at **c**. What does it mean to 'presuppose' that names have meaning? This may well be connected with the point that meanings play no part in logical syntax (3.33). (For 3.33 also speaks of 'presupposing'.) We might say: tautologies are expressed by means of *variables*, because they present logical *forms*. Now in order to be shown anything by a formula containing variables, we must have the ranges of the values specified (cf. 3.316*b*—the determination of the values of the variable *is* the variable). In the case of a simple tautology such as $p \vee \sim p$, it might be thought that what is 'presupposed' is that propositions have sense (to speak in the style of the present section); but propositions have sense only because the names of which they are composed have meaning— and *vice versa*. Thus to understand a tautology, we must know the ranges of values of the variables that occur in the tautology. And the 'connexion' (**c**) of the tautology with the world is this: all the propositions thus 'presupposed' must have the features displayed by the tautology. That $p \vee \sim p$ is a tautology does not say anything about any particular proposition (or about its constituents), but it shows that *any* particular proposition will necessarily be such that its sense cancels out the sense of its negation.

a **propositions of logic**: i.e. tautologies.

scaffolding (*Gerüst*): this image also occurs at 3.42 (3), 4.023 (5). In both places W. talks of a 'logical scaffolding'.

represent: I prefer 'present'.

b Literally 'They "treat" of nothing', or 'They are "about" nothing'.

The following dictum expresses the kind of logical realism that W. is attacking: 'Logic, I should maintain, must no more admit a unicorn than zoology can; for logic is concerned with the real world just as truly as zoology, though with its more abstract and general features' (Russell, *Mathematical Philosophy*, p. 169).

c **presuppose that names have meaning**: if names 'have meaning', elementary propositions will necessarily 'have sense'. But if there were no meaningful names, i.e. if there were no language, there would be no foothold for logical connectives, and hence no way of expressing 'logical propositions'. For the logical connectives are defined by means of truthtables which are, in turn, constructed out of elementary propositions. Logical propositions may, then, be said to 'presuppose' that there are significant elementary propositions (or, equivalently, that there are meaningful names), inasmuch as there could not be any logical propositions unless there were a language containing elementary propositions. (If the existence of a language is held to be a contingent fact, it might be inferred that the *significance* of 'logical propositions' is a contingent fact— e.g. that there is any role for $p.p \supset q: \supset q$ to play—but of course this does not make the *truth* of the logical proposition a contingent matter.)

connexion: used in approximately the same way as 'application' in 5.557 (the whole of which section is relevant here).

d Cf. 6.12 (1) (that certain propositions are tautologies shows formal properties of the world).

whose essence involves the possession of a determinate character: it shows something about the essence of the symbols occurring in, say, $p \lor \sim p$ that just *that* definite combination produces a tautology. Cf. 6.12 (3) for a reference to determinate structural properties.

THE CONNEXION BETWEEN LOGICAL PROPOSITIONS AND THE WORLD

I have previously discussed Wittgenstein's contentions that tautologies show that they are tautologies and show the logical form of their constituents (see notes on 4.461 (1) and 6.1201 above). Now I shall examine the view that the entire system of tautologies 'shows something about the world'—reflects the essence of the world.

I have argued previously that the first two kinds of ways in which tautologies show something do not suffice to establish a connexion between logic and the world. That a given tautology, say $p \vee \sim p$, is immediately recognized as a tautology (shows itself to be a tautology) might be held to be merely a consequence of the definitions of the logical connectives, '$\vee$', '$\sim$'. Unless it can be shown that these definitions are in some sense not arbitrary, it would be open to anybody to hold that the tautological character of the formula in question reveals only something about the original definitions, but nothing, so far, about the world. There is one entry in the *Notebooks* that seems to express this view: 'One cannot say of a tautology that it is true, for it is *made so as to be true*' (55 (14), italics in original). Consider the following analogy: It is open to us to introduce the two letters, k and l, as synonyms (with each, say, standing for the same living person). Then the equation $k = l$ would 'show by itself' that it said nothing (cf. 4.241 for Wittgenstein's view on definitions of this kind). But this would only remind us that we had chosen k and l as synonyms, and would obviously tell us nothing at all about the world. Of course, Wittgenstein held that the identity sign is not an essential constituent of an adequate language (5.533), but the signs of the logical connectives are also unnecessary in such a language (cf. 6.122 on getting along without logical propositions). If the tautological character of $p \vee \sim p$ is to show us anything about the world, it must do so in virtue of its 'essence', that remains invariant in every symbol by which it might be replaced. We must look, not to the specific definitions of the particular signs, '$\vee$' and '$\sim$', but rather to what is alleged to be shared by all notations for the truth-functions. We must consider the entire system of related expressions containing the logical connectives.

Similar remarks apply to the second kind of way in which, according to Wittgenstein, tautologies show something. If the tautology $\sim (p. \sim p)$ is supposed to show that p and $\sim p$ are mutually contradictory (cf. 6.1201) and hence to show something about the world, somebody might retort that the 'cancelling out' of complex symbols may only show how *we* intend the logical symbols to be taken and so far shows nothing about the world. Consider the following analogy: There are positions in chess in which there is 'nothing to be done', i.e. no legal move that can be made by either side. This may be compared with propositional formulas for which there is 'nothing to be done' by way of verification, because the symbolizing relations of the constituents 'cancel out'. We might therefore compare 'stalemate' in chess to a contradiction in Wittgenstein's sense. But the possible occurrence of stalemate tells us only something about the rules of chess, which are arbitrarily imposed. Similarly, it might plausibly be held that the possibility of contradiction and tautology tells us only something about the rules we have adopted for combining signs in the propositional calculus.

Another way, now to be examined, of defending Wittgenstein's conception of the connexion between logic and the world is to consider what is shown by the *entire system* of logical propositions. Let L be the entire set of formulas, expressed by means of single letters such as p, q, etc., and the two logical signs 'v' and ' $\sim$ ', that are tautologies according to the standard interpretations of these signs. And let K be the corresponding set of contradictions. The suggestion to be examined is that L's and K's having just *these* extensions—being composed of just those formulas that can be shown to be tautologies or contradictions by Wittgenstein's 'zero-method' or by truth-table calculation—may show something about the essence of the world.

Suppose we are given the following information concerning a system P of signs:

(*a*) P contains the signs p, q, ..., and also 'v' and ' $\sim$ ', with such brackets as are necessary, and the usual formation rules for combining these into complex formulas.

(*b*) Procedures are provided for generating all the members of a set L of the formulas of P (containing just those formulas that would count as tautologies on the standard interpretations of P) and another set K (consisting of just those formulas that would count as contradictions on the standard interpretations of P).

Commentary

(*c*) Each formula of P has one or the other of two 'values', t and f—but we are told nothing about the meanings of t and f, except that every formula must have either t or f associated with it, and cannot have both simultaneously.

(*d*) Rules are provided for calculating the 'values' of compound formulas in terms of the possible values of their components, which are such that the value of each member of L comes out as t, for all combinations of values of its components—and, similarly, the values of all members of K come out as f.

(It is to be noticed that we have not been told that the formulas of P are propositions, nor that t and f stand for truth and falsity respectively, and the meanings of the operation signs, '∨' and '∼', have been similarly left undetermined.)

I shall now consider the following problem about the set of all possible interpretations of P:

(*) Given the above information about the character of P, as set forth in clauses (*a*)–(*d*) above, choose an interpretation of P such that every well-formed formula of P becomes a proposition, and t and f mean truth and falsity respectively (so that 'p has the value t' comes to mean the same as 'p is true', and 'p has the value f' the same as 'p is false'). What, if anything, will follow, in *every* such interpretation, with respect to (i) the admissible meanings of the simple signs p, q, etc., (ii) the admissible meanings of the operation signs, '∨' and '∼'?

An analogous problem would be the following: Give an interpretation to the legal positions on the chess-board, such that every such position is interpreted as a proposition, a checkmate becomes a tautology and a stalemate a contradiction. What propositions if any can be used for such an interpretation, and what are the possible interpretations of the chess-moves that convert one position on the chess-board into another?

In both problems we are looking for certain invariants, in all the interpretations of a given formal system, that convert it into a set of propositions, tautologies, and contradictions, in a predetermined way. It might be said that we are trying to make a certain kind of inference from syntax to semantics.

334

Logic Presents the 'Scaffolding' of the World

I believe the problem stated above, (*), gives a plausible sense to Wittgenstein's question whether logic has a 'connexion' with the world. Any positive answer that might be supplied would certainly have a claim to be part of the truth about the world that logic, on Wittgenstein's principles, is supposed to manifest. For example, if the answer were to be, in part, that some of the propositions supplying an interpretation of P, in the manner stipulated above, must be mutually independent, something of great importance about logical space—about the logical form of the world—would have been revealed. If, on the other hand, it proved impossible to supply any definite solution to the formulated problem, Wittgenstein's view that logic reflects the world would become very dubious. I believe Wittgenstein would have expected that all interpretations of P, in the manner specified, would necessarily have certain things in common—in addition to their all being ways of interpreting the same formal system.

One way of interpreting P is, of course, to regard p, q, etc., as standing for a set of different and mutually independent propositions. Let us call this possible interpretation, I_1.

Consider, next, the following interpretation—I_2, say,—which has been described by Alonzo Church (for details see his 'Review of Carnap', p. 494).

Let a, b, c, d, be the following propositions:

a: There are 7 days in the week;

b: There are 14 days in the week;

c: There are 21 days in the week;

d: There are 42 days in the week.

Let every uncompounded sign, p, q, etc., be taken to express either b or c. If X is a formula identified with the proposition to the effect that there are x days in the week, let $\sim X$ be taken to be the proposition referring to $294/x$ days. (Thus if p is b, $\sim p$ will be c and *vice versa*.) If X and Y are propositions referring to x and y days, respectively, let $X \vee Y$ be taken to be the proposition referring to z days, where z is the highest common factor of x and y (thus if p is b, and q is c, $p \vee q$ is a).

Commentary

It is easy to check that this interpretation satisfies all the conditions stipulated in our problem (*). On the interpretation I_2, all members of L become tautologies, and all members of K contradictions. But this is a so-called 'non-standard' interpretation, because the meaning it assigns to ' $\sim$ ' is not that of negation and the meaning it assigns to '∨' is not that of disjunction. This follows at once from the fact that if p is b, $\sim p$ is c, where both b and c are false propositions; and from the fact that if p is b and q is c, $p \vee q$ is a, a true proposition.

Our conclusion must be that the formal structure of P does not suffice to restrict the possible interpretations of ' $\sim$ ' to negation, nor the possible interpretations of '∨' to disjunction. And if this is so, it would be idle to expect any useful outcome from our problem. If the structure of P is compatible with a world in which the only possible propositions are a, b, c, and d, and ' $\sim$ ' and '∨' have the meanings assigned by I_2, it is idle to expect P's structure to show anything about the world as it really is.

The case would be altered if further stipulations were added to the four conditions, (a)–(d), used in formulating (*). In particular, the further stipulation that any admissible interpretation must interpret $\sim p$ as false in any case in which p was true, and true in any case in which p was false, would have the effect of eliminating the non-standard interpretation, I_2. But this further stipulation would amount to giving ' $\sim$ ' the normal sense of negation. Wittgenstein's statement that logic only 'presupposes' that propositions have sense ($6.124c$) would have to be amended by adding that logic also 'presupposes' that ' $\sim$ ' means negation. Further stipulation would still be necessary to fix the meaning of '∨' (or, in equivalent systems, of the other logical connectives introduced). We should then have abandoned the hope of drawing inferences from the purely formal features of P.

6.124g   natural and inevitable: misleading. The sense is that the signs needed are of a nature that is necessitated.

h   any sign-language: because all other languages can be translated into that sign-language.

For further discussion of this issue, see Carnap's *Formalization*. The arbitrary features of the particular sign-language will not matter: it is bound to exhibit the necessary features of all language.

6.125 in advance: cf. 5.551 *a*.

the old conception: no doubt Russell's (perhaps the conception of logical truths as theorems in an axiom system).

W. seems to mean that we can give a description of the general form of all valid logical propositions. This is certainly so for the propositional calculus—but not for the predicate calculus.

6.1251 Echoed at 6.1261 *b*. But compare what is said immediately about proof in logic at 6.1262.

This section and the last are criticized by Carnap (*Syntax*, p. 101), on the ground of 'the *indefinite* character of the term "analytic"'. (A term is said to be 'definite' in the relevant sense if a finite number of steps according to a predetermined method will show whether or not the term should be applied to a given object.)

LXXVII

PROOF IN LOGIC

(6.126–6.13)

Wittgenstein seeks to break the grip of an ancient and still influential conception of logic as a deductive system in which theorems are inferred from self-evident axioms. Each logical truth, he claims, bears its own warrant upon its face, shows *by itself* that it is a tautology (6.127 *b*). That is why there is no unique inferential order among the propositions of logic (6.127 *a*), and why the 'proof' of logical conclusions from logical premises is merely a useful device for facilitating recognition of tautology in difficult cases (6.1262). Proof *in* logic (i.e. of conclusions that are truths of logic) is quite different from proof *by means of* logic (i.e. of contingent conclusions) (6.1263 *b*). For every logical proposition, unlike a 'genuine' proposition, can be conceived as having the 'form of a proof' (6.1264 *b*). 'Significant', contingent, propositions stand to one another in internal relations that are brought out by connecting premises with conclusions. But *all* logical propositions equally reflect the logical form of the world. There are no ontological priorities in logic.

6.126 (1) Cf. 6.113a (truth of logical propositions discernible in the symbol alone).

symbol: in view of what follows immediately, one might have expected 'sign' instead. The stress upon '*symbol*' is intended to exclude reference to contingent reality.

belongs to logic: i.e. is a tautology—cf. (3).

Inasmuch as 6.126a implies the existence of a general decision procedure for logic, it must be regarded as mistaken.

(2)b In accord with 3.33.

(3)b Most contemporary logicians, however, allow a contingent proposition to follow from a contradiction: W. no doubt would have demurred.

(4) Cf. 6.122 (dispensability of logical propositions), 6.127b (every tautology shows itself as such).

'*Logical propositions*, OF COURSE, all shew something different: all of them shew, *in the same way*, viz. by the fact that they are tautologies, but they are different tautologies and therefore shew each something different' (*Moore Notes*, 113 (2)).

6.1261a This statement is mentioned by W. in *Foundations* (1, §82). Both there and in the *Notebooks* (42 (10)) the equivalence of process and result is said to be a feature of mathematics as well as of logic.

equivalent: in deriving one tautology from another, we do not make any *discovery* (as, on the other hand, we would if we extracted a new chemical substance from a lump of rock). It is an internal feature of every tautology to be connected with every other tautology in the way that is rendered manifest by deriving one from the other. Thus (as explained in 6.1262) 'proof' in logic merely nudges our attention, helps us to see what we might conceivably have seen without it (cf. 6.127 (2)).

b Echoed at 6.1251.

6.1262 Cf. 6.1265.

'*Use of logical propositions*. You may have one so complicated that you cannot, by looking at it, see that it is a tautology; but you have shewn that it can be derived by certain operations from certain other propositions according to our rule for constructing tautologies; and hence you are enabled to see that one thing follows from another, when you would not have been able to see it otherwise. For example, if our tautology is of [the] form $p \supset q$, you can see that q follows from p; and so on' (*Moore Notes*, 111 (2)).

6.1263 b   **from the start**: rather, 'in advance' (*von vornherein*), a '*priori*'.
proof *in* logic: proof of a logical conclusion from logical premises.

'If we say one *logical* proposition *follows* logically from another, this means something quite different from saying that a *real* proposition follows logically from *another*. For so-called *proof* of a logical proposition does not prove its *truth* (logical propositions are neither true nor false) but proves *that* it is a logical proposition (= is a tautology)' (*Moore Notes*, 108 (6)).

6.1264 (**1**)   I read this as: 'A significant proposition says that something is the case and its proof shows that it *is* the case; while in logic', etc.

(**2**)   In the *Notebooks* (57 (8)) parallel remarks are made about mathematics.

The reference to *modus ponens* must not be taken literally. W. is thinking of the tautology $p \cdot (p \supset q) : \supset q$ as expressing a rule of inference—and similarly for *any* tautology having the form of an implication. (But his remark would not fit a case such as $p \vee \sim p$.)

'He is saying that the implication . . . is *as it were* a picture or proposition with the *modus ponens* as its sense' (Anscombe, *Introduction*, p. 115).

●   'Every tautology having the form of an implication can be regarded as an expression of a rule of inference.'

6.1265   **is its own proof**: in the sense of needing *no* proof—cf. 6.127 b.

6.127 (**1**)   **status**: or, 'warrant'. Cf. 5.454 on absence of classification in logic.

(**2**)   In the *Moore Notes*, W. says that tautologies of different forms each show 'something different' (113 (2)).

6.1271 bc   For similar strictures against appeal to 'self-evidence', see 5.1363, 5.4731.

'Logic and mathematics do not *rest* upon axioms—any more than a group [in the mathematical sense of that word] rests upon its defining elements and operations. *Herein lies the mistake* of regarding the obviousness, the evidence of the principles as a criterion of correctness in logic' (*Math. MS.* p. 541).

c   This seems unfair to Frege and especially to his sharp separation of logical from psychological considerations. Frege held 'that arithmetic is a branch of logic and need not borrow any ground of proof whatever from experience or intuition' (*Translations*, p. 148).

6.13 (1)   For logic as a mirror, cf. 5.511. For language as a mirror, see 4.121 (2).

(2)   transcendental: beyond experience, *a priori*. There is a similar remark about ethics at 6.421 *b*.

'[This remark] does not mean that the propositions of logic state transcendental truths; it means that they, like all other propositions, shew something that pervades everything sayable and is itself unsayable' (Anscombe, *Introduction*, p. 166).

LXXVIII

THE NATURE OF MATHEMATICS; MATHEMATICAL PROPOSITIONS AS EQUATIONS

(6.2–6.2323)

Wittgenstein's views about mathematics closely parallel his views about logic. Mathematics, like logic, shows the 'logic of the world' (6.22). So, mathematical propositions say nothing (6.21) and, like logical propositions, are 'pseudo-propositions' (6.2*b*), purporting to say what can only be shown. But mathematical propositions, according to Wittgenstein, differ from logical propositions in being *equations* (6.22, 6.2341) that show the identity of meaning of the expressions equated. So, Wittgenstein does not regard mathematics as reducible to logic, in the manner of Whitehead and Russell. On the other hand, what Wittgenstein has already called 'the peculiar mark of logical propositions' (6.113*a*), the possibility of perceiving their validity by inspection of the signs that express them, without reference to facts or any other external source of evidence, is equally characteristic of mathematical equations (6.2321). In view of this, the distinction between mathematics and logic must seem somewhat arbitrary. (If we are to isolate a special subject concerned with equations, why not do the same for the department of logic that handles implications?) This may be why Wittgenstein calls mathematics a '*logical* method' at the beginning of this instalment (6.2 *a*). Mathematics and logic are both grounded in 'logical syntax': the logical syntax of any sign language suffices to determine all the valid formulas of mathematics (to adapt what was said in the last sentence of 6.124 about logic).

6.2 (1) Echoed at 6.234.

(2) **pseudo-propositions** (*Scheinsätze*): this term is used at 4.1272, 5.534, 5.535 to refer to something 'which cannot be written' in a correct ideography (5.534). But here it is not W.'s intention to suggest that mathematical propositions are nonsensical. They are 'part of the symbolism' (4.4611 *b*) and have the genuine function of *showing* (6.22).

In discussing the proposed view of mathematics, Ramsey says: 'this is obviously a ridiculously narrow view of mathematics and confines it to simple arithmetic' (*Foundations*, p. 17). One difficulty raised by him is the presence in mathematics of inequalities (*op. cit.* p. 282). But the more serious difficulty, he holds, is that of accounting, on W.'s view, for the applicability of arithmetic (*op. cit.* p. 19).

6.21 'Mathematics consists (wholly) of calculations. In mathematics *everything* is algorithm, *nothing* meaning (*Bedeutung*); even there where it seems to be, since we seem to talk about mathematical objects (*Dinge*) by means of *words*. The truth is that we then construct an algorithm by means of those words' (*Math. MS.* p. 748).

6.211 (1) **in real life**: literally, 'in life' simply.

b It might be objected that we can, for example, *count* the roots of an equation.

(2) This is a comment upon (1), where W. has just been considering how mathematical propositions are used.

This passage can be regarded as an anticipation of the point of view later elaborated in *Investigations, passim*.

6.22 Cf. 6.1 (logical propositions are tautologies) and 6.2 (2) (mathematical propositions are equations).

It is hard to see how what is shown in equations can be assimilated in this way to what is shown in tautologies.

6.23 (1) *a* **sign of equality**: or, 'sign of identity'. For identities, cf. 5.5303 and 4.243 (1, 2). See also 6.24.

b Cf. 6.232*b*.

(2) Cf. 4.0141*a* on the importance of a rule for mutual substitutability of notations.

6.231 An illustration of 6.23.
construed: or, 'regarded'.

6.232 W. here rejects Frege's view that the senses of the expressions connected by the identity sign are essential to the sense of the identity (and so save the latter from degenerating into a useless repetition of the same reference). In saying that the identity of the meaning (= reference) 'can be seen from the two expressions themselves', W. may be taken to be adumbrating an alternative to Frege's conception of 'sense' (or, perhaps, merely an elaboration of it). For establishing identity of meaning in W.'s sense means attending to the *rules of use* for the expressions in question.

6.2321 can be perceived: either because we simply accept the 'propositions' or because we derive them by calculation—not by some act of privileged insight (cf. 6.233).

6.2322*b* A similar point is made at 4.243 (1, 2).
At one point in the *Notebooks* (4 (4)), W. says it makes sense to say that two *classes* (but not two things) are identical.

6.2323 equation: here better read as 'identity'.

LXXIX

MATHEMATICAL METHOD

(6.233–6.241)

Mathematical method, according to Wittgenstein, consists in transforming equations (6.2341), a process of 'calculation' (6.2331), with which 'intuition' in the ordinary sense of the word has nothing to do (6.233). Wittgenstein's remarks on this subject should be compared with what he has previously said about proof in logic (e.g. at 6.121*a*, 6.1262) and about self-evidence (e.g. at 5.4731). It is clear that Wittgenstein must regard all mathematical propositions as 'of equal status' (6.127*a*, cf. 6.2341*b*). Calculation in mathematics (6.2331), like proof in logic, is a discursive manœuvre for rendering logical form perspicuous. (It is the redundancy of our language, we might add, manifested in the existence of synonymous expressions, that makes mathematics both possible and useful.)

6.233 provides the necessary intuition: or. rather, makes any recourse to intuition in the conventional sense superfluous.

'The power of a living symbolism is the source of that insight into mathematics which is termed mathematical intuition' (Goodstein, *Formalism*, p. 11).

6.2331 (2) For the relations between calculation and experiment, see *Foundations*, pp. 95–7 and *passim*.

6.234 Cf. echo at 6.2.

There seems no reason here to stress 'method'. Mathematics is no more of a 'method' than logic is. W. may have been inclined at one time to regard mathematics as a department of logic, in view of his contention that mathematical formulas express identities of meaning. He may then have conceived of 'logic' as including more than such elaboration of identities— e.g. the expression of inferential connexions (cf. 6.1264).

6.2341*a* essential characteristic: or, 'essence'.

b **consequence**: this looks like a *non sequitur*, since complex equations may need elaborate calculation to unravel.

obviously true: this can hardly be intended as an invocation of self-evidence, in view of W.'s objections to such appeals (e.g. at 6.1271*c* above): *von selbst verstehen* might here be translated as 'self-sufficient'. Since an equation expresses an identity of meaning its correctness can be determined without reference to anything beyond the meanings of the signs occurring in it.

6.24 Cf. 6.23 (2) on substitution as indicating logical form.

6.241 Intended as an illustration of 6.24. For the notation, see 6.02.

W.'s proposed 'proof' is eccentric and would not satisfy contemporary standards of mathematical rigour. It may be pointed out, for instance, that he has provided no rules for the use of variable superscripts with the lamda symbol.

LXXX

SCIENCE AND THE 'A PRIORI';
INDUCTION; CAUSATION
(6.3–6.34)

Here Wittgenstein begins an interesting, though fragmentary, discussion of the philosophy of science. The topic is important, since scientific propositions are a test-case for the adequacy of Wittgenstein's theory of meaning. At 4.11, Wittgenstein has already assigned science, by implication, to the realm of the genuinely sayable. But that preliminary remark fails to distinguish scientific doctrine from any aggregate of contingent truths. One way in which scientific doctrines differ from mere collections of true statements about the world is in their high degree of organization by means of abstract laws and principles. These must be recognized as in some sense 'significant' (cf. 6.31a) and cannot be written off as expendable 'nonsense'. But how are the abstract propositions of science related to the world, on Wittgenstein's principles? In this instalment, Wittgenstein begins to give an answer that will be elaborated in the instalments that follow. The so-called law of induction, to begin with that, is neither a principle of logic, nor an *a priori* truth (6.31), and the same is true of the so-called 'principle of causality', the 'law of least action' and the other regulative principles of science. None of them fit snugly into any of the slots so far provided in Wittgenstein's theory of meaning. Wittgenstein's view about the relation of such regulative principles to the world seems to come to this: they express options for the syntax of possible languages of science (6.34, heavily glossed). On this view, the 'law of causation' must be a misleading title for a global feature of the syntax of one kind of language that can serve the purposes of science. It is not a law at all, but a grammatical prescription for bringing the 'description of the world' into 'a unified form' (6.341a).

6.3 Cf. 2.012 (which includes the converse of 6.3*b*), also 6.37*b* (only *logical* necessity), 6.375 (only *logical* necessity and impossibility).

6.31 proposition with sense: or, 'a significant proposition'. One that says something, unlike a 'logical law', which is shown. This seems to be in direct conflict with 6.363, where induction is said to consist in the choice of the simplest law harmonizing with experience. On the second view, the 'law of induction' would resemble the 'law of causality' (6.32) in being the 'form of a law' and so *a priori* after all.

Which 'law of induction' did W. have in mind? Perhaps, with echoes of Aristotle, one allegedly permitting an inference from 'Some *A*'s are *B*' to 'All *A*'s are *B*'?

● 'If you think of what people like to call a "law" of induction as a grand generalization about the universe—say, an affirmation that the conjunction of two characters in some observed instances is a reliable sign of their conjunction in unobserved instances—it will be an empirical statement that can be refuted by further observation. But this interpretation rests on a misconception.'

6.32 Cf. 6.34, 6.36*a* for amplification.

form of a law: elsewhere in the book, W. has linked 'form' with 'possibility' (2.033, 2.151). We might therefore suppose that W. takes the 'law of causation' to express the possibility of there being empirical generalizations of a certain kind. This reading agrees with the remarks that follow immediately (6.321–6.34), but seems to conflict with 6.36*a*, where a categorical sense is imputed to the 'law of causation'.

6.321 In a footnote to 6.32, in the Ogden edition (omitted from P.–McG.) Russell takes W. to mean that the causal principle stipulates that laws shall be 'of a certain sort'. But what sort? Possibly the kind that are expressed in physics by differential equations. But the line between such laws and others is bound to appear arbitrary: by the time we reach 6.36*a*, the 'law of causality' has been emptied of any determinate meaning.

6.3211 law of least action: first stated by Maupertuis in 1747. 'Maupertuis gave the name of "action" to the sum of the products of space (or length) and velocity, and, assuming for metaphysical reasons that *something* should be a minimum in such processes as the propagation of light, showed that the facts agreed with the supposition that light chose the path of least action' (Dampier, *History*, p. 191). The idea of such 'minimal' laws has been traced back at least as far as Hero of Alexandria. Fermat made a famous use of a similar idea; a well-known modern example of a law of this character is 'Hamilton's Principle' (1824), which asserts that the integral with respect to time of the difference between the kinetic and the potential energy of a conservative mechanical system is 'stationary'.

'Maupertuis really had no principle, properly speaking, but only a vague formula, which was forced to do duty as the expression of different familiar phenomena not really brought under one conception' (Mach, *Mechanics*, p. 460). Mach adds that the principle was subsequently changed by Euler 'into something new and really serviceable' (*op. cit.* p. 551).

'The laws of point mechanics can be stated in two entirely different forms, as differential and as integral laws. Each form contains initially unknown functions (F and L) of some or all of the variables of state, functions which experience only can yield' (Margenau, *Physical Reality*, pp. 185–6).

For a general discussion of such integral laws, with historical references, see Lindsay and Margenau, *Foundations*, pp. 128–36, and Yourgrau, *Principles*.

b **purely logical**: here, 'logical' cannot mean quite the same as it has done earlier in the book. At 6.124*gh*, logical propositions were said to be generated inexorably by the rules of logical syntax. In the present context, the relevant syntax must be that which governs the special 'language' of science, and W. is here emphasizing the *variability* of scientific systems of representation. We might say: what is '*a priori* certain' is the *conceivability*, the possibility, of laws of the causal sort.

6.33 a law of conservation: e.g. of conservation of momentum, conservation of energy, etc.

possibility of a logical form: if form is itself a possibility, the phrase shows redundancy.

6.34 principle of sufficient reason: or, 'law of causation'. In a letter to Russell (129 (2)) W. treats the two expressions as synonymous.

a priori **insights**: the Kantian echoes may well be deliberate. This passage should not be taken to impute some special faculty of 'intuition'. Cf. 5.4731 on the dispensability of 'self-evidence'.

LXXXI

THE NATURE OF SCIENTIFIC THEORY, ILLUSTRATED BY THE CASE OF MECHANICS

(6.341–6.35)

Newtonian mechanics illustrates the function of scientific theory in providing a 'form of description' for the world. Wittgenstein compares a system of mechanics to a network, having a predetermined pattern and an arbitrarily fine mesh, that is applied to a black and white surface for the purpose of describing it. The system of mechanics must be understood as a co-ordinate system, not as a set of substantial assertions about reality. (If we draw lines parallel to the co-ordinate axes through all the points on the axes that can be distinguished in practice, we get something like the 'network' of Wittgenstein's analogy.) The simile's appropriateness might well be contested, for Newton's 'laws of motion' have the air of being sweeping generalizations about the actual world (and were so conceived by Newton himself). But Wittgenstein wants to deny that a statement like 'Every body continues in a state of rest or uniform motion in a straight line unless acted upon by some external impressed force' is at all analogous to 'Water always flows downhill, unless compelled to do otherwise'. The latter is an empirical generalization; the former, in spite of appearances, is a covert way of defining what is to count as a 'body', as 'action', and as 'external impressed force'. Wittgenstein is right in saying that Newton's laws jointly provide a way of talking about nature. It is therefore misleading to call Newtonian mechanics either true or false, for the same reasons that render it misleading to assign a truth-value *simpliciter* to a given geometry. Yet, as Wittgenstein sees clearly, the choice of one system of mechanics rather than another, of one theoretical language rather than another, is not wholly arbitrary. Although no scientific language can fit the world perfectly, the extent of the adjustment needed to obtain empirical consequences of a predetermined accuracy is a measure of the theory's adequacy. The greater the number of observable phenomena that must be neglected, the less adequate is the system of description in question. The connexion of the theory with the world shows itself in the degree of elaboration (the fineness of the meshes, in Wittgenstein's analogy) needed for a given degree of accuracy to be attained within a prescribed mode of representation. As the shape of a suit tells something about the contours of its wearer, though the fit is imperfect, so the choice of the most suitable co-ordinate system tells something about the character of the actual world. In this way the theoretical sciences, however indirectly, 'still speak about objects in the world' (6.3431).

6.341 (1)*a* unified form: Newtonian mechanics provides a *single* 'form of representation' (or, as we might say, a single technical sub-language) for expressing all the physical facts—in terms of 'point particles', equal and opposite forces acting between pairs of such particles, etc.

THE ANALOGY OF THE NETWORK

Consider the task of making a systematic record of an irregular design of black patches on a white surface. It might be done, says Wittgenstein, by 'covering' the figure with a sufficiently fine network of square meshes, each of which is to be 'described' as being white or black. He might have added that a rule for giving the verdict is presupposed. The superimposed net is, of course, a rough set of co-ordinate axes: we might imagine the reference system drawn across the original design or a sheet of transparent squared paper placed over the design for the purpose of the description. (Similar methods are used for scanning photographs for reproduction on a television screen, where the original distribution of light and shade is simplified down to a set of discrete signals on a bank of cells.)

Wittgenstein uses this analogy to make the following points: (i) Any given figure can be recorded, to any desired degree of approximation, by a sufficiently fine measuring grid. (ii) The shapes of the meshes may be arbitrarily chosen: we are free to use, for example, a net composed of triangles (6.341 e) or one constructed of units having different shapes, say triangles and squares together (6.342 b). (iii) Use of a network brings the description into a 'unified form' (6.341 d). (iv) Some nets produce a 'simpler' description of a given figure than others do, inasmuch as a relatively coarser mesh suffices for a given degree of precision (6.341 f). (v) The properties of the net are given *a priori* (6.35 b), i.e. we know in advance for a given net the form of the resulting description. (vi) It is, however, an empirical truth that a net of a *given* fineness of mesh 'completely describes' the figure (6.342 e). (vii) Again, it is an empirical truth that one net furnishes a 'simpler' description than another (6.342 (2) b).

The first point is a mistake. On inspecting a square, we might find roughly the same proportions of black and white surface; whatever rule was employed to resolve the uncertainty, the report of the square's condition would be arbitrary, and if this happened in every cell, as it might, the resulting description would be wholly uninformative. Such a breakdown might happen at every level of precision, up to the point where the network would become too 'precise' to be used, because its lines could no longer be distinguished. Wittgenstein was too quick to assume his method was bound to work; echoing his language, we can say that it 'characterizes' the original design—is a contingent truth—that the method works at all. If the analogy holds, it must be a contingent truth that any theoretical science is possible.

Stripped of its picturesque trappings, Wittgenstein's view amounts to an emphasis upon the need in a theoretical science for a suitable *language* (the 'net'), complete with syntactical and semantical rules for its use. It cannot be an essential part of his conception that a physical network be used (although scientific measurement and observation need instruments). Even if all black and white figures came equipped with overprinted grids, it would still be necessary to establish conventions for reading and recording them: without such rules of interpretation a diagram would be inert and uncommunicative. There can be no question of literally applying a network to the weather, but we might use dates and record a series of readings of 'fine' and 'poor' weather; the dates would then function as the meshes of the net did, to identify portions of the field examined, so that suitable predicates might be applied. The general case Wittgenstein has in view is that of a technical vocabulary, some of whose members fix the subjects of the scientific propositions, while others are used, according to rules laid down in advance, to supply the predicates. The syntactical rules of the theoretical sub-language are the literal correlate of what Wittgenstein called the 'form' of the network; the semantical rules answer to the procedure for placing the net over the figure and obtaining a determinate verdict. Just as each mesh identified a region of the surface examined, we can imagine, in the general case, space-time divided into cells, to each of which the theoretical system then assigns predicates in a predetermined fashion. But this is too narrow a conception: we ought to include under 'application' any use of the theory to generate propositions of a lower order of generality than the constitutive principles of the theory itself. In order to adhere to Wittgenstein's conception, we must, of course, allow for a progressive series of technical vocabularies successively increasing in precision; alternatively, we can imagine such a series of vocabularies incorporated into a single language. The 'precision' of a given description might then be roughly measured by the number of independent symbols available in the sub-language actually employed. So far, Wittgenstein's account agrees pretty well with examples of scientific theory that come readily to mind.

Let us now consider what he says *about* the 'network' itself, i.e. about the general character of scientific theory. He says that the 'network' is 'unified' (6.341 *d*): mechanics, for instance, is an attempt to describe the world according 'to a single plan' (6.343). It is difficult to attach any useful sense to this idea. Wittgenstein is willing to allow the network of his analogy to be constructed of elements having different shapes (6.342 *b*): it is therefore unclear what type of scientific theory would have to be disqualified on his principles as insufficiently 'unified'. For example, a 'form of representation' of space using euclidean geometry in some regions and a non-euclidean geometry elsewhere would still have to count as 'unified' in the loose sense that is relevant. Similarly, there seems no reason against counting the present fluctuating uses of 'particle' and 'wave' representations in quantum physics as 'unified' in Wittgenstein's sense. It begins to look as if 'unified' means no more than 'complete', in the sense of providing for all contingencies by prior stipulations about how they shall be treated in the theory. But no theory can accommodate every kind of empirical datum that observation may supply—Wittgenstein's original network can be used only in connexion with surface designs, and has no provision for distinguishing chromatic hues.

What remains important in Wittgenstein's account is his stress upon the relative arbitrariness of scientific theory. This is perhaps too reminiscent of the conventionalism of Poincaré, Duhem, and others, to count as original, but it is a point of fundamental importance.

I have said that the 'propositions' comprising a given scientific theory, such as Newtonian mechanics, might be considered as having the function of syntactical rules for determining what shall count as a law and as an observation within that branch of science. It seems unimportant whether we call them 'rules' or, as some writers prefer, 'prescriptions' or 'recipes' for the construction of laws. Schlick, claiming to report Wittgenstein's views, treats natural laws as instructions (*Anweisungen*) for producing empirical propositions (*Gesetz*, p. 23), and Ramsey's treatment of scientific laws as 'variable hypotheticals' (*Foundations*, pp. 237–55) is also clearly indebted to Wittgenstein. His remark that 'a variable hypothetical...is not strictly a proposition at all, but a formula from which we derive propositions' (*op. cit.* p. 251) is quite in the spirit of the *Tractatus*. Both Schlick and Ramsey extend Wittgenstein's ideas about scientific theory to the derivation of scientific laws (general propositions relatively close to the crude observational data): I think Wittgenstein might have accepted this. On the other hand, it is hard to see how, within the framework of the *Tractatus*, he could have accepted the idea, taken for granted above, that semantical as well as syntactical rules are needed.

Wittgenstein's examination of scientific language must have had some tendency to relax the hold upon him of the 'picture theory'.

For the moral of such an examination is that the 'picture theory' is too simple to serve as a model for all uses of language. Wittgenstein had to choose between liberalizing his conception of the essence of language, because it failed to fit scientific propositions, or denying that science was really composed of propositions. Whatever choice is made, there results a liberalization of the *Tractatus* conception of language and its functions. (If we insist that scientific formulas are not propositions, we shall have to admit new senses of the *a priori*.) Once it has been conceded that scientific theory escapes the jurisdiction of the principle of extensionality, so that its formulas have empirical significance without being 'logical pictures', Wittgenstein's philosophy of language is ripe for reform. The recalcitrant case of scientific language can be accommodated to Wittgenstein's later views about the 'motley' of language without the shifts to which he was driven in the *Tractatus*.

6.341 (1) *e* **optional**: or, 'arbitrary'.

  the same result: rather, 'an equal success'. Any regular geometrical network would approximate as closely as desired to the contours of the irregular marks on the paper, if we made the elements of the net sufficiently small. (For example, we could simply record which of the elements contained at least one black point.)

f **description simpler**: the crucial idea. Since any kind of 'network' could be made to fit the given surface pattern to any desired degree of accuracy, the simplicity of a given form of representation has to be judged by the 'fineness' of the mesh. What is the literal meaning of this? Presumably, that in a given mode of describing a physical situation, a smaller number of propositions is required for a specified degree of accuracy than in another mode of description. It is, however, more plausible to hold that the 'simplicity' that concerns scientists is a matter of the avoidance of *ad hoc* supplementary hypotheses: the simpler theory is the one that successfully explains given observations without invoking arbitrary supplementary assumptions. The notion of 'simplicity' of scientific theories is very far from clear. For a good criticism of the idea, see Popper, *Logic*, ch. 7.

h The suggestion seems to be that the propositions of mechanics must follow from the axioms of the system (presumably with the aid of statements of initial conditions). Here a new conception of the form of representation determined by a given mode of formulating mechanics has been introduced—unless we regard the axioms themselves as prescriptions for the syntax of mechanics.

(2)   The axioms (conceived as prescriptions for the formulation of the propositions of the system) must provide for the approximate formulation of *all* propositions belonging to *mechanics*. But not all propositions belonging to physics, *pace* W., who here implicity identifies mechanics and physics. His assertion degenerates into truism: the system of mechanics must provide means for expressing all the propositions belonging to that system. The analogy with the number-system is far-fetched; the relation of physical propositions to the axioms of mechanics is manifestly different from that of an arbitrary number to its numerical components.

It may be noted that W.'s remarks about mechanics would equally apply to geometry.

'A characteristic example for my theory of the significance of descriptions in physics: The two theories of heat; heat conceived at one time as a stuff, at another time as a movement' (*Notebooks*, 37 (6)).

6.342 (1) *a*   What is the **relative position** of logic and mechanics? Presumably the rest of the paragraph is intended to be an answer. Perhaps: logic guarantees the possibility of a description according to the demands of a particular theoretical system, while mechanics supplies the details of the mode of description. (Logic tells us that a geometrical net *could* fit the phenomena to any desired degree of accuracy: mechanics then chooses the shape of the elements of the net.)

b   This sentence might more naturally be placed after 6.341 *d*. (Its object seems to be to stress the element of the arbitrary in the selected form of representation.)

e   **described** *completely*: only in the case of the analogy of the net. In scientific description, there is no such thing as 'complete' description and every measurement leaves room for further accuracy of specification.

(2)   'What experience teaches us is that one method of representation is more appropriate than another in the sense that a map of the earth is more appropriate on the surface of a sphere than on a plane' (Watson, *Physics*, p. 52).

'Thus what we have called the laws of nature are the laws of our method of representing it. The laws themselves do not show anything about the world, but it does show something about the world that we have found by experience how true pictures of the world of a certain degree of fineness or of a certain simplicity can be made by means of the methods which we have learned to use' (*ibid.*).

'Our choice of a method of representation is a real choice; we are guided by our experience in finding it' (Watson, *op. cit.* p. 53).

Frank says that W. has 'correctly described the relation of formal systems to physical laws' (*Science*, p. 107). Frank calls Newton's laws 'not a description of the world, but a machinery which can produce such a description if it is used in the right way; hence, the laws of mechanics are of no use if no advice is given on how to use this machinery' (*loc. cit.*). He continues, 'Part of the advice consists in the operational definition of the terms used in the laws' (*ibid.*).

NEWTON'S MECHANICS

Newton's celebrated laws of motion can be stated as follows (adhering closely to his original formulation):

(1) Every body continues in its state of rest, or uniform motion in a straight line, unless it is compelled to change that state by a force impressed upon it. (The so-called 'Law of Inertia'.)

(2) The change of motion is proportional to the motive force impressed; and is made in the direction of the straight line in which that force is impressed.

(3) Action is equal and opposite to reaction.

What empirical significance should be attached to these principles?

The voluminous literature on the subject includes almost every conceivable answer. Newton himself construed his principles as empirical generalizations of universal scope; Kant and many others have laboured to exhibit them as self-evident truths; for conventionalists, such as Duhem and Poincaré, they are a system of interconnected definitions; and it is not uncommon to find a blend of several of these views. For instance, a recent writer says that the second law is a 'mixture' of definition and 'statement of objective fact' (R. E. Peierls, *Laws*, p. 21).

As always when interpreting a scientific theory, we must distinguish between the syntactical connexions of the basic theoretical terms (expressed in the laws themselves) and the semantical rules, linking the theory with observation, that confer a physical meaning upon what would otherwise be an empty mathematical skeleton.

The terms to be discussed reduce to: *position, time, mass,* and *force,* of which the first two, though not explicitly mentioned, are obviously needed in determining velocities, the directions of forces, etc. To save space, I shall ignore difficulties about the empirical determination of mass. (Characteristic indices of mass can be assigned to bodies by comparing their momenta before and after collisions, or their relative motions under mutual attraction in relative isolation from other bodies.) I shall assume that the laws are intended to apply to 'particles', i.e. to bodies having negligible dimensions.

In order to assign a determinate empirical meaning to the first law, we need to choose a geometry, a chronometry (a system for determining temporal location and temporal interval) and some physical reference system with respect to which spatial location can be measured. I shall discuss only the last of these, assuming that a prior understanding has been reached as to how place and time are to be measured after a reference system has been chosen. Even so, there remain severe problems in justifying the choice of a particular reference system and in explaining how 'impressed force' is to have empirical significance.

As to the first, the standard procedure is to take as the fundamental reference system a set of rigid rectangular axes imagined as attached to those distant stars popularly called the 'fixed stars'. This can be justified as follows. We know, from astronomical observations, that if the co-ordinate system is chosen in this manner, bodies at great distances from one another will be found to be at rest or in uniform linear motion. If we accept Newton's first law, we shall have to conclude that such bodies—relatively isolated, we might call them—are free from external (= impressed) forces. Now this agrees with our vague, prescientific notion of a 'force': we think of a relatively isolated body (either too distant or too massive to be noticeably influenced by others) as 'on its own', and 'free from interference'. Newton's first law teaches us to expect to find such bodies moving *uniformly* (a fateful breakaway from the Aristotelian conception of *circular* motion as 'natural'): choice of the fixed stars for reference allows us, as observation shows, to fulfil this expectation. The empirical content of the first law can be partially summarized as follows: 'There *are* material reference systems (attached to the 'fixed stars' or moving uniformly relative to those stars) with respect to which bodies at great distances from others do have (approximately) uniform linear motion.

Let us now consider the empirical significance of 'impressed force'. The general case is that in which a body, observed to be moving non-uniformly with respect to the standard reference system of the fixed stars, is expected to be under the influence of an impressed force, according to the First Law. Where is such a force to be found? One plausible and widely accepted answer to this crucial question treats the first and second laws together as constituting a *definition* of 'force': in modern terminology, 'impressed force' is simply taken to *mean* the same as 'rate of change of momentum'.

This has the advantage of assigning a determinate and measurable interpretation to 'force', but it converts the first law into a tautology. For on this reading, the law of inertia reduces to the triviality that a body continues in its state of rest or uniform motion, unless its momentum is changing, i.e. unless it is *not* at rest or in uniform motion. As Eddington expresses this version (which he accepts), 'Every body continues in its state of rest or uniform motion in a straight line, except in so far as it doesn't' (*Physical World*, p. 124). On this view, the reference to 'force' in the principles of mechanics now becomes gratuitous, since the only variables needed are the remaining ones of position, time and mass. And the empirical content of the principles threatens to evaporate almost entirely. Roughly speaking, the 'laws', providing as they do, on this interpretation, for consistent determinations of position, time, and mass (defined in terms of relative accelerations), allude only to the empirical regularities that render such a system of determinations possible. The empirical content of mechanics begins to look like the empirical content of a physical geometry. For the latter can be reduced to the assertion that there exist 'rigid bodies' by means of which spatial measurements can be made conforming to the demands of the geometry in question; and the empirical content of the former reduces, likewise, to the assertion that there exist so-called 'inertial systems', e.g. the one to which the fixed stars approximate, by means of which the *motions* of bodies can be consistently described. Mechanics becomes a kind of geometry of position and motion, taken together.

This summary way of eliminating force from the foundations of mechanics, and thus erasing the problem of finding empirical correlates for the theoretical term, 'force', achieves only a specious economy, and overlooks a vital link between the notion of 'force' and certain general underlying and presupposed notions of causal explanation. In the background of Newton's thought, as in the thought of all of us, is the idea that forces must originate in bodies or other material agents (media, waves, etc.). The scientist, no less than the man in the street, is strongly predisposed to expect that every departure from a 'natural', 'free', unconstrained condition or state must be due to some determinate *material* agent. This regulative idea, which might be called the principle of substantial causality ('no causal effects without some responsible material agency') receives a precise formulation in Newton's laws. We have already seen how those laws define a 'natural' or 'free' motion as uniform motion in a straight line. A covert appeal to the principle of substantial causality now requires every deviation from uniform motion in a suitable system of reference (an 'inertial system' such as that of the fixed stars) to be explained by determinate causes originating in specifiable material bodies or material media. Finally, what is to count as a measure of a relevant cause or a relevant effect for the purposes of theoretical mechanics is specified by the choice of rate of change of momentum, according to the second law. The third law, stating that 'action' and 'reaction' are equal and opposite, imposes a further important condition upon the character of the admissible laws. (Roughly speaking, the forces conforming to the system's prescription are always to come in couples.) Taken all together, Newton's laws imply that deviations from the natural motions (i.e. as measured by the rate of changes of the momenta of the bodies in question) must be expressible as functions of the masses of the bodies and their mutual distances, the precise form of the function being left open for empirical determination. (Newton's law of gravitation is a famous example of such a determination, but many other instances may be found in other branches of physics. It is a tribute to Newton's genius that his scheme of explanation was later found to fit by analogical extension far beyond the scope of celestial motions. The search for mechanical forces conforming to his explanatory scheme proved effective in physical chemistry, thermodynamics, optics, and elsewhere. But the fact that after all it proved necessary in the end to modify and even abandon the Newtonian scheme strongly supports Wittgenstein's point about the partially 'arbitrary' character of such explanatory schemes.)

From the standpoint of common sense, it is by no means obvious that the mutual influences of the sun and the earth, or of any two other bodies upon one another, should be a function only of their masses and mutual distance: common notions of causal agency would have been just as well satisfied by some function of the bodies' velocities, accelerations, or other variable indicators of changes of state. To the extent that Newton's laws reject some of these abstractly possible types of functional connexion, they serve as a set of restrictive conditions upon the kinds of law that may be introduced into theoretical science.

To put the matter in another way: the choice of rate of change of momentum as the dependent variable (or, where the mass is constant, of the acceleration) has the consequence, as Poincaré pointed out (*Foundations*, p. 94), that the laws expressing the relative motions of material particles must be expressible by differential equations of no higher than the second order.

The foregoing discussion has emphasized three distinct things accomplished by Newton's laws of motion: (i) definition of what shall count as a 'freely moving body', (ii) choice of a criterion for establishing the existence of a disturbing force, (iii) restrictions upon the permissible specifications of the magnitude of the disturbing force as a function of spatial and dynamical variables.

(i) Anybody accepting Newton's laws commits himself to treating a body at rest or in uniform motion with respect to a suitably chosen 'inertial system' of reference (say the fixed stars) as 'moving freely' i.e. as not subject to external forces. It is tacitly understood that a motion of this kind is in *no need of further explanation*.

(ii) Rate of change of momentum is to count as defining the existence and scope of a deviation from the natural or free motion. It is not self-evident that the rate of change of momentum should be chosen as the sole feature of a non-natural motion requiring explanation. Of course, if uniform motion is taken to be 'natural', *any* deviation from such a motion will seem to need explanation, but it is not *a priori* clear that the rate of change of momentum will suffice.

(iii) Even if decisions conforming to the above account have been made about the character of 'natural motions' and the features of deviations from such motions that shall count as causally relevant, it is not self-evident that functional connexions of a predetermined form (differential equations expressed in terms of masses and their mutual distances) will in fact suffice for the desired causal explanations. Anybody accepting Newton's foundations of mechanics commits himself to a determinate, though schematic, method of explaining the motions of material bodies (second-order differential equations, or an equivalent system).

The point of adopting the Newtonian scheme of explanation can be made clearer by examining the consequences of its violation by the deliberate adoption of some variant definition of 'natural motion'. Let us consider the consequences of saying that a body shall count as moving 'freely' whenever it has progressively diminishing velocity in a straight line—say with a deceleration inversely proportional to its velocity at any given instant. If we still used rate of change of momentum as a measure of impressed force, we should have to conclude that a body moving uniformly *in vacuo* and far removed from other bodies would necessarily be subject to an *accelerating* force (to overcome the imputed natural deceleration). On the supposed hypothesis, the direction and magnitude of the requisite force could be easily calculated. Such a force would have the peculiarity of always acting along the line of the body's motion, but would have no material location or attachment; it could not be expressed as a determinate function of the states and positions of other bodies or of any enveloping medium. We should then be faced with the following awkward options: (i) to deny that such a motion was physically

359

possible, (ii) admitting it to be possible, to attribute the acceleration to some unobservable medium, (iii) to attribute its origin to the action of the *distant* bodies (i.e. to deny the possibility of isolation from causal influences), or, finally, (iv) to abandon our regulative standards of causal explanation by treating the existence of the un-attached accelerating force as an ultimate and inexplicable datum. The first of these choices would be incompatible with the known facts (our knowledge that uniform motion in relative isolation is possible), the second would amount to the introduction of a fictitious ether, the third would be a dodge, having no basis except our intention to find *some* material agent, at whatever price of implausibility, and the last would entail a drastic revision of categories of explanation, such as has since occurred in quantum mechanics. (We must not expect too much from the Newtonian scheme: circumstances may call for its abandonment, but not before its resources have been fully exploited.) I hope this simple example will help to show how the Newtonian system works and will suggest the considerations by which the choice of one theoretical system rather than another is ultimately justified.

The account given above of the use and import of Newtonian mechanics will serve, *mutatis mutandis*, for other theoretical systems, such as those of electro-magnetism and thermodynamics. (Some interesting examples are discussed in ch. 3 of Watson's *Physics*.)

According to the view I have been presenting the principles of mechanics are neither empirical generalizations, nor *a priori* truths. Taken together, they constitute an abstract scheme of explana-tion, within whose framework specific laws of *predetermined form* can be formulated and tested. If I am correct, Wittgenstein's central idea in his discussion of the philosophy of science has thus been vindicated.

6.343 For the emphasis on *true* propositions, cf. 4.11.

At the corresponding entry in the *Notebooks* (36 (2)), W. adds a reference to Hertz's 'invisible masses'. Hertz's 'single plan', we might say, consisted of his intention to represent all mechanical phenomena as arising from the free motions of systems of connected material particles. (But this forced him to introduce the unobservable 'invisible bodies'—the '*Schein-*

gegenstände' as W. calls them (*loc. cit.*). If this happened generally, we might expect that scientific description would always require the use of fictions—as if the description by means of the 'net', in W.'s analogy, compelled us to imagine the visible pattern of black spots supplemented by other invisible spots.)

6.3431   Can be read as a summary comment on 6.342 (2).
 however indirectly: delete (not in the original).

6.3432   To be read in connexion with 6.35 (1). Yet another facet of the view of the 'net' as *a priori*.

6.35 (1) *b   purely* **geometrical**: in the sense in which 'pure' geometry is commonly opposed to 'applied' geometry.

LXXXII

CAUSATION; THE 'PASSAGE OF TIME'; INCONGRUITY OF COUNTERPARTS
(6.36–6.362)

With respect to the 'law of causation', Wittgenstein's view seems to be that it is a prescription for the most general form of language compatible with the aims of science. Taken as something sayable, determinism would have to be equivalent to the pseudo-assertion, 'There are laws' (6.36*a*). Construed rightly, as a prescription for the syntax of a language of science, the 'law of causation' is so fundamental that what it excludes cannot be described at all (6.362). It would seem to follow, much current discussion notwithstanding, that the notion of an indeterministic law is an absurdity—an opinion that has much to recommend it. Wittgenstein supplies a couple of interesting corollaries of his analysis of causality. The principle of sufficient reason, to which he is in effect alluding in 6.3611 (3), follows from the necessity of a causal description of natural events. Absolutely symmetrical phenomena could not be distinguished, and any observable asymmetry would yield a differentiating cause-factor for one of the pair of occurrences. This is plausible enough. But the bearing of Wittgenstein's remarks about the problem of incongruent counterparts (6.36111) upon his theory of causality is unclear.

6.36 (1)   Cf. 6.32. In the present remark, W. is taking 'law of causality' more broadly than was implied at 6.321*b* above.

Since the 'law of causality' is the *form* of scientific laws (6.32, 6.36*a*) and accordingly belongs, like all propositions expressing forms, to the realm of the unspeakable (6.36*b*), it must be absurd to envisage a non-causal law (6.3611 (3)). An obvious retort might be that this generalizes the notion of 'causality' to the point of uselessness: for instance, it would require the dispute between determinists and non-determinists in quantum physics not to be about causation at all. W. should probably be read here as denying the significance of any notion of 'causality' (cf. his denial of the 'causal nexus' at 5.136). He might have agreed with other writers on the philosophy of science that the laymen's notion of 'cause' comes to be superseded by a notion of 'law', adding a caveat about the latter being a formal notion.

'On the view that we have been explaining, causal necessity is not a fact; when we assert a causal law we are asserting . . . a variable hypothetical which is not strictly a proposition at all, but a formula from which we derive propositions' (Ramsey, *Foundations*, p. 251).

(2)   makes itself manifest: or, 'shows itself' (*zeigt sich*). Not in the sense in which logical form 'shows itself'. Something is shown when we do in fact succeed in describing natural phenomena with a satisfactory degree of precision. (We might say that what here shows itself *need not* have shown itself had the universe been otherwise.)

Gasking ('Anderson', pp. 22–3) invites us to consider what we might mean by the sentence, 'There are no natural laws'. 'After a while it becomes clear that no matter what is proposed as the sense *we will reject it*—that we are not going to give *any* sense to the sentence. Thus the proposition does not express a proposition' (*op. cit.* p. 23).

'The uniformity of nature is not a hypothesis about the world at all—we are not prepared to substitute an alternative hypothesis—it is a statement concerning our method of representing nature' (Watson, *Physics*, p. 57).

6.361   Hertz's terminology: the allusion is obscure. W. may have been thinking of a passage such as the following: 'There exists a connexion between a series of material points when from a knowledge of some of the components of the displacements of these points we are able to state

Causation

something as to the remaining components' (Hertz, *Principles*, § 109). Here the notion of a 'connexion' is tied to the notion of a law-like relation between the things connected.

thinkable: we might instead say 'describable' (cf. 6.362).

6.3611 (1) ● 'In determining how long some occurrence or event lasts, it is senseless to speak of "comparing the event with the length of time elapsed"—here "comparison" must mean comparison with some other event, such as the movement of a minute hand.'

(3) ● 'To say that neither of two mutually exclusive but qualitatively identical events can occur, since neither could have a cause that the other does not have, is a misleading way of saying that we have no way of distinguishing the two events in the absence of some asymmetry.'

This remark connects neatly with W.'s conception of causality as a form of representation (6.34 and especially 6.362). Our choice of the causal form of representation *requires* us to look for an asymmetrical explanation for the occurrence of one event rather than the other.

***a* nothing to cause**: should be italicized, as in the original.

6.36111 Kant's problem: see Vaihinger, *Kommentar*, vol. 2, pp. 518–32, Kemp Smith, *Commentary*, pp. 161–6, Russell, *Principles*, p. 418. Also D. Pears, 'Counterparts'.

'The paradox consists in the fact that bodies and spherical figures [figures traced on spheres], conceptually considered, can be absolutely identical, and yet for intuition remain diverse' (Smith, *op. cit.* p. 164).

Kant's argument is as follows: two things exactly alike in all spatial respects ('counterparts', let us say) ought to fit the same space. But some such things (left and right hands, triangles drawn in the northern and southern hemispheres) do not coincide (are not 'replicas', we might say). Such counterparts must have an internal difference that cannot be grasped by the Understanding (cannot be 'described'?) but is revealed only by *external* spatial relations: '. . . und hier ist denn doch eine *innere* Verschiedenheit beider Triangel, die kein Verstand als innerlich angeben kann, und die sich nur durch das äussere Verhältnis im Raume offenbart' (*Prolegomena*, § 13). Kant used the argument several times—and to prove opposite conclusions. It was omitted from the second edition of the *Critique*—because, according to Kemp Smith, Kant had realized it was based 'upon a false view of the understanding' (*op. cit.* p. 165).

W. says that the impossibility of making counterparts fill the same space (at least without entry into a higher dimension) leaves their congruence unchallenged. But Kant would readily have agreed: W. does nothing to explain how the congruent counterparts can be numerically distinct, which was Kant's puzzle. On the face of it, the possibility of non-identical counterparts does not square with 6.3611 (3)—unless we take W. to be suggesting that the counterparts *must* have different causal antecedents by which alone they can be distinguished? (And this is now close to Kant's conclusion.)

(2) This is just a picturesque way of reiterating that the right hand and the left hand can be congruent. The reference to four-dimensional space cannot be taken literally.

6.362 This is even stronger than 6.32 and 6.36a, with which it should be compared. Here 'described' must mean described as conforming to some law, for W. surely did not mean to exclude the description of a chance event—say by means of an elementary proposition? But cf.: 'He [i.e. W.] also says that we could not say of a world not going according to law how it would look. So though he thinks that anything describable can happen, he would enquire whether the sun's not rising tomorrow is a describable event' (Anscombe, *Aristotle*, p. 14).

LXXXIII

INDUCTION AND THE 'LAWS OF NATURE'

(6.363–6.372)

The general tendency of Wittgenstein's remarks here is to disparage inductive procedure and, indeed, all scientific theorizing. There is no more than a 'psychological' basis for expecting the simplest laws to hold—or, to speak plainly, no basis at all (6.3631b). Our preference for simplicity has no power to sway the future (there is only '*logical* necessity', 6.37b) and we do not *know* that the sun will rise (6.36311). Explanation is as much of an illusion as prediction, since we rely upon the 'so-called' laws of nature (6.371). This is surely an excessively sceptical and deflationary view of the achievements and capacities of science. Like other rationalists, Wittgenstein is content with nothing less than the certainty to be found in logic and mathematics—and downgrades the natural sciences accordingly.

6.363 Resumption of the argument of 6.31. It will be noticed that the present remark does not square with the earlier one. Previously, W. has called the law of induction a 'significant proposition', but now he seems to be treating it as a rule of procedure. It is not a 'significant proposition' that the simplest laws will obtain: if we cannot say that laws obtain (6.36*b*), we also cannot say that the simplest laws obtain. It would have been more consistent for W. to have said that the truth of induction shows itself.

A similar remark occurs in *Phil. Bem.* (cf. *infra*), where W. also describes induction as a procedure according to a principle of economy. In the same place, the question of 'simplicity' is made to depend on the relative probabilities of the available hypotheses. This goes beyond the doctrine of the *Tractatus*—and in the right direction.

'My experience supports the view that *this* hypothesis will be able to represent my past and future experience *simply*. If it turns out that another hypothesis represents the stuff of experience (*Erfahrungsmaterial*) more simply, I choose the simpler method. The choice of a representation is a procedure (*Vorgang*) which rests upon so-called induction (not the mathematical sort)' (*Phil. Bem.* 130, 9).

accepting: or, 'assuming'.

as true: delete (not in the original).

6.3631 W. assumes here that there is no alternative to a 'logical' justification but a 'psychological' one, with an implication that the latter is not rational. Here I think he is taking too narrow a view of rational justification.

justification: or, 'basis' (*Begründung*).

6.36311 'So why does he say we do not know that the sun will rise? Not, I think, because the facts may falsify the prediction, but because there may not be any more facts: as in death the world does not change, but stops' (Anscombe, *Aristotle*, p. 14). The reference is to 6.431. This ingenious attempt to bring 6.35311 in line with 6.362 seems to me unsupported by the text.

do not *know*: cf. 5.1361*a* and the discussion on p. 243 above.

6.37 Cf. 6.3*b* (outside logic all is accident), 6.375 (only logical necessity).

6.371 If this is treated as a comment on the preceding remark, we might infer that W. held some *necessary* connexion to be required for a genuine explanation.

W.'s attitude towards the concept of explanation is distinctly unsympathetic. To insist that a genuine explanation must, *per impossibile*, demonstrate a necessary connexion between natural phenomena is to make an unconscionable demand and to ignore how explanation is actually used, in science and elsewhere. It is not unfair to say that in his brief remarks about explanation (as well as about induction and causality) W. merely exposes a rationalistic prejudice.

6.372 (2) **both**: the ancients and the moderns.

right: inasmuch as no experience can compel us to abandon the law—we can always add epicycles.

wrong: in supposing we are compelled to accept the law.

● 'But at least the ancients had a single mystery—God or Fate—while the moderns talk as if everything had been explained, although every ultimate law ought now to appear as a mystery to them.'

W. seems to be taking for granted here a somewhat far-fetched conception of scientific explanation.

LXXXIV

THE INDEPENDENCE OF THE WORLD FROM MY WILL

(6.373–6.374)

The first instalment of a number of remarks about questions connected with ethics. (Compare the further remarks about the will at 6.423, 6.43.) It is easy to see in what sense willing and wishing must, on Wittgenstein's principles, be 'independent' of 'the world'. The two propositions, 'I am determined that p shall be the case' and p, are logically independent of one another. My determination now that p shall be the case in the future, no matter how strong that determination, cannot guarantee that p shall in fact prove to be the case. (For there is only '*logical* necessity', 6.37.) If I take steps to bring about p, I am still at the mercy of the 'physical connexion' between the means and the desired end; and it is absurd to think of 'willing' a physical connexion (6.374). There is, as it were, an unbridgeable logical chasm between my determination that p shall be the case and the actual truth-value of *p*. If nothing less than the absurdity of trying to bridge this chasm will satisfy me, what happens *in* the world will easily seem ethically irrelevant (cf. 6.41 on the 'sense' of the world lying outside the world). As if all that can be right or wrong about my determination (my 'will') must be manifest in the act itself and hence independent of any contingent outcome. (There are similar thoughts in Kant and Schopenhauer.)

6.373 An application of 6.37: My willing a certain state of affairs is a fact; the actualization of that state of affairs is a different and independent fact. (Willing is directed to what is *not yet* the case.)

In the *Notebooks*, W. precedes the entry (73 (13)) by saying that since I cannot control the events of the world, I am completely powerless (*vollkommen machtlos*)—but I can render myself independent of the world (and so in a certain sense master it) by renouncing any influence over it.

For comment on this and the next section, see Anscombe, *Intention*, § 29.

6.374 no *logical* connexion between the will and the world: for a similar remark about *wanting*, see *Notebooks* (77 (9)).

LXXXV

THE INCOMPATIBILITY OF COLOURS
(6.375–6.3751)

We come now to a matter which at first seems to deserve no more than a footnote to Wittgenstein's main exposition. A little earlier, Wittgenstein said that there is only logical necessity (6.37*b*). Now, he repeats this statement (6.375) and, offering as an illustration the case of the exclusion of one colour by another at a point in a visual field (6.3751*a*), insists that here too logical impossibility must be in question. Then he reminds us that elementary propositions are mutually independent (6.3751 (3)*a*), with the obvious intention of concluding that propositions about the colours of points in the visual field cannot be elementary. But the conclusion is unwelcome.

The underlying trouble is that a proposition of the form '*X* (some point in my visual field) now has the colour *Y* (some absolutely determinate shade)' comes close to our conception of what an elementary proposition ought to be like. If a proposition of this form is not elementary, it seems that we can form no clear conception of what to expect of an 'elementary proposition'. Yet different propositions having the form in question are plainly incompatible with one another. Also, a similar problem seems inevitably to arise, no matter what form an elementary proposition is supposed to have. It is hard to conceive how the attribution of a specific property to an object could be compatible with the attribution to that same thing of *every* other property. The idea of the mutual independence of elementary propositions, so vital to Wittgenstein's conception, seems to be breaking in our hands.

Such considerations led Wittgenstein, in *Logical Form* (and in later unpublished writings, where he reverted to the same problems), to propose some radical revisions in the *Tractatus* theory of truth-functions. He suggested that while elementary propositions could not contradict one another, they might 'exclude' one another (see the notes on 6.3751 (3) *b* below). When this occurs, one line is missing from the corresponding truth-table. The proposed alteration is not at all trivial, and it is very hard to see how to fit it into the general scheme of the *Tractatus*. Here, it may be said, Wittgenstein's system begins to crack.

6.375   Can be read as a continuation of 6.37.

6.3751   Although this is presented as a very subordinate section, merely illustrating the general contention (6.37) that necessity pertains only to logic, the considerations raised prove very difficult to reconcile with some of the basic doctrines of the book (independence of elementary propositions, the theory of truth-functions).

(1) **logical structure** (*logische Struktur*): 'logical form' would be more consistent with W.'s usual terminology.

(2) **cannot be in two places**: presumably, if a particle had two different velocities at an instant t_0, it would have to be in two different places at any time t, if the interval $t - t_0$ were sufficiently small. It is hard to see how this could apply to the case of the colours, unless W. were thinking here of

the *physical* colours as wave-motions having 'velocities'. Even if what he suggests here were satisfactory (which is far from clear) there would remain difficulties about perceived colours, as in (3)*b*.

(3)*a* For the independence of elementary propositions, cf. 4.211, 4.27 (2), 5.134.

b Hence, a proposition ascribing a colour to a point in the visual field cannot be elementary. 'This implies that the apparently simple concepts red, blue (supposing us to mean by those words absolutely specific shades) are really complex and formally incompatible' (Ramsey, *Foundations*, p. 280).

In *Logical Form*, W. said 'The mutual exclusion of unanalysable statements of degree contradicts an opinion which was published by me several years ago and which necessitated that atomic propositions could not exclude one another [cf. 4.211]. I here deliberately say "exclude" and not "contradict", for there is a difference between these two notions, and atomic propositions, although they cannot contradict, may exclude one another' (p. 168). He went on to explain that such 'exclusion' would show itself in the 'disappearance' of one or more lines in the truth-table of the logical product. The truth-table for the product of two propositions that 'exclude' one another would have to be:

$$
\begin{array}{ccc}
p & \& & q \\
T & F & F \\
F & F & T \\
F & F & F
\end{array}
$$

Here we have to envisage some 'rule of syntax' that makes the missing line (*TFT*) 'nonsense'. Clearly, W. has introduced a drastic revision of the truth-table symbolism.

In *Phil. Bem.* W. repeats and develops the above ideas. He says: 'This is the way it is: The grammatical rules for "and", "not", "or", etc., are indeed not exhausted by what I said in the *Tractatus*, but there are rules for truth-functions, that also concern the elementary parts of the proposition' (34, 5). He goes on to compare propositions to rulers, in which coincidence with one mark automatically excludes coincidence with all the other marks: 'I do not apply the *proposition* as a measuring-rod to reality, but the *system* of propositions' (34, 6). And now 'The concept of "elementary proposition" in any case loses its former meaning' (35 (5)).

There is a clear transition here from an earlier view of the strict mutual independence of elementary propositions to the later emphasis (e.g. in *Investigations*) on the importance of the language-system (the 'language game') to which a given proposition belongs.

For this section, cf. *Blue Book*, p. 56, and Allaire, 'Tractatus'.

THE WORLD IS WITHOUT VALUE
(6.4–6.41)

Wittgenstein now resumes his discussion of ethics. Value is not 'in' the world, but 'outside' it (6.41 a). (This is irredeemable nonsense, not the nonsense that arises through the attempt to say what can only be shown. For how could it be shown that there is 'value' outside the world? What could at best be shown is that there is no value inside the world.) For Wittgenstein value must be something that is 'non-accidental' (6.41 (3)), something necessary, uncreated, indestructible, immutable. And of course nothing like this will be found in a contingent world. Nothing *in* the world can satisfy the mystical craving for essence.

6.4 of equal value: i.e. of no value—nothing of value is expressed by any significant proposition (6.41 c).

6.41 (1) sense of the world: or, as people commonly say, the 'meaning of life'—the purpose or end of life.

    would have no value: W. may be thinking here of the familiar position of the 'autonomy of ethics' argued by Hume and many others, whose central contention is that ethical conclusions cannot be inferred from factual premises.

(2) accidental: so W. is seeking for the *essence* of the ethical.

(4) This harmonizes with the view that the 'metaphysical subject' (5.633 a) is the *locus* of all value. Cf. 6.423 on the metaphysical will as the bearer of the ethical.

ETHICS; REWARD AND PUNISHMENT; THE WILL

(6.42–6.43)

There are no ethical propositions (6.42 a), so an attempt to formulate ethical laws must at best lead to irrelevance. The prospect of reward or punishment *in* the world has no ethical importance (6.422 b). Yet there is, we might say, an ethical way of life that leaves all facts unchanged, while transforming the metaphysical self, the 'limit of the world' (5.632). A life of happiness is to be attained by renouncing the world, by subduing all desire for the contingent. The world of 'the happy' is the world of those who have achieved self-abnegation.

6.42 (2) **what is higher**: anything having intrinsic, rather than instrumental value.

6.421 (2) **transcendental**: see the similar remark about logic at 6.13 b. We are entitled perhaps to infer that ethics can be *shown*, in spite of 6.421 a.

(3) 'The work of art is the object seen *sub specie aeternitatis*; and the good life is the world seen *sub specie aeternitatis*. This is the connexion between art and ethics' (*Notebooks*, 83 (6)). We might say: it is of the essence of both the aesthetic attitude and the ethical attitude as W. conceives them to be disinterested—not to be concerned with mundane or prudential considerations.

6.422 ● 'An ethical imperative provokes the question of the consequences of disobedience. But if that question can properly be raised we have not yet reached an absolute or intrinsic value. Ethics has nothing to do with reward or punishment in the ordinary senses of those words. And yet there must be a kind of intrinsic reward or punishment internal to the action itself.'

See also Anscombe, *Introduction*, p. 171.

We may guess that 'happiness' (cf. note on 6.43 (3)) is the 'reward' of right action.

Commentary

(1) *bc* 'Everything that happens with a view to reward or punishment is necessarily egoistic action and as such is without pure moral value' (Schopenhauer, *Preisschrift*, § 4).

(2) 'However different the religious dogmas of societies are, in all of them the good deed is accompanied by inexpressible satisfaction, the bad by infinite horror; no mockery shakes the first, there is no freedom from the second in any absolution of the father confessor' (Schopenhauer, *Die Welt*, § 12).

6.423 (1) **subject**: or, 'bearer' (*Träger*).

(2) **psychology**: cf. 4.1121 (3) *b* on the danger of entanglement in psychology.

6.43 (1) **acts of**: not in the original.
    limits of the world: at 5.632 and 5.641 (3), the 'metaphysical subject' is called a 'limit of the world'. 'Willing', W. suggests, changes the essential, the transcendental, ego.
    not what can be expressed by means of language: in the *Notebooks* W. adds: 'but can only be shown in language' (73 (15)).

(2) **their effect**: not in the original.
    wax and wane: the expression might suggest a change in the totality of facts, but this has already been excluded. In the *Notebooks* W. adds: 'As if by accession (*Dazukommen*) or loss (*Wegfallen*) of meaning (*Sinn*)' (73 (17)).

● 'For the good man, the whole world as it were becomes different (though the facts are unchanged) for *everything* now has value and significance.'

(3) 'The world of the happy is *a happy world*' (*Notebooks*, 78 (6)).
    'The point is not that the unhappy man knows or observes anything different from what happy people do' (Rhees, p. 389).
    happy (*glücklich*): has also a suggestion of 'fortunate' in the German. Many passages in the *Notebooks* are devoted to this concept. The happy man fulfils the purpose of existence (*Zweck des Daseins*, 73 (19)), is satisfied, is at peace (*befriedigt*), needs no purpose outside life (73 (20)), is therefore without fear even of death (74 (17)) and is without hope (76 (13)). He lives in the present, not in time (74 (18)), he is in accord (*in Übereinstimmung*) with the world—and this is what 'being happy' *means* (75 (4)). The happy life is self-justifying, the only *right* life (78 (11)), it can renounce the amenities of the world (81 (6)). It is to be achieved through the life of knowledge (81 (4)) and through contemplation of the beautiful (86 (9)).

LXXXVIII

DEATH AND IMMORTALITY

(6.431–6.4312)

That death is not an event *of* life (6.4311 *a*) is a sufficiently familiar thought. Wittgenstein uses it to stress again his conception of the unperceivable 'limit', the boundary of the world that we reach for, but can never experience. His remarks about 'temporal immortality' (6.4312) are an interesting example of the consistency with which he locates value outside the world. Continued and endless existence *in* the world would do nothing to solve the 'riddle of life', the unanswerable question about the purpose of existence. That 'riddle' can be solved only by causing it to vanish (6.521)—by extirpating the metaphysical craving for a 'higher' answer.

6.431   at death: in death 'my world' stops—the 'limit', beyond which there is no world, has as it were been reached. So, also, what happens 'outside' the world, at its 'limits' (6.43 *a*), is not a change *in* the world.

6.4311 (1)   In the *Notebooks* there follows: 'It [death] is not a fact of the world' (75 (2)).

(2)   live in the present: this is the 'happy' life (*Notebooks*, 74 (18)).

6.4312 *b*   some riddle: i.e. what the purpose is, the point, of our existence in space and time. Cf. 6.5 *b* (the riddle does not exist).

LXXXIX

THE MYSTICAL

(6.432–6.522)

The 'mystical feeling' is that the world is 'limited' (6.45 *b*), i.e. the feeling that there is something *beyond* the world. To the realm of the mystical belongs everything that Wittgenstein regards as having authentic value—aesthetics, ethics, religion—all that is 'transcendental'. It must be admitted that his attitude towards the 'mystical' is a vacillating one. On the one hand, it seems clear from remarks such as those of 6.522 that he conceives there to *be* the mystical. Yet, on the other hand, remarks like those of 6.5, 6.51, and 6.52 seem to say that any effort to express the mystical, whether by saying or by showing, must result in absurdity. Wittgenstein's mysticism has an equivocal character. That is why it has been possible for logical positivists to use the *Tractatus* as a text, while ignoring all its leanings towards mysticism. Such a bowdlerized reading cannot serve: Wittgenstein's 'mysticism' is far from being an irrelevant aberration. What he called 'the urge towards the mystical' (see note on 6.52 below) is one of the chief motive powers of the book.

6.432*a* **higher**: cf. the use of this expression in 6.42*b*.

b **God**: in the *Notebooks* W. says that the meaning of life can be called God (73 (8)). To believe in God means seeing that the facts of the world are not the end of the matter (74 (7), cf. 6.52*a*), seeing that there is a meaning of life (74 (8)). God is that on which we are dependent (74 (12)): to be 'happy' is to submit to his will (75 (5)) by being in accord with the world (75 (4)). Sometimes he identifies God with the world: 'God is, how things stand (*wie sich alles verhält*)' (79 (3)).

6.4321 **problem**: or, 'set task' (*Aufgabe*), like a piece of homework (cf. Anscombe, *Introduction*, p. 171).
'The facts [of science] are all parts of the mystical problem [why anything should exist] to be solved—not part of the solution of the problem' (Gasking, 'Anderson', p. 24).
'What we demand as an answer is something like a well-confirmed hypothesis whose consequent is *everything whatsoever*—the world contemplated *sub specie aeterni* as a *limited whole*, limited by an antecedent which is *something*, in spite of *everything* being in the consequent' (Gasking, *op. cit.* p. 25).

6.44 In the *Ethics Lecture*, W. describes an experience which is one *par excellence* to which he would want to attach 'absolute value': 'When I have it *I wonder at the existence of the world*. And I am then inclined to use such phrases as "how extraordinary that anything should exist" or "how extraordinary that the world should exist"' (p. 6). And later he adds: 'It is nonsense to say that I wonder at the existence of the world, because

I cannot imagine it not existing. I could of course wonder at the world round me being as it is. If for instance I had this experience while looking into the blue sky, I could wonder at the sky being blue as opposed to the case when it's clouded. But that's not what I mean. I am wondering at the sky being *whatever it is*. One might be tempted to say that what I am wondering at is a tautology, namely at the sky being blue or not blue. But then it's just nonsense to say that one is wondering at a tautology' (p. 7).

Why does W. say it is nonsensical to conceive of the world as not existing? (One is inclined to take the existence of the world as the supreme contingency.) Perhaps because in order to frame the supposition that the world does not exist, I must, as it were, *refer to* the world, and so presuppose that it *does* exist. (This is connected with 'the world' not being a class-description admitting of instances.)

things are in: not in the original, which runs, 'Not *how* the world is, is the mystical, but *that* it is'.

6.45 'The mystical feeling is the feeling that the world is not everything, that there is something outside it, its "sense" or "meaning"' (Ramsey, *Foundations*, p. 286).

(1) sub specie aeterni: this idea occurs in the *Notebooks* (83 (6)). W. there says that the work of art is an object seen '*sub specie aeternitatis*', and adds that the good life is the world seen *sub specie aeternitatis*.

(2) limited whole: to 'limit' anything is to contrast it with something else, as when in drawing a boundary line we contrast what is inside the line with what is outside. Thus to wonder at there being a world at all (6.44) is to conceive (*per impossibile*) that it might not have existed, i.e. to think of something other than the world as excluded. There is nothing absurd, of course, in considering what might have been but is not *the case*: mysticism springs from wonderment at the *substance* of the world and might be expressed as the thought, 'How strange that there should be any objects!'

mystical: rather, 'the mystical'.

This section is discussed by Anscombe (*Introduction*, p. 169).

6.5 (1) put into words: rather, 'expressed'.

(2) *The riddle*: cf. 6.4312*b* for another reference to this.

6.51*a* Scepticism: e.g. the scepticism of the solipsist, cf. 5.62*b*.

b Notice, however, that some of the pseudo-questions that W. here dismisses may still be set to rest by something that *shows* itself. (The 'deepest' questions may all have this character.)

6.52 This is preceded in the *Notebooks* by the remark, 'The urge towards the mystical (*Der Trieb zum Mystischen*) comes of the non-satisfaction of our wishes by science' (51 (3)).

This section is discussed by Anscombe (*Introduction*, p. 170).

6.521 In the *Notebooks*, W. interpolates between (1) and (2) the questions, 'But is it possible for one so to live that life stops being problematic? That one is *living* in eternity and not in time?' (74 (2)).

6.522 **things that cannot be put into words**: literally, 'the inexpressible' (*Unaussprechliches*). Cf. 6.42*b* and 6.421 for ethics and aesthetics as inexpressible. The literal rendering of O. is preferable here: 'There is indeed the inexpressible. This *shows* itself; it is the mystical.'

LXL

THE RIGHT METHOD OF PHILOSOPHY; HOW THE 'TRACTATUS' IS TO BE UNDERSTOOD
(6.53–7)

The book ends with celebrated and much-quoted statements that seem to accept utter defeat. The 'right method of philosophy' would be to abstain from positive remarks, contenting oneself with demonstrating that every attempt to 'say something metaphysical' results in nonsense. And the remarks of the *Tractatus* itself must be recognized as strictly nonsensical (*unsinnig*), to be abandoned once their true character has been revealed. The rest is silence. It may be noticed that in the preface to the book, Wittgenstein has quoted the very last remark (7) as part of the 'whole sense of the book': (What can be said can be said clearly and *poi basta*). The conclusion is profoundly unsatisfactory. That we understand the book and learn much from it is not to be seriously doubted. And the book's own doctrine of meaning and of the character of philosophical investigation must square with this. Wittgenstein may be too willing, at the very end, to

376

equate communication exclusively with 'saying'. There is much on his own principles that can be shown, though not said. There is much in the book that he has shown: this ladder need not be thrown away.

6.53 a nothing to do with philosophy: cf. 4.111 (philosophy distinct from science).

b **correct**: why does W. call the procedure described in this section the *only* correct method? Perhaps he is taking for granted that we can communicate only what can be said (cf. 7), i.e. that we cannot show another what shows itself to us (6.522 *b*). If this is so, the task of 'the heir of the subject which used to be called "philosophy"' (*Blue Book*, p. 28) can only be negative. It will be noticed, of course, that the method pursued in the *Tractatus* is *not* the 'correct' one.

6.54 (1) the ladder: this image occurs in Mauthner: 'If I want to ascend into the critique of language, which is the most important business of thinking mankind, I must destroy language behind me and in me, step by step: I must destroy every rung of the ladder while climbing upon it' (*Sprache*, vol. 1, p. 2, quoted from Weiler, p. 80).

'Just as it is not impossible for the man who has ascended to a high place by a ladder to overturn the ladder with his foot after the ascent, so also it is not unlikely that the Sceptic after he has arrived at the demonstration of his thesis by means of an argument proving the non-existence of proof, as it were by a step-ladder, should then abolish this very argument' (Sextus Empiricus, p. 489).

Stenius comments on this section: 'the "condemnation" of philosophy as "nonsense" is no true condemnation at all' (*Exposition*, p. 2) and adds that, according to W.'s conception, philosophizing may be 'meaningless' but yet not aimless.

(2) One might object that there is nothing for seeing the world 'right' (*richtig*) to be contrasted with; as one cannot think illogically, so one cannot see wrongly.

7 Ogden's version has become too familiar to be forgotten: 'Whereof one cannot speak, thereof one must be silent.'

Cf. 5.61 (4) (we cannot say what we cannot think).

What (*Wovon*): note the implication that there *is* something we cannot speak about, cf. 6.522 (there *is* the inexpressible).

'The silence with which W. ends recalls how Schopenhauer refused to give any appearance of positive description to that which is chosen when the Will turns round on its tracks; for us who are full of will, it is *nothing*; but, for those who choose it, "this so real world of ours, with all its suns and galaxies—is nothing"' (Geach, 'Review', p. 558).

'But what we can't say we can't say, and we can't whistle it either' (Ramsey, *Foundations*, p. 238).

> 'Schweig, Allerliebster, schweig: kannst du nur gänzlich schweigen,
> So wird dir Gott mehr Gut's, als du begehrst, erzeigen.'
>
> (Silesius, p. 59)

> 'Mensch, so du willst das Sein der Ewigkeit aussprechen,
> So musst du dich zuvor des Redens ganz entbrechen.'
>
> (Silesius, p. 65)

IS THE 'TRACTATUS' SELF-DEFEATING?

Nothing in the book has aroused more interest or provoked more scandal than its concluding remarks: 'My statements elucidate by leading anybody who understands them to recognize them eventually as nonsense—after he has climbed up them—by them, on them, over them. (He must as it were throw away the ladder, after he has ascended it.) He must overcome these statements: then he will see the world rightly. What can't be said must be left in silence' (6.54–7).

The 'elucidation' (*Erläuterung*) to be achieved is the same as that 'logical clarification of thought' which Wittgenstein earlier made the goal of philosophical method (4.112a–c). Discarding the nonsensical questions and answers of older philosophers (4.003), he invited us to an activity that would clarify thought by sharpening its boundaries (4.114). But now this programme faces self-condemnation: the very words in which our predecessors' errors were castigated have to be acknowledged as nonsensical, and we seem to be engaged in the same ancient and futile struggle to give impossible answers to questions that ought never to have been asked. Is this any better than the nonsense that resulted from earlier metaphysics? Even the conclusion that all that preceded was nonsense must itself be viewed as nonsensical and abandoned. For just as every tautology shows by itself that it is a tautology (6.127b), so every piece of nonsense must itself *show* that it is nonsensical, and the attempt to *say* so must be nonsensical. If metaphysical insight cannot be expressed, we cannot

378

say that it cannot be expressed—to say that we must be silent is already a violation of silence.

Our position begins to look desperate. The book's conclusion arose from considerations about the world, logical space, the essence of language, and so on. Wittgenstein now asserts that the conclusion implies the absurdity of its own reasons and even its own absurdity.

With what relish Frege would have assaulted this position. One can imagine him smacking his lips over the deliciously absurd notion that 'nonsense' can be understood. 'If we understand the conclusion', he might well have said, 'then it *cannot* be nonsensical. Since it implies its own lack of sense it must at best be false. For, if it were true, it would have to be nonsensical and hence without truth-value, which is a contradiction. So, the supposed conclusion is at best *necessarily* false. But all this is unnecessary—we can't begin to take seriously a statement that claims to imply its own absurdity.' No wonder that Popper was led to accuse Wittgenstein of recommending 'deeply significant nonsense' or that a critic as sympathetic as Ramsey could say, 'We must take seriously that it ["philosophy"] is nonsense, and not pretend, as Wittgenstein does, that it is important nonsense' (*Foundations*, p. 263). If we do take 'seriously' the conclusion that metaphysics is nonsense, it seems our confidence that we succeeded in understanding the book must have been a self-delusion. It is one thing to say we must throw the ladder away after we have used it; it is another to maintain that there never was a ladder at all.

These dismal reflections are premature, as I shall try to show. They arise from a too hasty equation of 'nonsense' with gibberish, and of what 'cannot be said' with what cannot be rationally communicated. It is quite certain that a sympathetic reader can make sense of the text of the *Tractatus* in a way which would be impossible if he were trying to decipher unintelligible absurdities. Wittgenstein's own practice provides numerous examples of a distinctively philosophical use of language that is neither irrational nor incommunicable and that need not be self-condemned. If we can understand what he is doing (and can resist the temptation to assimilate it with common-sense, with science—or, for that matter, with logic or mathematics)

379

we shall be able to see that it makes sense in its own fashion. Wittgenstein might perhaps be reproached for not having supplied a sufficiently perspicuous view of the philosophical activity he was advocating: in what follows, I shall try to do a little to remedy this deficiency, and to defend his own work against the condemnation that is encouraged by his own concluding remarks.

We shall go wrong at once if we fail to remember that 'sense', in Wittgenstein's use of that word, has two opposites (*sinnlos* and *unsinnig*), not one. When a sentence is inspected for its sense, or lack of it, three distinct cases may arise: it may have sense, i.e. it may be significant (*sinnvoll*), in which case it 'says something', expresses an empirical proposition; or, if not, it may either lack sense, be 'senseless' (*sinnlos*), or else be 'nonsensical' (*unsinnig*). The word 'senseless', practically a synonym for 'nonsensical' in ordinary English, strongly suggests something improper, absurd, and useless. These irrelevant suggestions would have been excluded if Wittgenstein had used, as he might, the less provocative word 'formal'. In his intended meaning, 'senseless' is not always used pejoratively, as is clearly shown by his contention that logical and mathematical statements are all 'senseless' (4.461 (3)). (Even 'pseudo-proposition', for which see e.g. 6.2*b*, is not pejorative in all its uses.) It was certainly no part of Wittgenstein's intentions to cast aspersions on logic and on mathematics, disciplines which he admired and respected. Logical and mathematical statements, he implies, are 'part of the symbolism' (4.4611) and serve to display 'the logic of the world' (6.22). Their function, as we have seen, is a peculiar one of showing something about the logic of their constituents, by combining them into 'limiting' statements whose empirical connexion with the world has been severed. But if we understand this, there is nothing wrong about constructing tautologies and equations, using them in calculations and otherwise, and no reason why our procedures should not be rationally communicated to others. The formal, 'senseless', statements of logic and mathematics are neither ineffable nor useless. Such statements, to be sure, 'show' but do not say; yet, what they show can be shown to anybody who understands their use. (An announcement of 'Checkmate' is not a move in chess, but there is nothing mysterious or absurd about such an announcement, even if it does put an end to the game. Tautologies, too, can be 'announced'.)

Now we can begin to see an escape from the nihilism of Wittgenstein's concluding remarks. His book cannot be held to 'say' anything, for it would be a howler to take it as consisting of empirical statements. But there remains the alternative of treating many of his remarks as formal statements, 'showing' something that *can* be shown. Then they will be in no worse case than logical and mathematical statements and there will be no theoretical barrier to their use in rational communication. A great many of Wittgenstein's remarks can be salvaged in this way—indeed all those that belong to 'logical syntax' or philosophical grammar. For all such remarks are *a priori* but involve no violations of the rules of logical syntax. For example, when Wittgenstein says that a proposition is not a complex name, he draws attention to an important feature of the grammar (or the 'logic') of the word 'proposition'. His remark is no more mysterious in principle than would be the announcement that a bishop is not a rook. (The important thing to be clear about is the situation in which such an announcement could serve any useful purpose.) It is a radical error to suppose that the difference between a proposition and a name is a matter of fact, but, the error once acknowledged, nothing forbids the relevant point of logical grammar from being expressed and communicated. Here we need no mystifying addendum about the need to 'overcome' the remark and to 'reject' it—here is one 'ladder' that need not be thrown away. The expression and communication of statements belonging to philosophical grammar is as reputable an activity as mathematics—and one equally articulate. Wittgenstein is not rallying us to the destruction of the *a priori* disciplines; he will be satisfied if we understand them and their 'peculiar position' in contrast to the sciences.

This line of defence applies to all cases in which Wittgenstein is seeking the 'essence' of something. In all such cases, his investigation, whether successful or not, results in an *a priori* statement that ought to be treated, on his principles, as the expression of a certain rule. There is no reason to maintain that such rules resist adequate formulation: if Wittgenstein thought otherwise, he was refuted by his own practice.

The defence I have so far offered, while it will apply to a large number of remarks in the book, will not rescue some of the most striking ones. Logical syntax cannot include such remarks as 'The world is everything that is the case' or 'The world is the totality of facts, not of things'. For expressions such as 'the world', 'a fact', 'a name', and many more, are used by Wittgenstein in invented or in stretched senses. It is therefore impossible to establish the correctness of the *a priori* statements in which they occur by reference to antecedent usage. Many of the most interesting of such statements must indeed be treated as 'nonsensical' (*unsinnig*), not merely 'senseless' (*sinnlos*). Their absurdity is irredeemable, and their ultimate fate must be rejection. But even these statements can have important uses, prior to being discarded, as I shall now try to make clear.

Our problem is that of understanding how a terminology can have a rational use, even if the ultimate verdict has to be that there is nothing better to do with that terminology than to discard it. In mathematics, as it happens, we can find many examples of this sort, which may provide the clue that has so far been lacking. For it is characteristic of the development of mathematical thought that imperfectly understood concepts are constantly extended—'experimentally', as it were—old symbols are used in ways that are strictly speaking unacceptable, or new symbols are introduced in advance of any satisfactory understanding of the logical and syntactical rules needed to regulate them. Mathematicians have often talked in the past as if the formulation of the appropriate rules of use were *discoveries*, when it would have been more appropriate to think of the activity involved as that of the *construction* and tentative *testing* of new concepts. But the types of procedure to which I am referring, however they are characterized, are sufficiently familiar to need no lengthy description. For example, the exponent notation, introduced as an abbreviation for the case in which a number is multiplied by itself any finite number of times (x^n) is governed by familiar rules for the addition, subtraction, and multiplication of the exponents. This system initially provides no meaning for an expression of the form x^0 which, in terms of the primary stipulations, ought to mean, absurdly, the result of multiplying *no* number of x's together. However, the possibility of writing x^0 as x^{n-n}, and then interpreting this, according to the subtraction rule for exponents, as x^n/x^n strongly suggests that the 'correct' value for x^0 must be 1. This result, because it can be consistently adhered to, then plausibly appears as a proof that x^0 must 'really' have meant 1 all along, though it took a while for the mathematician to discover it. What has really happened, of course, is that a new meaning has been assigned to a symbol, x^0, that turns out to be consistent with a certain extension of the antecedently established rules for symbols of the form x^n. Here, we may say, is a simple case of the extension of a mathematical concept. The point that deserves particular emphasis here is that x^0 had a determinate use for exploring a possible extension of a concept *before* its status had been legitimized. The same is true even in cases where the final verdict has to be that the intended extension of the concept in question is illegitimate. A simple example would be the attempt to assign a meaning to division by zero (i.e. to a symbol of the form $x/0$), consistent with the antecedently given rules for the division and multiplication of numbers. It very quickly appears that no such meaning can be assigned, since $x/0 = y$ would imply $x = y.0$ (by the rule for converting $u/v = w$ into $u = v.w$) and so we could infer $x = y.0 = 0$, which could not hold in the general case. Here, the problematic symbol $x/0$ is used in *determinate* ways in the calculations that lead up to its rejection. The rules for the use of the problematic symbol are dictated by the analogy that led to its tentative introduction. (For further examples of this sort, see Ambrose, 'Proof', pp. 439 ff.)

The following hypothetical example of an abortive attempt to extend a mathematical concept resembles Wittgenstein's actual practice in the text.

Somebody familiar with the series of natural numbers, $1, 2, 3, \ldots$, could be led to entertain the notion of 'the greatest of all numbers', which he might propose to denote by '∞'. As soon as he has introduced the new symbol, our hypothetical innovator has no trouble at all in deriving specific results, which will then appear to him as genuine discoveries. For example, he will 'prove' such results as the following:

$$\infty + 1 = \infty,$$
$$\infty + n = \infty,$$
$$\infty + \infty = \infty,$$
$$2 \cdot \infty = \infty,$$
$$n \cdot \infty = \infty,$$
$$\infty^2 = \infty,$$

and so on. The reason why he is able to proceed systematically in this way is that the new symbol was introduced by analogy with the symbols for the natural numbers, and is therefore assumed to be subject to the same rules, for the commutation of addition, etc., that governed the symbols of the original system. ∞, we might say, is understood to be like any other number, n, except that it is greater than all of them. The analogy exercises a control upon the use of the new symbol that prevents the calculations from degenerating into the idle play of arbitrary invention. Sooner or later, of course, things will go wrong, and our hypothetical innovator, if he is wise, will come to see that the introduction of ' ∞', in the way he originally intended, was illegitimate. Sooner or later he will encounter Cantor's demonstration that for every number, x, the number 2^x must be definitely greater—or find some simpler demonstration that the concept of '*the* greatest number' is incoherent and leads to contradiction. The only outcome of the investigation may be the well-grounded conviction that it makes no sense to talk of 'the greatest number', that the attempt to extend the series of natural numbers by imagining a final term 'beyond all of them' must lead to contradiction. The investigation might therefore be called an instance of 'the indirect proof of nonsense'. That the desired extension is inadmissible, though a negative result, is as valuable as such other negative results in mathematics as the impossibility of trisecting the angle, and the like. The work done to reach this result cannot reasonably be regarded as wasted—nor the method employed in reaching it as irrational. For very often it is not possible to tell in advance whether a proposed extension of a familiar mathematical concept will work or not. The attempt to give explicit definitions that would satisfy a logician's standards of clarity may well be premature, because the concept itself is still confused, but the analogy that prompts the use of the new concept and the new symbolism is sufficiently definite for an extended trial to be possible. The mathematician works *with* the new concept in order to discover for himself what the concept is—and, if necessary, in order finally to reject it. (The history of the infinitesimal calculus provides well-known and striking cases of this kind of development). The capacities and the limitations of the new concept are discovered by using it, and can often be discovered in no other way.

A metaphysician often works in a way that seems strikingly similar to the foregoing. He argues perhaps that just as the sum-total of all the existing things in his study is only a part of all the existing things in his house, while that in turn is merely a part of a larger class of existing things and so on indefinitely, it should be possible to conceive of 'the universe' as the largest class of all existing things. Like the mathematician who introduced the symbol, ' ∞', the metaphysician introduces a new expression, formed by analogy with familiar expressions, and therefore governed by determinate rules of use. The expression 'the universe' is not a piece of gibberish, but rather something that is subject to fairly strict antecedent controls. Whether the extension of language and thought that is being attempted will work is something that remains to be shown by the innovator's success in incorporating the new concept into his old system. Even if the outcome is negative, and the proper conclusion has to be that the desired innovation is illegitimate, the labour will not have been in vain.

I believe an account on these lines will do justice to Wittgenstein's procedure in the book (to the extent that this procedure is not sufficiently covered by my earlier remarks about logical syntax). In searching for the 'essence', he is constantly stretching words 'towards a generality foreign to their ordinary usage' (to use Whitehead's phrase). By the 'world' he does not mean the physical cosmos, but something vaster and philosophically more interesting; by a 'name' he means not the familiar names of persons and places, but the 'pure name' whose necessary existence follows from the over-arching conception of what language in its essence must really be like, and similarly for the other expressions that he uses in 'stretched' ways. Such an exercise in 'revisionary metaphysics' (to use Strawson's phrase) is neither absurd nor self-authenticating. Wittgenstein is trying out a new way of looking at the world, which forces him to twist and bend language to the expression of his new thoughts. His own conclusion that the new vision is incoherent was a result that had to be won by severe mental labour, and could not have been achieved by any short-cut—such as the automatic application of some principle of verifiability. A negative metaphysics, such as that of the *Tractatus*, has its own rules of procedure: the ladder must be *used* before it can be thrown away.

I have been arguing that a metaphysician is a man who is trying to enlarge and extend the given concepts of science and ordinary life in a way which will allow him to arrive at a more extensive, a more penetrating, and in some way more fundamental, view of the universe. In pursuing this aim, he proceeds by analogy and metaphor. He breaks through the bounds of the logical syntax he inherited, but without discarding *all* the linguistic principles in a single fell swoop. His adherence to some of the antecedent rules of logical syntax provides him with guarantees that his use of the new and only partially understood concepts shall be sufficiently systematic to render logical inference and elaboration possible. If the fullest examination of the new system of thought uncovers no internal contradictions, the philosopher will have managed to introduce a new language and a new way of looking at the world. But if the outcome is negative and the original attempt has in the end to be abandoned as abortive, it by no means follows that the metaphysical innovator was engaged in a futile and self-condemned enterprise. If this were the correct verdict then much of the most valuable and radical conceptual changes in scientific thought would equally have to be condemned as nonsensical in a pejorative sense of that word. For clarity arrives at the end of a conceptual investigation, not at its beginning. And if all were clear at the outset, there would be no point in the investigation.

SIGLA

A: a sign (3.203)

$=$: equality, identity (4.241, 4.242, 4.243, 5.5302, 5.531, 5.532, 5.5321, 5.534, 5.5351)

$\mathbf{v}$: sign of disjunction (5.42, 5.461, 5.515)

$\supset$: sign of implication (5.42, 5.461, 6.1201, 6.1203, 6.1221)

$\sim$: sign of negation (4.0621, 5.44, 5.515). See also: $\sim p$

$p\mathbf{v}q$: p or q (3.3441, 5.1311, 5.46, 5.513, 5.515)

$p.q$: p and q (5.1241, 5.513, 6.1203)

$\sim p$: not-p (3.3441, 4.061–4.0621, 4.431, 5.02, 5.1311, 5.254, 5.42–5.44, 5.451, 5.46, 5.51, 5.512, 6.1201, 6.1203)

$p|q$: neither p nor q (5.1311)

T: true (a truth-value) (4.31, 4.43, 4.44, 4.441, 6.1203)

F: false (a truth-value) (4.31, 4.441, 6.1203)

$(WWFW)(p, q)$: abbreviated representation of a truth-table (4.442, 5.101)

K_n: number of possibilities of holding and non-holding of n atomic facts (4.27)

L_n: number of possibilities of agreement and disagreement of a statement with truth-possibilities (4.42, 4.45)

W_r: number of truth-grounds of a statement, r (5.15, 5.151)

W_{rs}: number of s's truth-grounds shared by r (5.15, 5.151)

$\vdash$: Frege's assertion sign (4.442)

x: variable name (4.1272, 4.24)

fx: a function of one variable (4.24, 5.501, 5.52, 5.525)

$(x).fx$: a general statement ('for all x, f of x') (4.0411, 5.1311, 5.441, 5.521)

fa: a singular statement (4.1211, 5.1311, 5.441, 5.47, 6.1201)

$(\exists x)$: the existential quantifier (5.441, 5.451, 5.46, 5.47)

$(\exists x, y)$: the existential quantifier (two variables) (4.1272)

$(\exists x).fx$: the generalized statement ('there is an x such that f of x') (5.52, 5.521, 5.525, 5.46)

$(\exists x, \phi).\phi x$: a completely generalized statement (5.5261)

Sigla

$\phi(x, y)$:   a function of two variables (4.24)

$F(fx)$:   a function of a function (3.333)

aRb: sign for relational statement (3.1432, 4.012, 4.1252, 4.1273, 5.5151)

$(\exists x):aRx \cdot xRb$:   a term of a formal series (4.1252, 4.1273)

ξ: a variable statement (5.501, 5.502, 5.51, 5.52)

$(\bar{\xi})$:   Wittgenstein's sign for brackets containing statements (5.501)

$O'\xi$:   an operation (5.2521)

$[a, x, O'x]$:   general term of a formal series (5.2522)

$(\dots W)(\xi, \dots)$:   operation of simultaneous denial (5.5, 5.502)

$\mathcal{N}(\bar{\xi})$:   simultaneous denial (abbreviated form) (5.502, 5.51, 5.52, 6, 6.01, 6.001)

$\Omega'(\bar{\eta})$:   general form of operation for obtaining one statement from others (6.01)

$[\bar{p}, \bar{\xi}, \mathcal{N}(\bar{\xi})]$:   general form of truth-function (6)

$[0, \xi, \xi+1]$:   general form of an integer (6.03)

0:   zero (4.4611)

$1+1+1+1$:   example of an arithmetical expression (6.231)

$2 \times 2 = 4$:   the arithmetical formula so expressed (6.241)

$+_c$:   sign of addition for cardinal numbers (5.02)

$\sharp$:   sharp (in musical notation) (4.013)

$\flat$:   flat (in musical notation) (4.013)

GERMAN CONCORDANCE

Note: Words in square brackets are renderings in Ogden's translation that may be held dubious.

'**A denkt p**': '*A* thinks *p*' (an example). 5.541, 5.542

'**A glaubt, dass p der Fall ist**': '*A* believes that *p* is the case' (an example). 5.541, 5.542

'**A sagt p**': '*A* says *p*' (an example). 5.542

'**A urteilt p**': '*A* judges *p*' (an example). 5.5422

a priori: *a priori*. Cf. *analytisch, von vornherein*. 2.225, 3.04, 3.05, 5.133, 5.4541, 5.4731, 5.55, 5.5541, 5.5571, 5.634, 6.31, 6.3211–6.34, 6.35

abbilden: to depict, to picture, to represent. Ct. *darstellen*. 2.17, 2.171, 2.172, 2.18, 2.19, 2.201, 4.013, 4.016, 4.041

abbildende Beziehung: depicting, representing relationship. See *bezeichnende Beziehung, darstellende Beziehung*. 2.1513, 2.1514, 4.014

Abbildung: depiction, representation. Ct. *Darstellung*. 2.15, 2.151, 2.17, 2.172, 2.181, 2.2, 2.22, 4.015, 4.016

Aberglaube: superstition. 5.1361

Abgebildete: that which is depicted or represented. 2.16, 2.161, 2.2

abgeschlossen: closed. 5.4541

abgrenzen: delimit. Cf. *begrenzen, Grenze*. 4.112, 4.114

abhängen: to depend (upon). Ct. *unabhängig, selbständig*. 2.0211, 3.315, 3.342, 4.411, 5.231, 5.25, 5.474

'**Ablauf der Zeit**': passage of time. 6.3611

ableiten: to derive. 4.0141, 4.243, 6.127, 6.1271

Abmachung: agreement, convention, [adjustment]. Cf. *Übereinkunft. Festsetzung*. 4.002

abnehmen: to decrease, shrink, wane. Ct. *zunehmen*. 6.43

Abschluss: terminus. 6.372

absprechen: deny (a property). Ct. *zusprechen*. 4.124

abstrakt: abstract. Ct. *konkret*. 5.5563

Abzeichen: distinguishing mark. 4.43, 4.44

Addition, logische: logical addition, alternation. 5.2341

Additionszeichen: addition sign. 5.02

Ähnlichkeit: similarity. 4.0141, 5.231

ahnen: to anticipate, think, conceive. 5.4541

Ahnung: notion, idea. 4.002, 6.3211

alle: all. Cf. *sämtlich*. 1.11, 2.0124, 4.51, 4.52, 5.521, 5.524

'**alle Menschen sind sterblich**': 'All men are mortal' (an example). 6.1232

'**alle Rosen sind entweder gelb oder rot**': 'All roses are either yellow or red' (an example). 6.111

allgemein: general. Ct. *speziell*. 3.3441, 4.1273, 4.411, 5.156, 5.242, 5.2522, 5.46, 5.472, 5.526–5.5262, 6.1231, 6.3432

allgemeine Form: general form. 3.312, 4.1273, 6, 6.002, 6.01, 6.022, 6.03

allgemeine Regel: general rule. 4.0141

allgemeine Satzform: general statement form. 4.5, 4.53, 5.47, 5.471, 5.54

allgemeiner Bau: general structure. 5.5262

allgemeiner Satz: general statement. 4.1273

Allgemeineres: (something) more general. Ct. *Spezielleres*. 5.454

allgemeines Glied: general term. 4.1273, 5.2522

allgemeines Urzeichen: general primitive term. Cf. *Urzeichen*. 5.46

Allgemeingültigkeit: holding as a general truth, [general validity]. 6.1231, 6.1232

Allgemeinheit: generality. Cf. *Verallgemeinerung*. 5.1311, 5.521, 6.031

Allgemeinheitsbezeichnung: (the) generality sign, [notation for generality]. 3.24, 4.0411, 5.522, 5.523, 6.1203

allgemeinste: most general. 4.5, 5.46, 5.472, 6.01

allgemeinste Form: most general form. 5.46, 6.01

allgemeinste Satzform: most general statement form. Cf. *Form des Satzes*. 4.5, 5.472

allumfassend: all-encompassing. 5.511

Alten: (the) ancients. 6.372

'ambulo': (an example). 4.032

Analyse: analysis. 3.25, 3.3442, 4.221

analysieren: to analyse. Cf. *zergliedern, zerlegen*. 3.201, 4.1274

analytisch: analytic. Cf. *a priori*. 6.11

ändern: to alter, change. = *verändern*. 4.465, 6.43, 6.431

andeuten: to indicate. Cf. *anzeigen, hinweisen*. 4.24, 5.501

Angabe: (the) giving. Cf. *Beschreibung*. 3.317, 4.26, 5.501, 5.554

angeben: to give. Cf. *beschreiben*. 3.032, 3.251, 4.063, 4.1273, 4.5, 5.4711, 5.55, 5.5541, 5.5571, 6.35

angehören: to belong. = *gehören*. 3.323, 6.126, 6.211

Angenehmes: (something) pleasant, agreeable. Ct. *Unangenehmes*. 6.422

anlegen: to set against, apply. 2.1512

Annahme: assumption. 4.063, 6.4312

annehmen: to assume. 5.154, 6.363, 6.374

anschaulich: intuitive, pictorial. 6.1203

Anschauung: intuition. Cf. *Einsicht*. 6.233, 6.2331, 6.45

Ansehen: inspection. 5.551, 6.122

Antwort: answer. Cf. *beantworten*. Ct. *Frage*. 5.4541, 6.5, 6.51, 6.52

anwenden: (1) to apply; (2) to use. = *verwenden*. Cf. *successive Anwendung*. 3.202, 3.323, 3.5, 5.452, 5.5521, 6.123

Anwendung: application, use. 3.202, 3.262, 5.2521, 5.2523, 5.5, 5.557, 6.126

Anzahl: number. Cf. *Zahl*. 4.1272, 5.474–5.476, 5.55, 5.553, 6.1271, 6.341

Anzeichen: indication, mark [symptom]. Cf. *kennzeichnen*. 4.464, 6.111, 6.1231

anzeigen: to indicate, show. Cf. *andeuten*. 3.322, 4.0411, 4.442, 6.121, 6.124

Apparat: apparatus. 6.3431

äquivalent: equivalent. 5.232, 5.2523, 5.47321, 5.514, 6.1261

Argument: argument (of a function). See also *Wahrheitsargument*. 3.333, 4.431, 5.02, 5.251, 5.47, 5.523, 5.5351, 6.1203

Argumentstelle: argument place. 2.0131, 4.0411, 5.5351

Arithmetik: arithmetic. 4.4611

Art: (1) way. = *Weise*; (2) kind, sort. See also *Art und Weise*. 3.325, 3.34, 4.061, 5.132, 5.451, 5.501, 5.541, 5.5423, 6.126, 6.342, 6.422

Art und Weise: mode and fashion, [way]. 2.031, 2.032, 2.14, 2.15,

2.17, 3.14, 3.261, 3.321, 3.323, 3.3441, 4.013, 4.1273, 5.3, 5.4733, 6.12, 6.341

artikuliert: articulated. Cf. *gegliedert*. 3.141, 3.251

Ästhetik: aesthetics. 6.421

Asymmetrie: asymmetry. 6.3611

aufeinmal: once for all, [on one occasion]. See also *ohne weiteres*. 5.47

auffassen: to conceive. 3.314, 3.318, 4.1271, 5.541, 5.5421, 6.111, 6.1265, 6.231, 6.3611

Auffassung: conception. 2.1513, 4.062, 4.1213, 6.125

Aufgabe: task. Cf. *Problem*. 6.4321

aufheben: to cancel. 4.462, 5.253

aufhören: to cease. 6.431

Auflösung: dissolution. 3.3442, 4.466

Aufschluss: information. 3.3421, 3.3441

aufstellen: to set up, state (a rule), establish. Cf. *stellen*. 3.33, 4.12, 5.5542

Aufstellung: establishment [drawing up]. 3.331, 6.422

auftreten: to occur. = *eintreffen*, *eintreten*, *vorkommen*. 2.0122, 5.233, 5.4733, 5.523

aufweisen: to show forth, display, mirror. Cf. *spiegeln*, *zeigen*. Ct. *darstellen*, *sagen*. 2.172, 4.121

Aufzählung: enumeration. 5.501

Auge: eye. 5.633, 5.6331

Ausdruck: expression. Cf. *Klammerausdruck*. Pref.(3), 3.262, 3.31–3.314, 3.318, 3.323, 3.33, 4.03, 4.122, 4.126, 4.1272, 4.1273, 4.242, 4.243, 4.4, 4.431, 4.442, 5.22, 5.24, 5.242, 5.476, 5.503, 5.525, 5.526, 5.5351, 6.23, 6.232, 6.2322, 6.2323, 6.24

ausdrücken: to express. Pref.(1), (7), 3.1, 3.12, 3.13, 3.142, 3.1431, 3.2, 3.24, 3.251, 3.34, 3.341, 3.3441, 4.002, 4.013, 4.0411, 4.121, 4.124, 4.125, 4.126, 4.1272, 4.1273, 4.241,

4.43, 4.431, 4.441, 4.5, 5.131, 5.242, 5.31, 5.503, 5.5151, 5.525, 5.53, 5.5301, 5.535, 5.5352, 6.1203, 6.124, 6.21, 6.2321, 6.24, 6.42, 6.43

Ausdrucksform: form of expression. 3.143

Ausdrucksweise: mode of expression. 4.015, 5.21, 5.526, 6.361

auseinanderlegen: to take apart, analyse. Cf. *analysieren*, *zergliedern*, *zerlegen*. 3.261

ausgezeichnete Zahl: pre-eminent number. 4.128, 5.453, 5.553

auskommen: to get along with, make do with. 6.122

Aussage: assertion. See also *Satz*. 2.0201, 6.3751

aussagen: to say, assert. Cf. *aussprechen*, *behaupten*, *sagen*. 3.317, 3.332, 4.03, 4.1241, 4.242, 4.442, 5.25, 6.124, 6.1264, 6.342

ausschliessen: to exclude. 3.325, 6.3611, 6.362, 6.3751

aussehen: to appear, look. 3.031, 3.143

äussere Form: external form. 4.002

ausserhalb: outside, beyond. 2.0121, 2.173, 2.174, 4.0641, 4.12, 5.513, 6.3, 6.41, 6.4312

äusserlich: externally. 3.323, 3.325

aussprechen: to state, declare. Cf. *aussagen*, *sagen*. 3.221, 3.262, 4.116, 6.421, 6.5

Auszug: abstract, extract. 5.156

Axiom: axiom. 6.341

Axiom of Infinity: Whitehead and Russell's axiom of that name. 5.535

Axiom of Reducibility: Whitehead and Russell's axiom of that name. 6.1232 6.1233

Basis: base, basis. 5.21, 5.22, 5.234, 5.24, 5.25, 5.251, 5.442, 5.54

Bau: construction. Cf. *Gebäude*, *Gebilde*. 5.45, 5.5262, 6.341

bauen: to construct. = *bilden, konstruieren.* 4.002, 6.002

Baustein: building block, brick. 6.341

beantworten: to answer. Cf. *Antwort.* Ct. *fragen.* 4.003, 4.1274, 5.55, 5.551, 6.233, 6.5, 6.52

bedeuten: to mean, stand for. Cf. *bezeichnen.* 3.203, 4.002, 4.111, 4.115, 4.243, 4.3, 4.31, 4.43, 5.47321, 5.6, 5.62, 6.2322, 6.3

Bedeutung: meaning. Ct. *Sinn.* 3.203, 3.261, 3.263, 3.3, 3.314, 3.315, 3.317, 3.323, 3.328, 3.33, 3.331, 3.333, 4.026, 4.126, 4.241, 4.242, 4.243, 4.466, 4.5, 5.02, 5.31, 5.451, 5.461, 5.4733, 5.535, 5.55, 6.124, 6.126, 6.232, 6.2322, 6.53

Bedeutungsgleichheit: identity, [equality] of meaning. Cf. *Gleichung.* 6.2323

bedeutungslos: meaningless. Cf. *sinnlos.* 3.328, 4.442, 4.4661, 5.47321

bedeutungsvoll: meaningful. Cf. *sinnvoll.* 5.233, 5.461

bedingen: to imply, [guarantee]. 3.04

Bedingung: condition. See also *Wahrheitsbedingung.* 4.41, 4.461, 4.462

bedingungslos: unconditionally. 4.461

bedürfen: to need. = *brauchen.* 5.461

begrenzen: to demarcate. Cf. *abgrenzen, Grenze.* 4.113, 4.114, 4.463, 4.51, 5.5262, 5.5561, 6.45

begrenztes Ganzes: limited, bounded. whole. 6.45

Begriff: concept. See also *eigentlicher B., formaler B., Grundbegriff, Wahrheitsbegriff, Zahlbegriff.* 4.12721, 4.1273, 5.2523, 5.521, 5.555, 6.022

Begriff, eigentlicher. See *eigentlicher Begriff*

Begriff, formaler. See *formaler Begriff*

Begriffsschrift: concept script (or language), ideography, [logical symbolism]. See also *Notation.* 3.325, 4.1272, 4.1273, 4.431, 5.533, 5.534

Begriffswort: concept word. 4.1272

Begründung: foundation. Cf. *Grund.* 6.3631

behaupten: to assert. Cf. *aussagen, aussprechen, Urteilstrich.* 4.122, 4.21, 6.2322

Behelf: expedient. Cf. *Hilfsmittel.* 4.242, 5.452

beiläufig: incidentally, [roughly]. 2.0232, 5.5303

bejahen: to affirm. Ct. *verneinen.* 5.124, 5.1241, 5.44, 5.513, 5.514

Bejahung: affirmation. Ct. *Verneinung.* 4.064, 5.44, 6.231

bekleidet: clothed. 4.002

belanglos: irrelevant. 6.422

beliebig: arbitrary. Cf. *willkürlich, zufällig.* 4.466, 6.341

benennen: to name. = *nennen.* Cf. *Name.* 3.144

benützen: to use. Cf. *gebrauchen.* 3.11, 5.451, 5.461, 5.5351, 6.211

berechnen: to calculate out. Cf. *Rechnung.* 6.126

Bereich: scope. 4.0411

bereits: already. = *schon.* 2.012, 3.263, 3.333, 4.12721, 4.241, 5.47, 6.124

berufen, sich: to appeal. 5.525

berühren: to touch. 2.15121, 2.1515, 5.557

beschaffen: constructed. 6.121

beschreiben: to describe. Cf. *angeben.* See also *vollständig b.* 3.144, 4.016, 4.023, 4.063, 4.0641, 4.26, 5.501, 5.634, 6.124, 6.341, 6.342, 6.35, 6.3611, 6.362

Beschreibung: description. Cf. *Angabe, Weltbeschreibung.* 2.02331, 3.24, 3.317, 3.33, 4.023, 4.5, 5.02, 5.156, 5.4711, 5.472, 5.501, 6.125, 6.341, 6.3611

Besitz: possession. 4.1213

besitzen: to possess. 3.34, 4.04, 4.123, 4.1271, 6.111, 6.12

Bestandteil: constituent. Cf. *Element, Satzbestandteil.* 2.011, 2.0201, 3.24, 3.315, 3.4, 4.024, 5.4733, 5.533, 5.5423, 6.12

bestätigen: to confirm. Cf. *bewahrheiten.* Ct. *widerlegen.* 5.154, 6.1222

bestehen: (1) to obtain, hold, [exist]; (2) to consist. 2, 2.0121, 2.023, 2.024, 2.034, 2.04, 2.05, 2.06, 2.062, 2.11, 2.14, 2.1514, 2.201, 2.222, 3.14, 4.014, 4.0141, 4.1, 4.112, 4.122, 4.124, 4.125, 4.2, 4.21, 4.22, 4.221, 4.2211, 4.25, 4.27, 4.3, 5.131, 5.135, 5.55, 6.51

Bestehende: (that which) persists, exists. Cf. *Feste.* 2.027, 2.0271

bestimmen: to determine. Cf. *festsetzen, festlegen.* 1.11, 1.12, 2.0231, 2.05, 3.24, 3.315, 3.327, 3.342, 3.4, 3.42, 4.063, 4.0641, 4.1273, 4.241, 4.431, 4.463, 5.473, 6.341

bestimmt: definite, determinate. 2.031, 2.14, 2.15, 3.14, 3.251, 4.466, 5.475, 5.5151, 6.12, 6.124, 6.342, 6.3432

Bestimmtheit: definiteness. 3.23

Bestimmung: determination. 4.431, 5.473

bestreitbares Gebiet: controversial domain. 4.113

Beurteilung: judgement (of the truth of a statement). 4.063

bewahrheiten: to verify. Cf. *bestätigen.* 5.101

Bewegungsfreiheit: degree of freedom. 4.463

Beweis: proof. 6.126, 6.1262, 6.1263, 6.1264, 6.1265, 6.241

beweisen: to prove. = *erweisen.* See also *nachweisen, demonstrieren.* 4.5, 6.126, 6.1263, 6.2321

bezeichnen: to signify, designate. Cf. *bedeuten.* See also *symbolisieren.* 3.24, 3.261, 3.321–3.323, 3.325, 3.333, 3.334, 3.3411, 3.344, 4.061,

4.063, 4.126, 4.127, 4.1272, 4.243, 4.442, 5.42, 5.473, 5.476, 5.5541, 6.111

bezeichnende Beziehung: designating relationship. See *abbildende Beziehung, darstellende Beziehung.* 5.4733, 5.5261

Bezeichnete: that which is designated or signified. 3.317, 4.012, 4.061

Bezeichnung: designation, signification. Cf. *Zeichen.* See also *Allgemeinheitsbezeichnung.* 3.322, 5.02

Bezeichnungsweise: mode of designation or signification. 3.322, 3.3421, 4.0411, 5.1311

Beziehung: relation. See also *Relation.* Cf. *abbildende B., bezeichnende B., darstellende B.* 3.12, 3.1432, 3.24, 4.0412, 4.061, 4.1252, 4.4661, 5.131, 5.1311, 5.22, 5.42, 5.461, 5.5151, 5.5301

bezweifeln: to doubt. Cf. *Zweifel.* 6.51

Bild: picture. See also *logisches B.* 2.0212, 2.1–3.01, 3.42, 4.01, 4.011, 4.012, 4.021, 4.03, 4.0311, 4.032, 4.06, 4.462, 4.463, 5.156, 6.341, 6.342, 6.35

Bildelement: picture element. Cf. *Element.* 2.1515

bilden: to construct. = *bauen, konstruieren.* 2.021, 2.0231, 2.0272, 4.002, 4.51, 5.4733, 5.475, 5.501, 5.503, 5.512, 5.514, 5.5151, 5.555, 6.126, 6.1271

Bildhaftigkeit: pictoriality. 4.013, 4.015

Bindewort: conjunction. 4.025

bloss: mere. 6.126

böse: evil. Ct. *gut.* 6.43

brauchen: to need. = *bedürfen.* 4.464, 5.131, 5.5301, 5.552, 6.031, 6.211, 6.233, 6.343

Buchstabe: letter. 3.333, 4.24

Buchstabenschrift: writing by means of letters. 4.011, 4.016

Charakter: character. 6.111, 6.124
charakterisieren: to characterize. Cf. *kennzeichnen*. 3.31, 3.312, 5.25, 6.12, 6.23, 6.342
charakteristisch: characteristic. 3.311
charakteristischer Zug: characteristic feature. 4.126
Chronometer: chronometer. 6.3611
circulus vitiosus: vicious circle. 4.1273

darstellen: to present. = *vorstellen* (1). See *zeigen*, *abbilden*. Ct. *aufweisen*, *sagen*. 2.0231, 2.173, 2.201, 2.202, 2.203, 2.22, 2.221, 3.032, 3.0321, 3.312, 3.313, 4.011, 4.021, 4.031, 4.04, 4.1, 4.115, 4.12, 4.121, 4.122, 4.124, 4.125, 4.126, 4.1271, 4.1272, 4.31, 4.462, 5.21, 6.1203, 6.124, 6.1264, 6.3751
darstellende Beziehung: presenting relationship. See *abbildende Beziehung*, *bezeichnende Beziehung*. 4.462
Darstellung: presentation. 2.173, 2.174, 4.242
Darwinsche Theorie: the Darwinian theory. 4.1122
Dasein: existence. Cf. *Existenz*. 5.45
Deckung: coincidence. 6.36111
definieren: to define. Cf. *einführen*. 3.261, 5.42, 6.02
Definition: definition. Cf. *Einführung*. 3.24, 3.26, 3.261, 3.343, 4.241, 5.451, 5.452, 5.5302
definitiv: definitive. Pref.(8)
demonstrieren: to demonstrate. See also *beweisen*, *erweisen*, *nachweisen*. 6.121
denkbar: thinkable. Cf. *Sagbare*. 3.001, 3.02, 4.114, 6.361
denken: to think. Cf. *Gedanke*. Pref. (1), (3), 2.0121, 2.013, 2.022, 3.02, 3.03, 3.11, 3.5, 4.01, 4.116, 5.4731, 5.541, 5.542, 5.61, 5.631, 6.1233

Denkprozesse: process of thought. 4.1121
der-Fall-sein: be-the-case. 5.5542
derselbe (**dieselbe**, **dasselbe**): the same. Cf. *gleich*. Ct. *verschieden*. 3.203, 3.322, 3.323, 3.341, 4.1211, 4.241, 4.243, 4.465, 5.141, 5.41, 5.43, 5.441, 5.513, 6.232, 6.2322
Devise: motto. 3.328
Dimension: dimension. Cf. *Mannigfaltigkeit*. 5.475
Ding: thing. = *Gegenstand*, *Sache*. 1.1, 2.01–2.0122, 2.013, 2.02331, 2.151, 3.1431, 3.221, 4.0311, 4.063, 4.1272, 4.243, 5.5301, 5.5303, 5.5351, 5.5352, 5.553, 5.634, 6.1231
doppelte Verneinung: double negation. 5.44, 6.231
Druck: printing. 3.143
drucken: to print. 3.143, 4.011
Dualismus: dualism. 4.128
'Du sollst . . .': 'thou shalt . . .' (form of an ethical law). 6.422
durchgreifen: to reach through, extend. 3.42
Dynamische Modelle: dynamic model. 4.04

Ebene: plane. 6.36111
eigen: own. 5.251, 5.2521
Eigenschaft: property. Cf. *externe E.*, *interne E.*, *logische E.*, *materielle E.* 2.01231, 2.0231, 2.0233, 2.02331, 4.023, 4.063, 4.122, 4.123, 4.1241, 5.473, 5.5302, 6.111, 6.12, 6.231, 6.35
Eigenschaftswort: adjective. 3.323, 4.025, 5.4733
eigentlich: actual. Cf. *wirklich*. 3.3411, 4.1272, 5.46
eigentliche Relation: proper relation. 4.122
eigentlicher Begriff: proper concept. Ct. *formaler Begriff*. 4.126
eigentlicher Name: actual name. 3.3411

eigentliches Begriffswort: proper concept word. 4.1272

eigentliches Zeichen: proper sign. 4.1272

Eigentümliche: (the) peculiarity. 5.522

einfach: simple. Ct. *komplex*. 2.02, 3.201, 3.202, 3.21, 3.23, 3.24, 4.026, 4.24, 5.4541

einfache Relation: simple relation. 5.553

einfacher: simpler. 6.341, 6.342

einfaches Symbol: simple symbol. 3.24, 4.24

einfaches Zeichen: simple sign. Ct. *komplexes Zeichen*. See also *Name*. 3.201, 3.202, 3.21, 3.23, 4.026, 5.02

Einfachheit: simplicity. 5.4541

einfachste: (the) simplest (thing). 4.21, 5.5563, 6.363, 6.3631

einführen: to introduce. Cf. *definieren*. 3.42, 4.12721, 4.241, 5.451, 5.452, 5.46, 5.521

Einführung: introduction. Cf. *Definition*. 4.0411, 4.411, 5.451, 5.452

einheitlich: unified. 6.341

Einklang: harmony, agreement. 6.363

einleuchten: to be obvious. Cf. *klar, offenbar, von selbst verstehen*. 5.1363, 5.42, 5.4731, 5.5301, 6.1271

Eins: one (and the same). 2.027, 4.014, 5.621, 6.421

einsehen: to see, perceive. = *ersehen*. 6.2321

Einsicht: insight. Cf. *Anschauung*. 6.211, 6.34

eintreffen: to occur. = *auftreten, eintreten, vorkommen*. 5.153, 5.154, 5.155, 6.3611

eintreten: to occur. = *auftreten, eintreffen, vorkommen*. 5.441, 6.3611, 6.3631

einzigartig: peculiar. 6.112

Element: element. Cf. *Bildelement, Satzelement, Bestandteil*. 2.13, 2.131, 2.14, 2.15, 2.151, 2.1514, 3.14, 3.2, 3.201, 3.42

Elementarsatz: elementary statement. 4.21–4.221, 4.23, 4.24, 4.243–4.26, 4.28, 4.3–4.42, 4.431, 4.45, 4.46, 4.51, 4.52, 5, 5.01, 5.101, 5.134, 5.152, 5.234, 5.3–5.32, 5.41, 5.47, 5.5, 5.524, 5.5262, 5.55, 5.555–5.5562, 5.557, 5.5571, 6.001, 6.124, 6.3751

empfinden: to perceive. Cf. *wahrnehmen*. 4.012

empirische Realität: empirical reality. 5.5561

endlos: endless. Cf. *unendlich*. 6.4311

entbehrlich: dispensable. Cf. *überflüssig*. 5.4731

entgegengesetzt: opposed, opposite. 4.0621, 4.461, 5.1241, 5.513

entgehen: to avoid. 3.325

enthalten: to contain. 2.014, 2.203, 3.02, 3.13, 3.24, 3.263, 3.313, 3.318, 3.332, 3.333, 4.063, 5.02, 5.121, 5.122, 5.44, 5.47

entnehmen: to draw from, [understand]. 4.002, 5.132

entscheiden: to decide. 5.551, 5.553, 5.557, 5.62

Entscheidende: (the) decisive (thing). 6.124

entsprechen: to correspond. See also *vertreten*. 2.13, 3.2, 3.21, 3.315, 4.0621, 4.063, 4.28, 4.441, 4.466, 5.5542

entstehen: to arise. Cf. *zustandekommen*. 5.232, 5.233, 5.3

entwerfen: to sketch, [form]. 2.0212

Ereignis: event, occurrence. 5.1361, 5.153, 5.154, 5.155, 5.452, 6.3611, 6.422, 6.4311

Erfahrung: experience. 5.552, 5.553, 5.634, 6.1222, 6.363

erfinden: to invent. 5.555

Erforschung: investigation. Cf. *Untersuchung*. 6.3

erfüllen: to satisfy. 3.341, 4.463, 5.61, 5.47321
ergeben: to yield. 6.12, 6.1201
Erhaltungsgesetz: law of conservation. 6.33
erkennen: to recognize, perceive. Cf. *ersehen*. 2.223, 2.224, 3.05, 3.326, 4.002, 5.02, 6.113, 6.1203, 6.122, 6.1262, 6.54
Erkenntnistheorie: theory of knowledge. 4.1121, 5.541
erklären: to explain. 3.263, 4.02, 4.021, 4.026, 4.0412, 5.452, 5.5423, 6.1232, 6.372
Erklärung: explanation. 4.0412, 4.063, 4.431, 5.5422, 6.112, 6.371
erlaubt: permitted. Ct. *unerlaubt*. 5.473
erläutern: to elucidate. 6.54
Erläuterung: elucidation. 3.263, 4.112
erleben: to live through. 6.4311
erledigen, sich: to get dispatched, [disappear]. Cf. *verschwinden*. 4.1251, 5.535
erschaffen: to create. 5.123
erschliessen: to infer. 5.1361
ersehen: to perceive. = *einsehen*. Cf. *erkennen*. 5.13, 6.1221, 6.232
ersetzbar: translatable. 4.241, 6.23, 6.24
ersetzen: to replace, substitute, translate. 3.344, 3.3441, 4.241, 6.24
erwähnen: to mention. 5.5261
erweisen: to prove. = *beweisen*. 3.3421, 4.011, 5.452
erzeugen: to generate. = *hervorbringen*. 4.1273, 5.3, 5.44, 6.002, 6.126
Ethik: ethics. 6.42, 6.421, 6.422
ethisch: ethical. 6.422, 6.423
ethisches Gesetz: ethical law. 6.422
ewig: for ever. 6.4311, 6.4312
Ewigkeit: eternity. 6.4311
Existenz: existence. Cf. *Dasein*. 3.323, 3.4, 3.411, 4.1274, 5.5151

existieren: to exist. 3.032, 3.24
'existieren': the word 'exist'. Cf. '*ist*'. 3.323
Experiment: experiment. Cf. *Versuch*. 6.2331
Exponent: exponent. 6.021
extern: external. Ct. *intern*. 2.01231, 2.0233, 4.023, 4.1251, 4.1252
externe Eigenschaft: external property. Cf. *materielle Eigenschaft*. 2.01231, 2.0233, 4.023
externe Relation: external relation. 4.122, 4.1252

Faktum: (mathematical) fact. 5.154
Fall: the case. Cf. *So-Sein, Tatsache*. 1, 1.12, 1.21, 2, 2.024, 3.342, 4.024, 5.451, 5.5151, 5.541, 5.61, 6.23, 6.3631
fallen unter: to fall under (a concept), be an instance of. 4.126, 4.127, 4.12721
falsch: false. Ct. *wahr, richtig*. 2.0212, 2.17, 2.173, 2.18, 2.21, 2.223, 2.224, 3.24, 4.003, 4.023, 4.06–4.062, 4.063, 4.25, 4.26, 4.31, 4.431, 4.46, 5.512, 5.5351, 6.111
Falschheit: falsity. Ct. *Wahrheit*. 2.22, 2.222, 4.28, 4.41, 5.5262, 6.113, 6.1203
Farbe: colour. 2.0131, 2.0251, 4.123, 6.3751
Farbenraum: colour space. 2.0131
farbig: coloured. 2.171
Färbigkeit: colouredness. 2.0251
farbiges Bild: coloured picture. 2.171
farblos: colourless. 2.0232
Fehler: mistake. Cf. *Irrtum*. 3.325, 5.4731
Feinheit: fineness. 6.342
Feste: (the) fixed. Cf. *Bestehende*. 2.023, 2.026, 2.027, 2.0271
festlegen: to fix. Cf. *festsetzen*. 5.514
festsetzen: to fix, determine. Cf. *festlegen*. 3.316, 4.442, 5.501

Festsetzung: determination. Cf. *Abmachung, Übereinkunft*. 3.316, 3.317, 5.501

feststellen: to establish, [state]. 4.003, 4.0411, 5.154

Figur: figure. 3.032, 5.5423, 6.342, 6.35, 6.36111

fixiert: fixed, determined. Cf. *bestimmt*. 4.023

Fläche: surface. 6.341

Fleck: spot. 2.0131, 4.063, 6.341, 6.35

Folge: consequence. 6.422

folgen: to follow. 4.1211, 4.52, 5.11, 5.12–5.122, 5.124, 5.13, 5.131, 5.132, 5.1363, 5.14, 5.141, 5.142, 5.152, 5.43, 6.1201, 6.1221, 6.126

folgenschwer: of great consequence, [full of consequences]. 5.452

folgern: to infer. Cf. *erschliessen, ableiten, schliessen*. 5.132, 5.133, 5.134

Folgesatz: consequence. 5.123

fordern: to demand. 6.1223

Forderung: demand, requirement [postulate]. 3.23

Form: form. Ct. *Inhalt*. Cf. *Form, logische* and *Satzform*. See also *Ausdrucksform, Zeichenform*. 2.022–2.0231, 2.025, 2.033, 2.171, 2.174, 2.18, 3.31, 3.333, 4.002, 4.012, 4.063, 4.1241, 4.1271, 4.24–4.242, 5.231, 5.241, 5.2522, 5.46, 5.501, 5.5351, 5.542, 5.5422, 5.554, 5.6331, 6.1201, 6.1203, 6.1224, 6.341, 6.342, 6.35, 6.422

Form der Abbildung: form of depiction, form of representation. 2.15, 2.151, 2.17, 2.172, 2.181, 2.2, 2.22

Form der Darstellung: form of presentation. 2.173, 2.174

Form der Operation: form of operation. 4.1273

Form der Selbständigkeit: form of independence. 2.0122

Form der Tatsache: form of fact. 5.156

Form der Welt: form of the world. 2.026

Form der Wirklichkeit: form of reality. 2.18, 4.121

Form des Beweises: form of proof. 6.1264

Form des Gegenstandes: form of object. 2.0141, 2.0251

Form des Gesetzes: form of law. 6.32

Form des Satzes: form of statement. Cf. *allgemeine Satzform*. 3.311, 3.312, 4.0031, 4.012, 4.5, 5.131, 5.24, 5.451, 5.47, 5.5422, 5.54, 5.55, 5.556, 5.5562

Form des Sinnes: form of sense. 3.13

Form des Zusammenhangs: form of connexion. 2.0122

Form, logische: logical form. 2.0233, 2.18, 2.181, 2.2, 3.315, 3.327, 4.0031, 4.12, 4.121, 4.128, 5.555, 6.23, 6.33

formale Eigenschaft: formal property. 4.122, 4.124, 4.126, 4.1271, 5.231, 6.12, 6.122

formale Relation: formal relation. 4.122, 5.242

formaler Begriff: formal concept. Ct. *eigentlicher Begriff*. 4.126, 4.127, 4.1271, 4.1272, 4.12721, 4.1273, 4.1274

formales Gesetz: formal law. 5.501

Formenreihe: formal series. 4.1252, 4.1273, 5.252, 5.2522, 5.501

Formgebung: form allocation. 6.34

Fortleben: survival. 6.4312

Fortschreiten: (the) advance. 5.252

Frage: question. Ct. *Antwort, Streitfrage*. 4.003, 4.1274, 5.4541, 5.55, 5.551, 5.5542, 5.62, 6.1222, 6.1233, 6.211, 6.233, 6.422, 6.5, 6.51, 6.52

fragen: to question. Ct. *beantworten*. Cf. *sagen*. 4.1274, 5.5542, 6.51

Fragestellung: formulation of a question. Pref.(2), 6.422

Frege: Gottlob Frege. Pref.(6), 3.143, 3.3¹⁸, 3.325, 4.063, 4.1272, 4.1273, 4.431, 4.442, 5.02, 5.132, 5.4, 5.42, 5.451, 5.4733, 5.521, 6.1271, 6.232

fühlbar: palpably. 4.411

fühlen: to feel. Cf. *Gefühl.* 6.1223, 6.52

Fühler: feeler. 2.1515

Funktion: function. See also *Wahrheitsfunktion.* 3.3¹⁸, 3.333, 4.126, 4.1272, 4.12721, 4.24, 5.02, 5.2341, 5.25, 5.251, 5.47, 5.501, 5.52, 5.5301

Funktionszeichen: function sign. 3.333

Ganzes: whole. 6.43, 6.45

Gattung: kind. 5.5351

Gattungsname: class name. 6.321

Gebäude: structure. Cf. *Bau, Gebilde.* 6.341

Gebiet: domain. 4.113, 5.4541

Gebilde: structure. Cf. *Bau, Gebäude.* 4.0141, 5.4541

Gebrauch: use. 3.326, 4.123, 5.252

gebrauchen: to use. Cf. *benützen.* 3.328, 4.1272, 4.241, 5.156, 5.511, 6.124, 6.211

Gedanke: thought. Pref.(1), (3), (6), (7), (8), 3, 3.01, 3.02, 3.04, 3.05, 3.1, 3.12, 3.2, 3.5, 4, 4.002, 4.014, 4.112, 6.21, 6.422

Gefühl: feeling. Cf. *fühlen.* 4.1213, 6.1232, 6.45, 6.53

gegeben: given. 2.0124, 3.24, 3.42, 4.12721, 4.51, 5.442, 5.524, 6.002, 6.124, 6.341, 6.342

Gegenstand: object, thing. Cf. *Ding, Sache.* See also *räumlicher G., zeitlicher G.* 2.01, 2.0121, 2.0123–2.0124, 2.0131–2.02, 2.021, 2.023–2.0233, 2.0251–2.032, 2.13, 2.131, 2.15121, 3.1431, 3.2, 3.203–3.221, 3.322, 3.3411, 4.023, 4.0312, 4.1211, 4.122, 4.123, 4.126, 4.127, 4.1272, 4.12721, 4.2211, 4.431, 4.441,

4.466, 5.02, 5.123, 5.1511, 5.44, 5.524, 5.526, 5.53–5.5302, 5.541, 5.542, 5.5561, 6.3431

Gegenwart: the present. 6.4311

gegenwärtig: present, in the present. 5.1361, 6.4312

gegliedert: articulated. = *artikuliert.* 4.032

gehaltvoll: informative, having content, [substantial]. 6.111

gehorchen: to obey. Cf. *unterstehen.* 3.325

gehören: to belong. = *angehören.* 2.1513, 3.13, 4.442, 4.45, 4.4611, 5.632, 6.4321

gelten: (of statements) to hold. 5.4541, 6.1231, 6.1233, 6.342

gemein haben: to have in common. = *gemeinsam haben.* 2.022, 2.17, 2.18, 2.2, 3.31, 3.321, 4.12, 5.143, 5.152, 5.47, 5.4733, 5.513

gemeinsam: common. 2.02331, 2.16, 3.311, 3.317, 3.322, 3.333, 3.341, 3.3411, 3.343, 3.3441, 4.014, 5.11, 5.512, 5.5261, 5.5302

gemeinsam haben: to have in common. = *gemein haben.* 2.02331, 2.16, 3.341, 3.3411, 3.343, 5.5302

Gemeinsame: (the) common (thing). 3.322, 3.344, 3.3441, 5.143, 5.24, 5.512, 5.513, 6.022

genügen: to be adequate, satisfy. 4.0411, 5.5301, 5.5302, 5.5422, 6.1223, 6.123

Geometrie: geometry. 3.032, 3.0321, 6.35

geometrisch: geometrical. 3.411, 6.35

Gerüst: scaffolding. 3.42, 4.023, 6.124

gesamt: entire. 2.063, 4.11, 4.12

Gesamtheit: totality. 1.1, 1.12, 2.04, 2.05, 3.01, 4.001, 4.11, 4.52, 5.5262, 5.5561

geschehen: to happen. 6.362, 6.37, 6.374, 6.41

Geschwindigkeit: velocity. 6.3751

German Concordance

Gesetz: law. See also *Erhaltungsgesetz, logischesG., formalesG., Kausalitätsgesetz, Naturgesetz.* 3.031, 3.032, 3.0321, 4.0141, 6.1203, 6.123, 6.31, 6.32, 6.321, 6.3211, 6.3431, 6.35, 6.363, 6.422

Gesetz der kleinsten Wirkung: law of least action. 6.321, 6.3211

Gesetz des Widerspruchs: law of contradiction. 6.1203, 6.123

gesetzmässig: lawlike, lawful, [uniform]. 6.361

Gesetzmässigkeit: lawfulness regularity. 6.3

Gesichtsfeld: field of vision. 2.0131, 5.633, 5.6331, 6.3751, 6.4311

Gesichtszug: facial trait. Cf. *Zug.* 4.1221

gewiss: certain. 4.464, 6.3211

Gewissheit: certainty. Ct. *Möglichkeit.* 5.152, 5.156, 5.525

Gewusstes: that which is known. 5.1362

Glaube: belief. 5.1361, 5.1363

glauben: to believe. 5.43, 5.541, 5.542, 6.33, 6.3631

gleich: same. Cf. *identisch.* Ct. *verschieden.* 2.0233, 3.323, 3.325, 3.341, 4.0621

gleichbedeutend: having the same meaning. 4.243

gleichberechtigt: equally justified. 4.061, 6.127

gleiches Zeichen: same sign. 3.325

Gleichgewicht: equilibrium. 6.121

gleichgültig: indifferent. 5.501, 6.432

Gleichheit: identity. Cf. *Identität.* Ct. *Verschiedenheit.* See also *Bedeutungsgleichheit, Zahlengleichheit.* 5.53

Gleichheitszeichen: sign of identity. 3.323, 5.4733, 5.53, 5.5301, 5.533, 6.23, 6.232

Gleichnis: (1) likeness; (2) comparison. 4.012, 4.015, 5.5563

gleichsinnig: having the same sense. 5.515

Gleichung: equation, identity. 4.241, 6.2, 6.22, 6.232, 6.2323, 6.2341, 6.24

gleichwertig: having the same value. Cf. *Wert.* 6.4

Glied: member (of a series). 2.03, 4.1273, 5.232, 5.252, 5.2522, 5.501

Glücklicher: happy (person). Ct. *Unglücklicher.* 6.43

Gnade: grace, favour. 6.374

Gott: God. 3.031, 5.123, 6.372, 6.432

Grad der Wahrscheinlichkeit: degree of probability. 5.155

Gradation: gradation. 4.464

Grammatik: grammar. Cf. *Syntax, logische.* 3.325

Grammophonplatte: gramophone record. 4.014, 4.0141

Grenze: limit. Cf. *abgrenzen, begrenzen.* Pref.(3), (4), 5.143, 5.5561, 5.6, 5.61, 5.62, 5.632, 5.641, 6.43

grenzenlos: unlimited, unbounded. 6.4311

Grenzfall: limiting case. 3.313, 4.466, 5.152

'Grün ist grün': 'Green is green' (an illustration). 3.323

Grund: ground, reason. Cf. *Begründung.* See also *Wahrheitsgrund.* 5.451, 5.5562, 6.3631, 6.521

Grundbegriff: primitive concept. Cf. *Urbild.* 4.12721, 5.451, 5.476

Grundgedanke: fundamental thought. Cf. *Grundsatz.* 4.0312

Grundgesetz: basic law, axiom, [primitive proposition]. 5.43, 5.452, 6.127, 6.1271

'Grundgesetze der Arithmetik': Frege's book of that name. 5.451

Grundlage: foundation. 5.1

grundlegend: fundamental. 4.411

Grundoperation: fundamental operation. 5.474

Grundsatz: fundamental principle. Cf. *Grundgedanke.* 5.551

Gruppe: group. 4.45, 4.46

gut: good. Ct. *böse.* 6.43

Haken: hook, [catch]. 5.511
Hand: hand. 6.36111
handeln: to treat of, be about. 2.0121, 3.24, 3.317, 4.011, 4.122, 5.44, 5.641, 6.124, 6.35
Handlung: action. 5.1362, 6.422
Handschuh: glove. 6.36111
hängen, ineinander: to hang inside one another. 2.03
Härte: hardness. 2.0131
herausheben: to distinguish. 2.02331
herauskommen: to get outside. 4.041
herausstellen, sich: to become plain. 5.453
Hertz: Heinrich Hertz. 4.04, 6.361
hervorbringen: to produce, generate. Cf. *erzeugen*. 5.21
Hervorbringung: production, generation. 3.34
hervorheben: to emphasize, render prominent. 2.02331, 5.21, 5.522
Hierarchie: hierarchy. 5.252, 5.556, 5.5561
Hieroglyphenschrift: hieroglyphic script. 4.016
Hilfsmittel: expedient, resource. Cf. *Behelf*. 6.1262
hinaussteigen: to climb forth. 6.54
hindeuten: to indicate, [show]. = *hinweisen*. 5.461
hinschreiben: to write down. 6.341
hinweisen: to indicate, refer to. = *hindeuten*. See also *andeuten, anzeigen*. 2.02331, 5.02, 5.522
Höhe: pitch (of a note). 2.0131
Höheres: the Higher. 6.42, 6.432
Hypothese: hypothesis. 4.1122, 5.5351, 6.36311
hypothetisch: hypothetically. 5.154

Ich: I, the ego. Cf. *Subjekt*. 5.63, 5.64, 5.641
idealistisch: idealistic. 4.0412
identisch: identical. Cf. *gleich*. 2.161, 4.465, 5.41, 5.42, 5.473, 5.4733, 5.5303, 5.5352, 6.3751

'identisch': the word 'identical'. 3.323
Identität: identity. Cf. *Gleichheit*. 4.0411, 5.5301, 6.2322
Index: index. 4.0411, 5.02
indirekt: indirectly. 5.5151
Individuals: individuals (an English word). 5.553
Induktion: induction. 6.31, 6.363
Inhalt: content. Ct. *Form*. 2.025, 3.13, 3.31
'Inhalt des Satzes': statement content. Ct. *Satzform*. 3.13
innere: inner. Cf. *intern*. Ct. *äussere*. 4.0141, 5.1362
innere Notwendigkeit: internal necessity. Cf. *logische Notwendigkeit*. 5.1362
intern: internal. Cf. *innere, formal*. Ct. *extern*. 3.24, 4.1251, 5.131, 5.231
interne Beziehung: internal relation. = *interne Relation*. 3.24, 4.014, 5.2, 5.21
interne Eigenschaft: internal property. 2.01231, 4.023, 4.122, 4.1221, 4.123, 4.124
interne Relation: internal relation. = *interne Beziehung*. 4.122, 4.123, 4.125, 4.1252, 5.232
Interpunktion: punctuation. 5.4611
involvieren: to involve. 5.156
irren: to be in error. 5.473
Irrtum: mistake. Cf. *Fehler*. 3.325, 3.331
isolieren: isolate. 5.631
'ist': the word 'is'. Cf. *'existieren'*. 3.323

Kant: Immanuel Kant. 6.36111
Kardinalzahl: cardinal number. 5.02
Kausalität: causality. 5.1362
Kausalitätsform: causal form. 6.321
Kausalitätsgesetz: law of causation. 6.32, 6.321, 6.36, 6.362
Kausalnexus: causal nexus. 5.136, 5.1361

kennen: to know. Cf. *wissen.* 2.0123, 2.01231, 3.263, 4.021, 4.243, 5.156, 6.124, 6.2322

kennzeichnen: to characterize, determine. Cf. *charakterisieren.* 3.31, 3.3441, 5.241, 5.5261, 6.2323

Kette: chain. Cf. *Verkettung.* 2.03

Klammer: bracket. 4.441, 5.452, 5.46, 5.461, 5.5, 5.501, 6.1203

Klammerausdruck: bracket expression. 5.2522, 5.501

klar: clear. Pref.(2), 3.251, 4.112, 4.115, 4.116, 5.45, 5.46, 6.1221, 6.372, 6.521

Klarwerden: becoming clear. 4.112, 5.5301

Klärung: clarification. 4.112

Klasse: class. 3.142, 3.311, 3.315, 4.1272, 5.451, 6.031

Klassifikation: classification. 5.454

Kleid: garment, [clothes]. 4.002

kollidieren: to collide, [conflict]. 5.557

Kombination: combination. Cf. *Wahrheitskombination.* 4.27, 4.28, 5.46

Kombinationsregel: rule of combination. 4.442

Komplex: complex. 2.0201, 3.24, 3.3442, 4.1272, 4.441, 5.5423

komplex: complex. Cf. *zusammengesetzt.* Ct. *einfach.* 3.1432, 4.2211, 5.515

komplexes Zeichen: complex sign. Ct. *einfaches Zeichen.* 3.1432

kompliziert: complicated. 4.002, 6.1262

Konfiguration: configuration. 2.0231, 2.0271, 2.0272, 3.21

kongruent: congruent. 6.36111

konkret: concrete. Ct. *abstrakt.* 5.5563

können: to be able to. Cf. *möglich.* Pref.(2)–(4), 2.011–2.0122, 2.0231, 2.161, 2.171, 2.174, 2.18, 2.19, 3.031, 3.142, 3.144, 3.2, 3.221, 3.24, 3.261, 3.263, 3.31, 3.311, 3.341, 4.027, 4.0621 4.063, 4.12, 4.1212, 4.122, 5.123, 5.1311, 5.132, 5.1361,

5.1362, 5.233, 5.253, 5.254, 5.473–5.4732, 5.55, 5.5542, 5.5571, 5.61, 5.631, 5.634, 6.113, 6.122

konstant: constant. Ct. *variabel.* 3.312, 4.126, 4.1271

Konstant: constant. Ct. *Variable.* 3.313, 5.522

konstruieren: to construct. = *bauen, bilden.* 4.023, 4.5, 5.556, 6.343

Konstruktion: construction. 5.233

Kontinuität: continuity. 6.34

Kontradiktion: contradiction. Cf. *Widerspruch.* 4.46–4.464, 4.466, 4.4661, 5.143, 5.152, 5.525, 6.1202, 6.3751

kontradiktorisch: contradictory. 4.46

Koordinate: coordinate. 3.032, 3.41

Koordination: coordination. 3.42

koordinieren: to coordinate. 5.64

Kopula: copula. 3.323

Körper: body. 4.002, 4.463, 5.641

kreuzweise definieren: to define crosswise. 5.42

Kriterium: criterion. 6.1271

Kugel: sphere. 5.154

Lage: place, position. 3.1431, 5.551, 5.5541, 6.35

Lautsprache: spoken language, speech. 4.011

Lautzeichen: sound, audible sign. 3.11, 3.321, 4.011

leben: to live. 6.4311

Leben: life. 5.621, 6.211, 6.4311, 6.4312, 6.521

lebendes Bild: living picture. 4.0311

Lebensproblem: problem of life. 6.52

leer: empty. 2.013

Lehre: doctrine, theory. 4.112, 6.1224, 6.13

Leib: body. 5.631

Leiter: ladder. 6.54

liefern: to supply. 6.233

liegen: to lie (in). Pref.(4), 2.0121, 2.0123, 2.0131, 4.027, 5.513, 5.521, 5.525, 5.557, 6.41, 6.422, 6.4312

Logik: logic. Cf. *Satz der Logik*. 2.012, 2.0121, 3.032, 4.1121, 4.12, 4.126, 4.128, 5.02, 5.43, 5.45–5.454, 5.472–5.4731, 5.511, 5.551–5.5521, 5.555, 5.557, 5.61, 6.113, 6.1224, 6.1233–6.1265, 6.1271, 6.13, 6.234, 6.3, 6.342

Logik der Abbildung: logic of depiction or representation. 4.015

Logik der Sprache: logic of language. Cf. *Sprachlogik*. Pref.(2)

Logik der Tatsachen: logic of facts. 4.0312

Logik der Welt: logic of the world. 6.22

Logik des Bestandteiles: logic of constituent. 6.12

logisch: logical. Ct. *unlogisch*. 2.182, 4.032, 4.04, 4.112, 4.442, 5.233, 5.45, 5.47321, 5.555, 5.5562, 5.5563, 6.121, 6.1263, 6.3631

logische Addition: see *Addition, logische*

logische Allgemeingültigkeit: logical generality. 6.1232

logische Auffassung: logical conception. 4.1213

logische Eigenschaft: logical property. 6.12, 6.121, 6.126

logische Form: see *Form, logische*

logische Grammatik: logical grammar. 3.325

logische Konstruktion: logical construction. 5.233

logische Koordinate: logical coordinate. 3.41

logische Methode: logical method. 6.2

logische Multiplikation: see *Multiplikation, logische*

logische Notwendigkeit: logical necessity. Cf. *innere Notwendigkeit*. 5.1362, 6.37, 6.375

logische Operation: logical operation. 5.47

logische Scheinbeziehung: logical pseudo-relation. 5.461

logische Struktur: logical structure. 6.3751

logische Summe: see *Summe, logische*

logische Syntax: see *Syntax, logische*

logische Unmöglichkeit: logical impossibility. 6.375

logische Verbindung: logical connexion. 4.466

'logische Wahrheit': 'logical truth'. 6.1223

logischer Apparat: logical apparatus. 6.3431

logischer Bau: logical structure. 4.014

logischer Beweis: logical proof. 6.1263

logischer Fehler: logical error. 5.4731

'logischer Gegenstand': 'logical object'. Cf. *'logischer Konstant'*. 4.441, 5.4

logischer Grund: logical ground. 5.5562

'logischer Konstant': 'logical constant'. Cf. *'logischer Gegenstand'*. 4.0312, 5.4, 5.441, 5.47

logischer Ort: logical place. Cf. *logischer Raum*. 3.4, 3.41, 3.411, 4.0641

logischer Raum: logical space. Cf. *logischer Ort*. 1.13, 2.11, 2.202, 3.4, 3.42, 4.463

logischer Satz: see *Satz der Logik*

logischer Schluss: logical inference. 5.1362, 5.152

logischer Zusammenhang: logical connexion. 6.374

Logisches: that which is logical, the logical. 2.0121, 4.023, 6.3211

logisches Bild: logical picture. 2.181, 2.182, 2.19, 3, 4.03

logisches Gerüst: logical scaffolding. 3.42, 4.023

logisches Gesetz: logical law, law of logic. 3.031, 6.123, 6.31

'logisches Grundgesetz': 'logical principle'. 6.1271

logisches Operationszeichen: logical operation sign. 5.4611 logisches Problem: logical problem. 5.4541

logisches Produkt: see *Produkt, logisches*

logisches Urbild: logical proto-picture, [logical prototype]. Cf. *Urbild*. 3.315, 5.522

logisches Urzeichen: logical primitive-sign. 5.42, 5.45

logisches Zeichen: logical sign. 5.46

logisch-syntaktisch: logico-syntactic. Cf. *Syntax, logische*. 3.327

Lohn: reward. Ct. *Strafe*. 6.422

lösen: to solve. Pref.(8), 5.535, 6.4312

Lösung: solution. 5.4541, 6.233, 6.4312, 6.4321, 6.521

Manipulation: manipulation. 5.511

Mannigfaltigkeit: multiplicity. Cf. *Dimension*. 4.04, 4.041, 4.0411, 4.0412, 5.475

Märchen: tale. 4.014

Mass: measure. 5.15

Massstab: ruler. 2.1512

materielle Eigenschaft: material property. Cf. *externe Eigenschaft*. Ct. *formale Eigenschaft*. 2.0231.

materielle Funktion: material function. 5.44

materieller Punkt: material point. 6.3432

Mathematik: mathematics. 6.031, 6.2, 6.21, 6.211, 6.22, 6.234, 6.2341, 6.24

mathematisch: mathematical. Cf. *Satz der Mathematik*. 4.04, 4.041, 4.0411, 5.154, 5.475, 6.233

mathematische Methode: mathematical method. 6.2341

Mauthner: Fritz Mauthner. 4.0031

Mechanik: mechanics. 4.04, 6.321, 6.341, 6.342, 6.343, 6.3432

mechanisch: mechanical. 6.1262

mein Wille: my will. 6.373

meine Sprache: my language. 5.6

meine Welt: my world. 5.6, 5.62, 5.63, 5.641

meinen: to intend, [mean]. 3.315, 4.062, 5.62

Mensch: man. 4.002, 5.4541, 5.641, 6.4312, 6.521

menschenunmöglich: humanly impossible. 4.002

menschliche Seele: human soul. 5.641

menschlicher Körper: human body. 5.641

menschlicher Organismus: human organism. 4.002

merken: to observe, [note]. 5.633, 6.521

Merkmal: mark, criterion, defining property. 3.311, 3.317, 3.322, 4.0621, 4.126, 6.113

metaphysische Subjekt: (the) metaphysical subject. Cf. *Ich*. 5.633, 5.641

Metaphysisches: (something) metaphysical. 6.53

Methode: method. 4.1121, 5.631, 6.1203, 6.121, 6.2, 6.234, 6.2341, 6.24, 6.53

Mikrokosmos: microcosm. 5.63

Minimumgesetz: minimum-law. 6.321

Missverständnis: misunderstanding. Cf. *Verwechslung*. Pref.(2)

mitteilen: to communicate. 4.027, 4.03

Mittelding: middle thing, [middle course]. 5.153

Mittelpunkt: middle point. 5.143

Modell: model. 2.12, 4.01, 4.04, 4.463

modus ponens: the mode of inference having that name. 6.1264

möglich: possible. See also *können*. Ct. *unmöglich*. 3.02, 3.3421, 3.3441, 4.45, 4.46, 4.464, 4.5, 5.252, 5.46, 5.473, 5.4733, 5.525, 5.55, 5.555, 6.1222, 6.125, 6.34, 6.3611, 6.52

mögliche Notation: possible notation. 3.3441

mögliche Sachlage: possible state of affairs. 2.0122, 2.202, 3.11, 4.124, 4.125, 4.462

möglicher Sachverhalt: possible situation, possible atomic fact. 2.0124, 2.013

Möglichkeit: possibility. See also *Wahrheitsmöglichkeit*. 2.012, 2.0121, 2.0123, 2.014, 2.0141, 2.033, 2.15, 2.151, 2.201, 2.203, 3.02, 3.04, 3.13, 3.23, 3.3421, 3.411, 4.015, 4.0312, 4.2, 4.27, 4.28, 4.3, 4.42, 5.252, 5.42, 5.44, 5.525, 5.61, 6.33

Monismus: monism. 4.128

Moore: G. E. Moore. 5.541

Multiplikation, logische: logical multiplication. = *Produkt, logisches*. 5.2341

Musik: music. 4.011

musikalisch: musical. 3.141, 4.014

Mystische: (the) mystical. 6.44, 6.45, 6.522

Nachfolger: successor. 4.1252, 4.1273

nachträglich: subsequently. Ct. *von vornherein*. 2.0121, 2.0123

nachweisen: to demonstrate. Cf. *beweisen, demonstrieren*. 6.53

Name: name. Cf. *nennen, einfaches Zeichen*. See also *Personenname*. 3.142, 3.143, 3.144, 3.202, 3.203, 3.22, 3.26, 3.261, 3.3, 3.314, 3.3411, 4.0311, 4.126, 4.1272, 4.22, 4.221, 4.23, 4.24, 4.243, 4.5, 5.02, 5.526, 5.535, 5.55, 6.124

Natur: (1) nature, essence. See also *Wesen*. 2.0123, 3.315, 5.47, 6.124; (2) Nature. 6.34

Natur des Satzes: nature of a statement. 3.315

Naturerscheinung: natural phenomenon. 6.371

Naturgesetz: law of nature. 5.154, 6.36, 6.371. 6.372

naturnotwendig: necessitated by the nature (of something), essentially necessary. 6.124

Naturwissenschaft: natural science. 4.11, 4.111, 4.1121, 4.1122, 4.113, 6.4312, 6.53

naturwissenschaftlich: scientific. 6.111

Nebeneinander: side-by-side. 5.454

Negation: negation. Cf. *Verneinung*. 5.5, 5.502

negativ: negative. 2.06, 5.513, 5.5151

negative Tatsache: negative fact. Ct. *positive Tatsache*. 2.06, 4.063, 5.5151

negativer Satz: negative statement. 5.5151

nennen: to name, call. Cf. *benennen*. 2.06, 3.221

Netz: net. 6.341, 6.342, 6.35

Netzwerk: network. 5.511, 6.341

Newtonsche Mechanik: Newtonian mechanics. 6.341, 6.342

neu: new. 4.027, 4.03

Nichtbestehen: not holding. Ct. *bestehen*. 2.06, 2.062, 2.11, 2.201, 4.1, 4.2, 4.27, 4.3

nichtlogischer Satz: non-logical statement. 6.113

Nicht-Satz: non-statement. 5.5351

nichts sagen: to say nothing. 5.513, 5.5303, 6.121

Nichtübereinstimmung: disagreement (with). 2.222, 4.2, 4.4, 4.42, 4.43, 4.431

nicht-zufällig: non-accidental. 6.41

Notation: notation. Cf. *Zeichensprache*. 3.342, 3.3441, 5.474, 5.512, 5.513, 5.514, 6.1203, 6.122, 6.1223

Notenschrift: musical notation, [musical score]. 4.011, 4.013, 4.014

Notensprache: language of notes, [language of the musical score]. 4.0141

nötig: necessary, needed. Ct. *unnötig*. 5.452, 5.474, 6.233

notwendig: necessary. Ct. *möglich*. 4.0411, 6.232

Notwendigkeit: necessity. Ct. *Möglichkeit*. 5.1362, 6.37, 6.375

Nullmethode: null-method. 6.121

Nummer: number (identifying a theorem). 4.442

nur-möglich: merely-possible. 2.0121

Objekt: object. 2.173

Occam: William of Occam. 3.328, 5.47321

offenbar: obvious. Cf. *einleuchten, von selbst verstehen*. 2.022, 4.012, 4.221, 5.1311, 5.42, 5.5571, 6.31

offenbaren: to reveal. 6.432

ohne weiteres: forthwith, straight away, [off-hand]. 2.02331, 5.551

Operation: operation. Cf. *Grundoperation, Wahrheitsoperation*. 4.1273, 5.21–5.251, 5.2523, 5.253, 5.254, 5.47, 5.5, 5.503, 6.001, 6.002, 6.01, 6.021, 6.126

Operationszeichen: operation sign. 5.4611

ordnen: to order. 4.1252, 4.45, 5.1, 5.232

Ordnung: order. 5.634

Ort: place, position. Cf. *logischer Ort, Raum*. 3.4, 3.41, 3.411, 3.42, 4.0641, 6.3751

Paradox: paradox. 3.333

Partitur: musical score. 4.0141

passen: to fit, suit. 2.0121

Personenname: proper name. 3.323

Pfeil: arrow. 3.144, 4.461

Phänomen: phenomenon. 6.423

Philosoph: philosopher. Pref.(5), 4.003, 4.1121, 4.122

Philosophie: philosophy. 3.324, 3.3421, 4.0031, 4.111–4.113, 5.641, 6.113, 6.211, 6.53

philosophisch: philosophical. Pref. (2), 4.003, 4.112, 4.128, 5.641

'philosophische Satze': 'philosophical statements'. 4.112

Physik: physics. 3.0321, 6.321, 6.341, 6.3751

physikalisch: physical. 6.3431, 6.374

Plan: plan. 6.343

positive Tatsache: positive fact. Ct. *negative Tatsache*. 2.06, 4.063

positiver Satz: positive statement. Ct. *negativer Satz*. 5.5151

präjudiziert: prejudged. 2.012, 5.44

praktischer Erfolg: practical success. 5.47321

Präzedenzfall: precedent. 5.525

'Principia Mathematica': Whitehead and Russell's work of that name. 5.452

'Principles of Mathematics': Russell's book with that title. 5.5351

Prinzip: principle. 4.0312

probeweise: by way of trial, [for the sake of experiment]. 4.031

Problem: problem. Cf. *Aufgabe, Frage, Lebensproblem*. Pref.(2), (8), 4.003, 5.4541, 5.535, 5.551, 5.5563, 6.233, 6.36111, 6.4312, 6.521

Produkt, logisches: logical product, conjunction. Cf. *Multiplikation, logische*. 3.42, 4.465, 5.521, 6.1271, 6.3751

Projektion: projection. Cf. *abbilden, darstellen*. 3.11, 3.13, 4.0141

Projektionsmethode: method of projection. 3.11

projektive Beziehung: projective relation. 3.12

projizieren: to project. 4.0141

Projizierte: that which is projected. 3.13

Prozess: process. Cf. *Vorgang*. 6.1261

Psychologie: psychology. 4.1121, 5.541, 5.5421, 5.641, 6.423

psychologisch: psychological. 4.1121, 6.3631

Punkt: point. 2.15121, 3.032, 3.144, 4.063, 5.64, 6.3432, 6.3751

Rätsel: riddle. 6.4312, 6.5

rätselhaft: puzzling, enigmatic. 6.4312

Raum: space. Cf. *Ort, logischer Raum, Farbenraum.* 2.0121, 2.013, 2.0131, 2.0251, 3.032, 4.463, 6.3611, 6.36111, 6.4312

'Raumbrille': 'spatial spectacles'. 4.0412

räumlich: spatial. 2.0121, 2.0131, 2.171, 2.182, 3.0321, 3.1431, 4.0412

räumlicher Gegenstand: spatial object. 2.0121, 2.0131, 3.1431

räumliches Bild: spatial picture. 2.171, 2.182

Raumpunkt: space point. 2.0131

Realismus: realism. 5.64

Realität: reality. Cf. *Wirklichkeit, empirische Realität.* 5.5561, 5.64

Rechnung: calculation. Cf. *berechnen.* 6.2331

Recht: right. Ct. *Unrecht.* 6.372

rechtfertigen: to justify. 5.132, 5.136, 5.45, 5.453, 5.47321

Rechtfertigung: justification. 5.1363, 5.452

rechtmässig: legitimate. Cf. *richtig.* 5.4733

Rede: talk, discourse. 3.24, 3.33, 4.1211, 5.631, 5.641, 6.3432

reden: to talk. Cf. *sprechen.* Pref.(2), 3.323, 3.331, 4.122

Regel: rule. Cf. *Kombinationsregel, Zeichenregel.* 3.334, 3.343, 3.344, 4.0141, 5.47321, 5.476, 5.512, 5.514

reichen: to reach (up to). 2.1511

Reihe: series. Cf. *Formenreihe, Zahlenreihe.* 4.1252, 4.31, 4.442, 4.45, 5.1, 5.232, 5.2522, 6.02

Reihenfolge: sequence. 4.442, 5.501

rein: pure. 5.5562, 5.64, 6.3211, 6.35

Relation: relation. = *Beziehung.* Cf. *interne R.* 4.122, 4.123, 4.1251, 5.232, 5.42, 5.5301, 5.541, 5.553, 5.5541

Resultat: result. Ct. *Basis.* 4.112, 5.21, 5.22, 5.234, 5.24, 5.25, 5.251, 5.2521, 5.3, 5.32, 5.41, 5.442, 5.5, 6.001, 6.1261

richtig: correct. Ct. *unrichtig, falsch.* 2.17, 2.173, 2.18, 2.21, 3.04, 3.343, 4.1213, 4.1272, 4.431, 5.45, 5.46, 5.5302, 5.534, 5.5351, 5.5422, 5.62, 6.112, 6.422, 6.53, 6.54

Richtigkeit: correctness. 6.2321

rückgängig: reversed. 5.253

Russell: Bertrand Russell. Pref.(6), 3.318, 3.325, 3.331, 3.333, 4.0031, 4.1272, 4.12721, 4.1273, 4.241, 4.442, 5.02, 5.132, 5.252, 5.4, 5.42, 5.452, 5.4731, 5.513, 5.521, 5.525, 5.5302, 5.532, 5.535, 5.5351, 5.541, 5.5422, 5.553, 6.123, 6.1232

Russell's Paradox: the logical paradox known by that name. 3.333

Sache: thing. = *Ding, Gegenstand.* 2.01, 2.15, 2.1514, 4.1272

Sachlage: state of affairs. Cf. *mögliche Sachlage.* 2.0121, 2.0122, 2.014, 2.11, 2.202, 2.203, 3.02, 3.11, 3.144, 3.21, 4.021, 4.03, 4.031, 4.032, 4.04, 4.466, 5.135, 5.156, 5.525

Sachverhalt: atomic fact, atomic situation. Cf. *möglicher Sachverhalt.* 2–2.0123, 2.0141, 2.0272–2.032, 2.034, 2.04–2.062, 2.11, 2.201, 3.001, 3.0321, 4.023, 4.0311, 4.1, 4.122, 4.2, 4.21, 4.2211, 4.25, 4.27, 4.3

Sagbare: that which can be stated. Ct. *Unsagbare.* 4.115

sagen: to say. Cf. *sprechen, reden.* Ct. *aufweisen, zeigen.* See also *behaupten, beschreiben.* Pref.(2), 3.031, 3.1432, 3.221, 4.022, 4.062–4.063, 4.1212, 4.461, 4.465, 5.14, 5.142, 5.43–5.441, 5.47, 5.513, 5.5301–5.5303, 5.535, 5.542, 5.61, 5.62, 5.631, 6.001, 6.11, 6.342, 6.36, 6.51, 6.521, 6.53

sämtlich: all (together). Cf. *alle*. 2.0123, 2.02331, 3.315, 5.11, 5.123, 5.5, 5.501, 5.502, 5.52

Satz: statement, proposition. Cf. *Aussage, Elementarsatz*. See also *Wahrscheinlichkeitssatz*. 2.0122, 2.0201, 2.0211, 2.0231, 3.1–3.13, 3.141, 3.143, 3.1431, 3.144–3.202, 3.22, 3.221, 3.24–3.251, 3.263, 3.3–3.315, 3.317, 3.318, 3.323, 3.332, 3.333, 3.34, 3.341, 3.4, 3.42, 4, 4.001, 4.003–4.012, 4.016, 4.021–4.031, 4.0312, 4.032, 4.04, 4.05–4.11, 4.12–4.1211, 4.122, 4.124, 4.125, 4.1252, 4.126, 4.1272, 4.1273, 4.1274, 4.2, 4.221, 4.23, 4.243, 4.4–4.42, 4.431, 4.442, 4.46, 4.461, 4.463–4.466, 4.5–4.52, 5–5.02, 5.101–5.12, 5.123–5.131, 5.132, 5.1363, 5.14–5.151, 5.152, 5.153, 5.156–5.21, 5.23, 5.233, 5.2341, 5.24, 5.25, 5.2521, 5.3, 5.43, 5.44, 5.442, 5.451, 5.4541, 5.47–5.4711, 5.473, 5.4733, 5.5, 5.501, 5.503, 5.512–5.5151, 5.525–5.5262, 5.5301, 5.5302, 5.5321, 5.5351–5.541, 5.5422, 5.5562, 5.5563, 6–6.01, 6.1–6.1201, 6.1203–6.1222, 6.1231, 6.1232, 6.124, 6.125, 6.126, 6.1263–6.1271, 6.2–6.22, 6.2321, 6.2341, 6.241, 6.31, 6.34, 6.341, 6.343, 6.4, 6.42, 6.53, 6.54

Satz der Logik: logical statement. 5.02, 5.43, 6.1, 6.11, 6.111, 6.112, 6.113, 6.12, 6.121, 6.122, 6.1222, 6.124, 6.125, 6.126, 6.1264, 6.127, 6.22

Satz der Mathematik: mathematical statement. 5.43, 6.2, 6.21, 6.2321

Satz der Physik: statement of physics. 6.341

Satz, logischer: logical statement. = *Satz der Logik*. 6.112, 6.113, 6.121, 6.122, 6.1222, 6.1231, 6.1232, 6.124, 6.125, 6.126, 6.1263, 6.1271

Satz, mathematischer: mathematical statement. = *Satz der Mathematik*. 6.211

Satz vom Grunde: law of sufficient reason, [law of causation]. 6.34, 6.35

Satz vom kleinsten Aufwande: law of least effort. 6.34

Satzart: kind of statement, [kind of proposition]. 4.411

Satzbestandteil: statement component. Cf. *Bestandteil, Element, Wort*. 4.025

Satzelement: statement element, [propositional element]. Cf. *Bestandteil, Element*. 3.24

Satzform: statement form, [form of proposition]. Cf. *Form, Form des Satzes*. 4.5, 4.53, 5.1311, 5.156, 5.47, 5.471, 5.472, 5.54, 5.541

Satzgefüge: statement structure, [structure of proposition]. 3.3442, 4.442

Satzvariable: statement variable, [propositional variable]. Cf. *Variable*. 3.313, 3.314, 3.316, 3.317, 4.126, 4.127, 5.502

Satzverband: statement connexion, [propositional connexion]. 4.221

Satzzeichen: statement sign, propositional sign, sentence. Cf. *Zeichen*. 3.12, 3.14, 3.143, 3.1431, 3.2, 3.21, 3.332, 3.34, 3.41, 3.5, 4.02, 4.44, 4.442, 5.31

schaffen: to create. 3.031, 5.123

Schallwellen: sound waves. 4.014

scheinbar: seemingly, apparently. Ct. *eigentlich, wirklich*. 4.0031, 4.013, 4.0141, 5.441, 5.461, 5.61

Scheinbegriff: pseudo-concept. 4.1272

Scheinbeziehung: pseudo-relation. 5.461

Scheinsatz: pseudo-statement. 4.1272, 5.534, 5.535, 6.2

Schema: schema. 4.31, 4.43, 4.441, 4.442, 5.101, 5.151, 5.31
Schicksal: fate. 6.372, 6.374
schliessen: to conclude, infer. Cf. *folgern, erschliessen*. 2.062, 4.002, 5.1311, 5.132, 5.135, 5.633, 6.1224, 6.211
schliessen, in sich: to include. Cf. *enthalten*. 6.113
Schluss: conclusion, inference. 4.023, 5.132, 5.136, 5.1362, 5.152
'Schlussgesetz': 'law of inference'. 5.132
Schlüssel: key. 5.62
schon: already. = *bereits*. 2.0121, 4.063, 4.064, 4.0641, 5.123, 5.442, 5.46, 5.47, 5.524, 5.525, 5.5351, 6.002
Schrift: writing. 3.143
Schriftzeichen: written sign. 3.11, 3.1431, 3.321
schweigen: to be silent. Pref.(2), 7
Seele: soul. 5.5421, 5.641, 6.4312
sehen: to see. 3.24, 4.023, 4.0412, 5.5423, 5.633, 5.634
sein: to be. 5.5542
selbständig: independent. Cf. *unabhängig*. Ct. *abhängen*. 2.0122, 3.261, 5.461
Selbständigkeit: independence. 2.0122
selbstverständlich: obvious, self-evident. Cf. *offenbar, einleuchten*. 6.111, 6.35
sichern: to ensure. Cf. *verbürgen*. 5.5351
'simplex sigillum veri': 'simplicity is the hallmark of truth'. 5.4541
Sinn: sense. Ct. *Bedeutung*. Pref. (2), 2.0211, 2.221, 2.222, 3.11, 3.13, 3.142, 3.1431, 3.144, 3.23, 3.3, 3.31, 3.328, 3.34, 3.341, 4.002, 4.02–4.022, 4.027, 4.03, 4.031, 4.032, 4.061, 4.0621, 4.063, 4.064, 4.1211, 4.1241, 4.2, 4.431, 4.465, 4.5, 5.02, 5.122, 5.2341, 5.25, 5.46,

5.4732, 5.4733, 5.514, 5.515, 5.5302, 5.5542, 6.124, 6.126, 6.232, 6.41, 6.521
sinnlich warnehmbar: perceptible by the senses. 3.1, 3.11, 3.32
sinnlos: senseless. Ct. *unsinnig*. Cf. *bedeutungslos*. 4.461, 5.132, 5.1362, 5.5351
sinnvoll: having sense. Ct. *sinnlos*. 3.13, 3.326, 3.4, 4, 4.243, 5.1241, 5.525, 6.1263, 6.1264, 6.31
Skeptizismus: scepticism. 6.51
'Sokrates ist identisch': 'Socrates is identical' (an example of nonsense). 5.473, 5.4733
Solipsismus: solipsism. 5.62, 5.64
Sonne: the sun. 6.36311
sorgen: to care for, look after. 5.473
So-Sein: so-being. Cf. *Wie*. 6.41
speziell: special. Ct. *allgemein*. 3.3441, 4.12721, 5.511, 6.022
spezielle Form: special form. 5.554
Spezielleres: (something) more special. Ct. *Allgemeineres*. 5.454
Spiegel: mirror. See also *weltspiegelnd*. 5.511
Spiegelbild: mirror image. 6.13
spiegeln: to mirror, reflect. Cf. *aufweisen, zeigen*. 4.121, 5.512, 5.514
Spielraum: range. 4.463, 5.5262
Sprache: language. See also *Lautsprache, Notensprache, Zeichensprache*. Pref.(2), (4), 3.032, 3.325, 3.343, 4.001, 4.002, 4.014, 4.0141, 4.025, 4.121, 5.4731, 5.535, 5.6, 5.62, 6.12, 6.233, 6.43
'Sprachkritik': 'critique of language'. 4.0031
sprachlich: in speech. 4.125
Sprachlogik: logic of language. Cf. *Logik der Sprache*. 4.002, 4.003
sprechen: to speak. Cf. *reden, sagen*. 3.221, 6.3431, 6.423, 7
Standard: standard. 5.4541
Standpunkt: standpoint. 2.173, 6.2323

stehen: to stand (in a relation). 3.1432, 3.24, 4.014, 4.123, 4.211, 4.462, 5.131, 5.2

stehen für: to stand for. Cf. *vertreten*. 4.0311, 5.515

stellen: to place. Cf. *aufstellen*. 2.174

Stellung: position. 5.45, 5.452, 6.112, 6.342

stillschweigend: silently, tacitly. 4.002

stimmen: to agree. Cf. *übereinstimmen*. 3.24, 3.411, 5.123, 5.512

Strafe: punishment. Ct. *Lohn*. 6.422

Streitfrage: controversy, [disputed question]. 4.1251

Strich: stroke. 4.441, 5.501, 5.512, 6.1203

Struktur: structure. Cf. *logische S.* 2.032, 2.033, 2.034, 2.15, 4.1211, 4.122, 5.13, 5.2, 5.22, 6.12, 6.3751

sub specie aeterni: from the standpoint of the eternal. 6.45

Subjekt: subject. Cf. *Ich*. 5.5421, 5.631, 5.632, 5.633, 5.641

Subjekt-Prädikatsätze: subject-predicate statements. 4.1274

Substantiv: substantive, noun. 4.025

Substanz: substance. 2.021, 2.0211, 2.0231, 2.024

Substitutionsmethode: method of substitution. 6.24

successiv: by successive stages. 3.3411

successive Anwendung: successive application (of an operation). Cf. *anwenden*. 5.2521, 5.2523, 5.32, 5.5, 6.001, 6.126

Summe, logische: logical sum, disjunction. 3.42, 5.521

Symbol: symbol. Ct. *Zeichen*. 3.24, 3.31, 3.317, 3.32, 3.321, 3.323, 3.325, 3.326, 3.341, 3.3411, 3.344, 4.126, 4.24, 4.465, 4.4611, 4.5, 5.1311, 5.473, 5.4733, 5.513–5.515, 5.525, 5.5261, 5.5351, 5.555, 6.113, 6.124, 6.126

Symbolik: symbolism. 4.31

symbolisieren: to symbolize. = *bezeichnen*. 5.4733

Symbolismus: symbolism. 4.4611, 5.452

symmetrisch: symmetrical. 5.4541

Syntax, logische: logical syntax. Cf. *logisch-syntaktisch*. 3.325, 3.33, 3.334, 3.344, 6.124

System: system. Cf. *Zahlensystem, Zeichensystem*. 5.555, 6.341, 6.372

Tastsinn: sense of touch. 2.0131

Tätigkeit: activity. 4.112

Tatsache: fact. Cf. *Fall, negative Tatsache, positive Tatsache*. 1.1–1.2, 2, 2.0121, 2.034, 2.06, 2.1, 2.141, 2.16, 3, 3.14, 3.142, 3.143, 4.016, 4.0312, 4.061, 4.063, 4.122, 4.1221, 4.1272, 4.2211, 4.463, 5.156, 5.461, 5.5151, 5.542, 5.5423, 6.111, 6.113, 6.2321, 6.43, 6.4321

tatsächlich: actually. Cf. *wirklich*. 5.452, 5.5563, 6.35, 6.36111

Täuschung: illusion. 6.371

Tautologie: tautology. 4.46–4.4661, 5.1362, 5.142, 5.143, 5.152, 5.525, 6.1, 6.12–6.1203, 6.1221, 6.124, 6.126, 6.1262, 6.127, 6.22, 6.3751

tautologisch: tautological. 4.46, 6.1231

Teil: part. Cf. *Bestandteil*. 3.31, 3.315, 5.641

Teilchen: particle. 6.3751

Teilstrich: dividing line. 2.15121

Theorie: theory. 6.031, 6.111

'theory of types': Russell's theory of that name. Cf. *Type*. 3.331, 3.332

tiefste: deepest. 4.003

Tod: death. 6.431, 6.4311, 6.4312

Ton: note, tone. 2.0131, 3.141

Träger: bearer. 6.423

transcendental: transcendental. 6.13, 6.421

trennen: to separate. 5.521
trübe: muddy, opaque. 4.112
Type: type. Cf. *'theory of types'*.
3.332, 5.252, 6.123

Übereinkunft: agreement. Cf. *Ab-machung, Festsetzung*. 3.315, 5.02
übereinstimmen: to agree, accord with. Cf. *stimmen*. 2.21, 2.222, 4.2, 4.4, 4.42, 4.43, 4.431, 4.462
überflüssig: superfluous. Cf. *entbehr-lich*. 5.132, 6.031
Übergang: transition. 6.01
übergreifen: to trespass across, [over-lap]. 5.557
Überraschung: surprise. 6.1251, 6.1261
übersetzen: to translate. 3.343, 4.025, 4.243
Übersetzung: translation. 3.343, 4.0141, 4.025
überwinden: to overcome. 6.54
Umgangssprache: ordinary language, colloquial language. 3.323, 4.002, 5.5563
Umstand: circumstance. 4.063, 5.154, 5.155
unabhängig: independent. Cf. *selb-ständig*. Ct. *abhängen*. 2.024, 2.061, 2.22, 4.061, 5.152, 5.154, 5.451, 5.5261, 5.5561, 6.373
unanalysiert: unanalysed. 5.5562
Unangenehmes: (something) unplea-sant. Ct. *Angenehmes*. 6.422
unantastbar: unassailable. Pref.(8), 6.372
Unaussprechliches: (something) un-statable, [inexpressible]. 6.522
Unbeständige: the mutable [variable]. Cf. *Wechselnde*. 2.0271
Unbestimmtheit: indeterminateness. 3.24
'und so weiter': 'and so forth'. Cf. *successive Anwendung*. 5.2523
undenkbar: unthinkable. Cf. *Unsag-bare*. 4.123

Undenkbare: that which is unthink-able. 4.114
Unding: a non-thing, a nothing. 5.5421
unendlich: infinite. Cf. *endlos*. 2.0131, 4.2211, 4.463, 5.43, 5.535, 6.4311
unerlaubt: not permitted. 5.452, 5.473
Unglücklicher: unhappy (person). Ct. *Glücklicher*. 6.43
unlogisch: unlogical. Ct. *logisch*. 3.03, 3.031, 5.4731
Unlogisches: (something) unlogical. 3.03
unmittelbar: direct. 4.221
unmöglich: impossible. Ct. *möglich*. 2.0122, 2.0212, 2.02331, 4.243, 4.442, 4.464, 5.5422, 6.3751
Unmöglichkeit: impossibility. 5.525, 6.375
unnötig: unnecessary. Ct. *nötig*. 5.47321
Unrecht: wrong. Ct. *Recht*. 6.372
unrechter: wrong. 5.4732
Unregelmässigkeit: irregularity. 4.013
unrichtig: incorrect, wrong. Ct. *richtig*. 2.21, 5.525, 5.5351
Unsagbare: that which is unstatable. Ct. *Sagbare*. 4.115
Unselbständigkeit: dependence. 2.0122
Unsinn: nonsense. Ct. *sinnlos*. Pref.(4), 5.5303, 5.5351, 5.5422, 5.5571
unsinnig: nonsensical. Ct. *sinnlos*. 3.24, 4.003, 4.124, 4.1272, 4.1274, 4.4611, 5.473, 5.5351, 6.51, 6.54
Unsinnigkeit: nonsensicality. 4.003
Unsterblichkeit: immortality. 6.4312
unterscheiden: to distinguish. 2.0233, 4.04, 4.1241
Unterschied: difference. Cf. *Ver-schiedenheit*. 5.24, 5.241
unterstehen: to obey. Cf. *gehorchen*. 6.123

Untersuchung: investigation. Cf. *Erforschung*. 4.1121

unverallgemeinerter Satz: ungeneralized statement. Ct. *allgemeiner Satz*. 6.1231

unverbunden: unconnected. 4.466

unvollständig: incomplete. 5.156

unwahrscheinlich: improbable. Ct. *wahrscheinlich*. 5.153

unwesentlich: inessential. Ct. *wesentlich*. 3.317, 4.1121, 4.4661, 5.501, 6.126

unwichtig: unimportant. Ct. *wichtig*. 3.3421

unwiderleglich: irrefutable. 6.51

Unzeitlichkeit: timelessness. 6.4311

Urbild: proto-picture, primitive picture, indefinable, [archetype, prototype]. Cf. *Urzeichen*, and *logisches Urbild*. 3.24, 3.315, 3.333, 5.522, 5.5351

Urne: urn. 5.154

Ursache: cause. 6.3611

urteilen: to judge. 5.5422

Urteilstrich: assertion sign (of Frege). 4.442

Urzeichen: indefinable sign, primitive sign. Cf. *Urbild*. 3.26, 3.261, 3.263, 5.42, 5.45, 5.451, 5.46, 5.461, 5.472

variabel: variable (adj.). Ct. *konstant*. 3.312, 3.315, 4.1272, 6.022

Variable: variable. Ct. *Konstant*. Cf. *Satzvariable*. 3.313, 3.314, 3.315, 3.316, 3.317, 4.0411, 4.1271, 4.1272, 4.1273, 4.53, 5.24, 5.242, 5.2522, 5.501

variable Zahl: variable number. 6.022

variabler Name: variable name. 3.314, 4.1272

verallgemeinern: to generalize. 4.0411

verallgemeinerter Satz: generalized statement. 5.526, 5.5261, 6.1231

Verallgemeinerung: generalization Cf. *Allgemeinheit*. 4.52, 5.156

verändern: to change. = *ändern*. 5.5262

Verband: context. Cf. *Zusammenhang*. See also *Satzverband*. 2.0121

verbinden: to combine, connect. 4.0311, 4.4661, 5.131, 5.515, 6.12, 6.1201, 6.121, 6.1221, 6.23, 6.232

Verbindung: combination, connexion. See also *Zeichenverbindung*. 2.01, 2.0121, 4.221, 4.466, 5.451, 5.521, 6.1201, 6.1203, 6.1221, 6.124

Verbum: verb. = *Zeitwort*. 4.063

verbürgen: to guarantee. Cf. *sichern*. 3.4, 6.374, 6.4312

vereintliegen: to be united. 5.4541

vergleichen: to compare. 2.223, 4.05, 6.2321, 6.3611

Vergleichsobjekt: object of comparison. 3.05

verhalten, sich: to behave with respect to, be mutually related. 2.031, 2.14, 2.15, 2.151, 3.14, 3.328, 4.022, 4.023, 4.062, 4.5, 5.5423, 5.552, 5.633

verhindern: to prevent. 5.4731

verhüllen: to conceal. Cf. *verkleiden, verschleiern, verschlucken*. 5.1311

verkehren: to reverse. 5.2341

Verkettung: concatenation. Cf. *Kette*. 4.22

verkleiden: to disguise, conceal. Cf. *verhüllen, verschleiern, verschlucken*. 4.002

verknüpfen: to link, connect. 2.1511, 5.511, 6.12

vermitteln: to arrange, bring about. 6.2331

verneinen: to deny. Ct. *bejahen*. 4.0641, 5.1241, 5.44, 5.5, 5.512, 5.514

Verneinung: denial. Ct. *Bejahung*. 3.42, 4.0621, 4.064, 4.0641, 5.2341, 5.254, 5.44, 5.451, 5.512, 6.231

verschieden: different. Ct. *gleich,
dasselbe.* 2.0122, 2.022, 2.0233,
3.143, 3.321, 3.322, 3.323, 3.325,
3.333, 4.0141, 5.135, 5.4733, 5.535,
5.5423, 5.55, 5.553, 6.232, 6.2322
Verschiedenes: (something) different.
4.243
Verschiedenheit: difference. Ct.
Gleichheit. Cf. *Unterschied.* 5.53
verschleiern: to conceal. Cf. *verhüllen,
verkleiden, verschlucken.* 3.143
verschlucken: to swallow up, conceal.
Cf. *verhüllen, verkleiden, verschleiern.*
3.262
verschwinden: to vanish. Cf. *erledigen.*
5.143, 5.254, 5.441, 6.521
verschwommen: vague, blurred.
4.112
verständigen, sich: to communicate,
make oneself understood, [explain
oneself]. 4.026, 4.062
Verständnis: understanding. 4.002,
4.411
verstehen: to understand. Cf. *von
selbst v.* Pref.(1), 3.263, 4.003,
4.016, 4.02, 4.021, 4.024, 4.026,
4.243, 5.02, 5.451, 5.521, 5.552,
5.5562, 5.62, 6.54
Versuch: attempt, trial, experiment.
Cf. *Experiment.* 5.154, 6.343
vertreten: to stand for, take the place
of, go proxy for, deputize for, represent. Cf. *stehen für, entsprechen.* 2.131,
3.22, 3.221, 4.0312, 5.501
Vertretung: representation. 4.0312
verwechseln: to confuse, mistake.
5.02, 5.25
Verwechslung: confusion. Cf. *Missverständnis.* 3.324, 4.122, 4.126,
5.02
verwenden: to apply, use. Cf. *anwenden.* 3.325, 6.1202, 6.341
Verwendung: application, use. 3.327,
4.013
vollkommen geordnet: completely in
order. 5.5563

vollständig: complete. 2.0201, 3.201,
3.25, 4.26, 5.156
vollständig analysiert: completely
analysed. 3.201
vollständig beschreiben: to describe
completely. 2.0201, 4.023, 4.26,
5.526, 6.342
von innen: from within. 4.114
von selbst verstehen: to be self-
intelligible, to be self-evident, [follow
of themselves]. Cf. *offenbar, einleuchten.*
3.334, 6.2341
von vornherein: from the outset, in
advance, beforehand, [at first sight].
Cf. *a priori.* 4.411, 5.43, 5.47, 5.526,
6.125, 6.1263
vor: before. 5.552
vorausnehmen: to anticipate. = *voraussehen.* 5.557
voraussehen: to foresee. = *vorausnehmen.* 4.5, 5.556
voraussetzen: to presuppose. 3.311,
3.33, 4.1241, 5.515, 5.5151, 5.61,
6.124
Vorbereitung: preliminary. 4.0641
vorerst: first of all. 4.063
Vorgang: process. Cf. *Prozess.* 6.2331,
6.3611, 6.363, 6.3631
vorhanden: present. 5.1311
vorher: previously, beforehand. 5.02
vorkommen: to occur. = *auftreten, eintreten, eintreten.* 2.012, 2.0121,
2.0122, 2.0123, 2.0141, 3.24, 3.311,
4.0621, 4.1211, 4.23, 4.243,
5.25, 5.451, 5.452, 5.54, 5.541,
6.1203
vorstellen: (1) to exhibit; (2) to conceive, imagine. 2.11, 2.15, 4.0311,
5.631

wahr: true. Ct. *falsch, unrichtig.*
2.0211, 2.0212, 2.21, 2.223–
2.225, 3.01, 3.05, 4.022, 4.023,
4.024, 4.06–4.062, 4.063, 4.11,
4.25, 4.26, 4.31, 4.431, 4.442,
4.46, 4.461, 4.466, 5.123, 5.1363,

wahr: true (*cont.*)
5.512, 5.5262, 6.111, 6.113, 6.1232, 6.125, 6.343

Wahrheit: truth. Ct. *Falschheit.* Pref. (8), 2.22, 2.222, 3.04, 3.05, 4.28, 4.41, 4.464, 5.11, 5.12, 5.13, 5.131, 5.1363, 5.5262, 5.5563, 5.62, 6.113, 6.1203

Wahrheitsargument: truth-argument (i.e. of a truth-function). 5.01, 5.101, 5.152, 6.1203

Wahrheitsbedingung: truth-condition. 4.431, 4.442, 4.45, 4.46, 4.461, 4.463

Wahrheitsbegriff: concept of truth. 4.063, 4.431

Wahrheitsfunktion: truth-function. 3.3441, 5, 5.1, 5.101, 5.234, 5.2341, 5.3, 5.31, 5.32, 5.41, 5.44, 5.5, 5.521, 6

Wahrheitsgrund: truth-ground. 5.101, 5.11, 5.12, 5.121, 5.15

Wahrheitskombination: truth-combination. 6.1203

Wahrheitsmöglichkeit: truth-possibility. 4.3, 4.31, 4.4, 4.41, 4.42, 4.43, 4.431, 4.44, 4.442, 4.45, 4.46, 5.101

Wahrheitsoperation: truth-operation. Cf. *Operation.* 5.234, 5.3, 5.32, 5.41, 5.442, 5.54

Wahrheitswert: truth-value. 4.063

wahrnehmbar: perceptible. 3.1, 3.11, 3.32

wahrnehmen: to perceive. Cf. *empfinden.* 5.5423

wahrscheinlich: probable. Ct. *unwahrscheinlich.* 4.411, 5.153, 5.154

Wahrscheinlichkeit: probability. 5.15, 5.151, 5.152, 5.154, 5.155, 5.156

Wahrscheinlichkeitslehre: theory of probability. 4.464, 5.1

Wahrscheinlichkeitssatz: probability statement. 5.1511, 5.155, 5.156

Was: (the) what. Ct. *Wie.* 3.221, 5.552

Wechselnde: that which changes. Cf. *Unbeständige.* 2.0271

Weg: way. 3.261

Weise: way, manner. = *Art* (1). See also *Art und Weise, Bezeichnungsweise.* 2.0122, 3.251, 3.323, 5.135, 5.233, 5.3, 5.541

weisen: to show (the way). 3.261

Welt: world, universe. Cf. *Wirklichkeit, Realität.* 1–1.2, 2.021–2.022, 2.0231, 2.026, 2.04, 2.063, 2.19, 3.01, 3.031, 3.12, 3.3421, 4.014, 4.023, 4.12, 4.2211, 4.26, 4.462, 5.123, 5.4711, 5.526–5.5262, 5.551, 5.5521, 5.6–5.633, 5.641, 6.12, 6.1233, 6.124, 6.13, 6.22, 6.342, 6.3431, 6.373, 6.374, 6.41, 6.43, 6.431, 6.432, 6.44, 6.45, 6.54

Weltanschauung: world view, conception of the universe. 6.371

Weltbeschreibung: description of the world. Cf. *Beschreibung.* 6.341, 6.343, 6.3432

weltspiegelnd: world-reflecting. Cf. *spiegeln.* 5.511

Wert: value. Cf. *gleichwertig.* Pref.(7), (8), 3.313, 3.315, 3.316, 3.317, 4.127, 4.1271, 5.501, 5.502, 5.51, 5.52, 6.41

Wesen: essence. Cf. *Natur.* 3.1431, 3.342, 3.3421, 4.016, 4.027, 5.3, 5.471, 5.4711

Wesen aller Beschreibung: essence of all description. 5.4711

Wesen der Welt: essence of the world. 3.3421, 5.4711

Wesen des Satzes: essence of the statement. 5.471, 5.4711

wesentlich: essential. Ct. *unwesentlich, zufällig.* Cf. *formal, intern, logisch.* 2.011, 3.143, 3.31, 3.317, 3.34, 3.3411, 4.03, 4.112, 4.1121, 5.533, 6.1232, 6.124, 6.127

Wesentliches: that which is essential. 3.341, 4.013, 4.016, 4.465, 4.5, 6.232, 6.2341

Whitehead: Alfred North Whitehead. 5.252, 5.452

wichtig: important. 3.3421, 4.0621, 5.555, 5.631, 6.113

widerlegen: to refute. Ct. *bestätigen*. 6.1222

widersprechen: to contradict. 3.032, 4.1211, 5.1241, 6.1201

Widerspruch: contradiction. Cf. *Kontradiction*. 4.211, 6.123, 6.3751

Wie: (the) how. Ct. *Was*. 3.221, 5.552, 6.41, 6.432, 6.44

Wille: the will. 5.631, 6.373, 6.374, 6.423

Willensfreiheit: freedom of the will. 5.1362

willkürlich: accidental. = *zufällig*. Ct. *wesentlich*. Cf. *beliebig*. 3.315, 3.322, 3.342, 3.3442, 5.02, 5.473, 5.47321, 5.554, 6.124, 6.1271

wirklich: actual, actually. Cf. *eigentlich, tatsächlich*. Ct. *scheinbar*. 2.022, 4.0031, 4.431, 5.461, 5.633, 6.1233, 6.3631

Wirklichkeit: reality. Cf. *Realität, Welt*. 2.06, 2.063, 2.12, 2.1511, 2.1512, 2.1515, 2.17, 2.171, 2.18, 2.201, 2.21, 2.222, 2.223, 4.01, 4.011, 4.021, 4.023, 4.05, 4.06, 4.0621, 4.12, 4.121, 4.462, 4.463, 5.512, 6.3611

Wirkung: effect. 5.253, 5.46

wissen: to know. Cf. *kennen*. 3.05, 3.24, 3.334, 4.002, 4.024, 4.063, 4.243, 4.461, 5.1362, 5.156, 5.5542, 5.5562, 6.33, 6.36311

Wissenschaft: science. = *Naturwissenschaft*. 6.34

wissenschaftlich: scientific. 6.341, 6.52

Wollen: willing. Cf. *Wille*. 6.43

Wort: word. Cf. *Satzbestandteil*. 2.0122, 3.14, 3.143, 3.323, 4.002, 4.026, 4.123, 4.243, 5.452, 6.111, 6.211

Wörterbuch: dictionary. 4.025

Wörtergemisch: jumble (or mixture) of words. 3.141

wünschen: to wish. 6.374

Würfel: cube. 5.5423

Zahl: number. Cf. *Anzahl*. 4.126, 4.1272, 4.12721, 4.128, 5.154, 5.453, 6.02, 6.021, 6.022, 6.03

Zahlbegriff: number concept. 6.022

Zahlengleichheit: numerical equation. 6.022

Zahlenreihe: the series of integers. Cf. *Reihe, Formenreihe*. 4.1252

Zahlensystem: the system of numbers. Cf. *System*. 6.341

Zahlenzeichen: number sign, numeral. 4.126

zahllos: anumerical. 4.128

Zeichen: sign. Cf. *Bezeichnung*. Ct. *Symbol*. See also *Anzeichen, einfaches Z., Funktionszeichen, Lautzeichen, Operationszeichen, Satzzeichen, Schriftzeichen, Zahlenzeichen*. 3.11, 3.12, 3.1432, 3.201–3.203, 3.221, 3.261–3.263, 3.315, 3.32–3.322, 3.325–3.331, 3.334, 3.3442, 4.012, 4.0312, 4.061, 4.0621, 4.126, 4.1271, 4.1272, 4.211, 4.241–4.243, 4.431–4.441, 4.466, 4.4661, 5.02, 5.451, 5.46, 5.473, 5.4732–5.4733, 5.501, 5.512, 5.515, 5.5151, 5.53, 5.5541, 6.1203, 6.124, 6.1264, 6.53

Zeicheneinheit: sign element. 5.47321

Zeichenform: sign form. 5.5542

Zeichenregel: rule concerning signs. Cf. *Regel*. 3.331, 4.241, 6.02, 6.126

Zeichensprache: sign language. Cf. *Notation*. 3.325, 3.343, 4.011, 4.1121, 4.1213, 4.5, 6.124

Zeichensystem: sign system. 5.475

Zeichenverbindung: combination of signs. Cf. *Verbindung*. 4.466, 5.451

zeigen: to show. Ct. *sagen*. Cf. *anzeigen, aufweisen, spiegeln*. Pref. (2), (8), 2.02331, 3.262, 4.0031, 4.022, 4.0621, 4.0641, 4.121, 4.1211,

zeigen: to show (*cont.*)
4.1212, 4.126, 4.461, 5.1311, 5.24,
5.42, 5.5421, 5.5422, 5.551, 5.631,
6.12, 6.1201, 6.121, 6.1221, 6.126,
6.1264, 6.127, 6.22, 6.232

zeigen, sich: to show itself. Cf. *aufweisen, spiegeln.* 3.331, 4.122, 4.243,
5.24, 5.4, 5.513, 5.515, 5.5261,
5.5561, 5.62, 6.23, 6.36, 6.522

Zeit: time. 2.0121, 2.0251, 6.3751,
6.4312

Zeitdauer: temporal duration. 6.4311

zeitliche Unsterblichkeit: temporal
immortality. 6.4312

zeitlicher Gegenstand: temporal object. 2.0121

zeitlicher Verlauf: temporal passage.
6.3611

Zeitwort: verb. = *Verbum.* 3.323,
4.025

zerfallen: to divide. 1.2

zergliedern: to analyse. Cf. *zerlegen,
analysieren.* 3.26

zerlegen: to analyse. Cf. *zergliedern,
analysieren.* 2.0201

ziehen: to draw (a boundary). Pref.(3),
(4)

Zufall: accident. 2.0121, 6.1232, 6.3

zufällig: accidental. Ct. *wesentlich.*
Cf. *beliebig, willkürlich.* 2.012, 3.34,
5.4733, 6.031, 6.1232, 6.41

zufälligerweise: accidentally. 6.1231

Zug: feature, trait. Cf. *Gesichtszug.*
3.34, 4.1221, 4.126

zugeben: to concede, admit. 5.252

Zukunft: future. 5.1361, 5.1362

zunehmen: to increase, wax. Ct. *abnehmen.* 6.43

zuordnen: to correlate. 4.43, 5.526,
6.1203

Zuordnung: correlation. 2.1514,
2.1515, 4.44, 5.542, 6.1203

Zusammenfassung: combination.
3.24

zusammengesetzt: complex, composite. Ct. *einfach.* 2.021, 3.143,
3.1431, 4.032, 4.2211, 5.5261,
5.5421

Zusammengesetztheit: complexity.
5.47

zusammengestellt: put together.
4.031

Zusammenhang: connexion. Cf.
Verbindung, Verband. 2.0122, 2.15,
3.3, 4.03, 4.22, 4.23, 5.1311,
5.1362, 6.361, 6.374

zusammenhängen: to be connected
with. 2.032, 4.03, 5.634, 6.031

Zusammensetzung: composition.
3.3411, 5.55

zusprechen: to affirm (a property).
Ct. *absprechen.* 4.124

zustandekommen: to come to be.
4.221

zuwider: contrary. 3.031

zuwiderlaufen: to contradict. 3.0321

Zwang: compulsion. 6.37

Zweck: purpose. Pref.(1), 3.341,
4.002, 4.112, 5.47321, 5.5351,
6.1202

Zweifel: doubt. Cf. *bezweifeln.* 6.51,
6.521

BIBLIOGRAPHY

ALLAIRE, EDWIN B. *Tractatus* 6.3751. *Analysis*, **19** (1959), 100–5.

AMBROSE, ALICE. Proof and the theorem proved. *Mind*, **68** (1959), 435–45.

ANSCOMBE, G. E. M. Aristotle and the sea battle. *Mind*, **65** (1956), 1–15.

ANSCOMBE, G. E. M. *Intention* (Oxford, 1957).

ANSCOMBE, G. E. M. *An Introduction to Wittgenstein's Tractatus* (London, 1959).

ANSCOMBE, G. E. M. Mr Copi on objects, properties and relations in the *Tractatus*. *Mind*, **68** (1959), 404.

AUSTIN, J. L. Truth (symposium). *Proceedings of the Aristotelian Society* (suppl.), **24** (1950), 111–28. [Cf. Strawson.]

AUSTIN, J. L. Unfair to facts, in his *Philosophical Papers*, ed. by J. O. Urmson and G. J. Warnock (Oxford, 1961).

AYER, A. J. *Thinking and Meaning* (London, 1947).

BARTLETT, JAMES M. *Funktion und Gegenstand*. Inaugural dissertation (Munich, 1961).

BLACK, M. *The Nature of Mathematics* (London, 1933).

BLACK, M. *Problems of Analysis* (Ithaca, N.Y., 1954).

BOEHNER, P. *Ockham, Philosophical Writings* (Edinburgh, 1957).

BOLZANO, BERNARD. *Wissenschaftslehre*, ed. by W. Schultz (Leipzig, 1929).

BROAD, C. D. *Scientific Thought* (London, 1923).

BROAD, C. D. Are there synthetic *a priori* truths? (symposium). *Proceedings of the Aristotelian Society* (suppl.), **15** (1936), 102–17.

CARNAP, RUDOLF. *Der logische Aufbau der Welt* (Berlin, 1928).

CARNAP, RUDOLF. *The Logical Syntax of Language* (London, 1937).

CARNAP, RUDOLF. *Introduction to Semantics* (Cambridge, Mass., 1942).

CARNAP, RUDOLF. *Formalization of Logic* (Cambridge, Mass., 1943).

CARNAP, RUDOLF. *Meaning and Necessity* (Chicago, 1947).

CARNAP, RUDOLF. *Logical Foundations of Probability* (Chicago, 1950).

CASSIRER, ERNST. *The Philosophy of Symbolic Forms* (New Haven, 1953).

CHADWICK, J. A. Logical constants. *Mind*, **36** (1927), 1–11.

CHARLESWORTH, M. J. *Philosophy and Linguistic Analysis* (Pittsburgh, 1959).

CHURCH, ALONZO. A formulation of the simple theory of types. *The Journal of Symbolic Logic*, **5** (1940), 56–68.

CHURCH, ALONZO. *The Calculi of Lambda-Conversion* (Princeton, 1941).

CHURCH, ALONZO. Review of Carnap's *Formalization of Logic*. *The Philosophical Review*, **53** (1944), 493–8.

Bibliography

CHURCH, ALONZO. Review of Max Black's 'A translation of Frege's *Ueber Sinn und Bedeutung*'. *The Journal of Symbolic Logic*, **13** (1948), 152–3.

CHURCH, ALONZO. Review of A. Schmidt's *Mathematische Grundlagenforschung*. *The Journal of Symbolic Logic*, **17** (1952), 198–9.

CHURCH, ALONZO. *Introduction to Mathematical Logic*, I (Princeton, 1956).

COLOMBO, G. C. M. *Tractatus Logico-Philosophicus* (Milan, 1954). [Italian translation, with critical introduction and notes.]

COPI, IRVING M. *Tractatus* 5.542. *Analysis*, **18** (1958), 102–4.

COPI, IRVING M. Objects, properties, and relations in the *Tractatus*. *Mind*, **67** (1958), 145–65.

DAITZ, E. The picture theory of meaning. *Mind*, **62** (1953), 184–201.

DAMPIER, W. C. *A History of Science* (Cambridge, 1942).

DESCARTES, RENÉ. *Correspondance*, ed. by C. Adam and G. Milhaud (Paris, 1936).

DUMMETT, MICHAEL. Nominalism. *The Philosophical Review*, **65** (1956), 491–505.

EDDINGTON, A. S. *The Nature of the Physical World* (Cambridge, 1928).

FEIBLEMAN, J. K. *Inside the Great Mirror*. A critical examination of the philosophy of Russell, Wittgenstein, and their followers (The Hague, 1958).

FEYERABEND, PAUL. Wittgenstein's *Philosophical Investigations*. *The Philosophical Review*, **64** (1955), 449–83.

FINDLAY, J. N. *Meinong's Theory of Objects* (Oxford, 1933).

FRAENKEL, A. *Einleitung in die Mengenlehre* (Berlin, 1928).

FRANK, PHILIPP. *Philosophy of Science* (Englewood Cliffs, N.J., 1957).

FREGE, G. *Grundgesetze der Arithmetik* (Jena, 1893, 1903).

FREGE, G. *The Foundations of Arithmetic*, trans. by J. L. Austin (Oxford, 1950).

FREGE, G. *Translations from the Philosophical Writings of Gottlob Frege*, ed. by Peter Geach and Max Black (Oxford, 1952).

FREGE, G. The thought: a logical inquiry (trans. by A. M. and Marcelle Quinton). *Mind*, **65** (1956), 289–311.

FREGE, G. On the foundations of geometry (trans. by M. E. Szabo). *The Philosophical Review*, **69** (1960), 3–17.

FREUNDLICH, R. Logik und Mystik. *Zeitschrift für philosophische Forschung*, **7** (1953), 554–70.

GASKING, D. A. T. Anderson and the *Tractatus Logico-Philosophicus*. *The Australasian Journal of Philosophy*, **27** (1949), 1–26.

GÄTSCHENBERGER, RICHARD. *Symbola* (Karlsruhe, 1920).

GEACH, P. T. Subject and predicate. *Mind*, **59** (1950), 461–82.

Bibliography

GEACH, P. T. Review of Colombo's Italian translation of the *Tractatus*. *The Philosophical Review*, **66** (1957), 556–9.

GEACH, P. T. *Mental Acts* (London, 1957).

GERHARDT, C. I. (ed.). *Die philosophischen Schriften von G. W. Leibniz* (Berlin, 1875–90).

GOODSTEIN, R. L. *Constructive Formalism* (Leicester, 1951).

HADOT, P. Réflexions sur les limites du langage à propos du 'Tractatus logico-philosophicus' de Wittgenstein. *Revue de Métaphysique et de Morale*, **64** (1959), 469–84.

HALL, E. W. *What is Value?* (London, 1952).

HAMPSHIRE, STUART. Logical form. *Proceedings of the Aristotelian Society*, **48** (1947–48), 37–58.

HEMPEL, C. G. Some remarks on 'facts' and propositions. *Analysis*, **2** (1935), 93–6.

HERBST, PETER. The nature of facts. *The Australasian Journal of Philosophy*, **30** (1952), 90–116.

HERTZ, H. *The Principles of Mechanics* (New York, 1956).

HINTIKKA, J. J. Vicious circle principle and the paradoxes. *The Journal of Symbolic Logic*, **22** (1956), 245–9.

HINTIKKA, J. J. Identity, variables, and impredicative definitions. *The Journal of Symbolic Logic*, **21** (1957), 225–45.

HINTIKKA, J. J. On Wittgenstein's 'solipsism'. *Mind*, **67** (1958), 88–91.

HUME, DAVID. *A Treatise of Human Nature*, ed. by L. A. Selby-Bigge (Oxford, 1896).

HUSSERL, E. *Logische Untersuchungen* (Halle, 1900–1).

ISHIGURO, HIDÉ. Elementary propositions. B.Phil. thesis. Oxford, 1959.

JARVIS, JUDITH. Professor Stenius on the *Tractatus*. *The Journal of Philosophy*, **58** (1961), 584–96.

JOHNSON, W. E. The logical calculus. *Mind*, **1** (1892), 3–30, 235–50, 340–57.

KANT, IMMANUEL. *Kritik der reinen Vernunft*, in Hartenstein edn. of the collected works, III (Leipzig, 1867).

KANT, IMMANUEL. *Prolegomena zu einer jeden künftigen Metaphysik die als Wissenschaft wird auftreten können*, Hartenstein edn., IV (Leipzig, 1867).

KEILL, JOHN. *An Introduction to Natural Philosophy* (London, 1745).

KNEALE, W. *Probability and Induction* (Oxford, 1949).

KRIES, JOHANNES VON. *Die Principien der Wahrscheinlichkeitsrechnung* (Tübingen, 1927).

LAZEROWITZ, M. Tautologies and the matrix method. *Mind*, **46** (1937), 191–205.

LEIBNIZ, GOTTFRIED WILHELM. *The Monadology and Other Philosophical Writings*, ed. by Robert Latta (London, 1898). [See also Gerhardt.]

Bibliography

LEIBNIZ, GOTTFRIED WILHELM. *Philosophical Papers and Letters*, ed. by Leroy E. Loemker (Chicago, 1956).

LEWIS, C. I. and LANGFORD, C. H. *Symbolic Logic* (New York, 1932).

LINDSAY, R. B. and MARGENAU, H. *Foundations of Physics* (New York, 1936).

LUCAS, J. R. On not worshipping facts. *The Philosophical Quarterly*, **8** (1958), 144–56.

McGUINNESS, F. Pictures and form in Wittgenstein's *Tractatus*, in E. Castelli (ed.), *Filosofia e Simbolismo* (Rome, 1956), 207–28.

MACH, E. *The Science of Mechanics* (La Salle, Illinois, 1942).

MACH, E. *Space and Geometry* (La Salle, Illinois, 1943).

McTAGGART, J. McT. E. Propositions applicable to themselves, in his *Philosophical Studies* (London, 1934), 179–82.

MALCOLM, NORMAN. Wittgenstein's *Philosophical Investigations*. *The Philosophical Review*, **63** (1954), 530–59.

MALCOLM, NORMAN. *Ludwig Wittgenstein: A Memoir* (London, 1958).

MARGENAU, H. *The Nature of Physical Reality* (New York, 1950).

MARTIN, GOTTFRIED. *Kant's Metaphysics and Theory of Science* (Manchester, 1955).

MASLOW, A. *A Study in Wittgenstein's* Tractatus (Berkeley, 1961).

MAUTHNER, F. *Beiträge zu einer Kritik der Sprache* (Stuttgart, 1901).

MILNE, E. A. *Modern Cosmology and the Christian Idea of God* (Oxford, 1952).

MOORE, G. E. External and internal relations, in his *Philosophical Studies* (London, 1922), 276–309.

MOORE, G. E. Facts and propositions (symposium). *Proceedings of the Aristotelian Society* (suppl.), **7** (1927), 171–206.

MOORE, G. E. *Some Main Problems of Philosophy* (London, 1953).

MOORE, G. E. Wittgenstein's lectures in 1930–33, in his *Philosophical Papers* (London, 1959), 252–324.

PEARS, D. The incongruity of counterparts. *Mind*, **61** (1952), 78–81.

PEIERLS, R. E. *The Laws of Nature* (London, 1955).

PEIRCE, C. S. *Collected Papers of Charles Sanders Peirce* (8 vols., Cambridge, Mass., 1931–58).

POINCARÉ, H. *The Foundations of Science* (Lancaster, Pa., 1946).

POPPER, K. *The Open Society and its Enemies* (Princeton, N.J., 1950).

POPPER, K. Self-reference and meaning in ordinary language. *Mind*, **63** (1954), 162–9.

POPPER, K. Philosophy of science: a personal report, in C. A. Mace (ed.), *British Philosophy in the Mid-Century* (London, 1957), 155–91.

POPPER, K. *The Logic of Scientific Discovery* (London, 1959).

PRIOR, A. N. Categoricals and hypotheticals in George Boole and his successors. *The Australasian Journal of Philosophy*, **27** (1949), 171–96.

Bibliography

PROCTOR, G. L. Scientific laws and scientific objects in the *Tractatus*. *The British Journal for Philosophy of Science*, **10** (1959–60), 177–93.

QUINE, W. V. On the axiom of reducibility. *Mind*, **45** (1936), 498–500.

QUINE, W. V. *Mathematical Logic* (New York, 1940).

QUINE, W. V. *Methods of Logic* (New York, 1950).

RAMSEY, F. P. *The Foundations of Mathematics* (London, 1931).

REACH, K. The name relation and the logical antinomies. *The Journal of Symbolic Logic*, **3** (1938), 97–111.

RHEES, R. Critical notice of Cornforth's *Science Versus Idealism*. *Mind*, **56** (1947), 374–92.

RHEES, R. Miss Anscombe on the *Tractatus*. *The Philosophical Quarterly*, **10** (1960), 21–31.

RUSSELL, BERTRAND. *A Critical Exposition of the Philosophy of Leibniz* (Cambridge, 1900).

RUSSELL, BERTRAND. *The Principles of Mathematics* (Cambridge, 1903).

RUSSELL, BERTRAND. On the nature of truth. *Proceedings of the Aristotelian Society*, **7** (1906–7), 28–49.

RUSSELL, BERTRAND. *The Problems of Philosophy* (London, 1912).

RUSSELL, BERTRAND. The philosophical importance of mathematical logic. *The Monist*, **23** (1913), 481–93.

RUSSELL, BERTRAND. *Mysticism and Logic* (London, 1917).

RUSSELL, BERTRAND. *Introduction to Mathematical Philosophy* (London, 1919).

RUSSELL, BERTRAND. *Our Knowledge of the External World* (London, 1926).

RUSSELL, BERTRAND. *Logic and Knowledge. Essays 1901–1950*, ed. by Robert C. Marsh (London, 1956).

SCHLICK, M. Facts and propositions. *Analysis*, **2** (1935), 65–70.

SCHLICK, M. *Gesetz, Kausalität und Wahrscheinlichkeit* (Vienna, 1948).

SCHMIDT, ARNOLD. *Mathematische Grundlagenforschung* (*Enzyklopädie der mathematischen Wissenschaften*, Band II, Heft 1, Teil II) (Leipzig, 1950).

SCHOPENHAUER, ARTHUR. *Die Welt als Wille und Vorstellung*, ed. by W. Frhr. v. Löhneysen (Stuttgart, 1960).

SCHOPENHAUER, ARTHUR. Preisschrift über die Grundlage der Moral, in *Sämtliche Werke*, ed. by W. Frhr. v. Löhneysen (Stuttgart, 1962).

SCHWYZER, H. R. G. Wittgenstein's picture-theory of language. *Inquiry*, **5** (1962), 46–64.

SEXTUS EMPIRICUS. *Against the Logicians*, trans. by R. G. Bury (London, 1935).

SHWAYDER, D. S. D.Phil. thesis. Oxford, 1954.

SILESIUS, ANGELUS. *Der cherubinische Wandersmann*, ed. by Charles Waldemar (Munich, 1960).

SMITH, N. K. *A Commentary to Kant's Critique of Pure Reason* (London, 1930).

Bibliography

SPINOZA, BENEDICT DE. *Ethic*, trans. by W. Hale White (2nd ed., London, 1894).

STENDHAL (MARIE HENRI BEYLE). *The Life of Henry Brulard*, trans. by C. A. Phillips (New York, 1939).

STENIUS, ERIK. *Wittgenstein's Tractatus*. A critical exposition of its main lines of thought (Oxford, 1960).

STÖHR, ADOLF. *Algebra der Grammatik* (Leipzig, 1898).

STRAWSON, P. F. Truth (symposium). *Proceedings of the Aristotelian Society* (suppl.), **24** (1950), 129–56. [Cf. Austin.]

STRAWSON, P. F. *Introduction to Logical Theory* (London, 1952).

VAIHINGER, H. *Kommentar zu Kants Kritik der reinen Vernunft* (Berlin, 1922).

WAISMANN, F. Die Natur des Reduzibilitätsaxiom. *Monatshefte für Mathematik und Physik*, **35** (1928), 143–6.

WAISMANN, F. Logische Analyse des Wahrscheinlichkeitsbegriffs. *Erkenntnis*, **1** (1930–31), 228–48.

WAISMANN, F. Was ist logische Analyse? *The Journal of Unified Science* (*Erkenntnis*), **8** (1939–40), 265–89.

WASMUTH, E. Das Schweigen Ludwig Wittgensteins; über das Mystische im *Tractatus logico-philosophicus*. *Wort und Wahrheit*, **7** (November 1952).

WATSON, W. H. *On Understanding Physics* (Cambridge, 1938).

WEILER, G. On Fritz Mauthner's critique of language. *Mind*, **67** (1958), 80–7.

WHITEHEAD, A. N. *Modes of Thought* (New York, 1938).

WHITEHEAD, A. N. and RUSSELL, B. A. W. *Principia Mathematica* (Cambridge, 1910–13).

WHITTAKER, EDMUND. *Space and Spirit* (London, 1946).

WILDER, R. L. *Introduction to the Foundations of Mathematics* (New York, 1952).

WISDOM, J. W. T. Logical constructions. *Mind*, **40** (1931), 188–216, 460–75; **41** (1932), 441–64; **42** (1933), 43–66, 186–202.

WRIGHT, G. H. VON. *Form and Content in Logic* (Cambridge, 1949).

YOURGRAU, W. and MANDELSTAM, S. *Variational Principles in Dynamics and Quantum Theory* (London, 1960).

INDEX OF REFERENCES TO
PASSAGES FROM THE 'TRACTATUS' IN
OTHER WORKS

[NL], *Notes on Logic*; [MN], *Moore Notes*; [N], *Notebooks*; [A], Anscombe's *Introduction*; [S], Stenius's *Exposition*.

This index lists (i) passages in Wittgenstein's preparatory work for the *Tractatus* which coincide with or are similar to passages in the final text, (ii) places in the two commentaries where the respective passages are cited or discussed. References to [NL], [MN], and [N] are by page and paragraph number (each portion of text on a page starting with an indentation being counted as a paragraph) as previously explained. Thus '[MN] 112(3)' refers to the third paragraph of p. 112 of *Wittgenstein's Notebooks 1914–1916*, in which [NL] and [MN] are included as appendices.

INDEX OF PASSAGES PARAPHRASED

GENERAL INDEX

a priori, 271, 310, 325, 344
  whether such order in the world, 5
a priori insights, 346
a priori order, 267
a priori propositions, 95, 248
  and rules of use, 17
  certifiable by attention to meaning, 7
  manifest logical form of reality, 6
  say nothing, 6
abacus, 176
abbilden, meaning of, 74, 99
absolute simples, 8
accident, 10
acquaintance, principle of reducibility to, 58
acquaintance with objects, 10
actual infinite, 60
aesthetic attitude, 371
aesthetics, 10
affirmation, essential feature of, 280
aggregate, defined, 59
agreement, 207, 219, 220
  meaning of, 207
Alexander-mounted-on-Bucephalus (an example), 167
Allaire, E. B., 369
ambiguity, typical, 261
Ambrose, A., 383
amphiboly, 270
analysis, 26, 57, 58, 62, 107, 111, 305
  and definition, 58
  complete, 256; and grammar, 113
  'final', 208
  logical, 4
  of a sign, 154
  of meaning, 102
  of propositions, 111, 206–7
  postulate of, 208
  Russell's conception of, 25

analytic, 95, 337
  meaning of, 319
analyticity, 328
ancestral, 203–5
ancients, the, 366
'and so on', 205, 262
  and concept of operation, 259
angle sign, 180
Annahme, meaning of, 182
  see also supposition
Anscombe, G. E. M., 7, 41, 64, 84, 85, 91, 101, 106, 115, 116, 126, 127, 151, 158, 165, 177, 182, 183, 198, 199, 203, 209, 212, 223, 235, 244, 248, 260, 261, 262, 266, 275, 277, 279, 284, 285, 286, 289, 291, 297, 300, 301, 303, 306, 309, 312, 339, 340, 364, 365, 367, 371, 374, 375, 376
  on meaning of *Sachverhalt*, 39
application, 115, 306, 331, 350
  of signs, 114
  syntactical, 134
aRb, interpretation of, 77, 105, 106, 146
arbitrary (-iness), 36, 274, 275, 285, 304, 321, 332, 347, 358
arbitrary determination, 273
argument, 145, 285
  and index, 238–9
argument-place, 50
Aristotle, 27, 52
  on necessity, 244
arithmetic, 297, 316
  foundations of, 314–17
  logicist reduction to logic, 203
'arrays', defined, 67
arrow, 182, 232
  figure of the, 106
art and ethics, 371
Art und Weise, 86, 131

430

432

necessity
  inner, 244
  logical, 243
  Russell on, 286
negation, 177, 178, 225, 226, 263, 278, 326
  as unsubstantial, 225
  essence of, 280
  formal properties of, 321–2
  how introducible, 221
  joint, 276
  not an object, 181
  of entire propositions, 184
  of negation, 184
  of picture, 172
  'purpose' of, 225–6
  self-cancelling power, 278
  W.'s later view of, 225
  see also negation sign
negation-free atomic facts, 225
negation-free language, 221
negation-free propositions, 221, 225
negation sign, 179, 221, 224, 278
  dispensability of, 181
  not a name, 181
  occurrence not indicative of sense, 181
  reversal of its role, 180
negative, uniqueness of, 279
negative facts, 70–2, 181, 182, 280
negative proposition, 16
nennen, meaning of, 75
network, 183, 277, 347–52
  logical, 3
'new level' interpretation of truth-tables, 217
Newtonian mechanics, 53, 347, 348, 351
Newton's laws, 354
Newton's mechanics, 354
Newton's third law, 357
nexus, 209
  causal, 243, 244
Nicod, J., 276
nonsense, 97, 104, 133, 138, 139, 160, 161, 205, 272, 273, 289, 344, 378, 379, 380

indirect proof of, 384
irredeemable, 208, 307, 370, 382
'on stilts', 196
nonsensical, 18, 376, 380
notation, 153, 203, 242, 272, 290, 323, 324, 325
  conceptual, 294, 295
  essence of, 140
  essential aspects of, 278
  for truth-functions, 153
  irregularities of, 162
  meaning of, 153
  possibility of, 150
  systematic character of, 304
  transformation of, 162
Notebooks (W.), 2, 5, 6, 8, 12, 23–5, 38, 48, 50, 58, 77, 86, 96, 97, 102, 108, 112, 113, 124, 127, 131, 134, 151, 156, 159, 160, 164, 165, 166, 172, 173, 175, 177, 184, 188, 195, 202, 206, 214, 215, 218, 232, 235, 237, 244, 246, 251, 259, 262, 267, 271–4, 285, 288, 289, 305, 308–11, 328, 332, 338, 339, 342, 353, 360, 367, 371–6
Notes on Logic (W.), 2, 3, 4, 8, 23, 25, 26, 43, 61, 70, 77, 102, 103, 105, 106, 109, 113, 121, 126, 131, 133, 138, 147, 160, 178, 184, 186, 209, 221, 226, 242, 243, 264, 265, 266, 300, 301, 320
number, cardinal, 161, 202, 297
numbers, 313
numerical identity, 291

object(s), 10, 28, 31, 46, 49, 57, 58, 82, 329
  acquaintance with, 10
  as constituents of at least one fact, 115
  as interdependent, 9
  categorically different from facts, 28
  combinations of, 82–3
  contrasted with facts, 12
  discernibility of, 64
  form of, 57
  like co-ordinates, 9

General Index

world (*cont.*)
  general description of, 289
  how propositions are linked with, 11,
    13
  impersonal representation of, 289
  limits of, 307, 372
  order in the, 5
  substance of, 9
  see also universe

worlds, many satisfying general description, 287

Yourgrau, W., 346

zeigen, meaning of, 76
zero, 315
  as auxiliary symbol, 232